STAR TREK 365

THE NEXT GENERATION ®

BY PAULA M. BLOCK AND TERRY J. ERDMANN

INTRODUCTION BY RONALD D. MOORE

My first encounter with *Star Trek: The Next Generation* took place in a gas station.

Less than a year into my adventure as a college dropout, I was working as a medical records technician (otherwise known as a receptionist) at an animal hospital, all the while telling myself that I was actually a professional writer simply awaiting my inevitable discovery. After all, I was living in Studio City, whose name alone meant that I must be residing in a genuine film-and-television community, despite its lack of a single studio within its environs. To get to my place of (hopefully) temporary employment, I had to walk through the gas station parking lot, and I usually stopped in for a quick look at the "trades"—the *Hollywood Reporter* and *Daily Variety*—which at that time were the dominant sources of information and gossip about the entertainment industry I so fervently wished to join.

On this particular day, sometime in the fall of 1986, I saw a banner headline in *Variety* that literally made me stop and gasp: *Star Trek* was returning to television. I fumbled with whatever cash I had in my pocket, bought the paper, and proceeded to read the article over and over again for the next few weeks. All through the 1970s, when I first became aware of (and then obsessed with) *The Original Series*, my dream had always been that one day *Star Trek* would return to television. When *Star Trek: The Mo-*

tion Picture debuted in 1979 and spawned the movie franchise, I was of course thrilled, but the real grail was television. The *Star Trek* movies—by their nature—couldn't really do the kinds of interesting moral dilemmas and character stories that made the weekly series so brilliant. The movies had to be about enormous, galaxy-shaking events that could draw in a general audience. They couldn't just be about a planet with an interesting social problem, or about a half-human, half-alien character's sex drive, or about landing in an alternate reality where the *Enterprise* was a pirate ship. And it took years to make even one movie!

Star Trek was born as a TV series, and I, and many fans like me, yearned for it to return to its roots and once again provide a weekly voyage of adventure. So when I saw that announcement in the trades, it was the culmination of years of quiet hopes and dreams that one day it would really happen. And one year later, when I sat in my apartment and heard the now British-inflected words "Space, the Final Frontier . . ." come out of my tiny TV set, I can proudly say that tears of joy rolled down my cheeks as I saw my dream coming true.

I watched every episode and amassed a sizable collection of self-recorded VHS tapes (ask your parents), with every show carefully labeled as to title and airdate. After the initial excitement wore off, I had to admit to myself

that I wasn't that wild about that first season. Too many things had changed, too many things were different. Why'd they change the uniform colors? Kids on the *Enterprise*? "Where no *one* has gone before"? Really? Some of the stories creaked, others groaned, some were just bad.

But there were gems, too. The ship in particular grew on me every week. The new *Enterprise* was big and muscular, yet sleek and graceful. The vastness of her interior spaces seemed to promise something new and exciting to be found around every corner. But what really carried me along were the characters: the bald French captain with the British accent; his tall, stalwart, and gregarious Number One; the exotic counselor; the blind helmsman; the brainy doctor and her whip-smart son; the wide-eyed android; the spunky security officer . . . and then there was that Klingon on the bridge, whose presence both annoyed me (we're at peace with the Klingons now? where's the fun in *that*?) and intrigued me (when do we get to see the Klingon version of "Amok Time" or "Journey to Babel"?). The characters—even wearing the wrong uniform colors—pulled me in and gave me something to hold on to, even when the path they trod seemed rocky indeed.

Halfway into the second season, I began seeing a lovely girl named Bekah. (For the next decade I would literally date my life by *Trek* seasons. To this day, if you ask me about something that occurred in 1993, I have to think, "Well, let's see, that was the last season of *TNG* and the second year of *DS9* . . .") Bekah was sweet and she was kind, and when she somehow deduced that the Captain Kirk poster over my bed meant that I was a *Trek* fan, she offered to arrange a tour of the *Next Generation* set for me. She had worked for a time with the casting director on the pilot and she still had friends on the production and they had set tours all the time and it really wouldn't be a big deal to make a call. My heart leaped into my throat at the thought of actually being able to walk the corridors of the *Enterprise*—and it stayed firmly lodged there until she finally made the call and set up the visit. A long list of people wanted to experience the same thrill, so it would be six weeks before my turn would come. At the time, it seemed like an eternity to wait, but in retrospect, that month-and-a-half delay was the biggest gift of all, because it was during that period that I got the notion in my head to write an episode of *TNG* and bring it with me in hopes of getting someone on the show to read it and then buy it and produce it.

It was a ridiculous, hubristic fantasy that showed just how naive I truly was about the business I was trying to join. Fortunately for me, I didn't know any of that. Because when I actually brought that script with me and asked the man giving me the set tour to read it, he

took pity on my goofy earnestness (and wide-eyed idealism about how Hollywood really works) and actually decided to sit down and read it. And when Richard Arnold revealed that not only did he like the script, but he was, in fact, one of Gene Roddenberry's personal assistants and he would be happy to give the script to an agent he'd worked with for formal submission to the show, I still didn't realize how fantastically lucky I'd been. Seven months later, when Michael Piller took over the writing staff, found my script in the slush pile, and decided to buy it and produce it, I was ecstatic, but I still didn't understand what kind of odds I'd beaten. That realization didn't fully come until Michael brought me on staff midway though the third season and I got a glimpse at how many unsolicited scripts *TNG* received a year, which at that time was between two thousand and three thousand.

I was lucky and I was grateful and most of all I was filled with joy—not only for the opportunity to walk the halls of the *Starship Enterprise* any time I felt like it, but also for the chance to actually chart some of her voyages myself. "A dream come true" doesn't even begin to describe it.

The writers worked out of the William S. Hart Building on the Paramount lot, directly across from the production offices in the Gary Cooper Building, while the soundstages were on the

other side of the lot. During that third season of the show, the Hart Building felt like a war bunker. Writers had come and gone through a revolving door during the first two seasons—victims of fights with Gene, or studio politics, or their own frailties—and Richard Manning eventually made a large poster titled "The *Star Trek* Memorial Wall," on which were the names of all the "dead" writers who had gone before us.*

The upheaval in the writing staff during the first couple of years was indicative of the creative turmoil within the show itself, and the third-season staff was determined to smooth the waters and get the show on an even keel. Michael Piller decided that the way to do this was to refocus the storytelling on the characters—to stop making the shows about the guest stars and instead make each episode have some direct impact on Picard, Riker, Beverly, Troi, Data, Worf, Geordi, or Wesley. They were our heroes, and the audience wanted to see how the stories affected their lives. It was a crucial decision, and one that every writer embraced, even as we argued and fought with Michael over how to achieve it.

When the third season ended, all the writers left except me, and I dutifully added their names to the Memorial Wall, which had migrated to my office bathroom, before starting to work with a new staff on the fourth season. (I would continue to add names to that wall for the next four years, always dreading the possibility that I'd one day be adding my own.) We were well into writing new episodes when the third-season finale, "The Best of Both Worlds, Part I," was broadcast and all hell broke loose. That episode, *Trek*'s first cliff-hanger, touched a chord with the audience, and suddenly everyone was talking about *TNG*. We were seeing press clippings from all over the media with buzz about how wild it was to see Picard being Borgified into Locutus, and how stunning Riker's shout of "Fire!" was just before the final cut to black.

But perhaps more important than the fact that people were talking about the show was the *way* they were talking about it. Suddenly, we weren't "the new *Star Trek* series," we were *the Star Trek* series. Up until that moment, when you went to *Trek* conventions, you saw plenty of T-shirts and bumper stickers with disparaging remarks about *TNG* as the "pretenders" or the "upstarts," or with snide references to being fans of the "real" *Star Trek* with Kirk, Spock, and the gang. All that went away after "BOBW." We were "real" *Star Trek* after that, and we never felt like the new kids again.

Piller's dictum of starting stories with our characters redefined how the show was created week in and week out. Our one-liner notes on upcoming story lines always began with "A Picard story where . . ." or "A Troi story in which . . ." or "A Worf story about . . ." As we structured the season, we tried to balance the episodes accordingly, so that there weren't too many Data stories in a row, or maybe we hadn't done a Geordi story in a long time, so we should do one before that Riker story. It was all about the characters to us, and that, I think, connected with the audience, who tuned in week after week to hang out with a group of their friends who just happened to live on a starship.

The production ran on a firm, predictable calendar. Episodes would be filmed in seven days, with an occasional eight-day schedule for a big, expensive show (like a season cliff-hanger) or a six-day schedule to save money (like an episode where everyone's stuck in a shuttlecraft). For budgetary reasons, it was a soundstage-bound production, with only four or five days of location work allowed every year. The vast majority of the alien planets were realized on the Paramount soundstages, usually on Stage 16, which had the nickname "Planet Hell" on the production. We produced twenty-six episodes a year (except when the writers' strike shortened the second season), and that grueling schedule meant the writers typically got only two weeks' respite between seasons, though we sometimes kicked and screamed for three.

In the days of *TNG*, visual effects were created on film, and CGI was still in its infancy. The *Enterprise* and other ships were models,

not software, and every once in a while you could sneak off to the postproduction facility and see the ships themselves—and actually touch them, when no one was looking.

The scripts were written on computers—but to my horror, they were not the sleek, elegant Macs I'd used since college, but dinosaur machines with black-and-amber monitors that didn't even run Windows. I had to learn to use Word with a Scriptor style sheet, which was something less than an intuitive process. The files I created were then copied onto 5.5-inch floppy disks and physically walked downstairs to the script department, where they would be formatted (again) and finally printed out and distributed throughout the production. E-mail was unknown, and the Internet was something happening out there in a college lab as far as we knew. Changes and rewrites were written out by hand on the printed scripts, then handed back to the script department, who made the revisions and distributed copies once more. Looking back on those days now, it seems incredibly inefficient and time-consuming, but we thought we were on the cutting edge of technology and laughed at how generations of writers before us had to rely on the ladies in the Paramount typing pool to format their scripts.

As the years passed, we grew accustomed to the regularity of our high ratings and the comfortable knowledge of always being quaranteed a pickup for the next season. As the show approached season six, everyone felt it could easily cruise into a nine- or ten-year run without any difficulty. But with *The Original Series* movie franchise coming to a conclusion with *The Undiscovered Country*, Paramount began to feel the urge to transition the *TNG* crew into feature films and let *Deep Space Nine* and then *Voyager* carry the television franchise. So the voyages of the *Enterprise*-D were brought to a conclusion—and, as it turned out, just in the nick of time. That last year, season seven, was not a pleasant one in the writers' room. While season six had seemed bold and fresh and full of promise with shows like "Ship in a Bottle," "Frame of Mind," "Relics," "Chain of Command," and "A Fistful of Datas," season seven seemed tired and stale. We started pulling in tales of Geordi's mother, then Data's mother, then Worf's forgotten half brother, and the overall feeling in the room was one of creative exhaustion. If not for the triumph of the series finale, "All Good Things . . . ," we might well have walked away from the show with a feeling of regret instead of pride.

The fact that Brannon Braga and I wrote "All Good Things . . ." at the last second and under the competing pressure of writing the first *TNG* film, *Generations*, may actually have been the thing that saved us all in the end. For somehow —maybe because we didn't have time to think

about it—we managed to give the fans and ourselves a farewell valentine to the characters we'd lived with for the last seven years. The finale was all about them, about who they had been at the beginning, who they were in the present, and who they would be one day when they grew old and gray. Fittingly, it was the first and only *TNG* episode to be projected on a big screen for a full audience in Paramount's theater on the lot, and when the lights went up at the end and the crowd stood and cheered, I felt both pride in the accomplishment and sadness at the closure, but mostly I felt relieved that we hadn't embarrassed ourselves after all and had crafted a worthy conclusion to a great series.

Now, as I write this, over a decade has passed since that giddy night in the Paramount theater, yet I still feel like some part of me has never left the Hart Building. Every time I drive past those big gates on Melrose Avenue, I can't help but glance inside and wonder if any tangible thing is left there on the lot to mark our passing. The stages and offices have long since been turned over to other productions, and it's in the nature of multinational media conglomerates not to spend any time or money memorializing the past. So I know there's nothing physical left for me on the lot. But what do survive are the voyages. They're out there in the digital ether even now, letting new audiences boldly go where no one has gone before,

each and every day. I meet young writers all the time who tell me they grew up with Picard and Riker the same way I grew up with Kirk and Spock, and while it does make me feel old, it also makes me feel proud, very proud, to have been a part of this show.

Enjoy this trip through the voyages of the *Enterprise*-D that Paula and Terry have crafted for you, whether you're new to the trek or seasoned veterans of the Final Frontier. It's a good crew and a steady ship, and they'll always bring you home in the end.

Ronald D. Moore

*Author's note: See spread 339.

Ronald D. Moore served as story editor and producer for *Star Trek: The Next Generation*, contributing scripts for twenty-seven episodes, including the Hugo Award–winning finale, "All Good Things . . ." Moore also worked on the production staff for *Star Trek: Deep Space Nine* and *Star Trek: Voyager*, and cowrote *Star Trek Generations* and *Star Trek: First Contact*. Moore developed and executive-produced the Hugo and Peabody Award–winning reimagining of *Battlestar Galactica* for television, which aired from 2004 through 2009. He lives in California.

We first heard the rumor at a science fiction convention in 1986. One of the convention's organizers stepped up on the stage and stood before the microphone. His tone, when he spoke, was conspiratorial. He was about to share a very hot rumor with the thousand or so attendees—many already dressed for that evening's costume competition—who crowded the hotel ballroom.

"It seems that Paramount Pictures has *finally* approved a new *Star Trek* television show," he said.

A spontaneous cheer arose from the masses. They'd heard rumors of that possibility for years, but this was the first time they'd heard solid confirmation. At long last: *Star Trek* was going to return to television!

Their host raised a hand, signaling a pause in the hubbub. "I've only heard two things about it," he said. "It's going to take place a hundred years after the original five-year mission . . ."

A buzz of whispers filled the room. A *hundred* years? But what about—

"And there's going to be a C-3PO-type robot by the name of . . ." He paused, then, pronouncing the first syllable to rhyme with "fat," revealed the name: "Data."

The crowd uttered a collective, heartfelt moan. A *robot*? A robot with a stupid name?

"Yeah, that doesn't sound too promising, does it?" the man at the microphone agreed.

For the next hour, the fans engaged in a loud and at times heated discussion about whether the show would be, or ever *could* be, any good. Some in that room saw little to be optimistic about. In their minds, Paramount was *clearly* bent on corrupting Gene Roddenberry's perfect vision of the future. Never mind that Roddenberry himself was the man behind this new and *improved* (from his point of view) iteration of a "*Wagon Train* to the stars," or that "Data" (correctly pronounced with a long *a*) was a character that Roddenberry felt would win the affections of the most ardent Spock-lover in the viewership. To the doubters in that room, this new version of *Star Trek* couldn't possibly be as good as the original.

And yet, twenty-five years later, here we are, celebrating the miracle that was—and is—*Star Trek: The Next Generation*, arguably the most popular incarnation of *Star Trek*.

This book is the fulfillment of an audacious thought that we had while working on our previous tome, *Star Trek: The Original Series 365*: "If this book does well, maybe we'll be able to do one about *TNG*." We thank you, the readers who bought that book and spoke well of it, for playing a part in making that wish come true.

TNG is part of our joint history as a writing couple. In the mid-1980s, Paula was living in New York, editing magazines; Terry was living in Los Angeles, working in the publicity department of a major studio. We met, curiously enough, at a *Star Trek* event that was being held in the middle of the country. Terry was promoting science fiction films, and Paula was visiting some of her longtime Trekker friends. We began dating cross-country, which shouldn't have worked out, but somehow did, and Paula eventually relocated to the West Coast so that we could be together full-time. Then several things happened in very quick succession. Terry was hired as the production publicist on *Star Trek V: The Final Frontier*, and Paula landed a job at Paramount Pictures, overseeing the studio's licensed publishing program. A hundred yards from Paula's new office, just across the alley from where Captain Kirk helmed the *Enterprise*-A, was the bridge of Captain Picard's *Enterprise*-D. It was the very definition of confluence.

Although Terry continued to promote movies for other studios, he periodically returned to Paramount to lend a hand during the release of *Star Trek* films. In between, he wrote books about the entertainment industry. Meanwhile, Paula oversaw the development of all products containing *Star Trek* verbiage: books, comics, magazines, customizable card games, et cetera.

Because we were "there" during its production, writing this tribute to *Star Trek: The Next Generation* has been a pleasure. The words came from our memories of those halcyon days, and from those shared by the actors, writers, and behind-the-scenes people who worked on *TNG*. They were generous with their time and their mementos from the show: personal snapshots, costume sketches, concept art, paintings, storyboards, model shots, and more. Which was fortunate, because the studio's official photo archive has some gaps.

Oh, there is photography from nearly every episode; Paramount's television publicity department had diligently sent a professional photographer to the *TNG* set during each episode's production, but generally only for one or two days out of a seven-day shooting schedule. And that wasn't necessarily the day that we needed photography from. Thus, to obtain an image of the beautiful Minuet ("11001001")—who performed on a day when a photographer was not assigned—we required frame grab technology. The same is true of effects photography, which doesn't exist in tangible form. The only way to reproduce the show's groundbreaking visual effects (although *The Next Generation* was shot on film, the filmmakers used a videotape format to combine the individual elements of each effects sequence): once again, do a frame grab.

Obviously, this is not the first book to attempt to cover *TNG* in depth. In her years at Paramount, Paula personally green-lit such iconic works as the *Star Trek: The Next Generation Companion* (by Larry Nemecek), *The Continuing Mission* (by Judith and Garfield Reeves-Stevens), Starlog's extensive line of *TNG*-dedicated magazines (edited by Dave McDonnell), and even that indispensible repository of knowledge, *The Star Trek Encyclopedia* (by Michael and Denise Okuda). Each of these (and more) served as useful resources in jogging our memories while writing *Star Trek: The Next Generation 365*. We encourage you to add them to your personal library if you don't already have them.

As for this brick of a book you're presently holding in your hands, we hope that it possesses the power to invoke some wonderful memories from the 178 hours of quality television that are *Star Trek: The Next Generation*.

Make it so!

Paula M. Block
Terry J. Erdmann

THE THING
THAT
WOULDN'T
DIE

PREPRODUCTION

001

Star Trek was dead.

NBC had canceled the series in 1969. The sets had been struck. The actors, writers, and producers had moved on to new projects. But a funny thing happened on the way to the television graveyard.

Kaiser Broadcasting, a small division of industrial giant Henry J. Kaiser Company, put the show into syndication. Scheduling the series in a time slot carefully chosen to attract a youthful audience, Kaiser stations ran the episodes uncut and in order. When they got to episode number 78, the final episode produced, they started all over again. And then they did it again. And again. Viewership began to snowball, the reruns finding the core audience that had evaded *Star Trek* in its first run. And against all logic—there were no *new* episodes, after all—the snowball became an avalanche. A kind of Trekker nation took shape, its members participating in *Star Trek* clubs and sharing their own *Star Trek* stories. In 1972, the first *Star Trek* convention, held in New York City, drew more than three thousand enthusiastic attendees. The following year, a second convention doubled that number. Soon *Star Trek* conventions were taking place all over the country, with *Star Trek* creator Gene Roddenberry a much sought-after guest of honor.

Something was happening, that was clear.

None of this escaped the attention of Paramount Pictures, the rights holder to the show. But executives at the historic studio, located in the middle of Hollywood on Melrose Avenue, weren't quite sure what to *do* with this unexpected gift. After all, they weren't the ones who'd originally supported Roddenberry's vision of the future. That was Desilu Productions, a company that had since become an acquisition of Paramount's parent company. Was there a large enough audience to warrant bringing *Star Trek* to the big screen? Or, perhaps, a second attempt at the small screen? Plans changed from month to month. *A movie? Okay!* But the studio didn't like any of the submitted scripts. *A TV show on a brand-new Paramount network? Okay!* That idea got as far as preproduction. Actors were cast, sets were built, and scripts were written for a new series, tentatively called *Star Trek: Phase II*. But the brand-new network idea didn't pan out and plans for the series went *pffffft!*

By then it was 1977. *Star Wars* opened, and it was a mega hit. Cue more rumblings from behind the studio walls. *A movie?* But all that money had already been spent on the stillborn TV series. . . . *What if we take the script for the two-hour pilot and turn it into a movie?*

Two years later, *Star Trek: The Motion Picture* debuted on the big screen. It was successful enough to warrant sequel after sequel. Then, in 1986—the year of *Star Trek's* twentieth anniversary—the studio again took stock. *What if we continue to do the movies* and *also have another go at television?*

This time, the lights were green all the way down Melrose Avenue. . . .

"Twenty years ago, the genius of one man brought to television a program that has transcended the medium. We are enormously pleased that that man, Gene Roddenberry, is going to do it again."
   —Mel Harris, President, Paramount Television Group

By October 1986, plans regarding a new *Star Trek* television series had proceeded to the point where Paramount felt comfortable spilling the beans at a studio press conference. Stalwart *Star Trek* fans had been hearing rumors through their own grapevine for quite some time, and they had mixed feelings. They wanted a new show, of course, but they weren't thrilled to hear that it would take place a century after *The Original Series* and feature a brand-new crew.

For the powers that be at Paramount, it was a logical decision. Weekly television necessitates a grueling pace; why would actors who'd been earning goodly sums to do a *Star Trek* movie every two years want to return to the lower paycheck and unpredictable hours of series television?

For its part, the press was intrigued by Paramount's announced intention to distribute the show itself, rather than sell it to an established network. Paramount initially had offered the show to the four major players (by this time, Fox, too, had its own network, along with ABC, CBS, and NBC), but the networks had balked at Paramount's conditions: commit to a full season of episodes, a guaranteed time slot (with *no* preemptions), and an expensive promotional push. So Paramount execs did the math and made a bold decision. They would produce the series themselves and syndicate the new episodes to the same stations that were airing *The Original Series*. While syndication of reruns was a tried-and-true moneymaker, syndication of a new program was a risky strategy. In the long run, it could pay off handsomely. In the short run, however, if the show was not a hit . . .

Paramount decided to chance it. As Mel Harris would later explain, "We realized that nobody else was going to care as much about *Star Trek* as we did."

During this early development period, Gene Roddenberry was gathering a team of talented people to help him put the show—soon to be christened *Star Trek: The Next Generation*—together. Among them were four who cared very much about *Star Trek*,

and who had, in fact, been closely associated with *The Original Series*: producers Robert H. Justman and Edward K. Milkis, and writers Dorothy "D.C." Fontana and David Gerrold. All four would make important contributions to the series, but for various reasons, all would depart within *The Next Generation*'s first year of production.

Elsewhere on the Paramount lot in 1986, on a separate career path, was a man whose fate would soon become irrevocably intertwined with *Star Trek*. His name was Rick Berman.

In 1984, Rick Berman left a career in television production (including PBS's Emmy Award–winning *Big Blue Marble* and HBO's *What on Earth*) to become a "suit"—that is, a studio executive who supervises the work of producers. As director of current programming for Paramount Television, he was charged with overseeing successful sitcoms such as *Cheers* and *Family Ties*. Within a year, he was promoted to executive director of dramatic programming. In 1986, he was bumped up again, this time to vice president of longform (over sixty minutes) and special projects, and it was in that position that he received *the* phone call. He was to meet with producer Gene Roddenberry the following day.

Berman arrived to find Roddenberry arguing with a group of studio executives about a proposed new series. Berman quietly observed the back and forth and refrained from interjecting his own opinions. As he later noted in his foreword to the book *Star Trek: The Next Generation—The Continuing Mission*, he was unfamiliar with the subject under discussion and didn't *have* an opinion. But in the midst of all the shouting, Roddenberry had noticed him. Their eyes met, and Berman, admittedly amused by the scene playing out before him, smiled at Roddenberry.

The smile, apparently, told the producer everything he needed to know about this unknown exec— if nothing else, that Berman wasn't simply sitting in the room agreeing with his fellow suits on principle. In fact, Roddenberry read even more into the expression. He later told Berman that it seemed to say, "Can you believe what assholes these guys are?" Berman, however, holds to his conviction that "it was nothing more than a slightly mischievous smile."

The upshot of that enigmatic smile was life-changing. The day after the meeting, Roddenberry invited Berman to lunch. The producer discussed his past, and Berman discussed his own. Roddenberry was particularly interested in Berman's early stint as a globe-trotting documentary filmmaker, which perhaps mirrored Roddenberry's own love of adventure. Per Berman, the subject of *Star Trek* never came up—until the next day, when Roddenberry conveyed an invitation for Berman to quit his job with the studio and come work for *Star Trek* as a producer.

Perhaps Roddenberry had been right about their connection, because Berman took a leap of faith and accepted the offer. He had no idea that he would be responsible for overseeing the entire *Star Trek* franchise within a few short years.

On the opposite page is a relic of sorts: a photo that captures Berman (left) during the brief period in 1986 when he was Paramount Television's "studio guy," responsible for riding herd on special projects. Next to Berman is John Ferraro, then a development executive for Paramount's TV Group, and on the far right, Peter S. Greenberg, vice president of TV development. Today, Ferraro is an independent film producer. Greenberg is currently the travel editor for CBS News, producing travel segments across all CBS broadcast platforms and hosting his own nationally syndicated radio program.

Like the Constitution of the United States, a television series bible is considered a "living, breathing document"—not set in stone but, rather, subject to change via the inclusion of "amendments." And just as the first bible for the original *Star Trek* series included elements that would change with casting choices and network provisos, so, too, did the initial bible for *Star Trek: The Next Generation*.

The twenty-three-page document, dated November 26, 1986, covered the show's format, central premise, characters, and technology. Some details would "stick"—like perfectly cooked spaghetti thrown at the wall—while others quickly morphed into aspects more familiar. Frenchman "Julien" Picard maintained his Franco heritage through the transition to "Jean-Luc" Picard, but ultimately spoke with a British accent due to the casting of Patrick Stewart. Deanna Troi, who had telepathic abilities that were the result of her "one-eighth" Betazed heritage (from her father's side of the family), became a more clear-cut half-blood Betazoid with empathic skills, thanks to her Betazoid mom. Security Chief Macha Hernandez, said to be inspired by Vasquez, the plucky Latina character in the film *Aliens*, was rechristened with

a Ukrainian moniker—Natasha "Tasha" Yar—when blonde, blue-eyed Denise Crosby landed the role. And perhaps no character went through as large a physical transition as Leslie Crusher, the petite, winsome fifteen-year-old *girl* who accompanied her mom, Doctor Beverly Crusher, to the *Enterprise*. (Mom, by the way, was said to have had "a natural walk more suitable to a striptease queen" than a scientist.) Interestingly, there wasn't a Klingon officer named Worf to describe at this point (which explains why Michael Dorn didn't appear in the earliest group shot, seen on the opposite page); Gene Roddenberry initially was reluctant to add alien species that had played a significant role in *The Original Series*. He considered them "retread" characters.

The series was set in the early twenty-fifth century on the *Enterprise*-G, the *eighth* starship to bear that name. It later was recalibrated to take place in the twenty-fourth century—just one hundred years after *The Original Series*—on the *Enterprise*-D (i.e., the *fifth* starship to carry that name). Communicators were conceived as "wrist devices" (as previously seen in one of the early *Star Trek* films), but ultimately became the familiar insignia badges. And one new

bit of technology—the "landing envelope"—never happened at all, possibly due to the strain it would have placed on the effects budget and the writing staff (not enough danger!). The device would have placed "a protective power field envelope around a person or landing party, allowing away teams to visit planets with much more hostile environments than was possible in the past."

Casting for *Star Trek: The Next Generation* began in March 1987. By April 13, the list of potential crew members for the *Enterprise* had been whittled down to a select group. Many of the actors who did not make the final cut clearly were impressive enough to be called back to the *Star Trek* franchise at a later date. Mitchell Ryan, a contender for Picard, would show up in the series' second season as Will Riker's father, Kyle. Rosalind Chao, reading for the role of Tasha Yar, would pop up during *TNG*'s fourth season as semi-regular Keiko Ishikawa O'Brien, bride of Transporter Chief Miles O'Brien; she would accompany him to *Star Trek: Deep Space Nine* two years later. Tim Russ, later cast as Tuvok on *Star Trek: Voyager*, was a contender for the role of Geordi La Forge (as were Reggie Jackson and Wesley Snipes, neither of whom made it to *Star Trek*). And while Eric Menyuk didn't win the coveted role of Data, he did win a consolation prize when he was cast as the Traveler, guesting three times over the course of *TNG*'s seven seasons. At first, Belgian actor Patrick Bauchau (perhaps best known to audiences as Sydney in the television series *The Pretender*) seemed a favorite to capture the role of Picard, but Robert Justman was relentless in his campaigning for

Patrick Stewart, who'd greatly impressed the producer in a Shakespeare seminar at UCLA. Roddenberry agreed that Stewart clearly had talent, but . . . "Gene did not like the idea of a bald English guy stepping into the shoes of William Shatner," said Rick Berman in a 2006 interview for the Archive of American Television. "He just didn't match his image of what a captain should be." With Berman adding additional weight to Justman's arguments, Roddenberry finally agreed to let Stewart audition in front of the studio reps who would make the final call—but only if Stewart wore a wig. Stewart complied and was sent over to meet with John Pike, then president of Paramount's network television division. Following the meeting, Berman recalls, Pike's decision was succinct. "He said, 'Go with the English guy, but *lose the wig.*'"

"CAPTAIN JEAN-LUC PICARD (played by Patrick Stewart): Picard deserves the description 'distinguished.' A born explorer and superbly experienced starship commander, he served on an incredible 22-year voyage as captain of the legendary deep space charting vessel, the *U.S.S. Stargazer*.

"Born in Paris, France, Picard betrays a Gallic accent only when deep emotions are triggered. Quite often, however, there's a touch of French phrasing in his speech. He is in prime physical condition. Definitely a 'romantic,' he sincerely believes in concepts like honor and duty, although on issues that affect the safety of his crew and starship, he can be completely pragmatic and tough as hell.

"Picard demands absolute authority in his role as starship captain. On the other hand, he has learned that there are many more times at which a leader needs advice, counsel, and even critical comment from his subordinates. He invites this and expects his crew to know when the situation does or does not permit it. Picard's vast experience has left him capable of arranging which one he needs—when he needs it.

"He enjoys the privileges that go with his rank and vessel—also the eccentricities permitted. He knows that a certain amount of selfishness is healthy and necessary to the captain of a starship this vast, engaged in missions of this importance and under so much emotional pressure. He does not hesitate to make his prejudices known to his crew, an example of which is his insistence that he does not like children. . . ."

—from the *Star Trek: The Next Generation* writers'/directors' guide '88–89, second-season revision

"COMMANDER WILLIAM T. RIKER (played by Jonathan Frakes): Number One (whom the U.S. Navy would call the 'Executive Officer') is in his early thirties, considered by Starfleet to be a top quality captain-in-training. His principal responsibilities are:

" to constantly provide the Captain with a top condition vessel and crew, and,

"2. to command away missions.

"Like all First Officers, Riker feels highly possessive about the *Enterprise*—considers it *his* ship, quite understandably since he is the one responsible for keeping the vessel polished and efficient. (From time immemorial First Officers have considered the ship captain as one who merely *uses* the vessel.) This creates no friction between Picard and Riker since, after all, Picard was the same kind of proud First Officer before becoming a Captain. . . .

"One of Riker's special charms (shared also by the actor) is the 'twinkle' in his eye which suggests a very special sense of humor.

"Riker is called 'Number One' by the Captain. Only rarely is he called that by an *Enterprise* crewmember and never by anyone not part of the *Enterprise*. Socially, his friends call him *Will*.

"Riker was born in Valdez, Alaska, and there is a strong outdoors pioneer quality in his personality. . . . Like the legendary 23rd century Kirk (when in his early thirties), our Number One is very strong and agile and has a tendency toward 'derring-do.' Also like Captain Kirk, Riker has a healthy sex drive."

—from the *Star Trek: The Next Generation* writers'/directors' guide '88–89, second-season revision

"LIEUTENANT COMMANDER DATA (played by Brent Spiner): An android so perfectly fabricated that, on applying for a Starfleet commission years ago, he tested out as *alive*. This is a point of some pride to Data, whose Starfleet psychiatric profile ('medical eyes only') lists the android as having the 'impossible dream of somehow, some day becoming human. . . .'

"Data is so perfectly fabricated that from appearances, you would never know he is not composed of normal flesh and blood. Data's artificial skin is gold, his eyes an eerie yellow; otherwise, his appearance is that of a human in his mid-thirties. . . .

"Data's mind/instincts/needs/et cetera are remarkably humanlike—not perfectly so, but in that we find this character's special qualities. As a Starfleet Academy graduate, he is totally loyal to Starfleet and its regulations—but also capable of being puzzled enough by some Starfleet practices to ask sensible (make that *too* sensible) questions about them. . . .

"Data serves the vessel as something of a 'walking library' with commensurate mental dexterity and reading speed. . . . He is also enormously strong and agile. . . .

"He is completely incapable of understanding human *humor*, and this has become a running joke in the series. Through his experiences, he has learned many 'lessons' about human behavior.

"His most exciting character facets, however, involve his weaknesses and the things he *cannot* do. He is anything but a 'cool character' and constantly exhibits an almost childlike naïveté—which, in fact, has become something of his 'trademark.' He is also literal to a fault. . . ."

—from the *Star Trek: The Next Generation* writers'/directors' guide, special edition 1992–93

"LIEUTENANT COMMANDER GEORDI LA FORGE (played by LeVar Burton): He is racially black and birth-defect blind . . . Totally without optical nerves from birth, his intelligence and spirit captivated a top medical/electronics team. It led to the scientific effort to produce a sensor capable of modifying the electromagnetic spectrum and carrying these readings to the human brain. With his VISOR (Visual Instrument and Sensory Organ Replacement), Geordi's infra-red vision can 'see' the warmth of a recent footprint, use ultra-violet light to 'see' through an opaque substance, and much more . . .

"After having spent a year on the *Enterprise* as a Bridge Officer (as required by Starfleet regulations), Geordi [was] promoted . . . and returned to what he was trained to be: the ship's Engineering Officer. . . .

"Unlike Riker's sense of humor, Geordi's is highly vocal and visible and irreverent. For example, when something dangerous appears on the Main Viewer, Geordi is likely to say something like, 'Oh, oh, *big* trouble!' . . . He is the starship's 'blithe spirit . . .'"

—from the *Star Trek: The Next Generation* writers'/directors' guide '88–89, second-season revision; and the '89–90 third-season revision

"DOCTOR BEVERLY CRUSHER (played by Gates McFadden): "She is one of the most talented and insightful physicians in Starfleet. She and Picard have known each other for many years.

"Doctor Crusher is an intelligent and strong-willed diagnostician. She has a profound sense of medicine, the kind of skill that takes years to develop. . . . She is first and foremost a brilliant ship's doctor.

"She is a beautiful woman and looks considerably younger than her age. Her wit and intelligence have not escaped the Captain's eye either, and though they have had their differences in the past, they have developed a solid friendship and mutual admiration.

"Beverly's husband, Jack Crusher, was killed while serving under Captain Picard on the *U.S.S. Stargazer*. Beverly has long since forgiven Picard for any anger she felt over Jack's death, and she knows it is not logical to blame him. . . .

"Beverly's son Wesley lived on board the *Enterprise* with her when she signed on during the first season. Wesley stayed on the *Enterprise* during the second season while Beverly left the ship to head Starfleet Medical for a year . . ."

—from the *Star Trek: The Next Generation* writers'/directors' guide, special edition 1992–93

LT. WORF/COUNSELOR DEANNA TROI

"LIEUTENANT WORF (played by Michael Dorn): A Klingon, the only one to have graduated so far from Starfleet Academy, Worf is in charge of security for the *U.S.S. Enterprise*, a rather appropriate position for one from a race which considers military expertise the highest of all virtues. As a child, Worf lost his parents during a Romulan attack on the Federation Outpost at Khitomer. Worf was the only Klingon survivor, and was adopted by a human Starfleet family. Although his emotions and some of his values are Klingon, Worf is totally loyal to Picard and the *Enterprise*.

"In addition to his expertise on starship security, Worf is also of value to Picard as an expert on armaments of all types. . . .

"Worf has little sense of humor, at least none that humans can translate. His speech pattern, however, can provide humor to us. He speaks in short declarative statements. When on a world featuring lovely half-naked women ('Justice'), he summed up his impressions with, 'Nice planet!'"

—from the *Star Trek: The Next Generation* writers'/directors' guide '88–89, second-season revision

"COUNSELOR DEANNA TROI (played by Marina Sirtis): An attractive and very witty Starfleet professional, she is the starship's Counselor, a position of vital importance on space vessels of the 24th century; the success of a starship's mission depends as much on efficiently functioning human relationships as on the vessel's mechanisms and circuitry. Troi is a master in human and alien psychology, also Starfleet-trained as a bridge officer. Her mother was a Betazed alien and she has inherited a form of telepathic ability that allows her to 'feel' the emotions of others.

"Troi and Riker are old friends who had a tempestuous relationship sometime in the past. Somehow it didn't work and, with both on the same vessel, now that fire is only embers, a warm and comfortable friendship."

—from the *Star Trek: The Next Generation* writers' guide, March 23, 1987; and the writers'/directors' guide '88–89, second-season revision

"LIEUTENANT NATASHA 'TASHA' YAR (played by Denise Crosby): Despite the fact that she is only 28 years old, Tasha has been selected by Captain Picard as the starship's Security Chief, one of the few of the crew who performs the same function both aboard the ship and off.

"Accounting for her almost obsessive devotion to protect the ship and its crew, Tasha comes from an unfortunate colony where a combination of harsh environmental change and fanatical leaders had made existence there a hellish nightmare. She managed to escape this ugliness as a teenager, but carried with her a desperate hunger for peace and order in life. . . .

"Tasha's (unspecified) Ukrainian descent gives her an unusual quality of conditioned-body beauty. . . . With fire in her eyes and a muscularly well-developed and *very* female body, she is capable of pinning most crewmen to the mat—or being just an exciting, sensual and intellectual challenge to males who enjoy (win or lose) full equality between the genders."

—from the *Star Trek: The Next Generation* writers' guide, March 23, 1987

"WESLEY 'WES' CRUSHER (played by Wil Wheaton): A highly intelligent and winsome boy who came aboard with his mother, Beverly Crusher, the *Enterprise*'s Chief Medical Officer. He has a special relationship with Picard, based on Wesley's father having been killed while serving under Picard's command years ago. . . .

"Wes's unusual intelligence won him an acting-ensign appointment from Captain Picard. He has an eidetic memory in areas of starship engineering and related sciences. Several centuries ago he might have been one of the young *electronic wizards* who were introducing computers to a puzzled world. . . .

"His remarkable abilities are *not* limited merely to being able to visualize broad categories of starship design and functioning. . . . He can visualize . . . the *potential* of the designs he has called up from memory. In other words, he can visualize things that the *Enterprise*'s engines and circuitry *could do* if re-patterned or re-arranged. . . .

"In all other ways, he's a normal boy, filled with questions and enthusiasms of his years. He . . . enjoys being able to hold down the conn bridge position, but would enjoy it a lot more if a girl his own age could see him at it. . . ."

—from the *Star Trek: The Next Generation* writers'/directors' guide '89–90, third-season revision

"DOCTOR KATHERINE PULASKI (played by Diana Muldaur): Doctor Pulaski came to the *Enterprise* as Chief Medical Officer as a result of Doctor Beverly Crusher's strong recommendation. We gather that on leaving the *Enterprise* to become head of Starfleet Medical, Beverly had made use of her new position and her knowledge of the *Enterprise* to force Doctor Pulaski's appointment. . . .

"She has abrasive edges to her personality and is not at all uncertain of herself and her opinions. She is also the intellectual equal of Captain Picard. Fortunately, she also understands the realities of command and Picard's years of deep space experience and carefully defers to him in those areas. . . .

"Pulaski is a few years younger than her Captain. . . . A 24th Century woman in almost every way, she is amused by pretension. Marriage being just one of many options in this era, she has three grown children by three different men. . . .

"Pulaski is a humanity lover, passionately fond of the human species. . . . She is the only crewmember who treats Data like a machine."

—from the *Star Trek: The Next Generation* writers'/directors' guide '88–89, second-season revision

"GUINAN (played by Whoopi Goldberg): Guinan is an alien female from a very distant planet. Picard, when a young officer on the *U.S.S. Stargazer*, was fascinated by members of her life-form that he met. Now Captain of one of the vast *Galaxy*-class starships with its immense crew and facilities, he has discovered that this very kind of person would be a perfect choice to operate the *Ten-Forward* facility. . . .

"We do not know Guinan's age. She is a *humanoid* with many similarities to the human form, but also with some subtle differences. . . . She combines the loveliness of wisdom and child. We'll learn from Picard that she is at least 'several centuries' old. . . .

"She is a born catalyst, able to fit into a 'customer's' mood. . . . As Picard discovered long ago, Guinan is a member of a *Listener* life-form. Something about her life-form *encourages others to be honest when they speak*—and perhaps old-style bartenders had something of the same ability."

—from the *Star Trek: The Next Generation* writers'/directors' guide, special edition 1992–93

"THE *U.S.S. ENTERPRISE* – NCC 1701-D: The *fifth* starship to carry the name *Enterprise. Twice the length of the original starship* and thus approximately *eight* times the interior size.* She retains much the same symmetry, which includes an engineering module with twin nacelles and, of course, a great saucer-shaped *command module*.

"The starship is designed to be home (*home* in a very literal sense) to 1,012 persons. Gone is the metallic sterility of the original ship, the reason being that the last century or so has seen a form of technological progress which 24th-century poets call 'Technology Unchained'—which means that technical improvement has gone beyond developing things which are smaller, or faster, or more powerful, and is now very much centered on improving *the quality of life*. . . .

"As humanity probes deeper and deeper into space with ten-year or longer missions becoming the norm, Starfleet has been encouraging crew members to share the space exploration adventure with their families. . . . Previous experiences in space exploration have underscored the lesson that people need people for mental and physical health. . . .

ship's engines are channeled or metered through dilithium crystals. . . . However, unlike the past, we now know how to recrystalize dilithium and are far less likely to experience significant problems with the ship's crystals. . . .

"The saucer section is detachable from the battle section. The saucer part of the *Enterprise* contains living decks and the main bridge. While it has its own impulse engines, it does not have warp drive capability. The battle module contains the engineering section, the main cargo bay, and the two nacelles containing the warp drive engines. The battle section has impulse engines as well as warp drive capability; it also has its own bridge, to which the ship's command officers evacuate in time of battle. The saucer section is then detached and the battle module is ready for action."

—from the *Star Trek: The Next Generation* writers' guide, March 23, 1987

*The new *Enterprise* was estimated to be exactly the size of the Paramount Studios lot, as demonstrated by an illustration from the writers' guide.

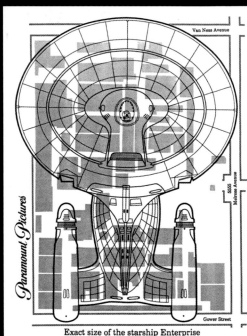

Exact size of the starship Enterprise
compared with 55 acre studio lot.

Andrew Probert had worked as a production illustrator on *Star Trek: The Motion Picture*, so when he heard an announcement that a new *Star Trek* production was being launched, he called the studio. The call paid off, and only days later he found himself sitting in Gene Roddenberry's office. "The bridge is the most important set," Probert recalls Roddenberry saying, "so we want to bring someone in early to do bridge designs." The memory makes Probert smile. "I was the fifth person hired on *The Next Generation*," he says.

"Although I was brought on to design the bridge, naturally I wanted to design the exterior of the ship if given the opportunity. I was doing little doodles of what I would like to see the new ship look like, and I tacked one of those doodles on the wall in front of me. One day, David Gerrold came in to talk, and he glanced up and said, 'Hey, is that the new ship?' I said I didn't know, so he said, 'Let's find out,' and he pulled it off the wall and left. A little while later he came back, slapped it down on my desk, and said, 'Yup. That's the new ship.'"

Gerrold, it turns out, had walked into a meeting with Roddenberry, Robert Justman, and coproducer Herbert Wright and shown them the four-inch by six-inch drawing (black-and-white sketch on the opposite page, bottom row). They all liked it. "There were no notes or anything on it," Probert says with a shrug. "It was just a scribble on a piece of paper."

And so Probert started finessing the design. Originally, he planned it to be two thousand feet long, twice the length of Kirk's *Enterprise* in *The Motion Picture*. "When Gene reviewed the finished drawing, he said, 'The nacelles look too short—I'm used to the engines of the older ship. Can you lengthen these a bit?' So I lengthened them as little as I could get away with," he says, chuckling. "I extended the nacelles l80 feet. Now the ship is an overall 2,180."

Noting that Probert had created a ship with a bridge located in the center of the saucer, Roddenberry asked for one other change. "He said, 'I really would like to have the bridge back on top. I feel it gives people an idea of the scale of the ship, because once they see the bridge interior, they will understand the exterior size relationship.'

"Those are the only two changes Gene asked for," Probert says. "It was pretty mind-blowing."

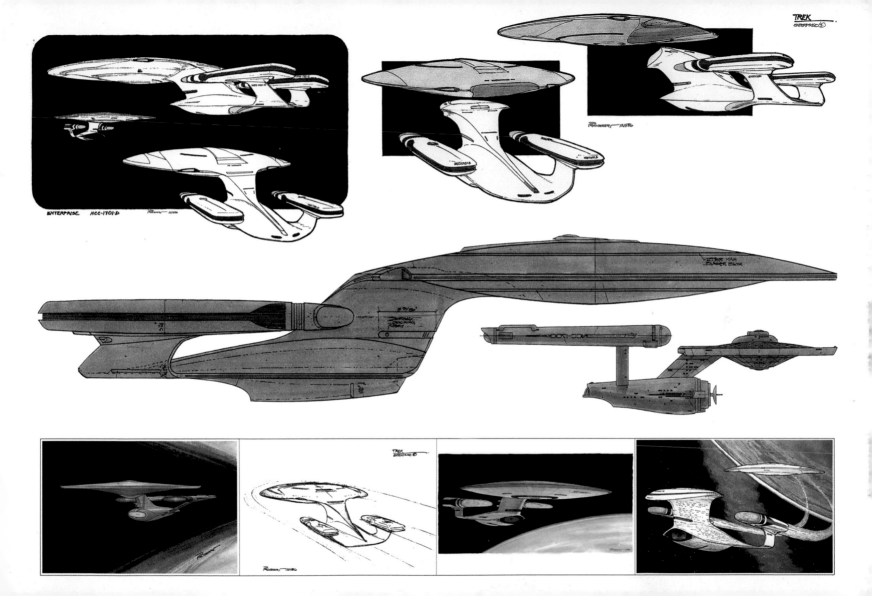

"THE MAIN BRIDGE: Because of this starship's level of automation, the Bridge on the *Enterprise* looks very different from the one in the original series. Gone is the need for officers to report to work to what seems a giant cockpit lined with rows of duty stations studded with clusters of instrumentation and controls.

"Much the same kinds of things happen here as in the old Bridge, but with less emphasis on the mechanics of steering the starship. It is a place where the starship officers with either *aboard* or *away* responsibilities can meet, check out information, make plans, et cetera.

"Who actually drives the *Enterprise*? The job of starship command and control is handled by two Bridge duty officers at positions known as *CONN* and *OPS*.

"*CONN* (for vessel "control" and navigation). Usually manned by a supernumerary ensign (male or female).

"*OPS* (vessel "operations," including Engineering and Life Support). Position usually manned by Data . . .

"The COMMAND AREA of our Main Bridge is a semi-circle of control seats where the Captain and his next-in-command and advisors are located. Just ahead of this are two FORWARD STATIONS, OPS and CONN positions. . . .

"The forward part of the Main Bridge is a large wall-sized 'Viewer.' This Main Viewer is usually on and will dominate the Bridge and the action as the original framed viewscreen could never do.

"The rear of the Bridge has a raised semi-circular area, separated from the Command Area by a railing which is also a set of console stations. This is the TACTICAL CONSOLE. At this position, Worf plus any necessary assistants are responsible for weaponry, defensive devices (shields, etc.), plus ship's internal security.

"The rear wall of the Bridge is an additional set of duty stations called AFT CONSOLES. These five stations represent functions which will also be ordinarily unsupervised unless called for by a story situation. . . ."

—from the *Star Trek: The Next Generation* writers' guide, March 23, 1987

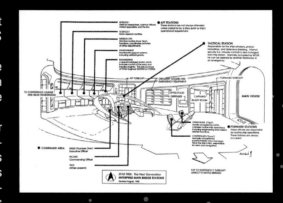

"Gene had a sort of laundry list of what he wanted the bridge to be like," says Consulting Senior Illustrator Andrew Probert. "He wanted it to be larger than the original, because the ship was going to be larger. And he wanted it to look more like an office lounge, in a way, rather than a control room with 'people hunched over their workstations.' And he wanted the viewscreen to dominate the front of the bridge like no other viewscreen had."

Roddenberry's story plans put the *Enterprise* on an extended mission, with families aboard, so the ship's design would include plants and warm colors. "That's where I headed with the bridge," Probert says. "Gene wanted it to be comfortable, so I gave it a softer look than Kirk's bridge." The modifications included a ramp rather than steps to the upper level. "I'm very much into equal access, and I wanted critters and people of all physical abilities to be able to go from one level to another," the designer says. "I also provided a bridge 'head' [bathroom] door, that was only used once, when you see somebody coming out wiping his hands."

A foam core model of an early design (spread 21) included a conference table between the two ramps. "That was Bob Justman's idea," Probert notes, "and we held a lot of meetings about it. But the idea of the captain getting up from his command chair and going around to a table behind to sit and talk about a situation just didn't seem believable." In the end, the conference table gave way to a conference lounge, just behind the bridge. Also visible in the model: sunken conn and ops stations. "They're depressed into the floor because of concerns about seeing over their heads," Probert explains. "But then Bob pointed out that would make it hard for the camera dolly to traverse. So to make it easier to film, it became one deck. The conn and ops stations stayed separated in order to allow Picard to walk between them if he wanted to address the screen directly. Kirk always had to walk around the stations."

"While creating these designs with Herman Zimmerman, we heard a tremendous amount of angst among the fans that we were 'replacing their [original] show,'" Probert says. "So I included clues that hopefully would calm their concerns." Those clues include chasing lights below the viewscreen, and a ship's diagram and dedication plaque similar to those from *TOS*. "Instead of being at the back of the bridge, they're on either side, near the front," he adds. "Just above the food replicators—which were *never* used."

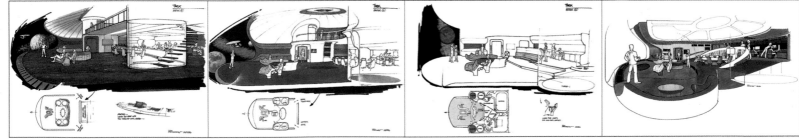

"The production designer is responsible for everything you see on the screen—except for the acting," says Herman Zimmerman, *TNG*'s production designer for the show's first season. Overseeing all the visual elements that must come together in each scene of every episode is a huge responsibility—but sometimes it's more about translating than it is about creating. Take, for example, the *Enterprise* bridge. According to Zimmerman, "I didn't design the bridge, I just kept it from being impossible to construct."

The bridge design was the brilliant work of Andrew Probert, who'd joined the show prior to Zimmerman's arrival. Probert had been hard at work on this crucial set for some time, but as beautiful as his approved bridge design looked on paper, the concept was, Zimmerman recalls, "almost unbuildable because it's got compound curves in every direction. But that's also what makes that bridge *unique*. It was important that I do the best I could to make it a reality, and I hired some of the best set designers in the business to help me translate Andy's drawings into something that could be made in feet and inches."

Another problem was that *huge* viewscreen at the front of the set. The audience at home probably

doesn't realize it, but that screen isn't always there. Whenever the script calls for an exciting space visual to appear, the camera operator turns his equipment in the direction of the viewscreen and a green screen is lowered into place; in the meantime, the visual effects department starts working on whatever image they ultimately will lay in. If the script *doesn't* call for a viewscreen visual, the green screen is raised and the camera operator is free to shoot the action from other directions—even from outside the set, looking in through the empty space where the green screen was.

If it sounds simple, it isn't. Or rather, it wasn't, until Zimmerman solved a problem. "It was almost an impossibility to shoot," he recalls, "because the lower edge of the viewscreen frame was only eighteen inches high." That wasn't enough space for the bottom of the green screen to completely disappear behind the wall when in place, so the effect didn't look real. But Zimmerman knew just what to do.

"We cut a hole in the soundstage floor and made a huge trapdoor—so huge that it had to be engineered—that dropped down on hinges and allowed the screen to go down below floor level," he says. "And when we were done shooting the screen, we'd

bring it back up and use that space for other things . . . like simply walking behind the set!"

Below: a composited visual effect from "Where No One Has Gone Before." Opposite: an angle that the audience *never* sees, for obvious reasons.

The start-up process on a new television production is far from glamorous. It means hours of mind-numbing work squeezed into a period that is inevitably too short. Sounds a bit like hell, or at the very least purgatory, right?

Wrong. "I was in heaven," Michael Okuda says of *The Next Generation*'s preproduction phase, when he was charged with designing the control panels for the new *Enterprise*. Herman Zimmerman had challenged Okuda to create something "cool," with a sense of "technical credibility." Equally important: something "affordable on a tight television budget." "It was an exhausting process," shares Okuda, "but it was way more fun than anyone should be allowed to have.

"Gene Roddenberry said that he wanted his new ship—called the *Enterprise*-7 and the *Enterprise*-G during the early days of preproduction—to be far more advanced than the ship in *The Original Series*," Okuda recalls. "So advanced that it would be highly simplified and elegant. For me as graphics designer, that was both daunting and exciting. Daunting because it meant that I couldn't fall back on [*TOS* designer] Matt Jefferies's brilliant futurism or the cool stuff from the *Star Trek* movies." And *exciting* be-

cause it meant that Okuda would get to create a whole new look for something that would be seen by viewers in every single episode of the new series.

"I started by looking at the way prop control panels were made for sets," he continues. "Because cost was such an important factor, I looked at ways to make those panels as inexpensive as possible. If I could make them affordable, the new ship could have a lot more panels! I felt that the entire control panel, including control keyboards, instruments, and display screens, could all be simulated with backlit photo art on acrylic plastic sheets. Then, when you put lights behind the panel, it would look very dramatic and (hopefully) futuristic, like high-tech stained glass."

By creating the panels entirely as artwork, Okuda freed himself from the need to employ conventional —and expensive—buttons and dials. "I tried to come up with something that implied great sophistication of system design, that would make sense, even when seen out of focus, behind an actor, in the background of a shot," he adds.

Okuda ultimately named this design style "LCARS," for "Library Computer Access and Retrieval System." The easily readable, highly recog-

nizable interactive panel displays became standard throughout *TNG*—and virtually all the permutations of *Star Trek* to follow. But outside of scripted dialogue spoken by the characters, few would mention the LCARS acronym when referring to the colorful displays. In a tip of the hat to their creator, they became more widely known to cast, crew, and *Star Trek* fandom-at-large as "Okudagrams."

While Gene Roddenberry was reluctant to recycle certain iconic elements from *The Original Series*, he saw no problem with rehiring some of the same behind-the-scenes department heads who'd been so creative the first time around. Thus, when the time came to create uniforms for his new crew, he again called on the man who'd designed the first Starfleet uniform: William Ware Theiss.

In the two decades since Theiss had collaborated with Roddenberry, he'd worked steadily as a costume designer, on cult favorites like *Harold and Maude*, *Bound for Glory*, *Goin' South*, and *Heart Like a Wheel*, and most recently on a series of TV movies for Disney. But he hadn't lost his unique *Star Trek* touch, and as he set to work, he deliberately steered away from the military-inspired uniforms worn by Captain Kirk and company in the recent franchise movies. Instead, Theiss designed a variety of stylish outfits, including the unisex "skant" (skirt/pant hybrid) worn by Deanna Troi in the pilot, and periodically by background players during the first season. Eventually, the producers expressed their preference for one-piece jumpsuits, and during repeated "wardrobe meetings," Theiss (here in a plaid shirt) brought in models to demonstrate a variety of

possibilities. Roddenberry, Rick Berman, and Robert Justman chose the prototypes seen on the opposite page. "They're a simple, uncomplicated design," explained Theiss. "I try not to make my designs too complex, visually."

Theiss retired from the show after only one season. He passed away in 1992.

"One of the most perplexing design projects was Geordi La Forge's VISOR," relates scenic artist Michael Okuda. "Gene wanted it to look like cool, advanced technology that wouldn't distract from LeVar Burton's good looks. This was an important project, so illustrators Andrew Probert and Rick Sternbach gave it the full-court press under the guidance of Herman Zimmerman. As the show's graphic artist, I had more than enough work with the ship's control panels, and I was content to watch the cool stuff that emerged from their drawing boards.

"In any design project, it's normal for the first few concepts to be rejected, as designers get a feel for what the producers want. But this process lasted longer than anyone expected. Through many sketches and prototypes, Gene just wasn't seeing what he wanted. Even set decorator John Dwyer got into the fray, bringing in a dizzying array of sunglasses from funky stores on Melrose Avenue—to no avail. And time was running out.

"I'd just moved to Los Angeles from my hometown of Honolulu. I hadn't even found an apartment. My friends Jeff and Kiku Annon were kind enough to let me crash at their home. One morning, I noticed that Kiku had an interesting-looking hair clip. Its pat-tern of 'teeth' caught the light, but it wasn't overly complicated. As a bonus, you could see through the teeth, which would be important if LeVar had to wear it.

"I asked Kiku if I could borrow the clip, and she said 'Sure!' even though *TNG* was so secretive at this point that I couldn't tell her what I wanted it for.

"I brought the clip to Herman, who studied it closely. Like Gene, Herman always tried to think 'outside the box,' and I hoped it might inspire some new thoughts for our illustrators. A moment later, Herman said, 'I think you may have solved a very difficult design problem.' He had the clip spray-painted, then headed to Roddenberry's office. I returned to my duties; I was still racing to finish the control panel graphics for the bridge.

"The next morning, a delivery person stopped by my desk with a bottle of champagne and a thank-you card from Gene Roddenberry! And for the next seven years, Geordi La Forge wore a visual prosthetic gizmo based on my friend's hair clip.

"Sadly, Kiku never got it back. It got lost at the prop shop. Sorry, Kiku!"

Right: Susan Duchow—Denise Crosby's stand-in—models the original spray-painted hair clip.

Opposite: Rick Berman and Gene Roddenberry study an early version of Geordi's VISOR modeled by an unidentified body double from Central Casting.

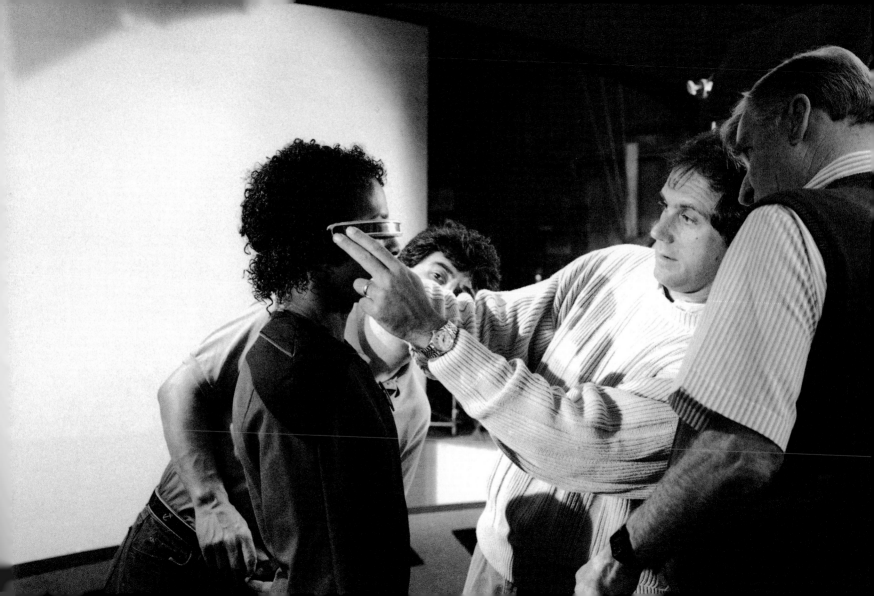

"What's in a name?" Juliet asked.

Good question. But when a big, expensive television show is being mounted, the people in charge expect the label to be a perfect fit from the get-go. The wrong title could turn off potential viewers, even the ones who'd waited twenty years for *Star Trek* to return to the airwaves.

Everyone knew that the name *Star Trek* had to be in there, but they also knew it had to be followed by something else, something that suggested, yes, this is the *offspring* of that other show, but it's about a different ship, a different era, a different crew. Lists of suggestions came from the writers and producers, interoffice memos fluttering into in-boxes and tossed into trash cans:

Star Trek: Future Trek

Star Trek: A New Beginning

Star Trek: The Second Generation

Star Trek: The New Generation

Meanwhile, over in the art department, Andrew Probert (pictured with an early foam core model of the *Enterprise* bridge) was trying to create a visual for something that didn't yet have a name. "They were looking for something to put on their scripts and call sheets," he recalls, "and the name of the show hadn't been locked in. So I'm playing with 'The New Star Trek,' 'The New Generation,' 'The Next Generation' . . . and I'm thinking, '*I don't know what this is*—'

"And suddenly my brain went, '*Screeech!* Wait a minute,'" Probert says with a laugh. "I remembered that I'd come up with a logotype back when I was working on *The Motion Picture* and I'd tacked it up on the wall, right next to the shuttle pod and the Vulcan shuttle paintings I was doing for the movie." (Photo inset, opposite.)

That sleek, streamlined logotype hadn't been used for the film, so Probert quickly resurrected it, and sent it on to the producers. Once the producers reached a consensus on the final title, the modified logotype was slapped onto scripts, call sheets, and, eventually, the series' opening credits. Not to mention every piece of spin-off merchandise imaginable.

Probert's montage of assorted logotypes is also interesting for the small sketch in the lower corner. It's Probert's own concept for "saucer separation."

"After I had designed this beautiful smooth shape for the *Enterprise*, the producers said, 'Oh, by the way, it has to separate.' They told me, 'The ship has a battle section.' I didn't know what they meant," Probert admits. "So that little drawing was my first idea for a battle section. It even has its own warp nacelles. But when they saw it, they said, 'No, no— the *whole* saucer separates. The battle section is the *engineering hull*.'"

Probert subsequently divided his single sleek design into the double-hulled version that viewers saw on-screen. Happily, like the once unused logotype, Probert hung on to his tantalizing original idea, shown here for the first time.

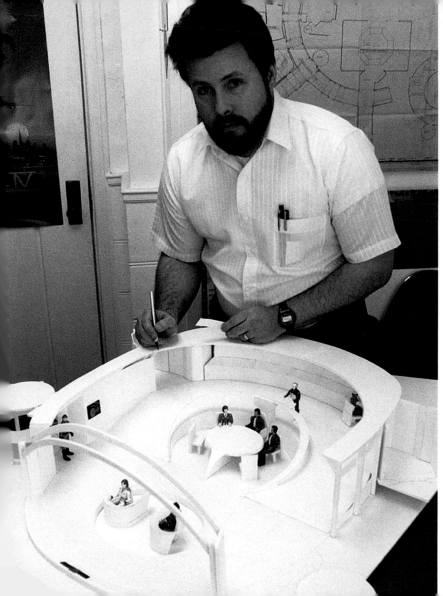

STAR TREK
THE NEXT GENERATION

STAR TREK

STAR THE NEW STAR TREK

STAR THE NEW STAR TREK

STAR TREK

STAR TREK
THE NEW GENERATION

STAR TREK
THE NEXT GENERATION

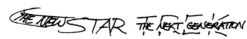

THE NEW STAR THE NEXT GENERATION

Photography on the pilot was scheduled for June 1987, but in the days that preceded the first call of "Roll film!" a thousand tiny details needed tending. Many of those details had to do with how the actors looked—or rather, how their characters *should* look on-screen. Data's skin color was a particularly popular topic of discussion. "When we first started testing Brent [Spiner's] makeup for Data, I didn't have a specific concept in mind for him," says makeup supervisor Michael Westmore (seen touching up an "almost there" version of Spiner's makeup at right). "We worked for three or four days, trying every possible combination of hair and makeup you can imagine, until we found something that looked sufficiently 'android-like.'" Over the course of a series of makeup tests, Data's skin color was pink, green, blue, and even battleship gray. Ultimately, the producers decided on a pale metallic gold with matching yellow contact lenses.

Jonathan Frakes was luckier. They played with his hair a bit—combing it back, tousling it forward, moving the part slightly—even giving him the quintessential classic *Star Trek* pointed sideburns (scrutinized here by classic sideburn expert Robert

As the clock ticked down, it was Marina Sirtis who seemed to draw the most attention. Though they'd cast her for her exotic looks, the producers weren't quite sure how *Troi* should look. The actress's dark, naturally curly hair was pushed into a tight bun, tweaked into a playful updo that screams "1980s," and finally allowed to cascade wildly behind a wide headband—at least for the pilot. After that, they went back to the bun (leading her costars, Sirtis recalls, to affectionately refer to her as "bunhead"), which she dutifully wore for the rest of the first season.

Seen opposite is a rare shot of the youthful Sirtis modeling her poufy updo and just *one* of the very dark contact lenses that testify to her Betazoid heritage. Sirtis's natural eye color is a lighter hazel.

Those who worked closely with Gene Roddenberry attest to the fact that, for any shortcomings they had to complain about, he truly was touched with genius. His optimistic view of the future, and particularly his view of mankind living in that future, never faltered. He fought hard to re-create *Star Trek* on his own terms. But ironically, even as the series went into production, he no longer had the physical stamina to lead the way. Robert Justman, in his 1996 memoir *Inside Star Trek* (cowritten by former Desilu exec Herbert Solow), recalls that during the initial preparation of *Star Trek: The Next Generation*, it was clear to him that Roddenberry, overweight and suffering from cardiovascular disease, was in bad shape physically: "He would be out of breath after walking a hundred feet, and he had to drive a golf cart to visit the stages or other parts of the lot."

Roddenberry increasingly delegated responsibilities to people on his team, including Justman, Rick Berman, and Leonard Maizlish, Roddenberry's attorney/business manager. But, as with any collaboration between multiple participants, frequent miscommunication resulted in friction and frustration among staffers. After completing production on "The Neutral Zone," Justman departed, citing hy-

pertension due to stress. Berman stayed on, playing a larger and larger role as the series progressed, but he steadfastly maintained that the show was Roddenberry's baby. "It's not about my vision of the future," he says. "It's about Gene Roddenberry's vision of the future."

"Let's see what's out there." —Picard

Captain Jean-Luc Picard's first assignment aboard Starfleet's new flagship, the *U.S.S. Enterprise* NCC-1701-D, is intriguing: solve the mystery of Farpoint Station. Because the station is on distant Deneb IV, a planet located far beyond the explored portion of the galaxy, Picard's goal is to negotiate a friendly agreement that will allow Starfleet to use the base. Before he does that, however, he must determine how the low-tech Bandi, the owners and operators of the station, managed to construct such an impressive high-tech facility. Captain Picard's efforts to reach Farpoint are hampered by Q, the arrogant representative of an all-powerful species that considers humanity too barbaric for space exploration. Appointing himself judge, jury, and executioner, Q indicts the *Enterprise* crew as members of "a grievously savage race," and threatens to sentence them accordingly—unless Picard can find a tangible way to prove that the human race has matured.

"I will not promise never to appear again." —Q

"He was mad, bad and dangerous to know."

Actor John de Lancie found himself thinking about Lady Caroline Lamb's famous assessment of Lord Byron as he read about the character of Q in the "Encounter at Farpoint" script. That may account for his devilishly charming and occasionally sinister portrayal of the omnipotent Q. "I think of him as kind of a naughty boy," says de Lancie. "You're not quite sure what's going to happen with him. *I'm* not sure what's going to happen."

Although Q is one of the most popular guest characters in the *Star Trek* pantheon (so popular that he later made appearances on *Star Trek: Deep Space Nine* and *Star Trek: Voyager*), he likely wouldn't exist at all if it hadn't been for a disagreement between Paramount studio execs and Gene Roddenberry.

Roddenberry had asked *Star Trek* veteran Dorothy "D.C." Fontana—story editor on *The Original Series* for two of its three seasons—to write the pilot for *The Next Generation*. He instructed her to write an hour-long pilot; the studio, however, was pushing for a two-hour TV movie. The studio ultimately won the dispute, so to flesh out the piece, Roddenberry in-

serted the subplot about Q into Fontana's completed script. At least superficially, Q seems to have a great deal in common with Trelane, the omnipotent child-god from the *TOS* episode "The Squire of Gothos." But in the hands of the talented de Lancie, what might have been an annoying retread became an audience favorite, at once an eternal gadfly to Captain Jean-Luc Picard and, at the same time, a perversely motivated being who occasionally seems to have the best interests of humanity at heart.

01 026

A clever combination of physical special effects, makeup, wardrobe, and an actor with a plentiful amount of patience briefly transforms bold security chief Tasha Yar into a shapely human Popsicle.

"This is a new ship, but she's got the right name. Now you remember that, you hear. You treat her like a lady, and she'll always bring you home." —Admiral Leonard McCoy

Although he knew comparisons were inevitable, Gene Roddenberry didn't want the success of *Star Trek: The Next Generation* to coast on fond memories of *The Original Series* (*TOS*), nor did he wish to be accused of repeating himself. Thus, he initially resisted the idea of giving prominent roles to species like Klingons and Vulcans because they had been featured so often in the first show. The same was true of the actors who had appeared on *Star Trek* . . . until it wasn't. Several performers eventually would reprise their iconic *TOS* roles in *TNG* episodes, including Leonard Nimoy (Spock), James Doohan (Scotty), and Mark Lenard (Sarek, Spock's Vulcan father). But only one of them would show up in *the pilot*—and at Gene Roddenberry's request. Serving as a touchstone to the faithful who had long supported *Star Trek*'s return to television, DeForest Kelley's appearance as the eccentric unnamed Starfleet admiral who'd rather *not* use the transporter was both humorous and poignant. Ever the easygoing, good-

natured Southern gentleman, Kelley reportedly refused to accept more than SAG scale for the walk-on role as Doctor Leonard McCoy. Fans lauded Kelley's appearance, which was memorable enough to merit a special collectors' edition action figure—complete with the admiral's "Starfleet issue" sweater—from toy manufacturer Playmates. The actual sweater that Kelley wore in the episode—a cardigan of silver-gray wool, trimmed with black and gray braid, metallic fabric elbow patches, and epaulets—was sold at the 2006 Christie's auction "40 Years of *Star Trek*: The Collection."

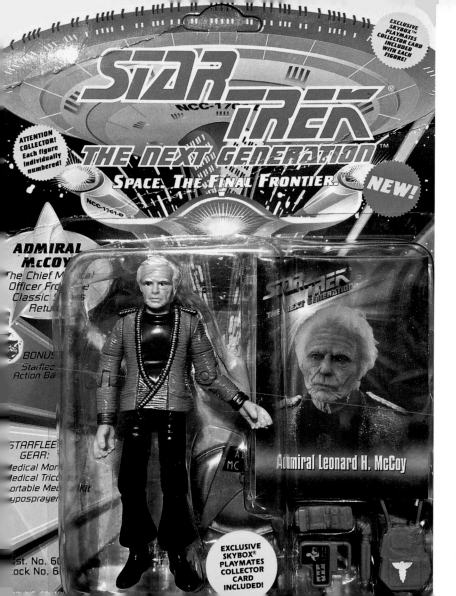

In autumn of 2006, forty years after the debut of the original *Star Trek*, the world-famous Christie's auction house offered for sale a large quantity of authentic *Star Trek* costumes, props, and other memorabilia that had been provided by series franchise owners CBS and Paramount Pictures. The auction was a massive success, with even the humble items utilized by *Star Trek* personnel who worked behind the scenes selling for surprising sums.

Case in point: a binder containing extensive costumer's notes and an annotated script from "Encounter at Farpoint." These notes provided scene-by-scene descriptions of each character who appeared in the episode, with Polaroid reference photos of actors in costume and his or her shooting schedule.

Documentation of this type is not unique to *Star Trek* productions. Costumer continuity notes are an essential tool used by all wardrobe department personnel. They are filled out carefully and referred to throughout each shooting day to ensure accuracy in the look of the costumes.

The notes pages are split into four columns, and titled, from left: Change, Scene Nos (or Numbers), Set, and Description.

"Change" identifies a particular costume; in any production, an actor may have multiple costume changes. The notes for Michael Dorn identified Worf's Starfleet uniform as "Change #1."

"Scene Numbers" lists each of the various scenes in which the costume was worn.

"Set" indicates on which stage set the costume was worn, in other words, "Main Bridge," "Engine Room [*sic*]."

"Description" details all of the various elements that are included in this particular costume so that it can be located amid other similar costumes it may be stored with. Worf's uniform, for example, includes a "Gold imitation woven leather sash w/ fringe." Picard's doesn't.

The photographs are included to demonstrate how the costume was worn in each scene. Often a costume will need subtle modifications as shooting progresses, so multiple photographs are taken to show the details and nuances. If Worf were to get into a fight and lose his sash, or tear his sleeve, essentially he would still be wearing Change #1, but the modifications would be recorded in the notes and a new picture would be taken and labeled accordingly. This process continues, page after page, until the character is seen in different clothing (for instance, off-duty garb). In that case, a new note page would be started for Change #2. Worf, as it happens, didn't have a Change #2 in this episode. Q, on the other hand, had many changes.

As shooting continues over days or weeks, the notes get filed into a continuity book. Each character filmed gets his or her own "chapter," with a new book started for each episode.

Opposite: This particular lot, initially estimated at a value of $600 to $800, sold at auction for $4,000.

If you have unlimited time and money, there's no shortage of ways to do something "right." When both are severely limited, it helps to have bosses who appreciate unique solutions.

"Gene had initially asked that the bridge control panels be very clean, almost stark in simplicity," explains Michael Okuda. "He told me to keep blinkies or other activity to a minimum because he wanted to show that the ship's technology was *so* advanced that it had become simple. He wanted most of the panels to remain off, except in an emergency. That's why the bridge panels in 'Encounter at Farpoint' have few lights on, and virtually no blinking.

"But after 'Farpoint,' producer Bob Justman came up to the art department and told me that he and Rick Berman had decided to add more activity to the bridge panels. The problem, of course, was that now that we had built the bridge for the pilot, there was very little money or time for changes. 'You'll have to think of something,' he said with a grin. Bob knew me well enough by then to know that I loved a challenge.

"I originally had wanted to install video monitors on the bridge, but that had been deemed too costly, as were numerous other cool electronic gizmos that were commonplace in sci-fi movie spaceships. Blinking lights on the panels might have been a possibility, but the effects department's budget was limited . . . and Gene still didn't want a lot of blinkies.

"I remembered seeing low-tech backlit signs that utilized polarized light spinners to create the illusion of shimmering motion. They used to be popular in store displays and at trade shows. And also in bars. I called around until I found a company on the East Coast that made the polarizers, and immediately had a bunch of them rushed to my desk at Paramount. There were only a few days left until we were scheduled to start filming 'The Naked Now,' the first regular episode.

"Within hours of the polarizers' arrival, our mechanical effects department had a working prototype for a bridge panel. Herman Zimmerman had been understandably skeptical of this strange gizmo, but when he saw the effect in action, he loved it. He immediately ordered the bridge aft panels retrofitted for installation of polarized spinners, and I set about modifying my panel designs to take advantage of what I called 'beer sign technology.' The technique was very limited in the kinds of animation it could do, but it was fast, inexpensive, and it fit with our existing panels. Initially, all it could do was shimmer, but eventually I incorporated it into graphics to suggest flowing warp plasma, pulsing force fields, and even a turbulent solar photosphere for 'The Naked Now.' Polarized motion graphics became a vital (and inexpensive) part of the *Enterprise*-D's graphic style."

Opposite: The master situation monitor in engineering featured Okuda's "beer sign technology."

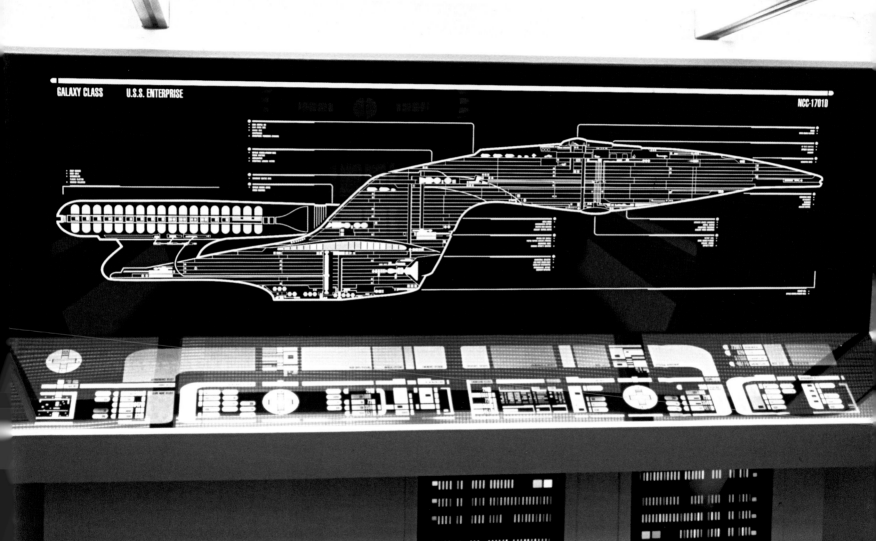

GALAXY CLASS   U.S.S. ENTERPRISE

NCC-1701D

"We are more alike than unlike, my dear Captain. I have pores. Humans have pores. I have fingerprints. Humans have fingerprints. My chemical nutrients are like your blood. If you prick me, do I not leak?" —Data

Rendezvousing with the science ship *Tsiolkovsky*, the *Enterprise* crew discovers that all aboard the small vessel apparently have died as a result of their own self-destructive behavior. As Doctor Crusher attempts to figure out what could have triggered the researchers' actions, members of Picard's own crew begin acting strangely, exhibiting symptoms that resemble extreme intoxication. Surprisingly, information on the bizarre malady is already in the *Enterprise*'s medical database; it infected Captain James T. Kirk's crew aboard the NCC-1701 a century ago. But the virus has mutated since then and the old antidote doesn't work anymore. When the dying star that *Tsiolkovsky*'s crew had been monitoring begins to collapse, the *Enterprise*'s immediate priority is to clear out of the area. Unfortunately, Wesley Crusher has commandeered engineering and the computer controls are offline. All of which means . . . the ship isn't going anywhere.

During *TNG*'s first season, says Rick Berman, "the characters were all kind of stumbling to find themselves. And the writers were kind of stumbling to find them as well." A case in point would be the first *TNG* episode to be produced after the pilot: "The Naked Now," an update of the *TOS* episode "The Naked Time" (written by John D. F. Black, who also receives shared story credit for the *TNG* version). The producers referred to it as an "homage" to the original, not a redo, and included references to pertinent points in the earlier script as a demonstration of their honest intent. The motive here, as in the first version, was to give the show's audience a glimpse into the inner longings of key members of the *Enterprise* crew. The realization of that effort, however, pleased neither the fans nor the author of the teleplay, Dorothy "D.C." Fontana, who replaced her name on the final product with the pseudonym "J. Michael Bingham." Particularly irksome to fans was the writers' use of young Wesley Crusher, whose science project—the portable tractor beam seen at right—provides the deus ex machina that saves the ship at the last minute.

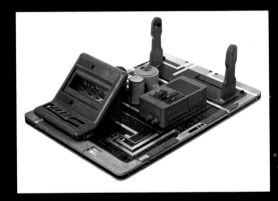

Picard: "You speak of a code of honor. But what you are saying now, according to our customs, is called an act of war."
Lutan: "This is not an act of war, but of love."

The *Enterprise*'s mission on Ligon II—treaty negotiations to obtain a lifesaving vaccine—is complicated when the planetary leader abducts Security Chief Tasha Yar with the intention of making her his new wife. The Prime Directive demands that the crew abide by Ligon's strict code of honor, meaning they can't just beam Yar home. But when Picard learns that Yar and the leader's current wife are expected to engage in a battle to the death, he realizes that something other than simple diplomacy will be required.

Ask any *TNG* cast member for his or her least favorite episode and chances are the name of this episode will come up. "The worst and most embarrassing . . . was that horrible, racist episode from the first season, 'Code of Honor,'" Jonathan Frakes shares with audiences at convention appearances. Wil Wheaton says much the same in venues that in-

clude his humorously acerbic *TNG* episode reviews at TVSquad.com, although his primary gripe is the show's similarity to an episode from *The Original Series*. "It borrows way too heavily from 'Amok Time,' immediately after an episode that was essentially a rewrite of another *TOS* classic," Wheaton states. "We were still proving that we deserved the right to carry the *Star Trek* mantle, and when I look back at 'Code of Honor' . . . I'm astonished that we weren't canceled by mid-season."

The original script by Katharyn Powers and Michael Baron reportedly focused on an alien species whose moral code was similar to that of Japan's ancient samurai. While the script indicated that two of the guards who protected the planetary leader were racially black, somewhere along the way a decision was made to transform the entire Ligonian culture into one more akin to tribal Africa (or, more precisely, a dated, politically incorrect portrayal of tribal Africa)—and casting followed suit. The result was an episode that rubbed just about everyone the wrong way.

"Could you please continue the petty bickering? I find it most intriguing." —Data

Plans for a bout of rest and relaxation on the idyllic planet Haven are scuttled when Counselor Troi receives an unanticipated—and unwelcome—visit from her outlandish Betazoid mother, Lwaxana. Mrs. Troi is accompanied by the Miller family, longtime friends of Deanna's deceased human father. Apparently, they've all arrived for a festive occasion: the time has come for the fulfillment of Deanna's prearranged bonding vow to the Millers' son, Wyatt. Neither Deanna nor Wyatt is thrilled about the impending union. The counselor doesn't want to leave her post on the *Enterprise* (or her former lover, Will Riker), and Wyatt is disappointed that Deanna isn't the beautiful blonde woman he's had visions of since childhood. For tradition's sake, however, the young couple is prepared to make the best of the situation. At least, until the arrival of a mysterious plague ship changes everyone's options.

"I am Lwaxana Troi. Daughter of the Fifth House, Holder of the Sacred Chalice of Rixx, Heir to the Holy Rings of Betazed. Who are you?"
—*Lwaxana*

"Gene came home one day and said to me, 'Majel, I have a great part for you, and guess what—you don't have to act!'"

Majel Barrett loved to tell the story of how she became Deanna Troi's mother. She told it onstage at *Star Trek* conventions and to reporters for all manner of publications, from fanzines on up.

As the story goes, Barrett had no idea what the role called for. All she had to go on was husband Gene Roddenberry's intriguing description of the character as "the 'Auntie Mame' of the Galaxy." The character of Auntie Mame (whose exploits were the basis for a novel, a musical, and a motion picture) is best described as "free-spirited," and apparently Roddenberry felt that phrase fit his wife to perfection. Barrett took up the gauntlet, transforming herself into Lwaxana Troi, a true force of nature, alternately haughty, horny, and happy-go-lucky. She was the oversolicitous mother-from-hell of Counselor Troi, and the fearsome manhunter of

an embarrassed Captain Picard (among others).

She played it broad during her first few *TNG* appearances, pulling out all the stops for a character who often bordered on caricature. However, later episodes allowed her to flesh out Lwaxana's personality and give fuller performances, revealing a woman as capable of feeling soul-wrenching sadness as joy. That those episodes coincided with the physical decline and ultimate death of her husband may have played a part in the metamorphosis.

Prior to meeting Gene Roddenberry, Majel Barrett had enjoyed a successful career as an actress, appearing in numerous movies (*The Buccaneer*, *Will Success Spoil Rock Hunter?*, *The Quick and the Dead*) and television shows (*Whirlybirds*, *The Untouchables*, *Leave It to Beaver*). In 1962, she met Lucille Ball in an acting class and soon appeared on *The Lucy Show*. A year later she was cast in *The Lieutenant*, a Desilu production created by her future husband. *The Lieutenant* was short-lived, but the relationship forged between Roddenberry and Barrett continued. He created the role of "Number One" for her in the failed pilot for *Star Trek*, but the character—a high-ranking intelligent female officer—didn't please the network. Undeterred,

Roddenberry cast her again once the show was on the air, this time as Nurse Christine Chapel, who appeared in twenty-five episodes of *The Original Series* and two *Star Trek* films. Lwaxana graced six episodes of *The Next Generation* and three episodes of *Star Trek: Deep Space Nine.* Over the course of the entire *Star Trek* franchise, Barrett was heard as the voice of Starfleet's shipboard computers in 236 episodes and six motion pictures.

After Gene Roddenberry's passing in 1991, Barrett went on to produce two successful television series that her husband had created: *Earth: Final Conflict* and *Gene Roddenberry's Andromeda*. She died in 2008, remembered by friends and fans alike as "The First Lady of *Star Trek*."

Picard: "Where is this place?"
Data: "Where none have gone before."

While testing an alleged advanced propulsion system, the crew of the *Enterprise* find themselves over one billion light-years from their own galaxy, thrown into a region of space where thought becomes reality. Kosinski, the arrogant Starfleet engineer who claimed responsibility for the advance, doesn't know how to get the ship home. That's because it was actually Kosinski's assistant, a mysterious alien known only as "the Traveler," who was behind the ship's astounding journey through time and space. The Traveler claims to have the ability to magnify and utilize the energy of thought, but the excursion outside of the galaxy has left him on the brink of death. And without the Traveler, there is no way home.

Eric Menyuk, who played the Traveler in this and two subsequent episodes of *TNG*, was the first runner-up in the casting competition for the role of Data. Although Brent Spiner was chosen for the part, the producers liked Menyuk, and welcomed the opportu-

nity to cast him as the Traveler. In a way, *not* winning the role of everyone's favorite android was a far more significant stepping-stone for Menyuk than a permanent position in *Star Trek* would have been. For the next twelve years, Menyuk made guest appearances on dozens of television series, including *Cheers*, *L.A. Law*, *Wiseguy*, *Married with Children*, *Matlock*, and *Diagnosis Murder*. Then, in 1998, he quit acting entirely and took up a new profession: law. That was the year he graduated from Loyola Law School (the acting jobs had paid for his education) and began working as a litigator. He wound up at Newman Aaronson Vanaman, a firm that specializes in providing assistance to children with disabilities—in fact, the first firm in Southern California to provide representation for disabled children in their struggle to receive appropriate educational programs. It was the perfect fit for Menyuk, who had in the past sought the assistance of such advocates on behalf of his son, who had been in special education since fourth grade.

"Merde." —*Picard*

The *Enterprise* becomes the first Federation ship on record to have a face-to-face encounter with the mysterious Ferengi after members of the mercenary species steal an energy converter from a Federation outpost. When both the *Enterprise* and the Ferengi vessel lose power above a planet that once belonged to the extinct Tkon Empire, the two sides call a tentative truce so that teams from both ships can join forces to investigate the abandoned outpost below. But since the Ferengi don't share the Federation's value system, is it any surprise that they double-cross Commander Will Riker's away team soon after beaming down?

Although Klingons and Romulans are prominent in *Star Trek: The Next Generation*, Gene Roddenberry did not want to use them as the primary villains of his new show. He charged coproducer Herbert Wright with creating a brand-new species to plague the crew of the *Enterprise* on a recurring basis. Wright recalled that the inspiration for the rift between the Federation and the Klingon Empire in *TOS* was Cold War–era hostility between the United States and the USSR, and he searched for a contemporary (1980s) equivalent. Although the film *Wall Street*, with its pervasive "Greed is good" sentiment, would not be released until the end of 1987, there already was a palpable feeling that the nation's financial sector was full of amoral barbarians. This, Wright decided, was just the straw horse he was looking for: a species of ruthless robber barons whose entire society was built on the principle that profit is the most important thing in the galaxy. Wright especially liked the sharp contrast between this new species—dubbed the Ferengi—and the enlightened men and women of the *Enterprise*-D, who had no need or desire for money.

With Roddenberry's blessing, the development of the Ferengi got underway. A great deal of time and energy went into the appearance of the Ferengi—far more, in fact, than had gone into the look of the original Klingons. Ferengi would be short in stature, and their faces, by our standards, would seem grotesque. Andrew Probert created a series of impressive concept designs, later modified by makeup supervisor Michael Westmore. With huge ears—the better to hear potential profit in the wind—and piranha-like teeth, they looked suitably aggressive, as did their sharp-edged Marauder starships (another design by Probert, inspired by the shape of a horseshoe crab).

Unfortunately, when the species made its on-camera debut in "The Last Outpost," the general reaction was disappointment; the Ferengi were no Klingons. What did them in? For one thing, their costuming—a caveman-like fake fur sarong worn atop what appeared to be loose gray pajamas—resembled something left over from the oft-criticized third season of *The Original Series*. An ill-conceived decision to have them "jump up and down like crazed gerbils" (per Armin Shimerman, who played one of the episode's three Ferengi) did not jibe with their reputation as dangerously crafty aggressors. And the prospect of Picard regularly squaring off against a race of cutthroat capitalists was a nonstarter with the audience. The most negative elements would be modified in future episodes, and solid character development of the species in sister show *Deep Space Nine* would actually win fans, but the damage here was done: the Ferengi would not be the key bad guys of *TNG*. That role ultimately would be played by the Borg.

Yar: *"I must ask where you were during this vessel's Earth hours of eighteen-hundred last night and zero-seven-hundred this morning."*
Antican: *"Eating."*
Yar: *"Sir, we're talking about hours here."*
Antican: *"It was a large meal, Lieutenant Yar. And a very interesting animal."*

A mission to ferry two groups of adversarial diplomats to a Federation conference is disrupted when the *Enterprise* passes through a strange energy cloud and inadvertently picks up a non-corporeal life-form. After inhabiting several crew members' bodies, the entity decides that Picard is the most compatible "host." The command crew is horrified when the joint being announces its intention to beam back to its cloud while within Picard's body.

The *Enterprise* crew may not have been fond of the wolfish Anticans or the snake-headed Selay, but they were two of Michael Westmore's favorite first-season creations. Inspired by concept art by Andrew Probert, Westmore's team created the Antican masks in the tiny makeup lab on the Paramount lot, but due to space considerations, they sent the Selay head sculpt to a different lab for manufacture of the masks. The completed headgear *looked* great, but unlike the lightweight, pliable Antican masks, "they were as heavy and rigid as rocks," mourns Westmore. He had time to recast only two of the Selay snakeheads in lighter foam rubber prior to filming. "The background actors who had to wear the heavier ones were very uncomfortable," he admits, although it appears they bore up well under the pressure.

Some of the key visual effects in this episode already were familiar to fans of the era's most popular science fiction films. A cloud tank—a large water tank used in creating a variety of atmospheric effects (primarily clouds, hence the name) of the sort seen in *Close Encounters of the Third Kind*—was utilized for the "energy pattern cloud" from which the *Enterprise* picks up its cosmic hitchhiker. Lightning-like animated energy bolts, similar to the ones the Emperor uses on Luke Skywalker at the end of *Return of the Jedi*, conveyed the otherworldly powers of the sentient cloud being.

Below: An image of the havoc wrought by the cloud being's energy blasts *prior* to the insertion of postproduction effects. The captain/cloud being has already left the bridge, but the blinded bridge crew is not yet aware of that fact.

It doesn't always happen. There are, of course, close bonds within all *Star Trek* productions—long-term friendships, an occasional marriage, and even, in one instance, an unplanned pregnancy quickly worked into that series' ongoing story line. But *Star Trek: The Next Generation* stands out for its on-set harmony and tight familial atmosphere, which contributed to the believability of the on-screen relationships.

"Whether by design or by accident, Gene [Roddenberry] picked a bunch of people who hit it off immediately," says Marina Sirtis.

"We had a good solid week of rehearsal together before we actually started shooting," LeVar Burton recalls. "I *liked* these people. We seemed to get along real well." He chuckles, noting that at the time he wondered how long it would last.

Somehow, the camaraderie between the core cast members never dissipated throughout *TNG*'s seven-year run, even as the group of primarily unknown actors became household names, and the excitement of landing a full-time gig inevitably became . . . a job. "I think we were well cast," reflects Jonathan Frakes, "in that people who were spending seventy, eighty hours a week together still managed to laugh and enjoy each other's company."

They may, in fact, have enjoyed each other's company a bit too much. "There was a running joke on the set that guest directors hated doing the show," script coordinator Eric Stillwell recalls, "because the cast was always goofing off so much that they couldn't get any work done."

Makeup artist Doug Drexler begs to disagree. Yes, there was rabble-rousing—but the work always got done. "The later the nights wore on, the more fun it became," he says with a smile. "The bridge became a high-tech nightclub, and there was huge silliness, with singing, wrestling matches, water-bottle bowling with Frakes, Spiner practicing his Jimmy Stewart impression or honing his phaser quick draw, and Patrick reciting poetry in the native tongue. I never saw them do a serious rehearsal, and the appreciative stage crew was usually roaring with laughter. But I'll tell you what: when the bell rang and the clapboard clapped, they were right on the money. It was uncanny."

"Nice planet." —Worf

The planet Rubicun III seems to be the perfect place for a bit of rest-and-recreation, a pastoral paradise populated by the scantily clad Edo, who believe in living life to its sensual heights. But if the rules governing the attainment of pleasure on Rubicun are simple, so are the rules for breaking the law. Death is the sentence for any and every infraction, even tromping on some flowers, which is Acting Ensign Wesley Crusher's crime—leaving Captain Picard with a difficult choice between upholding the Prime Directive or saving Wesley's life.

What do the crew of the *Enterprise*-D, employees of the Los Angeles City Sewage Department, comedian Pauly Shore, students at Starfleet Academy, and Austin Powers have in common? They've all visited, filmed at, or beamed down to the Donald C. Tillman Water Reclamation Plant in L.A.'s San Fernando Valley. The futuristic-looking facility was designed by Mr. Tillman, L.A.'s city engineer from 1972 to 1980, as a sanctuary where the public could

enjoy peaceful surroundings while, just beneath their feet, tunnels, pipes, and filtering equipment removed organic and inorganic particles from 40 million gallons of incoming wastewater every day. The landscape, including a lovely 6.5-acre Japanese garden (which is more prominently featured in other *TNG* episodes), is open to the public—and, not coincidentally, to movie and TV production crews.

But as lovely as Riker and his away team found this portion of Rubicun III, it is not the most beautiful park in Los Angeles. That distinction arguably belongs to Huntington Botanical Gardens, twenty-three miles to the east—the location used as the setting for Wesley's misadventure in one of the Edo's "forbidden zones." Open to the public since 1919, what was once railroad and utility magnate Henry Huntington's private ranch has, over the past century, evolved into a living public showcase of outdoor beauty, 120 acres featuring over 14,000 varieties of plants in fourteen distinct gardens. Wesley's disastrous game of catch was shot near the Lily Ponds, the first garden established at the Gardens, and home to turtles, bullfrogs, and koi. On any given day, garden visitors will find sights nearly as entrancing as those that greeted Riker's away team—although

greetings from the Huntington docents likely won't be quite as effusive as those of the Edo.

have done. **I dropped into high warp, stopped right off the enemy vessel's bow, and fired with everything I had."** —*Picard*

Captain Picard receives a strangely generous gift from a Ferengi *DaiMon* (captain) named Bok: the *Stargazer*, the now derelict vessel that Picard once commanded. Nine years earlier, Picard and his then crew abandoned *Stargazer* after it was badly damaged in an attack by an unidentified enemy ship. Bok casually reveals that the enemy ship was Ferengi; he claims his only interest in the matter is returning an abandoned ship to its rightful owner. Picard, troubled by an unusual headache and increasingly powerful remembrances of the battle aboard *Stargazer*, is too distracted to question much. However, the discovery of forged log tapes on the old ship leads Geordi, Data, and Riker to suspect that Bok may be attempting to discredit Picard's role in what the DaiMon refers to as "the Battle of Maxia"—a battle in which, not so coincidentally, Bok's son died.

Right: The Ferengi "thought maker" device— which doesn't look nearly as threatening when it

"Hello, old friend." —Picard

It's the age-old question: which came first, the *Stargazer* starship or the *model* of the *Stargazer* starship?

The answer is: the model came first—sort of.

The little model is a permanent part of the set dressing in Picard's ready room: a curious quadruple-nacelled ship resting on the credenza. It represents a collaborative effort by Andrew Probert and illustrator Rick Sternbach. "Andy and I began fleshing out the *Stargazer* during the preproduction phase, based on a mention of Captain Picard's previous command in the *TNG* writers' bible," Sternbach says. Following a conversation with set decorator John Dwyer about adding a model of the ship to Picard's ready room, the pair "threw a bunch of ideas together, did a few doodles, and settled on using four nacelles to suggest that the *Stargazer* was a fast science vessel," recalls Sternbach. "Then I did most of the actual fabrication and detailing." The model was painted in a desert yellow semigloss to harmonize with the ready room's warm tonal palette—not a traditional Starfleet hue but one that *could* be rationalized as "a specialized hull coating used in initial warp field tests."

Although never identified in episode dialogue as a model of the *U.S.S. Stargazer*, the intention seemed clear. Or at least it did until the script for "The Battle" came in, signaling the need for a larger-scale representation of Picard's ship, suitable for shooting purposes. As Sternbach recalls, "There was some talk about using the *Enterprise* refit (the filming model that had been created for the *Star Trek* movies). But ultimately, they decided to go with the *Stargazer* as we'd designed it."

Ironically, there's a lot of the refit in the *Stargazer*. Sternbach had built Picard's ready room piece with parts from two commercial toy store–variety *Enterprise* refit model kits. He mounted two pairs of nacelles on newly fashioned pylons and turned them ninety degrees, then glued together two top hull pieces (discarding the bottom halves) to form the oversize saucer. To add texture to the surfaces, Sternbach included "plant-on" bits from Japanese anime kits. When master model maker Greg Jein built the four-foot shooting model of the *Stargazer* for "The Battle," he duplicated these details, right down to a tiny anime robot Sternbach had attached to the bottom of the ship. And yet there are differences: the four-foot model is painted in standard Starfleet shades of gray, making it forever distinguishable from its progenitor. Another difference: the official *Stargazer*'s registry number displayed on the shooting model is NCC-2893. The ready room model is numbered NCC-7100 because Sternbach had used decals from the *Enterprise* refit kits he bashed. "We didn't believe it would ever be seen close enough to read," he admits.

"No one has ever offered to turn me into a god before." —Riker

As part of a wager he's made with the Q Continuum, Q returns to the *Enterprise* and bestows upon Commander Riker "a gift beyond all other gifts": the omnipotent powers of the Q. Thus equipped, promises Q, Riker will be able to do *anything* he can imagine, from raising the dead to granting his crewmates' fondest wishes. Giving sight to Geordi La Forge, turning Wesley Crusher into a grown man, making Data a human—it's all mere child's play. But are these gifts worth making a deal with the devil . . . or rather, the Q?

Q's force field grid was a simple reuse of an effect originally created for "Encounter at Farpoint," although storyboarded "FX notes" provided by newly hired visual effects coordinator Dan Curry suggest modifications that might be required to make the element work within "Hide and Q." Curry was brought in to take the pressure off Rob Legato, whose role as the show's sole visual effects coordinator had become prohibitively time-consuming. Curry would now share those responsibilities, with one man typically overseeing the odd-numbered episodes produced during a season, and the other handling the even-numbered ones.

HIDE AND "Q"

VARIOUS FX NOTES
(OUT OF ORDER)

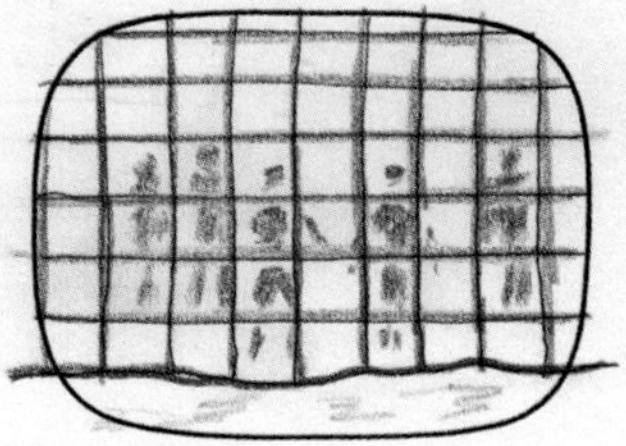

3-116   GR-1

Q - GRID IN FOREGROUND

– MAY HAVE TO RE-TRANSFER TO
MAKE GRID BRIGHTER

WIPE LINE .... TO CREATE ILLUSION
THAT GRID IS RESTING ON GROUND

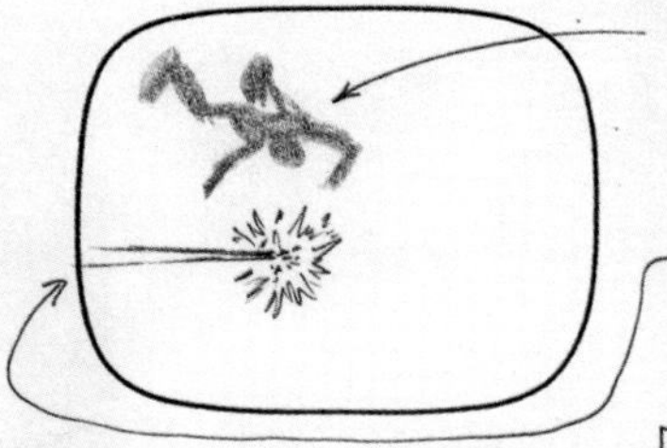

DURING FIREFIGHT –
CHARACTER LEAPS UP OUT OF WAY
OVER BLAST FROM Q-SOLDIER'S WEAPON

Q-SOLDIER FIRE GOES UNDER
LEAPING CHARACTER

NO NEED FOR PIN REG. TRANSFER

DATA

2 MOONS IN SKY FOR
23-22 & 23-32
AND ~~POSSIBLY~~ ONE OTHER SHOT WITH Q

MOONS MOVE VERY SLIGHTLY ...
NEARER MOON MOVES FASTER ...
LATER SHOTS SHOULD CONTINUE
PERSPECTIVE OF MOON MOTION

NO NEED FOR PIN REG. TRANSFER

WHORF
STAYS

DATA

KLINGON FOX "Q"S OUT OF BRIDGE

← NEED MATTE LINE TO KEEP FX BEHIND CONSOLE

↙ WILL NEED A SEPARATE MATTE FOR SPLIT
TO KEEP DATA ON

The *Enterprise* escorts aging Admiral Jameson, a man renowned for his diplomatic skills, to the planet Mordan IV, where he's been summoned to resolve a hostage situation. Forty years ago, Jameson successfully negotiated peace on this world. Or so the legend goes. In fact, he supplied arms to Karnas, the planetary leader—then went behind Karnas's back to supply similar weapons to opposing factions. This resulted in four decades of civil war, leaving Karnas determined to exact revenge on Jameson. But he may not need to; in preparation for their encounter, Jameson has been dosing himself with an alien compound to restore his youth—with dire effects.

The *TNG* art department staff always faced more than enough tasks to fill the average workday, yet when scenic artist Michael Okuda and illustrator Rick Sternbach saw an opportunity to contribute a bit more, they volunteered posthaste. Such was the case when they created the futuristic buildings and arid vista seen through the window of Karnas's office on Mordan IV. "Creating models wasn't really our job," notes Okuda. "We weren't set up for model mak-

ing in the art department, and we were lucky enough to have the services of Paramount's effects shop, as well as talented outside vendors like [professional model makers] Greg Jein and Tony Meininger. But we tried to help out when the vendors were too busy, or if there was something small that we thought was cool but the budgets didn't allow."

Okuda and Sternbach's contribution to "Too Short a Season" was not elaborate; in fact, Okuda won't even go so far as to call it a model. "Mostly we painted a few found objects and a tabletop to create a loose impression of a cityscape. I recall that we used a big wok for the dome of one large building."

Right: Karnas's office, with the artificial "view" beyond.
Opposite: A partial view of the Mordan city, complete with wok.

"So this is the big goodbye. Tell me something, Dixon. When you've gone, will this world still exist? Will my wife and kids still be waiting for me at home?" —McNary

En route to a delicate diplomatic mission with the irritable Jarada species, Captain Picard attempts to relax by inviting his friends to participate in an adventure in the upgraded holodeck—specifically, an adventure based on the fictional life of a hard-boiled twentieth-century private detective named Dixon Hill. Unfortunately, a scan by the Jarada triggers a glitch in the holodeck system, preventing anyone from entering, exiting, or shutting off the program. Picard's crew can't communicate with him to let him know anything's amiss—likewise, after one of his guests is critically wounded by a supposedly "unreal" bullet, Picard can't let the crew know that the once amusing program has turned deadly.

Produced precisely halfway through the series' first season, "The Big Goodbye" was the first true sign of what *Star Trek: The Next Generation* would

become. Everyone involved invested heart and soul into the story, from executive story editor Tracy Tormé, who wrote it following a suggestion from Gene Roddenberry, to costume designer William Ware Theiss, who received 1988's Primetime Emmy Award for Outstanding Costumes for a Series, to the on-camera regulars, who finally seemed to relax and settle into their roles. As Wil Wheaton noted in an online critique of the episode, "There isn't an actor in the world who doesn't love playing a period piece, and I think our real joy in filming 'The Big Goodbye' cascaded into our performances. . . . This is one of the very first times where the audience could really feel the actors—and therefore their characters—coming together."

Tormé turned Roddenberry's suggestion of "a detective story on the holodeck" into an affectionate film noir pastiche, with characters whose names and performances owed much to films like *The Maltese Falcon*. Tormé and director Joseph Scanlan wanted to push the envelope further by actually filming the holodeck sequences in black and white, but producers Rick Berman and Robert Justman nixed the idea, reportedly because they felt the holodeck program couldn't physically transform Picard and company

into black and white. (Berman eventually altered his opinion, allowing the holodeck sequences in *Star Trek: Voyager*'s Flash Gordon–influenced "Captain Proton" episodes to be shot in glorious monotones.)

Although primarily played for laughs, the episode, which won the *Star Trek* franchise its one and only Peabody Award, also works in some philosophical soul-searching when the holodeck characters discover there's another reality outside their own. Two of them pay the ultimate price for that information, literally dissolving when they try to escape into the real world, while Dixon Hill's fictional buddy McNary is left to ponder if he'll still exist after Hill/Picard exits the program. The *TNG* writers would take the intriguing theme of "self-aware holograms" even further in subsequent episodes, as would the writers for *Deep Space Nine* and *Voyager*.

"Shut up, Wesley!" —Picard, Doctor Crusher

The *Enterprise* travels to Omicron Theta, once home to a group of colonists who mysteriously vanished some twenty-six years ago. Omicron Theta is also the planet where Starfleet officers discovered the android Data, unactivated. In the lab that belonged to Data's creator, Dr. Noonien Soong, the *Enterprise* away team finds the parts of a second android: a twin to Data, named Lore. When Lore is reactivated, he claims that he was disassembled because the colonists found him "too perfect," but it soon becomes obvious that this isn't the truth. In fact, Lore was responsible for the terrible fate that befell the colonists—a fate Lore now intends for the crew of the *Enterprise*.

"Datalore" presented viewers with their first look inside Data—literally—after the evil android Lore kicks him, exposing the circuitry in Data's forehead. The scripted effect might have presented a challenge for Michael Westmore if *TNG*'s makeup supervisor didn't already have on call just the right man to assist him: son Michael Westmore Jr. As a scion of one of Hollywood's most famous makeup dynasties, it was, perhaps, inevitable that Michael Jr. would be drawn into the family business in some capacity— although his personal talents steered him down a very specialized path. "I started developing computer systems with a friend as a hobby in high school," he explains. From there it wasn't a huge leap to designing and building the systems and circuits that are integrated within some of his father's most intricate makeup designs. Their first collaboration was on the blinkers that attach Geordi's VISOR to the sides of his head. Then came the script for "Datalore," which set the standard for the way the pair would combine prosthetics and circuitry for Data in future episodes. Per Michael Sr., "First we pick an area we want to 'open up,' then I build a thin fiberglass shell that fits over it and a foam latex appliance that goes over the top of that. Meanwhile, Michael Jr. builds

his electronics into the shell, and we glue the shell and the latex appliance together. The cords usually run through Brent Spiner's hair, and down his back to an off-camera control panel."

Right: A life cast of Brent Spiner's face, used as a template for both Lore's dummy head and for the transparent "epidermal mold" that Data tries on in the remains of Soong's lab.

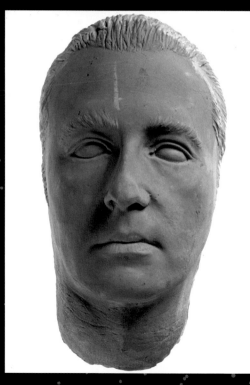

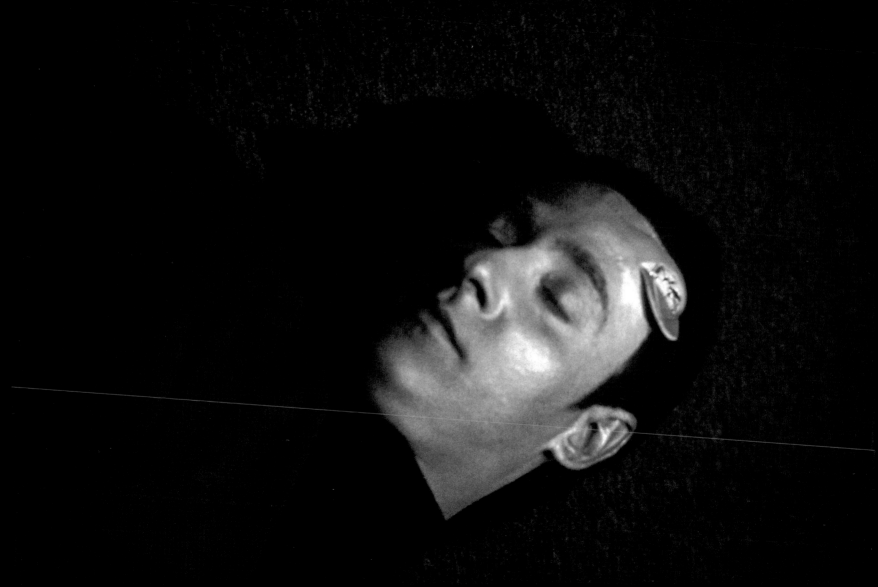

Scenic artist Michael Okuda almost played Data's infamous creator, Dr. Noonien Soong, in "Datalore."

Almost. As Okuda recalls:

"Although the elusive doctor wasn't seen in that episode, an early draft of the script called for our heroes to study a computer screen that showed his biography. As the show's graphic designer, it would be my job to create the screen display. I knew that in the finished episode, the text on the screen would probably be too small to read, so I thought it might be a good idea to include a photo of Dr. Soong, which would help make it clear that this was bio-graphical info. At the preproduction meeting, our producers agreed.

"'What should I do for a photo of Dr. Soong?' I asked. Remember, Soong was not going to be seen in this episode, and it would be nearly two years be-fore anyone thought of casting Brent Spiner in the role of Data's maker. This was a potentially expen-sive question because I was really asking them to cast someone in the role.

"As Bob Justman looked at me from across the table, I noticed a gleam in his eye. That generally meant he was going to cut the budget or pull a zinger. Oddly enough, this time it was both. He ex-changed a glance with Rick Berman, and they both smiled at me. 'How about you, Mike?'

"The plan was to use a photo of me as Soong in the bio screen. As one of the few Asian-Ameri-can staffers on the show, I was delighted to be asked. And since this meant that they wouldn't be hiring an actor to play Dr. Soong, the ever-frugal Mr. Justman had found another ingenious way to stretch the show's budget.

"Sadly, the scene with the bio graphic was cut from the final version of the script, so I didn't get to play Data's maker. It was just as well. 'Brothers,' in *TNG*'s fourth season, would present Soong in the flesh, this time played by the talented (and funny) Brent Spiner.

"But it would have been fun."

"But will you still respect me in the morning?"
—*Riker*

The *Enterprise* tracks survivors of the lost freighter *Odin* to the matriarchal world of Angel One, where Riker's away team receives a chilly reception from Beata, the elected planetary leader. They soon learn that the survivors from the freighter—all males—are in hiding because they refused to accept the social status quo of Angel One's female-dominated society. Riker promises to remove the fugitives, but, unfortunately, the missing men don't want to leave; they've taken wives and now think of Angel One as their home. Beata announces her intention to execute them—leaving Riker searching for a diplomatic way to save their lives.

An interesting plot thread lies buried beneath this routine tale of a society where women rule the roost. The *Enterprise* receives word that Romulan vessels are converging near Federation outposts along the border to the Neutral Zone. Why? Viewers don't find out in this episode. In fact, although the *Enterprise* will have a face-to-face encounter with the Romulans in the first-season finale ("The Neutral Zone"), the lost plot thread doesn't connect until Q introduces the crew to the Borg ("Q Who?"), halfway into season two. Still, while this Romulan tease is only a third-ranking subplot in "Angel One"—a B-story about the shipboard virus laying waste to the crew receives more attention—it does provide the episode with a requisite "ticking clock" that goads everyone to quickly work out the standoff so the ship can race to the Neutral Zone.

Opposite: When is an objet d'art not an objet d'art? When it's an execution device posing as a decorative set piece. Here we see members of the away team supplicating themselves to Beata when they first arrive on Angel One. The set detailing in this reception area is sparse. There is, however, a nice vase, prominently placed on a platform directly behind Riker. But this is no ordinary platform. It's Angel One's final solution (or rather, its "final alternative"): a disintegration machine! And it's sitting right out in the open, available to anyone who wishes to activate it—or accidentally stumbles into it.

MOIRÉ PATTERN WIPES INTO L-SHAPED WHITE PANELS... WIPE LINES MOVE FROM TOP AND BOTTOM AND MEET AT CENTER...

AT THE CONTACT POINT LIGHTNING-LIKE BEAMS EMINATE FROM LIT "DIODES" WORKING FROM CENTER UP AND DOWN AND COVERING VASE...

THE VASE IS BATHED IN SIZZLING ENERGY AS IT DISSAPPEARS...

LEAVING A RESIDUAL VAPOR AS THE MOIRÉ PATTERN FADES

For a television series set in the twenty-fourth century, *Star Trek: The Next Generation* displayed a much more casual attitude toward the show's flashy hardware than did *The Original Series*. The camera didn't waste time lingering on Picard's appealingly compact desk monitor or on those wafer-thin padds everyone carried around the *Enterprise*. Instead, it zoomed in on whatever plot-related graphics their monitors displayed. The producers didn't bother to explain what these magical devices did or how they worked. They knew that the show's audience *got* it.

In the twenty years between the two *Star Trek* series, real-world technology had advanced at such a rapid pace that the notion of devices like these was no longer remarkable to viewers. Home computers, cordless telephones, and early mobile phones were already in use. They were clunky, to be sure, but it wasn't hard to imagine a future with beautiful streamlined versions. Joe Fan didn't have a padd of his own, but he was pretty sure that he would someday (and, in fact, he probably does today).

Gene Roddenberry had imagined as much when he began developing *TNG*. He understood that he didn't need to reinvent the wheel. The future technology utilized in *TOS* already had captured the imag-ination of a generation of viewers. All he needed to do was update it, demonstrating the passage of time between Kirk's generation and Picard's.

Thus, *TNG*'s preliminary bible included a page titled "Technology Unchanged (but improved)." It listed all the iconic items: turbolifts, deflectors, tractor beams, phasers, photon torpedoes, and sensors, to name a few. The tricorder, that crucial staple of every landing party, was back, but smaller and packed with more functions. If the *TOS* version resembled the portable cassette player/recorders of the sixties, the new one, decreed the bible, would be "Walkman-sized," small enough to fit in one's pocket (if only Starfleet uniforms *had* pockets).

To Roddenberry, the phaser was something of a necessary evil; he was never fond of reminding his audience that his ostensibly peace-minded Starfleet explorers boldly went while packing potentially lethal firepower. Following his directive to minimize the visual impact of the crew's weaponry, an early version of the *TNG* phaser—nicknamed "the cricket" by behind-the-scenes personnel—was so small and inconspicuous that it was difficult to spot in an actor's hand. Later versions of phasers were easier to see, but they looked more like futuristic tools than the pistol-like weapon that Kirk often carried. In fact, the curvy phaser type-II, used for only two seasons, was affectionately dubbed "the dustbuster" because of its resemblance to the popular household appliance. Phasers took on their more familiar angular configuration in *TNG*'s third season.

Of all of *TOS*'s technological wonders, none underwent a greater transformation than the handheld communicator. Initially reimagined as a wristband, the *TNG* communicator ultimately was incorporated into the Starfleet insignia worn on each crewmember's uniform.

Opposite, top, left to right: Desktop viewer; communicator; tricorder.

Bottom, left to right: Cricket; padd; Starfleet phaser type-II.

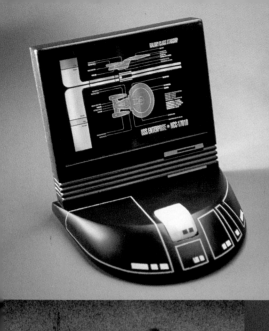

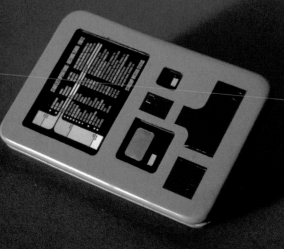

"What's a knockout like you doing in a computer-generated gin joint like this?" —Riker

The *Enterprise* stops at Starbase 74 for a computer system upgrade, scheduled to be performed by a quartet of Bynars. The diminutive species has evolved to become so dependent upon computers that they speak to each other in binary language. Instead of attending to the upgrade, however, the Bynar team programs the *Enterprise* computer to fake an emergency that will trick most of its crew into evacuating. Once the ship is empty, they plan to take it to their homeworld. But Picard and Riker would rather destroy the *Enterprise* than allow it to fall into the alien species' hands.

One of the first season's more memorable episodes, "11001001" recycled some old but effective tricks from the pilot of *The Original Series* to create the Bynars. By casting very petite women as the episode's four computer-dependent humanoids, manipulating the vocal track in postproduction to lower the pitch of the Bynar speaking voices, and hiding the actresses' gender beneath asexual clothing and makeup, the behind-the-scenes crew gave this brand-new species a childlike "alien" quality. More than twenty years earlier, the big-brained Talosians of "The Cage" had been created in much the same way. Michael Westmore's Bynar makeup consisted of a large appliance that fit over each woman's head like a bathing cap, then ran down across the bridge of the nose, over the cheekbones, and around the neck. To save time, Westmore used headpieces cast from the same mold for all four women, then cut and trimmed them to custom-fit each one. Although the heads were bald, the makeup team applied a bit of purple hair to the side of each character's neck to hide the join line between latex and skin.

Riker comments at the end of the episode that Minuet, the Bynars' very special holodeck program, will be difficult to forget—and indeed she was. Riker apparently is still thinking about his holographic soul mate three years later when a young alien named Barash finds her image in the commander's mind and mistakenly assumes she is a real woman ("Future Imperfect"). Actress Carolyn McCormick, better known to viewers as Dr. Elizabeth Olivet on *Law & Order*, plays Minuet in both episodes.

"Darkness. Death. Terrible. Must go home to wet sand. War over." —Velaran microbrain

Picard's crew discovers that the death of an engineer at a terraforming station on Velara III wasn't an accident—it was murder. The culprits: the planet's microscopic indigenous life-forms, which the terraformers inadvertently have been destroying as they attempt to turn Velara III into a planet capable of supporting humanoid life. And after Data and Geordi bring one of the life-forms back to the ship for study, the tiny being decides to declare all-out war on the humans aboard the *Enterprise*.

Some members of the *Star Trek* audience probably first learned about "terraforming"—the process of deliberately modifying a planetary body's atmosphere, temperature, topography, and ecology to make it habitable for terrestrial organisms—from *Star Trek II: The Wrath of Khan* in 1982. The concept had, however, been around for decades. Author Jack Williams coined the term "terraforming" in 1942 in his short story "Collision Orbit," which appeared in the magazine *Astounding Science Fiction*. By 1988, when "Home Soil" hit the airwaves, terraforming was old news. Still, the subject matter had never been covered in a *Star Trek* television episode, and the *TNG* producers no doubt were hoping their audience would enjoy this take on it. Unfortunately, the technology utilized by the engineers on Velara III was far less interesting than that postulated in *The Wrath of Khan*, and the story line itself seemed more than a little derivative of the classic *TOS* episode "The Devil in the Dark." As in that script, humans come to an apparently unoccupied planet and start digging, inadvertently harming indigenous life-forms—which respond (understandably) by seeking violent retribution until someone from the *Enterprise* manages to explain that "we mean no harm." Still, it did bring into *Trek* semantics the expression "Ugly Bags of Mostly Water," the microbrain life-form's wonderfully snide yet scientifically accurate euphemism for the unwelcome humanoids.

Opposite: The matte painting of the terraforming station is the work of artist Syd Dutton, cofounder of Illusion Arts (IA), a company that provided thousands of hand-painted mattes to film and television productions from 1984 to 2009. Done in oil on Masonite, the painting was photographed and composited for *TNG* by Dutton's partner at IA, visual effects supervisor Bill Taylor.

The inhabitants of the cloaked world Aldea—a place long held to be a myth—create a nightmare for parents aboard the *Enterprise* when they kidnap a group of children, including Wesley Crusher, to perpetuate their species.

"They enter cautiously. In the center is a shiny black box that pulsates with a glowing light."

That one line from the shooting script was all visual effects coordinator Rob Legato had to go on when he was charged with creating the power source for Aldea's "Custodian." There weren't any other specifics provided, but Legato immediately understood one thing. "It needed to be something that left you awestruck—something that was about one hundred feet tall," he explains.

Budget-wise, creating a set piece that massive wasn't possible. But Legato knew how to make a smaller item *look* that big. "We made an octagonally shaped box out of old [toy] model parts—pieces from old aircraft carriers, tanks, planes, and cars," he says. "It actually was about two feet tall." Juxtaposed against the box was a deep shaft with a small

ledge built into it. The script called for the characters to come through a door and step out onto the ledge to gaze up at the hundred-foot structure. Legato shot them separately, with a bright white light rising behind them.

After this image was layered with the footage of the model, audiences were presented with this illusion: a huge glowing monolith stands in the middle of a cavernous shaft; a large door rises vertically in the wall of the shaft; light spills out into the dark cavern, backlighting a group of silhouetted characters standing in the doorway, their shadows stretching out across the ledge.

The effective sequence came in at a modest $3,000!

Right: Michael Westmore dabs a bit of makeup on a young extra who bears a curious familial resemblance. As with *The Original Series* episode "Miri," producers looked within their own ranks to fill out the cast roster for "When the Bough Breaks." The three children in nonspeaking roles were Wil Wheaton's younger brother and sister, and this young lady: McKenzie Westmore. This was not McKenzie's first acting role; at the age of three, she

appeared in *Raging Bull*. She would go on to appear in *Star Trek: Voyager*, *Friends*, *Dexter*, and the daytime drama *Passions*, and host Syfy's makeup competition series *Face Off*.

It may *look* like child's play, but very stringent child labor laws govern the participation of young actors in television and motion picture production. Children under six months of age may not be present at the work location (e.g., the soundstage) for more than two hours per day, and during that period they may "work" (be photographed) for an accumulated total of twenty minutes. The work time allotment tiers upward with the age of the child. Thus, when Wil Wheaton was cast as Wesley Crusher at age fifteen, he was allowed to remain on location for nine and a half hours each day, and during that period he could work a total of three hours. The rest of Wheaton's set time had to be divided between "school" (three hours), "rest and recreation" (one hour), and "meal break" (half an hour). Which left him two hours of free time to do homework, observe the production, or hang out with his friends in the cast and crew. But being educated in an informal setting doesn't mean that the assignments are any easier than they'd be in a classroom. Production companies employ "studio teachers"—tutors trained specifically for the production environment—who place an emphasis on the same difficult subjects that might be part of the traditional curriculum at, say, North Hollywood High.

Math is tough no matter where you study.

Those aren't the only restrictions. In order to be allowed to work while the rest of his young peers are in school, the child actor must be enrolled in an Independent Studies Program, either a state-regulated homeschool curriculum or a private or public school that has a program in place to accommodate working students.

Of course, when not actively employed on a specific production, the child actor must attend classes at regular schools just like everyone else. Wil Wheaton participated in one semester of regular high school before he was cast on *The Next Generation*. "I hated it," he confessed in a 2003 blog on wilwheaton.net. "I was really shy, and awkward, and nerdy . . . I felt like I was in a foreign country." Already a minor celebrity because of his role in the film *Stand by Me*, Wheaton says that his shyness came off as arrogance. "It was hard for me to make friends . . . I missed out on homecoming, and prom, and football games . . . but I had a good time being on *Star Trek*. I don't know if I ever would have made friends in high school."

At Relva VII, where Wesley Crusher faces tough competition for the sole opening at Starfleet Academy, Captain Picard receives a surprise visit from his old friend Admiral Quinn. But Quinn, accompanied by Lieutenant Commander Remmick of the Inspector General's office, makes it clear that it's not a social call. There's something very wrong on the *Enterprise*, he says, and he's brought Remmick to pinpoint what it is. Picard presses for an explanation, but Quinn will state only that the captain and his officers are to cooperate fully with the investigation. Remmick's confrontational questions quickly put everyone on edge, leaving Picard to wonder what's really behind the inquisition.

Like Wesley Crusher, a Benzite named Mordock made the final list of candidates for entry to Starfleet Academy. Unlike Wesley, Mordock needed a respiration device to help him breathe in the Class-M environment of Relva VII. His breathing apparatus evolved from an early concept drawing by Rick Sternbach into the final version seen in the episode. Makeup designer Michael Westmore describes Mordock's appearance as one of his most elaborate creations for *TNG*'s first season. "We had one piece that covered most of the head, and additional pieces for the upper lip, chin, and eyelids," Westmore explains. "The lids folded into themselves like a set of venetian blinds. There was also a set of catfish-like feelers around the mouth area, and another set of tendrils hanging from each earlobe." A year after this episode aired, Westmore resurrected the makeup design in "A Matter of Honor" for a Benzite named Mendon, who—not so coincidentally—looked *exactly* like Mordock. Viewers were told that the resemblance was natural since the two Benzites were from the same "geostructure," but a more likely reason was that actor John Putch played both characters, which allowed Westmore to use the same facial mold.

Right: Worf ponders a piece of cake at a surprise party thrown for Wesley's sixteenth birthday. Although filmed, the scene was cut for time.

Trek . Alien Breathing
device

pouch

cover

sternbach

"What burns in their eyes, fires my soul. I hear their words, and I see it all as it was. Part of me longs for that time." —Worf

Lieutenant Worf is forced to choose between his warrior heritage and his loyalty to Starfleet when renegade Klingons who despise the alliance between the Federation and the Klingon Empire attempt to hijack the *Enterprise*.

There's something odd about the Klingons that Picard and company encounter in "Heart of Glory." It's not their desire to indulge in some good old-fashioned mayhem (even Worf admits to feeling a similar bloodlust). No, it's their unnatural native dialogue: a few mushy bits of gobbledygook that don't sound authentic to the well-trained Klingon ear. And there's a reason for that.

"The first time the *Star Trek: The Next Generation* writers used Klingon language, they made it up themselves," explains linguist Marc Okrand. Okrand should know. In 1984, while working as a consultant on *Star Trek III: The Search for Spock,* he established

the foundations for what scholars today recognize as the official language of the guttural warrior race. A year later he expanded upon the vocabulary and grammatical rules that he'd laid out for Kruge and his compatriots in the book *The Klingon Dictionary*, a huge-selling seminal work that's still in print today. But while fandom took the book to heart, *TNG*'s writing staff wasn't aware of it, or of Okrand. After "Heart of Glory" aired, someone brought the book to the staff's attention and the writers "began using it to look for words," says Okrand. "Later, when I was working on the feature *Star Trek V: The Final Frontier*, the writers heard I was on the Paramount lot and asked me to come to the *TNG* production office. I made up some lines for them and they put them in 'A Matter of Honor,' the episode where Riker was a 'foreign exchange student' on a Klingon ship."

And so it was that honor was restored to the ungobbledygooked Klingon language.

"The name of my ship is the Lollipop *. . . It's a good ship." —Riker*

The *Enterprise* travels to the planet Minos to investigate the disappearance of the *U.S.S. Drake*. But upon arrival, the crew finds no sign of the *Drake*, or of the inhabitants of Minos, whose civilization was renowned for its devotion to the manufacture of weaponry. While investigating, automated attack drones imperil members of an *Enterprise* away team, and Doctor Crusher is badly injured when she and Captain Picard tumble into a cavern. In the meantime, Geordi La Forge, left in charge of the *Enterprise*, clashes with the higher-ranking chief engineer as he attempts to keep a killer drone from destroying the ship.

"To be totally armed is to be totally secure. Remember, the early bird that hesitates gets wormed." —Minos arms salesman

After a commissioned prop was deemed too big and unwieldy to use as Minos's flying drone robot, Dan Curry went home and made one out of items he liberated from the Curry household. He assembled the final version of the menacing drone from a large plastic Easter egg, a bottle that had once held a children's shampoo, and a L'eggs panty-hose container. "I didn't bother doing a sketch," notes Curry. "I just pieced it together intuitively."

But if the drone—referred to as "Echo Papa Series 607" by the holographic arms salesman—looked a bit goofy, so did the technician who operated it onstage. "Everyone thought I was crazy," Curry says with a chuckle, "but I decided to do the shots with Echo Papa as a puppet, rather than floating around via standard motion control photography. I mounted it upside down on a rod, made a large shield for myself out of green screen, and shot in front of a green screen. I guided the little drone around, doing it all by hand using Tai Chi movements. I thought this would convey a more natural sense of a drone flying

through the planet's foliage, as it would not have the perfection of motion control movement. We were able to do all the shots of the drone in one morning."

Curry also built the little space drone that creates havoc for Geordi up on the *Enterprise*. "That one was painted black, with streamers attached that were made out of white plastic shopping-bag strips," he says. "That drone *was* mounted to a motion control rig to create the illusion of an invisible drone entering the atmosphere and heating up—which is how Geordi was finally able to locate it. We kept the camera's shutter open for five seconds per frame, using a fan to keep the plastic strips fluttering in the breeze. I figured the resulting blur would resemble the flames and hot gases that surround a space capsule as it reenters the atmosphere."

Opposite, left: Dan Curry's son Devin shows off his father's prototype for the drone robot in 1988.

Ever wonder why the likenesses of licensed action figures are so hit or miss? That's partly due to the size of the figures; it's hard to put much detail into a face that measures less than an inch across. Then there's the matter of references—artistic references, that is. A standard studio head shot doesn't give a toy manufacturer much to work with. Given the track record of spin-off merchandise related to *The Original Series*, Paramount's licensing department felt that *Star Trek: The Next Generation* action figures were likely to be very popular with fans . . . particularly if they actually resembled the actors. The department put through a request to the production office, and *TNG*'s new cast of actors, intrigued by the prospect of toys in their own image, agreed to pose for turnaround shots that would serve as references for licensee Lewis Galoob Toys. Shown on the opposite page are a few of Denise Crosby's turnarounds, taken outside a *Star Trek* soundstage during a break in filming. Crosby's *TNG* alter ego, Tasha Yar, would be one of the first six characters released. Ranging from 3.75 to 4 inches tall, the figures were generally lauded by fans for their realistic features and nicely detailed uniforms.

Action Figures

Join Captain Jean-Luc Picard, Commander William Riker, Lt. Commander Data, Lt. Tasha Yar, Lt. Geordi La Forge and Lt. Worf on all their adventures. Collect all six 3¾" poseable figures.

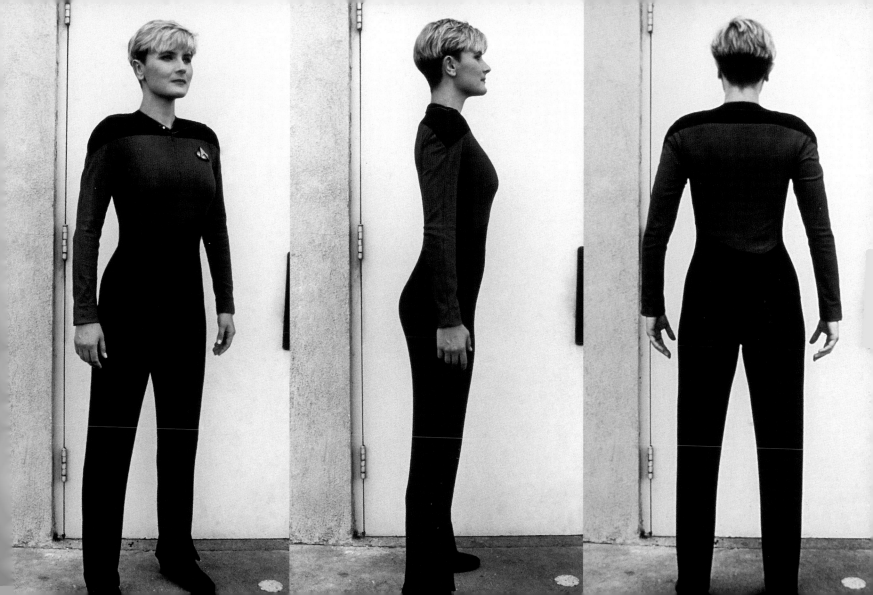

"We are here to honor our friend and comrade, Lieutenant Natasha Yar. Coming to terms with the loss of a colleague is perhaps the most difficult task we must face in the work we have chosen to pursue. We will all find time to grieve for her in the days that are ahead. But for now, she has asked that we celebrate her life. . . ." —Picard

Counselor Troi's shuttlecraft crash-lands on Vagra II, home to Armus, a malevolent alien life-form created from the cast-off negative emotions of the planet's former inhabitants. As an away team from the *Enterprise* mounts a valiant effort to rescue Troi, Armus, who derives pleasure from the suffering of others, tortures and taunts the counselor's closest friends—and kills one of them, simply because it can.

Filmed prior to "Symbiosis," but broadcast a week *after* that episode, "Skin of Evil" confirmed a widespread rumor the fans had been hearing but hadn't wanted to believe: Denise Crosby was leaving *Star Trek: The Next Generation*. In fact, by the halfway point in the episode, the character of Tasha Yar was dead.

The decision was Crosby's. Although she enjoyed working on the show and loved her coworkers, she felt she was spending too much time standing around on the bridge, reciting uninteresting technical lines. She wanted more to do on the show, and the producers made it clear they couldn't guarantee that. The series, they explained, was about Picard, Riker, and Data. The other characters—the rest of the regular crew, the aliens-of-the-week, the special guest stars—were there to fill in the gaps.

And that, Crosby professed, was not acceptable to her. The producers granted her request to be released from the series, and they parted on friendly terms. She went on to make guest appearances in numerous television series, and won a major role in the motion picture *Pet Sematary*, but the beefy parts she'd been looking for didn't seem to be out there.

Ironically, two years after she abandoned the *Starship Enterprise*, she was back as Tasha Yar in the third season's "Yesterday's *Enterprise*." Her appearance was just a one-shot—but it was a standout role in an episode that resonated with the fans, and which later led to a series of stints on the show as Tasha Yar's daughter.

So in a way, Crosby did get what she'd asked for . . . although she had to die to get it.

Opposite: Rick Sternbach's dramatic concept art for Armus, Vagra II's living oil slick.

"So much has happened with optical effects over the years that we probably could come up with more effective visuals today," Michael Westmore says, "but back then, when we filmed 'Skin of Evil,' everyone was thrilled with the way we did it."

Well, maybe not *every*one.

"There was this black slime in a pit," Jonathan Frakes recalls. "I said to the prop master, 'What is this stuff?' He said, 'It's Metamucil and black printer's ink. It'll be fine. Go ahead. Get in it.'" Frakes, figuring this is what an actor does, agreed. "And so," he says, "I immersed myself, over my head, with black Metamucil."

While "Metamucil" was an easy way to shorthand the identity of the substance for the actor, it wasn't entirely accurate. The goo that Armus called home was a mix of water-soluble printer's ink and methylcellulose, a chemical compound derived from plant tissue. It's a key component of a whole variety of consumer products, including toothpaste, shampoo, artificial tears, personal lubricants (like K-Y Jelly), and constipation relievers like Metamucil. When dissolved in cold water, it forms a clear viscous solution (hence the need to color it with the ink). It's nontoxic—but considering the effects

of Metamucil, one hopes that Frakes and stunt actor Mart McChesney—the guy in the Armus suit—didn't swallow much of it.

Frakes actually had it easy compared to McChesney, who spent four days immersed in the stuff. "We'd designed a head for him to wear," Westmore explains, "and it had three holes so if we had to, we could stick our fingers inside the mask and clean the gunk out of his mouth in a hurry. While he was under, we had to time the scene with a stopwatch. In retrospect, it would have been a good idea to build a small oxygen tank into the head."

Wearing a suit provided by the wardrobe department, McChesney was fine. The suit, on the other hand . . . "The goo was supposed to be inert," Westmore comments, "but for some reason we've never been able to explain, it started to fall apart at the seams. We made a quick call to the manufacturer to make a few more—and every one of them fell apart. And that oily black goo was tremendously messy," he adds. "We hooked up a hose outside the stage door to rinse it off. Everyone was filthy with the stuff."

"There was an elevator built into the pit, and it forced me up through the slime and then vomited me

onto the beach," Frakes relates, flashing his characteristic grin. "And one of my favorite moments in *Star Trek* took place just *after* I was vomited up on the beach, covered with the black slime. LeVar Burton comes over, leans over me, and says, 'Oh, Frakes, I would *never* have done that!'"

The *Enterprise* comes to the aid of a disabled freighter transporting valuable cargo from one world to its planetary neighbor. Picard learns that for two centuries the Brekkians—owners of the freighter—have been supplying the Ornarans with a drug called felicium, which the Ornarans need to battle a terrible plague on their world. In exchange, the Ornarans have been supporting the Brekkians' comfortable lifestyle. But while the two species fight over payment of the undelivered shipment, Doctor Crusher realizes that the Ornarans were cured of the plague long ago; felicium now serves only as a narcotic—and the Brekkians know it! Although Crusher's first instinct is to enlighten the Ornarans, Picard warns her that the Prime Directive prohibits telling the beleaguered Ornarans that their neighbors have turned them into drug addicts. However, he *does* have a solution—one that will be painful to both species.

The year was 1988, and the "Just Say No" campaign against recreational drugs—launched by first lady Nancy Reagan—was in full swing. More than twelve thousand "Just Say No" clubs were in oper-

ation across the country and around the world, according to the Ronald Reagan Presidential Foundation and Library, and Mrs. Reagan spent much of her spare time making public appearances to support the crusade. Although the campaign was lauded by many, it was belittled by those who felt that the program didn't go far enough in addressing the many social issues—such as unemployment, poverty, and family dissolution—that are often conducive to drug use.

Star Trek episodes have often served as metaphors for social issues, but the "Just Say No" campaign seems an odd choice for a *TNG* "message" episode. The various *Star Trek* series, and, in fact, creator Gene Roddenberry, were more likely to lean left than right when taking a scripted stance. Still, there it was: a conversation between Tasha Yar and Wesley Crusher toward the end of the episode that easily could have served as a "Just Say No" public service announcement.

WESLEY: *How can a chemical substance provide an escape?*
TASHA: *It doesn't, but it makes you think it does. You have to understand, drugs can make you feel*

good. They make you feel on top of the world. You're happy, sure of yourself, in control.
WESLEY: *But it's artificial.*
TASHA: *It doesn't feel artificial until the drug wears off. Then you pay the price. Before you know it, you're taking the drug not to feel good, but to keep from feeling bad.*
WESLEY: *And that's the trap?*
TASHA: *All you care about is getting your next dosage. Nothing else matters.*
WESLEY: *I guess I just don't understand.*
TASHA: *Wesley, I hope you never do.*

A distress signal leads the *Enterprise* to a science outpost on Vandor IV, where Dr. Paul Manheim has been performing experiments in nonlinear time. Manheim's wife, Jenice, is an old flame of the captain's, and while it's obvious to the crew that Picard's feelings about her are unresolved, it's her husband's work that soon has everyone's undivided attention. His most recent experiment has created an opening between dimensions that, if left open, could destroy the interdimensional fabric of space itself.

"Stunt casting"—hiring a name actor to play a supporting role, ostensibly to pull in a larger audience—is a recent addition to the *Oxford English Dictionary* (a 2011 subordinate entry under the existing word "stunt"). However, it's not new. In fact, it's been standard practice on television since the days of *I Love Lucy*, which featured a multitude of appearances by prominent actors of the day, usually playing comically tweaked versions of themselves.

Star Trek (like *Lucy*, a Desilu production—at least initially) is no stranger to stunt casting. *The Original Series* was restrained in its use of the gimmick,

Melvin Belli being the somewhat garish exception, but *The Next Generation* was more than willing to go there. If a famous person was a fan of *Star Trek*, chances were that he or she would show up sooner or later on *TNG*, whether said person was an actor (Jean Simmons, Paul Winfield, Kelsey Grammer, Bebe Neuwirth), stand-up comic (Joe Piscopo), recording artist turned actor (Mick Fleetwood, Theodore Bikel, Ben Vereen), astronaut (Mae Jemison), scientist (Stephen Hawking), sports star (James Worthy), or *Star Trek* icon (Leonard Nimoy, DeForest Kelley, James Doohan, Mark Lenard, Majel Barrett).

By the time *Star Trek* fan Michelle Phillips turned up on *TNG* as Picard's old flame Jenice, she was well established as an actress, with recurring roles on shows like *Knots Landing*, *Fantasy Island*, and *The Love Boat*. But her iconic status as a sixties superstar (as a former member of the Mamas and the Papas, the renowned folk-pop vocal group that scored eleven Top 40 songs between 1965 and 1968) likely didn't hurt during the casting process.

01 ‖ 063 "CONSPIRACY"

"Something is beginning. Don't trust anyone. Remember that, Jean-Luc." —Walker Keel

Picard is alarmed when his close friend Walker Keel warns him of a possible conspiracy within Starfleet's upper ranks. Not long after, Picard learns that the *Horatio*, Keel's ship, has been destroyed with all hands aboard, possibly legitimizing the man's paranoia. Uncertain who to trust, Picard takes the *Enterprise* to Earth, determined to uncover the truth. Upon arrival, all appears normal; Picard is greeted casually and invited to dinner with senior members of Starfleet Command. With Picard occupied at Starfleet Headquarters, Admiral Quinn pays a "friendly" visit to the starship. Per Picard's orders, Riker sticks close to the older man, keeping an eye out for suspicious behavior. Nevertheless, he's completely unprepared when the admiral attacks him with a display of inhuman strength. In the meantime, dinner turns out to be a bowl of wriggling maggots, and Picard realizes that his "Starfleet" hosts are something other than human.

Opposite: Andrew Probert's appropriately icky concept art for the alien parasites, including a vivid depiction of Remmick's demise, was realized almost exactly in the final production.

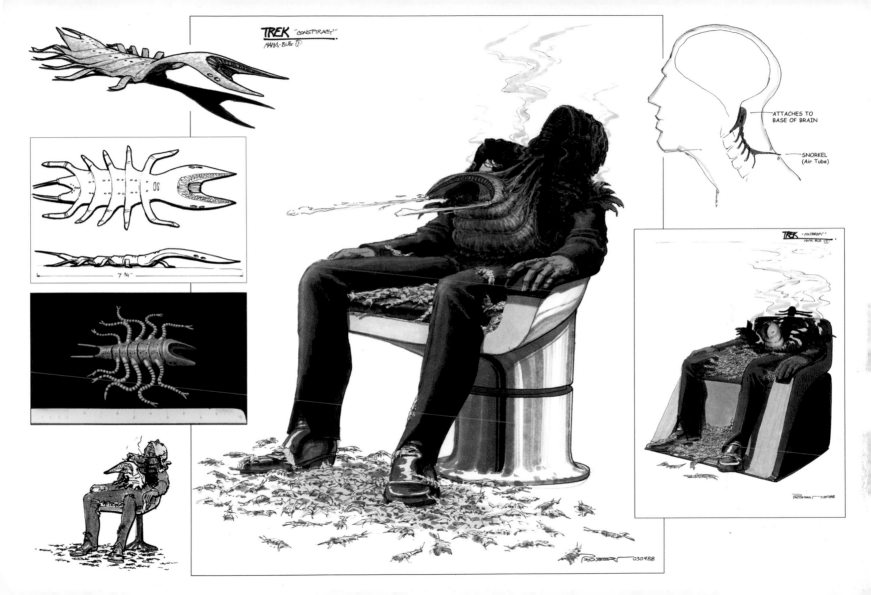

TREK "CONSPIRACY"
MAMA-BUG ①

7 ¾"

ATTACHES TO
BASE OF BRAIN

SNORKEL
(Air Tube)

TREK "CONSPIRACY"
MAMA-BUG ②

ROBERT 030488

"Conspiracy" was conceived as a *Seven Days in May*–style thriller set in the hallowed corridors of Starfleet Command. The notion that something was very wrong within Starfleet had been hinted at in "Coming of Age," but Gene Roddenberry felt strongly that Starfleet officers were above politics and subterfuge. And so the conspirators were transformed into outsiders—alien parasites.

Shifting the episode's focus from thriller to near horror show challenged a coalition of "up for it" effects teams. The latex and flexible wire "baby" creature crawling up Remmick's arm was shot by David Stipes, using stop-motion techniques he had employed while animating the Pillsbury Doughboy for commercials. "We also made partial sections of the baby so it could appear to crawl into Remmick's mouth," reveals visual effects coordinator Dan Curry, "starting with a half creature, and then a hollow tail that fit over the actor's tongue. For the final entry, he just pulled his tongue back."

To help sell the effect, Michael Westmore applied a "skin sleeve" to actor Robert Schenkkan's neck and knelt behind him, blowing through tubes into a series of bladders, giving the impression of a parasite moving in Remmick's throat.

Remmick's head—the one that blew up, that is—was made from a randomly chosen mold obtained by Dick Brownfield, *TNG*'s special (physical) effects master. "It was labeled 'Paul Newman,'" says Curry, smiling. "We packed it with raw meat and explosive squibs, creating the shape of a head," he explains. "Then we blew it up."

So Paul Newman was on *Star Trek*?

Curry considers. "Briefly."

By over-cranking the footage, they slowed the action down to approximately three hundred frames a second, allowing the audience to get a good look at the mayhem.

Property master Alan Sims manipulated the gruesome "Mother" (a latex hand puppet with mechanical jaws built, like the baby, by North Hollywood–based Makeup & Effects Laboratories) from underneath the headless Remmick corpse. "There was a hole in the bottom so Alan could reach up into the body with the puppet," says Curry. "We packed the body cavity with cotton candy and placed little water spritzers inside. When the spritzers went on, the cotton candy turned into red goo—which was the gory effect we wanted, but it ran down the hole and poor Alan got bathed in the sticky stuff."

Opposite: Dan Curry, the *real* "head" of the "Conspiracy" . . . or at least of the episode's grim visual effects.

Data: "Computer, this is Lieutenant Commander Data. Please access all Starfleet Command orders to starships, starbases, and colonies for the past six months."
Computer: "Working."

Although "Conspiracy" was a serious, even dark, episode, an "Easter egg" planted by the art department provided one of the show's few light spots. As Data reviews recent orders from Starfleet Command, a variety of images flash on the monitor: a Klingon ship, a Starfleet shuttlepod, a few odd charts . . . and one *very* odd graphic of a big green bird with a human head. Fans who spotted it decided that it was "the Great Bird of the Galaxy," the mythic creature playfully invoked by Lieutenant Sulu in an episode of *The Original Series* ("The Man Trap"). They were correct; it was inserted here as a playful tribute. The name of this beast also was an inside joke; it had long been producer Robert Justman's nickname for Gene Roddenberry. The graphic on Data's monitor (right) was based on a painting rendered by consulting senior illustrator Andrew Probert. Probert had created the original full-color version as a gift for Roddenberry on his sixty-sixth birthday in 1987.

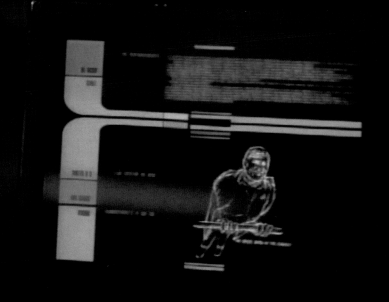

"Do you understand my meaning, Captain? We are back." —Commander Tebok

Following an investigation of a derelict space capsule, Data takes it upon himself to bring the vessel's occupants—three cryogenically preserved humans who were launched from Earth three hundred years ago—back to the *Enterprise*. While the survivors reacclimate aboard the ship, Captain Picard receives disquieting news: Federation outposts along the edge of the Romulan Neutral Zone are disappearing. Starfleet has not heard a peep from the Romulans for fifty-three years—but Picard suspects that this activity near the Neutral Zone means that the hostile species has decided to make its presence felt in Federation territory once again.

With the first season winding down and production on "The Neutral Zone" beginning, Andrew Probert sensed an opportunity. "I didn't have any information except that the Romulans were coming back and that we had never seen their ship before [in *TNG*]," he says. "Since the *Enterprise* is so hori- zontal, I wanted to contrast it with a vertical ship." But when he designed and submitted a tall, skinny ship concept (opposite page, far left lower panel), it didn't fly.

"At this point we didn't see Gene Roddenberry anymore," Probert says. "Gene had always been open to suggestions. I was in awe of how he had created the show, and my respect for him was enhanced by the fact that he would sit and listen to your ideas. He may not have always used them, but he would always listen. I felt that if I had shown him the vertical warbird and explained my reasoning, he would have considered it."

But that didn't happen. Instead, the designer was told by another producer, "Let's make it horizontal instead." "So I created new preliminary drawings [shown opposite, across the bottom], and being that it was a war *bird*, I continued the birdlike motif from my earlier sketches."

Eventually Probert added a bottom wing to the horizontal design. "I hadn't thought about putting a bottom wing on there, but I looked sideways at one of my earlier vertical drawings and thought I'd add a loop to see how that worked.

"I drew that final image as a scale reference to the *Enterprise*, just to show the difference in size," he says. "I love even numbers, so the warbird is 4,440 feet long. The thing is, I provided this image to the producers purposely to suggest that the scene be filmed with the *Enterprise* in front, obviously closer to us, yet the warbird is still larger. Unfortunately, the visual effects people reversed the shot and you really had no idea how much larger the Romulan ship was."

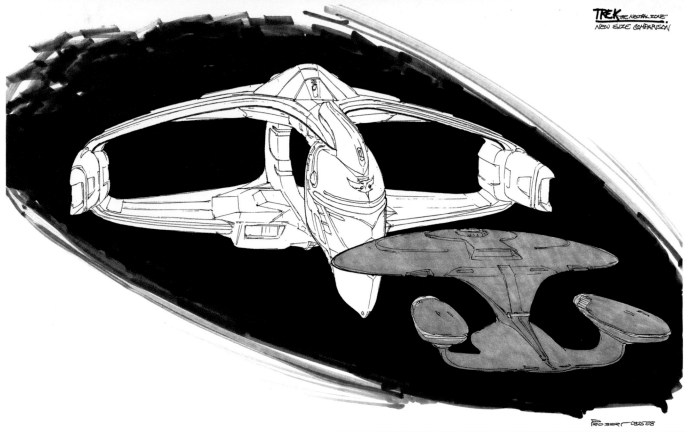

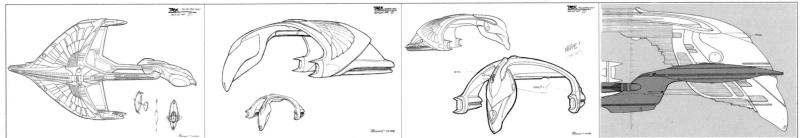

The *Enterprise*'s sensors are monitoring an ancient capsule, possibly from Earth. Worf suggests activating a tractor beam. But Riker responds, "I think not, Mr. Worf. It's just a piece of space debris. . . . Leave it be. Let nature take its course."

What's wrong with this picture?

Seeing as the above scene appears in an episode of *Star Trek*, just about everything. That capsule represents *exactly* what the *Enterprise*'s mission is all about, from *seeking out new life* to *boldly going*. Yet Riker seems content to let it float off to oblivion.

A few scenes later, it's Picard's turn. Informed that the capsule held three human occupants whom Data decided to retrieve, the captain is vexed. "They were *already dead*," Picard chides. "What *more* could have happened to them?" Worse yet, now that Doctor Crusher has *revived* them, the captain grumbles, "We're going to have to treat them as living human beings."

Really, Captain? You'd have preferred to let this historic opportunity pass you by? To leave the dead drifting in space for eternity rather than helping to restore their lives?

Charitable viewers might justify the above behavior by speculating that, this early in the series, neither the writers nor actors had solidified the characters' personalities; Riker and Picard had not yet developed into the noble beings they would become in the later seasons. But in truth, that wasn't the reason at all. It was *bad timing*.

In late February 1988, nine thousand members of the Writers Guild of America were preparing to go on strike against the Alliance of Motion Picture and Television Producers. Their main argument was that, under a proposed contract, writers of one-hour dramas wouldn't receive proper residual payments for their work when it was syndicated after its original airing. The previous contract, from 1985, ruled that writers be paid an entire amount of estimated royalties when a series was first sold. Producers wanted to modify that into payments on a sliding scale, arguing that many series didn't qualify for syndicated rerun status because they didn't last until the necessary one-hundredth episode. Each group had legitimate concerns: the producers lost money on shows that aired only once; the writers made most of their money on residuals. Negotiations ended in a stalemate; starting the first week of March, writers showed up outside their offices carrying picket signs.

Leading up to the strike, some hour-long dramas already had assembled enough scripts to complete their season. Not so with *Star Trek: The Next Generation*. Working from an idea that had been pitched by two freelance writers, producer Maurice Hurley had just a day and a half to complete a filmable teleplay before the current contract expired. Then the strike commenced, leaving no time to smooth out rough dialogue or finesse questionable characterization.

Thankfully, there *was* time for the craftsmen behind the scenes to make the sequence *look* plausible. Rick Sternbach built the cryosatellite model, its damaged solar panels contributed by scenic artist Michael Okuda.

Have you ever wondered why the Romulans of the *TNG* era—with pronounced browridges and a curious dip in the middle of the forehead—look so different from the Romulans of *The Original Series*? According to Michael Westmore, it's because the producers wanted to make them appear more menacing than their forefathers. "From the very first moment they appeared on-screen, the viewer had to take them seriously, rather than seeing them as stereotyped villains with pointed ears," he explains. "The two races [Vulcans and Romulans] were completely different on a cultural level, but it wasn't that easy to tell them apart physically. They had the same basic skin color, they wore the same hairstyle, and both races had pointed ears and archless eyebrows. Aside from dressing them in different clothes, what were we going to do to bring out the diversity between them?" For Westmore, who often gravitates to the anatomical region between the hairline and the nasal bridge when he establishes a new alien look, the solution was simple. "I devised a forehead that had a dip in the center, and then I hollowed out the temple area," he says. "We wanted to stay close to their natural forehead, not making them look Neanderthal, but giving them a built-in

sullen expression they couldn't get away from."

Of course, at the time *TNG* reintroduced the Romulans to the *Star Trek* universe, the show's writers had not yet weighed in on their genealogical relationship to Vulcans. *TOS*'s "Balance of Terror" had established only that the two races shared similar roots. In that episode, Spock described them as a likely "offshoot of my Vulcan blood." But by *TNG*'s fifth season, personnel in the writers' room—and their opinion about the Vulcan-Romulan relationship—had changed.

"I hated the foreheads on the Romulans," comments writer Ronald D. Moore, who joined the series during its third season. "The backstory [established in 'Unification'] was that they were basically the same race, yet somehow the Romulans got these different foreheads at some point."

But if there's anything about the Romulans that Moore dislikes even more than their furrowed brows, it's their threads—not because the uniforms conflict with the backstory, but because he and his fellow writers thought they were *ugly*. "We *hated* the Romulan outfits. Big shoulder pads, the quilting. They were just dopey. And Rick [Berman] would defend them. It became this whole weird in-house political

thing. We'd say, 'Can't we just get new uniforms for them?' And he'd say, 'We established them before any of you people were on the show, so . . .'"

Although modifications would be made over the seasons, Romulan gear would hew closely to William Theiss's first-season costume designs for years, as entrenched in *Trek* lore as the blood feud between Romulans and Klingons.

Opposite: Actor Marc Alaimo shows off *TNG*'s new look for Romulans. Alaimo's later appearance as the show's first Cardassian (in "The Wounded") would lead to his casting as the villainous Gul Dukat on *Star Trek: Deep Space Nine*.

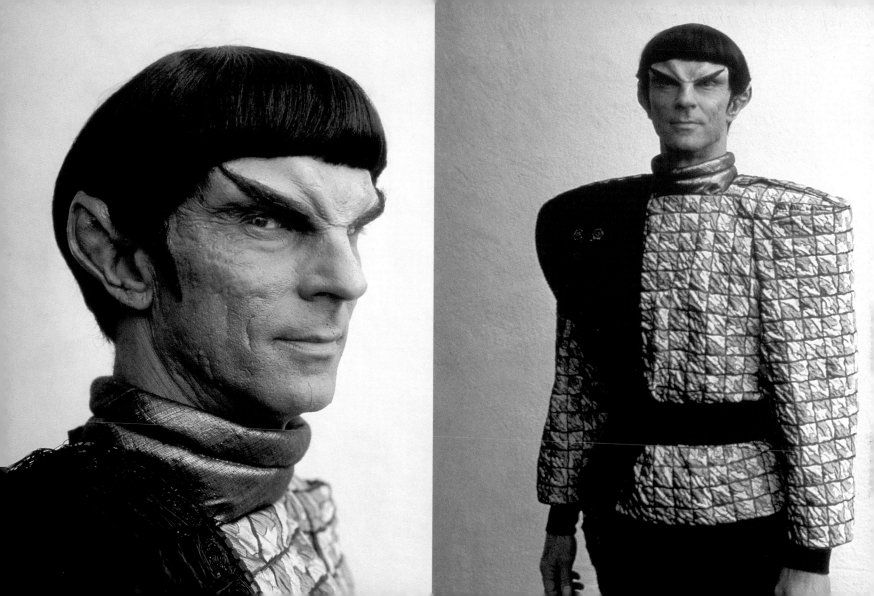

"When we first started, the audience was very, very skeptical," says Jonathan Frakes. "The fans were loyal to classic Kirk, Spock, and Bones, and skeptical of who we were and why we were there. The fear, I think, from talking with fans about it, was that we somehow were trying to re-create what they'd had on *Star Trek*—and we weren't."

It wasn't only the fans who were concerned about the new show; everyone from the actors' agents to the studio financial execs initially hedged their bets.

"Nobody believed that the series would ever become the success that it did," Patrick Stewart explains. "In fact, one of the reasons that I signed on was that I was assured that the six-year contract that I was signing was meaningless, that this series would do one, perhaps two years at the most, because nobody expected it to be successful."

"We had three different contracts," Frakes clarifies. "We had a contract for the pilot, a contract for the first half of the first season, then a contract if, in fact, it was to be extended. Somewhere near the end of the first season, it was clear that we weren't going away. The numbers turned out to be better than projected, so they doled out the additional signings."

Right: In the early years of *Star Trek: The Next Generation*, Paramount Domestic Television Advertising and Promotion created a number of eye-catching ad slicks featuring characters from the series for prominent placement in newspapers and magazines. The clear purpose of these two, designed to promote the episodes "11001001" and "Heart of Glory": draw in new viewers, particularly those who might appreciate a shapely forehead.

Opposite: Despite the concerns of cast and crew, *Star Trek: The Next Generation* almost immediately found a coveted niche with the viewers that mattered most: teens and young adults. Paramount Television proudly crowed about the results of a ratings survey conducted by Nielsen Syndication Service with this ad in late 1987.

STAR TREK #1
THE NEXT GENERATION IS #1

"Star Trek: The Next Generation" is the highest rated first-run syndicated show in all young adult demos. It is #1 with men and women 18-34 and 18-49, and it is #1 with teens.*

"Star Trek: The Next Generation's" powerful delivery not only beats every weekly series in these demos, but outdelivers every strip program including "Wheel of Fortune" and "Jeopardy."

In fact, "Star Trek: The Next Generation's" young male audience appeal is so strong that only two shows on all television can beat it: "Moonlighting" and "L.A. Law."

"STAR TREK: THE NEXT GENERATION," THIS SEASON'S ONLY NEW HIT SERIES.

*Source: NSS Pocket Piece Season average through Nov. '87 Sweeps.

For six of *The Next Generation*'s seven seasons, the *Enterprise* sets were on Paramount stages 8 and 9, conveniently located side by side in the center of the lot. But when the show was being mounted in 1987, Stage 8 wasn't available, so the bridge and the crew members' living quarters were constructed on Stage 6, a much smaller soundstage just across a narrow alley from Stage 8. "Thank goodness, when the first season was over, Michael Schoenbrun [then vice president of production for Paramount Television] found the money to move the set from Stage 6 to the larger Stage 8," recalls Herman Zimmerman. "And in doing so, they made improvements—like adding removable walls—to things that hadn't been easy to shoot before."

In a way, Schoenbrun's inordinate largesse was payback. "When we did the pilot," Zimmerman says, "the coordinator in charge of the whole investiture for the sets didn't keep very good books, and when the accountants finally caught up, we were $400,000 over budget—which would be equivalent to about a million dollars today. Understandably, the studio was not happy about that. I spent the whole of the first season being as cheap as possible with everything that I could, and by the end of the season

we were only about $2,000 per episode over budget. In other words, I made up $370,000 of that $400,000 by being frugal with the money we spent on sets. Of course, Mike Schoenbrun was the only one who thanked me for it," he says, laughing.

When the bridge was relocated, Zimmerman wasn't around to supervise; he'd left *TNG* to serve as production designer on *Star Trek V: The Final Frontier*, and wouldn't return to the *TNG* bridge set until the two franchises came together in 1994, for *Star Trek Generations*. Throughout the filming of *Generations*, he thought the spacious set looked the same—until the crew told him about one small difference.

"In the entertainment business, when a set is struck [taken down], it's struck by the grip department, not the carpenters," he explains. "And when it's put back up again, if there are no changes required, it's reassembled by the grips, and not the carpenters. But the grips apparently didn't understand the set well enough to get it together right. They went all the way around the oval and found they had eighteen inches too much set. So they just cut it off on one side. And they 'sewed it up' like that. And here I am, the guy who's always standing in the middle looking for right and left symmetry,

and *I* never noticed it. It wasn't picked up by the camera either," he says, chuckling. "Had they never confessed to me that they made that mistake, I *still* wouldn't know."

"Last night, while I slept, something which I can only describe as a presence entered my body." —Troi

The *Enterprise*'s mission to transport samples of a deadly plague to a science station is disrupted by the revelation that Counselor Troi is pregnant. The details are sketchy; she's been impregnated by a non-corporeal alien entity whose intentions, Troi believes, are not malevolent. The life she carries within her matures at a phenomenal rate; she gives birth in just thirty-six hours, and the child, whom she names Ian, grows from an infant to an eight-year-old child within a day—however, beyond that he appears to be a normal humanoid boy. But an unknown source of radiation aboard the *Enterprise* is causing the plague samples to grow so rapidly that they'll soon pose a health threat to the entire crew—and Ian might be the cause.

The first episode of season two was overflowing with changes both on and off camera, among them: the arrival of a new chief medical officer (Diana Muldaur as Dr. Katherine Pulaski), an expansive new set (Ten-Forward) hosted by a new recurring character (Whoopi Goldberg as Guinan), and modifications to various crew members' hair and wardrobe. Troi was assigned a more figure-

flattering jumpsuit. Riker adopted a dashing beard. Wesley Crusher got an official uniform to go with his status as acting ensign. And newly appointed Chief Engineer Geordi La Forge and Chief of Security Worf were switched from red to gold uniforms, as befit their permanent positions in the ship's operations division. Worf also received a new baldric. The old one, a holdover from the wardrobe of *Star Trek*'s original Klingons, was showing signs of wear and tear. Durinda Rice Wood, *TNG*'s new costume designer, made him a new one from bicycle chains and strips of leather.

One significant element *wasn't* new: the script for "The Child," a reworked version of a ten-year-old draft by Jaron Summers and Jon Povill for the unproduced television series *Star Trek: Phase II*. The recycling effort was triggered by the ongoing Writers Guild of America strike against the Alliance of Motion Picture and Television Producers, which dragged on for a record 155 days. Having a fundamentally sound script in hand allowed the producers to get a jump start on the episode's preproduction phase as the strike dragged into its final days. When it officially ended on August 7, 1988, co-executive producer Maurice Hurley dived into a rewrite to make the story more relevant to *TNG*, and the episode moved into production.

STAR TREK II

"THE CHILD"

Written by

by

Jaron Summers

and

Jon Povill

Return to Script Department
PARAMOUNT PICTURES CORPORATION
5451 Marathon Street
Hollywood, California 90038

Gene Roddenberry - Executive Producer

Harold Livingston
Bob Goodwin   - Producers

UNREVISED FINAL DRAFT

January 9, 1978

Of all the gin joints in the galaxy, she walked into theirs.

"I needed one hell of a bartender or hostess for this new lounge," Gene Roddenberry explained in a 1988 interview. "And we were thinking that we'd get the most beautiful girl in creation to play this part. And thank God, Whoopi called up and said, 'I am a *Star Trek* fan. I was a *Star Trek* fan before I became Whoopi Goldberg, and if there's some part I can play in your show . . .'"

She was, at the time, a Golden Globe Award winner (for *The Color Purple*) who'd already been nominated for both an Oscar and an Emmy, a renowned comedian whose one-woman show ran for 156 sold-out performances on Broadway. Is it any wonder that the producers of *Star Trek: The Next Generation* had trouble taking the phone call seriously?

Goldberg, however, was serious. "This is one of the few shows that took place in the future that I saw as a kid," she explains. "I saw Lieutenant Uhura was there. And Asian people. All kinds of folks. That gave me a lot of hope. It's very important that the future be hopeful, and that's what [*Star Trek*] is."

Goldberg's timing was excellent. The show only needed a bartender for a few episodes a year, which suited Goldberg's busy schedule. It wasn't like adding a new cast member; it was like having a great guest star in the wings for special appearances.

Diana Muldaur also came to the show in a limited capacity, with each appearance listed in the guest credits, rather than in the opening title credits. Reportedly the actress's choice, it may have been a premonition of what would prove to be a brief tenure.

Gates McFadden's absence came as a surprise to viewers. The general word was that McFadden, dissatisfied with her character's development, had left to "pursue other creative endeavors." But the truth, revealed by Rick Berman in a 2006 interview with the Archive of American Television, was that she'd been fired.

"After the first season, Gene Roddenberry decided to step back and leave everything to me and Maurice Hurley," Berman recalls. It was Hurley who campaigned to replace McFadden. "And I," admits Berman, "let it slide."

Pulaski was cut from a different mold than Crusher. "Crusty" is the adjective most often used to describe her. The writers gave her several of Doctor McCoy's personality quirks: she hated transporters, believed in speaking her mind, and loved to pick on the unemotional science officer. But what had endeared McCoy to the audience worked against Pulaski, and her gruff character never seemed to gel with the rest of the cast. The fans wrote letters. "They didn't like that Gates had been let go for whatever reason," Berman says. When Hurley left the show at the end of the season, Berman reevaluated his friend's decision. "I decided it would be healthier for everyone involved to bring Gates back."

Ten-Forward was constructed on Paramount's Stage 8 during the hiatus between seasons one and two. Conceived as a location for the *Enterprise* crew to take shift breaks, grab a meal, or simply relax after hours, it presented an interesting challenge to Herman Zimmerman, who designed the set before he left the series. "I wanted it to be on the bottom lip of the saucer so that in addition to simply looking out, you could see *below* the ship when you were at the windows," he says. In order to make that work without digging *another* hole in the stage floor, Zimmerman built the set on a platform, leaving plenty of room below to accommodate the all-important star field located beyond the windows. "Most of the time the star field was a black velvet curtain with rhinestones," he explains (a similar curtain was situated behind the conference room windows). "But occasionally a script would call for other visuals, and they would put a green screen out there."

Ten-Forward is a good-size set, but not nearly as big as it looks on television. "I put in mirrors on the right and left sides of the main room, so when they were shooting a side angle it looked as if the window openings went all the way around on either side of the room," Zimmerman explains. "You really got the

impression that you were on the front lip of the saucer of a ship moving through space."

While *TNG*'s production designer could see all this in his head before it was built, others could not easily make the mental leap between a two-dimensional blueprint and the final three-dimensional reality. For this reason, the art department staff occasionally would create foam core models of new sets so that the show's directors and actors could stop in, take a peek, and get the proper "perspective." "It seemed to help them more than a detailed sketch might," notes illustrator Rick Sternbach. "A director would come in and see the model and say, 'I want to put the camera through this window *here*.' When we built this model, we took a couple of little pocket mirrors and made a periscope so you could see into the set at the proper camera height and look all around the inside of Ten-Forward. We even built the windows and added little cut-out figures. I remember Jonathan Frakes stopping by and he was so amazed he just blurted out, 'Holy shit!' It was like he actually had a camera looking around inside."

Nagilum, an alien life-form, traps the *Enterprise* and its crew within a strange featureless void. The creature claims to be curious about human life, particularly the species' mortality, and announces plans to kill as many as half of the crew to see the different ways humans can die. In response, Picard sets the *Enterprise* on automatic self-destruct. Better to kill everyone at once, he reasons, than allow Nagilum to use his shipmates as lab rats.

What the heck *is* Nagilum? Perhaps a more pertinent question is: What's behind that ultra-weird face of his?

The simple answer is Earl Boen, the actor credited as Nagilum. If the name isn't familiar, the face—his real face—might be. He's appeared in three *Terminator* films and dozens of television shows over the past forty years. But more important to the producers was his extensive experience as a voice actor, because he wasn't going to appear on-camera . . . much.

Boen was directed to deliver his lines in front of a blue screen and told to avoid moving his head. "We planned to keep Earl's eyes and mouth [as part of the final effect] to lend verisimilitude to facial expressions and retain the actor's performance of dialogue," relates Dan Curry. "It must have been a challenge to deliver a meaningful performance while keeping his head frozen. But it was necessary in order to map him onto a simple computer-graphics face structure that we could manipulate in compositing, allowing Nagilum to look around the bridge. The technology was extremely primitive by today's standards. After hours of testing, [associate producer] Peter Lauritson approved this look from one of the many different versions created in the edit bay."

Right: Director Winrich Kolbe sets up a shot from the episode. This was his first *Star Trek* assignment. A quick, creative director known for his skill in helming action-packed dramas like *Magnum, P.I.*, *T.J. Hooker*, and *Spenser: For Hire*, Kolbe found himself challenged by "Where Silence Has Lease." A classic bottle episode—one designed to utilize existing sets as much as possible to help keep the budget under control—shooting was restricted to the bridge for much of the story. Kolbe kept things fresh by carefully choreographing movements of the camera and the actors. Apparently, the experience didn't sour

him on *Star Trek*; in subsequent years, he'd become one of the franchise's primary go-to directors, helming an additional fifteen *TNG* episodes (including the two-hour finale "All Good Things . . ."), plus thirteen episodes of *Star Trek: Deep Space Nine*, eighteen of *Star Trek: Voyager*, and one of *Star Trek: Enterprise*.

"Whatever I was when this began, I have grown. I am understanding more and more. And I am able to use the power at my fingertips."
—*Moriarty*

Knowing that Data appreciates Sherlock Holmes stories, Geordi La Forge programs the holodeck to create a Holmes adventure for Data to participate in. But because Data's computer-like brain has memorized every published Holmes story, the adventure isn't much of a challenge. Dr. Pulaski challenges La Forge to have the holodeck come up with a new adventure—and an opponent who could actually beat the android. The holodeck simulator responds by making Professor Moriarty, Holmes's fictional nemesis, a self-aware entity within the program—whereupon Moriarty promptly kidnaps Dr. Pulaski and threatens to take over the ship. His ultimate goal: freedom from the confines of the holodeck.

In the twenty-fourth century, there doesn't seem to be a heck of a lot of difference between an android whose mental processes are the product of a positronic brain (which is, for all practical purposes, a very advanced computer) and a hologram whose mental processes have been programmed by a very advanced computer like the one on the *Enterprise*-D. While "The Measure of a Man" soon would be lauded for its well-reasoned take on an android's rights as a sentient being, the rights of something far less tangible—a sentient hologram—set the stage here for many an intriguing *Star Trek* episode to come.

Data's behavior operates within the parameters established by Dr. Noonien Soong, the man who designed that marvelous brain. But, initially, the Professor Moriarty hologram in "Elementary, Dear Data" can behave only within the parameters of his fictional counterpart in Sir Arthur Conan Doyle's Sherlock Holmes books. However, thanks to Geordi's ill-conceived programming directive (he tells the computer to create an adversary "capable of defeating Data"), the Moriarty hologram "evolves" to a sentience that rivals Data's.

The artificial intelligences (AIs) that Captain Kirk encountered during his travels a century earlier weren't nearly as complex as the ones that Picard and, later, *Voyager*'s Captain Janeway meet up with. Kirk could easily trip up the logic circuits of twenty-third-century AIs, and push the not-quite-sentient constructs into "force quit" mode. But Moriarty (and presumably the mysterious Minuet created by the Bynars) is virtually human. So is *Star Trek: Deep Space Nine*'s holosuite character Vic Fontaine, and any number of holograms introduced on *Star Trek: Voyager*, particularly the ship's Emergency Medical Hologram (EMH), who, like Data, ultimately goes to court to press for the rights inherent to sentient technology.

What hath science wrought? Is sentience in a conglomeration of light and energy particles a good thing or a bad thing? The jury's still out on that. In the meantime, unless a hologram has access to an autonomous holo-emitter like *Voyager*'s EMH, he's pretty much stuck on the holodeck.

"Take my Worf—please." —Data

Captain Picard's decision to help a charmer named Okona repair his spaceship draws the *Enterprise* crew into an unpleasant confrontation with the rulers of two nearby worlds. Each demands that Picard turn over Okona; one claims that the young man stole a sacred jewel, while the other says that the rogue impregnated his daughter. Picard realizes that if he gives Okona to either accuser, the action may trigger an interplanetary war. On the other hand, if he doesn't comply with either man, the two worlds are likely to open fire on the *Enterprise*.

It's the closest Han Solo ever got to *Star Trek*.

As played by actor William O. Campbell (better known as Billy Campbell these days), Thadiun Okona seems cut from the same cloth as *Star Wars'* intrepid space smuggler. But it's another well-loved space traveler that Campbell almost saw among his character credits: if not for a "thumbs-down" from one high-ranking Paramount executive, he would have been cast as Commander William Riker. Executive John Pike, the same man who'd told the producers to go with Patrick Stewart, *sans* wig, as the captain, shot down Campbell's big break. "He didn't feel [Billy] had a sense of command," recalls Rick Berman. "He said he wouldn't follow him into battle."

Perhaps it's just as well that Campbell didn't win the role. In the twenty-five years since *The Next Generation* hit the airwaves, he's appeared in regular or recurring roles in nine television series and a number of motion pictures, including fan favorite *The Rocketeer*—and yet he's a man who passionately loves his free time. When Campbell was offered a role in *The 4400*—a sci-fi television series that ran for four seasons—he told the producers, "I'll do your TV series, but I'm sailing around the world for a year." The producers, including Ira Steven Behr, writer and producer on *TNG*'s third season, were convinced that Campbell was right for the role and cast him anyway. Then they accommodated his adventurous spirit by assassinating his character in the middle of the show's second season and resurrecting him a year later when the actor returned to dry land—after having sailed into twenty-five ports of call.

While *TNG*'s producers were taken with Campbell's performance as Okona, Paramount's television publicity department had eyes only for then-popular comedian Joe Piscopo. Which is why the department's still photographer for the episode focused not on the main story line, but on Piscopo's appearance in the B story as The Comic, a holodeck character who (unsuccessfully) attempts to teach Data how to be funny.

"It is a beard, Geordi. A fine, full, dignified beard. One which commands respect and projects thoughtfulness and dignity. Well? Opinions?" —Data

Responding to a call for help, the *Enterprise* travels to the research facility of Dr. Ira Graves, the brilliant but eccentric scientist who mentored Data's creator Dr. Noonien Soong. It was Graves's young assistant Kareen who summoned the ship, in the hopes that someone aboard could help the scientist. Unfortunately, it's quickly determined that Graves's illness is terminal and he has little time left. Graves strikes up a friendly rapport with Data, and shares his last breakthrough with the android: a device capable of transferring a human personality into a computer. After Graves dies, Data begins displaying uncharacteristically human tendencies, including a profound yen for the attractive Kareen, leaving Picard to wonder just what happened down in Graves's laboratory.

Data's never-ending quest to become more like his shipmates takes a giant leap in the wrong direction with his hirsute effort to emulate Riker's new (as of season two) facial adornment. As was so often the case, Data's effort is served up for laughs, a lightweight prelude to the episode's central plot: Ira Graves's far more successful attempt to humanize the sentient android—by replacing Data's consciousness with his own.

Over the course of the series, virtually all of Data's personal attempts to "improve" himself were failures, arguably because he was already the kindest, gentlest person on the ship. To paraphrase Kirk's eulogy (in *Star Trek II: The Wrath of Khan*) for his own allegedly unemotional science officer: of all the souls we would meet in our travels aboard the *Enterprise*-D, his was the most human.

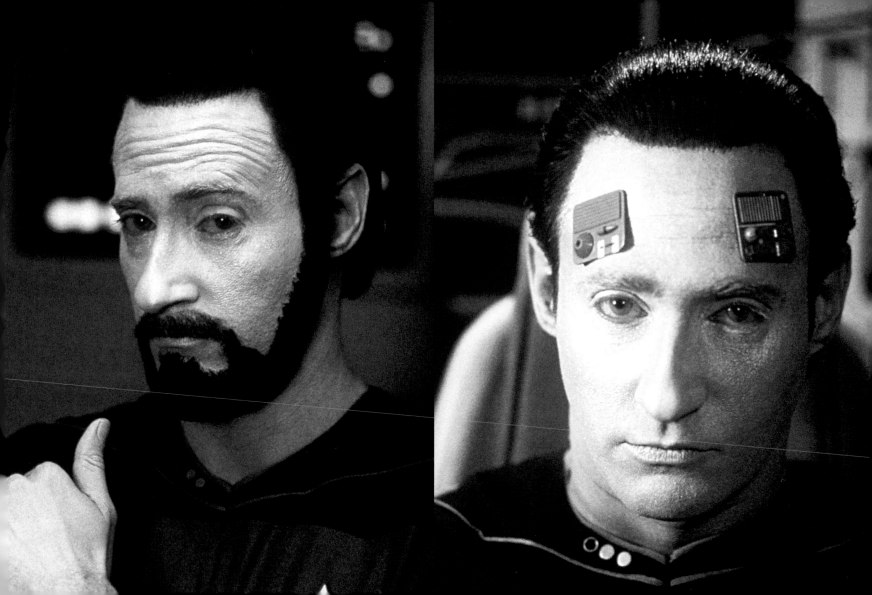

Riker: *"Deanna, I don't understand what he's going to do. How can he mediate without his interpreters? He won't even be able to talk to them."*

Troi: *"Riva is going to teach them sign language."*

Data (speaking as Riva): *"Yes, it is turning a disadvantage into an advantage. Learning sign will be a part of their process of learning how to live together in peace."*

The *Enterprise* carries the renowned mediator Riva to Solais V, where the inhabitants have waged a bitter civil war for centuries. Riva is congenitally deaf; he "speaks" via a telepathic chorus of interpreters who convey his thoughts. It's an eloquent method of communication, but one that proves to have its drawbacks. When Riva attempts to open negotiations on Solais, a terrorist opens fire and kills Riva's three interpreters. Suddenly "voiceless," the traumatized mediator withdraws and refuses to deal with either the people of Solais or the crew of the *Enterprise*, leaving the fate of the strife-torn planet in limbo.

Born deaf, actor Howie Seago didn't learn American Sign Language (ASL) until high school; his hearing parents felt that he'd be better equipped to deal with the world if he spoke out loud. Seago later became adept in his use of ASL, but he is also vocally fluent.

Seago's career breakthrough came when avant-garde American theater director Peter Sellars cast him in the title role of Sophocles's tragic play *Ajax*. Convinced that the classic drama would be the perfect vehicle for the deaf actor, Sellars changed the play's traditional Greek "chorus" into five interpreters who follow Ajax around and speak for him. "Each of them," Seago recalls, "interpreted according to my character's mood."

The production toured successfully in America and Europe, and made it possible for Seago to acquire a Hollywood agent. Not long after, Seago's wife made a seemingly off-the-wall suggestion: do a *Star Trek: The Next Generation* episode. "She loves *Star Trek*," Seago says, admitting that he wasn't as passionate about the show. "It's hard to lip-read aliens," he says with a laugh.

Seago's agent contacted a producer at Paramount Pictures. At the time, the Hollywood studios were on an imposed hiatus because of a writers' strike. "It's the only reason I got in to see the producer," the actor jokes. "He had nothing else to do." Six months later, Seago's agent called the theater where he was working to say, "*Star Trek* wants you."

In the original script, mediator Riva carried a device that allowed him to hear and speak. At a critical point in negotiations, the device breaks. "That was lame," Seago notes, and he expressed that feeling to the show's producers. They offered up a solution suited to Seago's accomplished linguistic skills: Data would teach Riva to speak overnight.

But Seago nixed that idea as well. He didn't want his performance to give the parents of deaf children the false hope that their children could instantly become clear speakers. Every deaf child is different; not all are as successful at vocalizing as he is.

Drawing on his background, Seago told them about the translators who'd followed him around in *Ajax*. Suppose Riva has a chorus, he proposed—and they *die*. And then Data must learn sign language in order to communicate with Riva.

It was a good suggestion, made better when the writers took it a step further, having Riva decide to teach the warring factions to sign.

By the second season, *TNG*'s popularity was such that Soundstages 8 and 9—where the standing *Enterprise* sets were located—became a "must see" destination for VIPs who had other business on the Paramount lot. Generally, requests to stop by and meet the crew were accommodated if the filming schedule for that week's episode hadn't fallen too far behind. It was good for publicity, after all, and the actors typically enjoyed the interaction with men and women whose paths likely would never have intersected with their own out in the "real world."

And so it was in February of 1989 that Jonathan Frakes and Patrick Stewart got to meet the man who was, at the time, the highest-ranking military officer in the United States Armed Forces. As the *Los Angeles Times* reported the next day, "The nation's top military man was on the bridge of the *Enterprise* Monday. Admiral William J. Crowe, chairman of the Joint Chiefs of Staff, was at Paramount to do a cameo in *Cheers*, and asked to visit the nearby set of *Star Trek: The Next Generation*. Knowing when he was outranked, the head man of the *Enterprise*, Captain Jean-Luc Picard (Patrick Stewart), graciously relinquished his chair to the admiral during the brief visit."

Responding to a distress call from the *U.S.S. Lantree*, the *Enterprise* crew is shocked to learn that *Lantree*'s entire ship's complement has died of old age. Picard orders the *Enterprise* to the *Lantree*'s last port of call, the Darwin Genetic Research Station, where he discovers that Darwin's lab personnel also have been afflicted, apparently with a virus that causes rapid aging. The stricken staff members at Darwin are more concerned about the status of the genetically bred children whom they have in isolation; they want to release them so they can live normal lives. Picard worries that the children are the source of the disease, but the researchers deny it—until Dr. Pulaski becomes infected with the virus after examining one of the children.

Aging an actor via elaborate makeup techniques is always a tremendous challenge, explains Michael Westmore. That's particularly true when it's done for television, where, unlike feature films, there's little time built into the production schedule for makeup tests. "It has to work the first time," notes Westmore. "And it has to look 'real' or the audience will notice it right away."

By the time he became the makeup designer on *The Next Generation*, Westmore was quite skilled at applying old-age makeup, thanks to his work on features like *Raging Bull*, *True Confessions*, and *2010*. But the ticking clock on a weekly television show can be a killer. For a variety of reasons, Westmore hadn't been happy with the look of eighty-year-old Admiral Jameson in the first season's "Too Short a Season." Clayton Rohner, the actor who played Jameson, was actually in his twenties, which meant the transformation Westmore had to pull off was extensive: a bald cap, a forehead, eyepieces for the upper and lower part of the eye, a throat piece, jowls, and a wig. The schedule for that episode, Westmore admits, brought him to the brink of nervous exhaustion. Still, he learned a great deal from the experience—particularly in terms of pacing himself—and he was quite pleased with his next feat of extreme aging in "Unnatural Selection." The task was made easier by the fact that Diana Muldaur had a more mature face than Rohner. "We were able to make intermediate changes by using highlight, shadow, and a little stretch rubber," Westmore says. "With Rohner, it was impossible to make those changes without using appliances." Westmore did create some appliances for Muldaur to convey the final stage of her aging, but the work involved was far less extreme. "Overall, I was very happy with the end result," he says with a smile.

"If Klingon food is too strong for you, perhaps we could get one of the females to breast-feed you." —Klag

An exchange program gives Commander Riker the opportunity to become the first Starfleet officer to serve on a Klingon ship. After studying up on Klingon dietary habits and receiving vital tips from Worf about the ways of Klingon crews, Riker proves that he can hold his own with the warrior race aboard the *Pagh*—or so it seems until he faces a real challenge. A nasty strain of bacteria is eating away the hull of the Klingon vessel, and the *Pagh*'s captain believes that the *Enterprise* is responsible. If Riker doesn't help the crew attack the Federation starship, he can count on the *Pagh*'s second officer to follow Klingon tradition by assisting him into "honorable retirement" . . . via assassination.

"When Ten-Forward came about in our second season, it created a tremendous opportunity for me to make food," says *TNG*'s property master Alan Sims. "I wanted to make something different, very specialized food of the future. Especially for 'A Matter of Honor,' where Riker had to become acquainted with Klingon food. I was in my heyday because I was able to create something that had never been seen before. And being a fan of things that frighten people . . ." Sims's voice trails off with a chuckle. "As it was written [in the script], it was supposed to be pretty frightening, and that opened up the floodgates for me. For '*pipius* claw,' I bought chicken feet and eliminated the middle toe so that it looked like a devil's fork kind of thing. I got the organs from the butcher. 'Heart of *targ*' was an actual [beef] heart. I had a liver and more. The Asian market [offered] a plethora to me. Different kinds of fish with eyes—and I just used eyes and fins. I can't tell you how much fun I had. Then when Riker actually went to the Klingon ship, there was a whole Klingon feast! I used squid and octopus, but I did different things with them. And the actors had to eat this stuff!"

"A Matter of Honor" was the only episode of *Star Trek: The Next Generation* to be turned into one of View-Master's licensed 3-D reel products. The View-Master device had been developed by Sawyer's Photo Services in the early twentieth century, conceived as a product that would enable consumers to view photographic images in stereo. Essentially an updated stereoscope that utilized then-new Kodachrome 16-mm color film, each View-Master disk contained seven pairs of matching film frames. When a pair of matching images was viewed simultaneously, one with each eye, the consumer experienced a simulation of binocular depth perception. Initially marketed as a 3-D alternative to scenic postcards—popular subject matter included Carlsbad Caverns and the Grand Canyon—Sawyer's branched out into licensed entertainment in the 1950s with images of Disney characters and scenes from the newly opened Disneyland park. Licensing expanded in 1966 when the company was acquired by GAF, which began producing disks that capitalized on the popularity of such television series as *The Man from U.N.C.L.E.*, *The Beverly Hillbillies*, and *Star Trek* ("The Omega Glory").

Over the years, View-Master licensed a number of Star Trek titles from Paramount, including "Yesteryear," from *The Animated Series* (released as "Mr. Spock's Time Trek"), *Star Trek: The Motion Picture*, *Star Trek II: The Wrath of Khan*, and this one *TNG* title.

Why "A Matter of Honor"? One can only guess at this point, but the Klingon-heavy episode had proven to be an audience favorite, bringing the series its highest Nielsen rating to date; that alone would have made it a logical candidate for Ideal Toy Company (the third owner of View-Master) to add to its line.

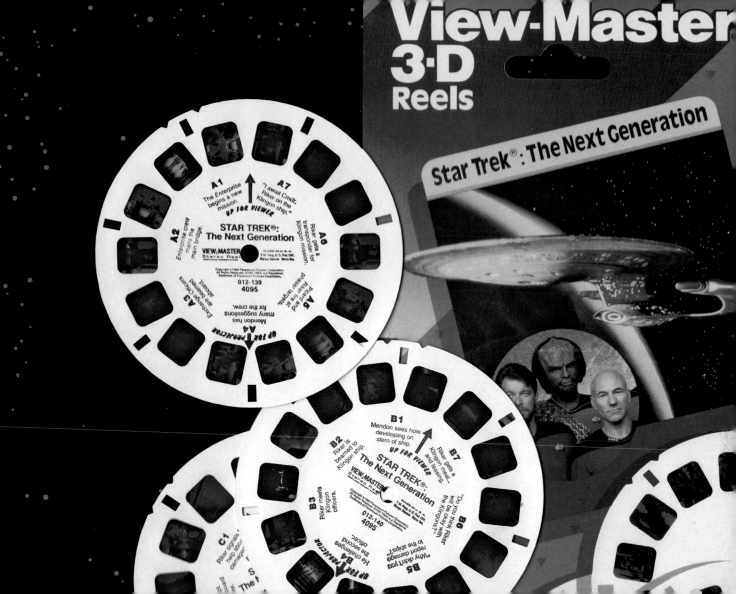

During the final months of 1988, anyone walking down Paramount's Avenue P couldn't help but feel a bit of temporal disturbance. On the east side of the avenue, a group of people buzzed about, fully concerned with the twenty-third century; on the west side, another group worked within the twenty-fourth. And for a select, very busy few, such as members of the art department, the futuristic centuries came and went, back and forth, as they crossed a nonexistent center line.

On the east, work crews and costumed characters hustled in and out of three soundstages, occupied with filming the feature *Star Trek V: The Final Frontier*. On the west, similar activities around two stages defined the filming of TV's *Star Trek: The Next Generation*. Just standing in the middle of the street was enough to make a grown fan smile.

And a grown actor, too. The proximity of the stages offered a perfect opportunity for the various cast members to become acquainted and exchange pleasantries. They had one thing in common, after all: each was proudly serving on the *U.S.S. Enterprise*. And that crossed all boundaries, temporal and otherwise.

"Pinocchio is broken. Its strings have been cut." —Riker

Is Data a piece of Starfleet equipment? A noted robotics specialist has received Starfleet's approval to disassemble the unique android. His goal: to create more androids like Data. But when Data learns that the specialist may not be able to put him back together again, he refuses to submit to the experiment and resigns his commission. In response, Starfleet proclaims that Data *can't* resign because he's Starfleet property, a position that leads Picard to argue Data's rights as a sentient being in a court of law.

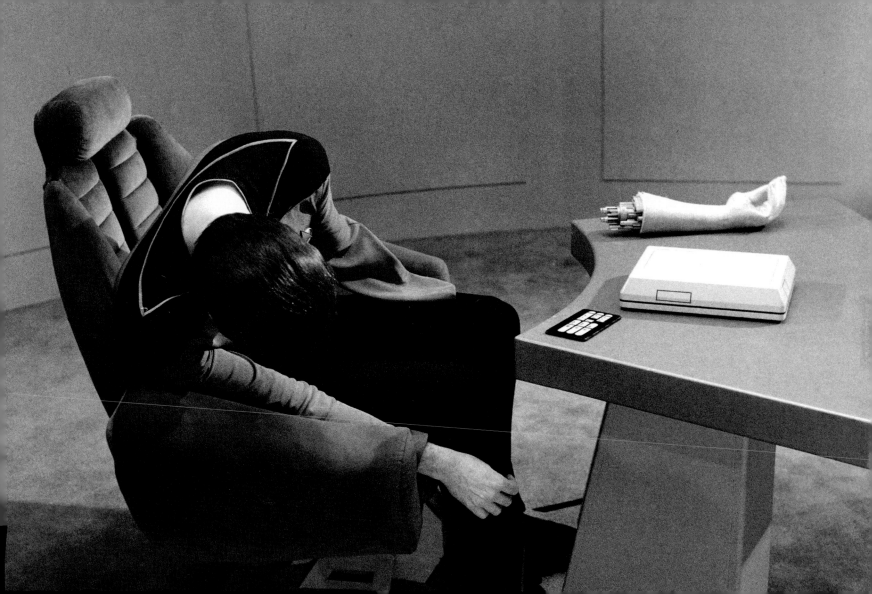

"The ultimate measure of a man is not where he stands in moments of comfort and convenience, but where he stands at times of challenge and controversy." —Martin Luther King Jr.

Many people think of "The Measure of a Man" as the quintessential Data story. But Data is not the "man" referenced in the episode's title. In fact, he isn't a man at all. He is, in his own words, "an automaton made to resemble a human being."

Certainly Data's plight is the catalyst for the episode's action, but this really is Picard's story. It is Picard who bears the burden of proof to defend the rights of his friend. For if Data is judged a mere piece of Starfleet property, with no rights and no say about his own future, then he can be taken apart and duplicated ad infinitum. And all of those duplicates will be property as well: in essence, a race of high-tech *slaves*. So Picard acts, knowing that an inadequate defense will not only cost Data his freedom, but very likely cause "something unique, something wonderful" to be lost from the universe. It doesn't matter that Data isn't a "man." He is an individual—conscious, self-aware, and intelligent—and that is what Picard must make the judge comprehend.

Thus, it is the captain—and perhaps all of his Starfleet peers—who bear the weight implicit in the title. The purpose of Starfleet, as is pointed out at the beginning of every episode of *The Next Generation* and *The Original Series*, is to "seek out new life." And here, in one of *TNG*'s finest pieces of oration, Captain Jean-Luc Picard reminds the people gathered in the courtroom of that noble purpose:

"Your Honor, the courtroom is a crucible. In it we burn away irrelevancies until we are left with a pure product, the truth for all time. Now, sooner or later, this man or others like him will succeed in replicating Commander Data. And the decision you reach here today will determine how we will regard this creation of our genius. It will reveal the kind of a people we are, what he is destined to be. It will reach far beyond this courtroom and this one android. It could significantly redefine the boundaries of personal liberty and freedom, expanding them for some, savagely curtailing them for others. Are you prepared to condemn him and all who come after him to servitude and slavery? Your Honor, Starfleet was founded to seek out new life. Well, there it sits. Waiting. You wanted a chance to make law. Well, here it is. Make a good one."

"This case has dealt with metaphysics, with questions best left to saints and philosophers. I'm neither competent nor qualified to answer those. I've got to make a ruling, to try to speak to the future. Is Data a machine? Yes. Is he the property of Starfleet? No. We have all been dancing around the basic issue. Does Data have a soul? I don't know that he has. I don't know that I have. But I have got to give him the freedom to explore that question himself. It is the ruling of this court that Lieutenant Commander Data has the freedom to choose." —Phillipa Louvois

It is, as she herself has described it, a Hollywood Cinderella story. At the urging of her good friend, writer/producer George R. R. Martin, novelist Melinda M. Snodgrass wrote a spec script for *Star Trek: The Next Generation*. Both Martin and her agent warned her that a spec script was "just a calling card," meant to demonstrate a writer's level of skill at creating characters and crafting dialogue. If she were lucky, she'd be invited to meet with the producers and pitch a few story ideas. Snodgrass delivered the script to her agent in 1988, the day before the writers' strike commenced. At which point, *Star Trek* production came to a standstill.

The strike dragged on for months, far longer than anyone anticipated, and when it ended, it left *TNG* staffers hustling to fill the very large holes in the show's production schedule. Scripts could now be commissioned, of course, but the process from pitched story concept to final shooting script is never a quick one. Suddenly the office "slush pile" looked very attractive. . . .

Every book publisher, talent agency, and production office has a slush pile of unsolicited scripts or manuscripts. The bulk of these literary efforts never see the light of day; it's too time-consuming to assign someone to read through them and separate the gold from the dross. But after the strike, those slush piles were potential show-savers.

In October 1988, Snodgrass received a call informing her that the *Star Trek* staff wanted to see her. She flew from her home in New Mexico to Los Angeles, prepared to pitch some different ideas for episodes. But instead, Snodgrass was told that everyone loved her script, and that they wanted to buy it—could she make the necessary changes right away?

She could. In fact, the final script was so well received that it won her a position as *TNG*'s story editor. Snodgrass possessed expert knowledge on the subject matter; prior to taking up writing as a profession, she'd practiced law. "The Measure of a Man" was nominated for a Writers Guild award—quite an accomplishment for a first effort at screenwriting. The episode remains, to this day, a fan favorite.

Worf: "Men do not roar. Women roar. Then they hurl heavy objects. And claw at you."
Wesley: "What does the man do?"
Worf: "He reads love poetry. He ducks a lot."

The *Enterprise* ferries Salia, a sixteen-year-old girl, and Anya, her overprotective guardian, to the troubled planet she is meant to rule. Salia and Wesley immediately hit it off, but Anya is fiercely determined to keep them apart. Troi senses that there is something odd about the two women—but nothing quite as odd as what Wesley discovers when he and Salia attempt to meet in secret.

Morphing software, which allows a visual effects artist to take two pictures and seamlessly change one into the other as if it were transforming before your eyes, is common today, but it didn't exist in early 1989, when "The Dauphin" was in production. Thus, as is his wont, Dan Curry resorted to using a few old-fashioned, low-tech methods in order to create the high-tech effects required for this episode.

For all of the transformations, including Anya's morph into Salia's fuzzy little playmate (depicted opposite in this ad slick that Paramount Domestic Television distributed to the syndicated stations that carried *TNG*), "we did a painted morph, literally hand-animating the transformation frame by frame," explains Curry. "I had done something similar a few years earlier for *Jason Lives: Friday the 13th Part VI*, using oil paintings and quick dissolves for the stages of the transformation. In this case, I asked the late Steve Price, a terrific artist and animator, to do it on a digital paint system. We shot a locked-down plate of the actress (Paddi Edwards) and then one of the person wearing the allasomorph costume (Cindy Sorenson), and then a clean plate with no actors. Then Steve did a half-way digital painting using elements from both characters, and

then kept doing in-betweens until the transition was the correct length."

In the same episode, rather than creating virtual asteroids for the sequence in which Wesley takes Salia on a holographic visit to Rousseau V, Curry actually went shopping for them. "All of the asteroids were pieces of lava rock—the kind you'd use in gardening—that I bought at a local building supply place," he says. "I took a bucket and carefully selected each rock for its 'appropriateness' as an asteroid. One of the guys working in the supply yard got very curious, watching me pick up these things one at a time. Finally, he came over and said, 'Hey man, I've never seen anyone so particular about rocks as you!' When I explained what they were for, I wasn't sure if he thought I was crazier than he had in the first place!"

"They also serve who only stand and wait."*
—John Milton, "On His Blindness"

*(or lie)

"Fate protects fools, little children, and ships named Enterprise.*" —Riker*

Responding to a distress call issued by the *U.S.S. Yamato*, the *Enterprise* crosses into the Romulan Neutral Zone, arriving just in time to witness the *Yamato*'s destruction. Although the crew initially suspects Romulan malfeasance, they quickly learn that the explosion of the ship—a *Galaxy*-class vessel like the *Enterprise*—was triggered by widespread computer malfunctions. Retracing the *Yamato*'s most recent course, the crew finds itself at the legendary planet of Iconia, home to a long-dead civilization of advanced beings who traveled via gateways through time and space. But Picard's excitement over the discovery is short-lived; the *Enterprise* has been infected with the same computer virus that destroyed the *Yamato*. Making matters worse: the Romulans are extremely displeased to see the *Enterprise* on the wrong side of the Neutral Zone.

It's hard to imagine, but just twenty-five years ago, writers used *typewriters* to transfer words from their imagination into physical reality. But by the mid-1980s, with personal computers increasingly available, the writing—so to speak—was on the wall: time to upgrade.

This change was both exciting and unnerving for writers—even writers of science fiction. They were excited by the new technology, but few of them knew what to ask for when they went into a computer store. Which is why, when Gene Roddenberry decided to take the big leap and purchase his first desktop computer, he went directly to Beth Woods, the manager of a computer store located near the Paramount lot. Both Dorothy Fontana and David Gerrold had recommended Woods, and that was enough for Roddenberry. Woods not only sold him a computer, she taught him how to use it. Not long after, *TNG* hired Woods to implement a computer system for the staff writers; Paramount, at this time, did not have an extensive IT department, and, in fact, few offices at the studio used computers.

Learning that Woods was, like countless others in Hollywood, a struggling writer, Roddenberry invited her to pitch some ideas for his new series. Woods had never sold anything for television, but she felt that her friend Steve Gerber—yet another person she'd met through her job at the computer store—might be a good collaborator.

Gerber wasn't exactly an unknown. He was a superstar in comic book circles, best known for creating cult favorite Howard the Duck (the comic character, not the movie). With stories appearing in imprints of virtually every U.S. comic publisher, Gerber had more recently served as story editor on a variety of animated television projects, including *G.I. Joe*, *Thundarr the Barbarian*, and *The Transformers*. He was also a longtime *Star Trek* fan.

The writing team got a positive response to their pitch about the mysterious explosion of a *Galaxy*-class starship and the subsequent infection of the *Enterprise*'s computer system. Conversations with Roddenberry as they were developing the script generated an angle related to the ancient civilization of the long-dead Iconians (and, in the process, established Picard's passion for archaeology). Despite a few predictable tweaks made after they turned in their final draft, both writers were pleased with the result—except, ironically, for one thing: the way the *Enterprise* was "cured" of its computer malady. Sim-

ply rebooting, they explained, would likely have rebooted the virus as well. But they accepted that the in-house fix was much less complicated than their more technically appropriate solution.

Following her television debut, Woods focused on writing computer how-to books. Gerber, noting that he'd fulfilled a lifelong ambition to write a *Star Trek* episode, went back to writing comics and animated television shows until his death in 2008.

Opposite: Michael Dorn, Patrick Stewart, and director Joseph Scanlan double-check continuity with script supervisor Cosmo Genovese.

After recovering a bit of space refuse that appears to have come from a twenty-first-century Earth spacecraft, Riker, Worf, and Data beam down to an uninhabited planet and find themselves trapped within an artificial environment that resembles an old casino. Inside one of the hotel rooms, they find the remains of the astronaut who piloted the spacecraft. On a bedside table is a novel called *The Hotel Royale,* and also the astronaut's diary, which reveals his fate—and perhaps predicts their own.

"The Royale" is another unloved child of *The Next Generation*'s early years, disowned by its progenitor Tracy Tormé (who removed his name from the final product and replaced it with the pseudonym Keith Mills) and regarded as inconsequential by the fans. Originally titled "The Blue Moon Hotel," it had been one of the first story concepts that Tormé pitched to *TNG*'s producers, although he wasn't given the green light to go to script until season two. Tormé's draft was reportedly unsettling and surreal, and more than a little influenced by his admitted fondness for the classic 1960s television series *The Prisoner*. The as-

tronaut's life in the hotel was based not on a cheesy novel, but on a fragment of a pleasant memory that the mysterious resident aliens had pulled from his mind. But even a pleasant memory can become a nightmare if one is never permitted to leave. Tormé's version of the story featured a central role for the hapless astronaut—which caused conflict between the writer and the producers. "They made a big point at the time, 'We don't want to do big guest roles,'" Tormé stated in a 2002 interview with *Star Trek: The Magazine.* "So the astronaut then became a skeleton and everything about him in the piece was gone. That was the biggest thing I had a problem with in the rewrites. He was the heart of the story for me."

The clash apparently took the heart out of Tormé's involvement with the series as well. The son of singer Mel Tormé made plans to move on to other projects at the end of the season, and contributed only one additional script—"Manhunt"—to *TNG*, choosing to use a pseudonym (Terry Devereaux) on that one as well.

The crew comes upon a disabled shuttlepod that apparently is from their own starship. Inside the shuttlepod is a disoriented double of Captain Picard. The twin is just as real as the Picard presently on board, but tests show he is from six hours in the future. Apparently, at that time, the *Enterprise* will encounter a gigantic energy whirlpool and be destroyed, leaving the captain as its only survivor. With the future version of himself unable to communicate, the present Picard must decide on the correct course of action to prevent the catastrophe from occurring . . . *again*.

Gene Roddenberry's concept of "beaming" via "transporter" provided *Star Trek* producers with a quick, easy, and (production-wise) cheap way to get their characters from the ship to a planet's surface. And once the visual effect ("transporter sparkle") was in the can, it could be used repeatedly at little additional cost.

The alternate way of making that ship-to-shore journey—via shuttlecraft—was quite expensive. So expensive, in fact, that *The Original Series* had to do without until plastic model maker AMT, a *Star Trek* licensee, offered to build a shuttle for the show (which, in turn, allowed AMT to sell *Galileo 7* shuttlecraft model kits).

Twenty years later, the producers of *The Next Generation* faced a similar problem. They recognized the value of having an alternative means of transportation, but they had already pushed their budget to the limit for standing sets. Then writer Sandy Fries submitted his script for "Coming of Age," in which the theft of a shuttlecraft by one of Wesley's friends provides the story with an exciting beat. The producers loved Andrew Probert's design for a new twenty-fourth-century shuttlecraft, but felt it would prove too expensive to construct. So they built only a small filming model, along with a partial interior. The following season, a partial exterior was created and utilized, to so-so effect, in episodes like "Unnatural Selection."

It wasn't until "Time Squared" that *TNG* got a shuttle with a full exterior that could be photographed from any angle. Smaller and lacking the graceful curves of the original Probert design, this economical little workhorse, designated the *El-Baz* (after former NASA planetary geoscientist Farouk El-Baz), was a two-person "Type-15 shuttlepod," primarily limited to short interplanetary hops. It was designed by Rick Sternbach and set designer Richard McKenzie.

Another three years would pass before the budget was expanded to the point where a larger, full-scale Federation shuttlecraft could be introduced on the show.

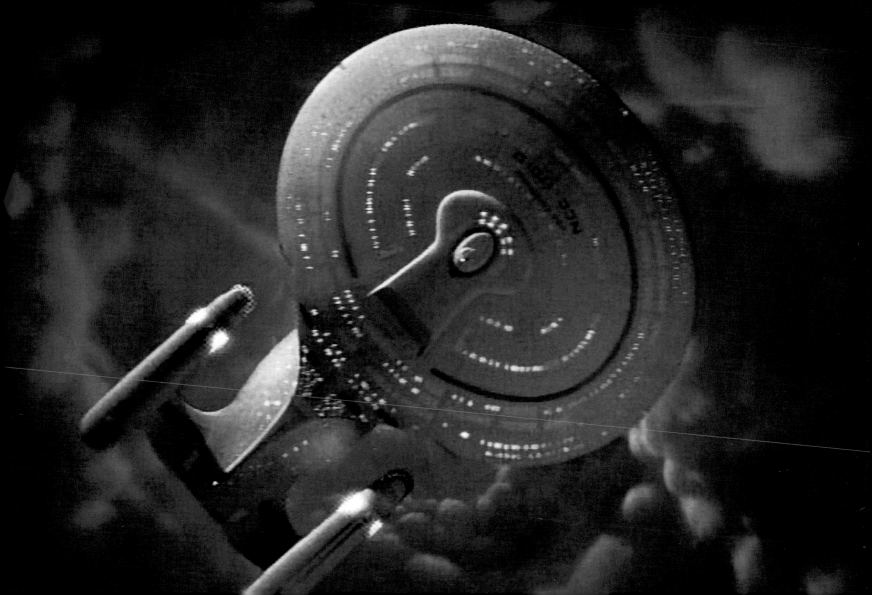

Riker ponders accepting command of his own starship and leaving the crew he's come to think of as family. Complicating the decision is an unanticipated reunion with his father, Kyle, from whom he has been estranged for fifteen years. At the same time, members of the crew learn that Lieutenant Worf's uncharacteristically hostile behavior toward them has to do with his feelings of cultural isolation. He's missed out on a ritual marking the tenth anniversary of his "Age of Ascension." Wesley's solution: use the holodeck to program some warriors who will poke Worf with the Klingon equivalent of a cattle prod, thus allowing him to admit his "most profound feelings under extreme duress."

"Right now, the best place for me to be is here." —Riker

In Greek mythology, Icarus was the son of Daedalus, a master craftsman. Daedalus created the means for the two of them to escape from exile: wings fashioned from wax and feathers. Daedalus cautioned Icarus not to fly too close to the sun, a warning his son ignored, to fatal effect.

Why title this episode "The Icarus Factor"? Yes, it's about a father/son relationship, but who's strapping on wings? Who's flying too near the sun?

Admittedly, it's a stretch—but it's certainly not the first time a *Star Trek* episode has attempted to elevate its subject matter by giving the title a classical reference, say a Shakespeare quote ("By Any Other Name") or a line from an ancient Greek play ("Whom Gods Destroy").

Will Riker could easily make the case that his father gave him nothing, that he got his own wings and rose through the ranks of Starfleet without getting burned. But is it mere coincidence that Kyle, his long-absent father, shows up at the *precise* moment Will is offered the opportunity to fly even higher as captain of the *Aries*?

Will has always wanted his own command, even though he passed on the *Drake* to take the second-banana position on the *Enterprise*. Kyle is present to brief Will on the dangerous mission he'd be taking on as captain of the *Aries*—so dangerous that Worf wants to go with Riker because of the potential "to die a true hero."

Kyle Riker feels his son will accept the transfer "*because* it is dangerous." After all, *he'd* do it. "We aren't so different, Will and I," he says.

Ah, but they *are*. During the anbo-jyutsu match, Will realizes that his father cheats, and that he's *always* cheated. According to Kyle, it was the only way to hold Will's interest and keep him coming back for more. "I had to keep you challenged," Kyle explains.

Will has an epiphany: competition is the only way Kyle knows how to interact; the death of Will's mom left him incapable of relating to others on an emotional level. That's why Kyle prefers a life of challenge and danger.

That's not Will—at least, not anymore. Apparently Kyle *did* give him wings. Will's ambitious desire to move up the career ladder while a young man—we'll learn in "Second Chances" that this is what

destroyed his romantic relationship with Troi—was fueled by that old competition with Dad. It compelled Will to fly higher and higher. But in his heart, he wanted more. That's why he bypassed the *Drake*. On the *Enterprise*, Will found a sense of the family life he lacked as a boy.

Seeing his father again brought that home to him. Will doesn't need to compete to obtain emotional satisfaction. Someday he'll leave this cozy nest and stretch his wings. But the demons that drive Kyle won't drive Will; he may fly close to the sun, but never so close as to fall.

While the view outside the windows in Ten-Forward is always breathtaking, crew members who spend much time in the room eventually find their eyes drawn to the view behind Guinan's bar. It's an ever-changing panorama of shape and color, designed not by some alien artist on Tau Alpha C but by Earthman Rick Sternbach, as part of Herman Zimmerman's overall design for the new set.

"Behind the bar there's a piece of dimensional artwork surrounded by some static fluorescent lights, and if you watch it, you'll see that it appears to be moving all the time," informs Zimmerman. "That's because of the color wheels we situated in that wall. As they move, the colors shift and progress. We didn't want to interfere with the actors with a piece of machinery, so we made it very subtle, as subtle as possible. And this painting, or I guess you would call it a sculpture, enriches the background with this slow change of color."

Although it looks abstract, Sternbach intended it as an impressionistic view of the Milky Way galaxy.

Right: The sculpture as the audience never sees it—with the power off. Filling in for Guinan: one of the authors of this book (circa 1989).

"Oh, Data. Your whisper from the dark has now become a plea. We cannot turn our backs."
—*Picard*

Picard finds himself in an untenable position when he learns that Data has broken Prime Directive guidelines to communicate with a young girl in an unstable planetary system. As the girl pleads for help from her unseen "pen pal" Data, Picard reluctantly allows Data to help ensure the girl's safety. In the meantime, Wesley, given responsibility for the survey mission assigned to investigate the dangerous geological events on the girl's planet, learns that managing his team is as important as conducting the scientific research.

You might call Rick Sternbach a nuts-and-bolts kind of guy. During the run of *The Next Generation*, he was most often called upon to submit sketches for the ships and props referenced in the scripts. Every now and then, however, he'd get to deal with animate objects. "I didn't really design aliens," he explains. "But sometimes Michael [Westmore] would ask me for some concepts," Data's Dreman pen pal Sarjenka, for example. "I don't recall exactly what the script said, but I seem to remember 'different skin,' 'different hair,' and 'little skin splotches,' like we're famous for. Someone on staff once made up a fake script cover: 'Attack of the Aliens with Bumps on Their Heads.' If there was a new alien makeup, chances were they got bumps or splotches."

In Westmore's hands, Sarjenka lost the elongated ears but kept the shag haircut (courtesy of a spiky wig). Her mottled orange skin was accented with gold glitter to give it a metallic sheen, Westmore says. "I also made long finger extensions for her, which were made out of clear plastic and fitted over her own fingers. They were translucent, so that when she held up her hands, the light would shine through them, producing a wonderful effect. Unfortunately, in filming the episode, the effect was never focused upon."

"You judge yourselves against the pitiful ad-versaries you have encountered so far. The Ro-mulans, the Klingons. They are nothing compared to what's waiting. Picard, you are about to move into areas of the galaxy containing wonders more incredible than you can possibly imagine, and ter-rors to freeze your soul." —Q

After Captain Picard declines Q's request to be-come a member of the *Enterprise* crew, Q hurls the starship into a distant region of the galaxy, toward an encounter for which Q predicts the intrepid ex-plorers are poorly prepared. Almost immediately, the crew spots a gigantic cube-shaped vessel manned by a species known as the Borg: cybernetic beings that are part organic and part machine, linked via a group mind. After studying the *Enterprise*'s capabil-ities, the Borg call for the starship's surrender. In-stead, Picard engages the massive ship in battle. Both ships sustain damage, but the Borg ship, like its crew, adapts to the *Enterprise*'s onslaught, and regenerates quickly. As casualties mount aboard the *Enterprise*, Picard has no choice but to retreat. How-ever, with the ship's shields failing and warp drive gone, escape does not appear to be an option.

By the end of *TNG*'s second season, the production budget would be running on empty—in part because of "Q Who?" The episode that introduced the Borg reportedly went $50,000 over budget, thanks to the enthusiastic contributions of all the creative departments. Still, there's no denying that the money, as they say in the trade, "was all up on the screen."

That's particularly true for the knockout visual effects sequences provided by Dan Curry and his team. Their work established the template for Borg visuals that would be used and built upon in subsequent episodes (not to mention the film *Star Trek: First Contact*).

Curry's biggest challenge in "Q Who?" was the sequence where the Borg carve up the *Enterprise*, "like a roast," per Riker. Cutting a hole in the production's only filming model obviously was out of the question, so Curry commissioned an oversize model of just the necessary portion of the saucer surface. He also ordered a model to represent the tubular core that the Borg remove from the ship—a small section of four decks that are "stacked up like coins," as Curry puts it. Details of that model included severed power cables, furniture, carpeting, and a Federation wall plaque—everything a visitor (albeit a tiny one) to the *Enterprise* might expect to see on those decks. The core fit neatly into a hole cut in the oversize saucer segment, and was pushed upward with a hydraulic ram to simulate the Borg's tractor beam action.

Opposite: Curry's storyboard pages from 1989 track the entire sequence. Note how closely the completed effect (below) came to Curry's illustrated suggestion for scene 41A.

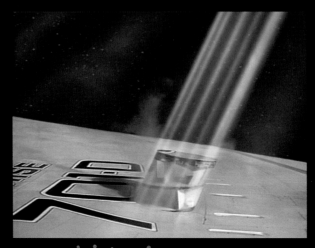

Sc. 37C

BORG TRACTOR BEAM ATTACHES
TO ENTERPRISE SAUCER

[ADD ANIMATION TO COMP FOR (Sc.35)]

Sc. 39

ENTERPRISE FIRES PHASERS ATTEMPTING
TO STOP BORG TRACTOR BEAM... BORG
BEAM HOLDS

ENTERPRISE: IMAGE G-Z
          ROLL 137/031 T.C. 01:00:50.12

BORG SHIP: [B-C]

Sc. 41 AS THE TRACTOR BEAM HOLDS

ANOTHER BEAM LEAVES THE BORG
SHIP AND CUTS INTO ENTERPRISE...
INTERMITTENT PHASER FIRE

ENTERPRISE: IMAGE G-D H.F.
          ROLL 116/031 TC: 01:00:31.15

BORG SHIP: [B-D]

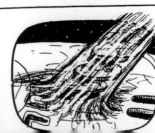

Sc. 41 A

TIGHT ON ENTERPRISE HULL...
BORG CUTTING BEAM SLICES
OUT A CORE SAMPLE...
TRACTOR BEAM STARTS TO
REMOVE IT.

-INSERT + HARRY ANIMATION

When costume designer Durinda Rice Wood joined *The Next Generation* during its second season, she found that certain established aspects of couture were off limits. "I said, 'I would really like to redesign the uniforms,' but they had spent so much money on them that they didn't want to change them, at least not at that point," Wood says with a sigh. Her most memorable contributions to the show were in garments she created for new characters, like Guinan, and new aliens. And no new species made a bigger impression on *Star Trek*'s audience than the Borg.

"They were to be the new bad guys of the universe," Wood recalls. "Typically, we were given a week to work on designs, but the Borg were important enough that we were given *two* weeks. The producers wanted them to be scary, and part of that scariness was their uniformity, and their asexualness. I was tired of the streamlined, stainless steel concept of 'scary,'" she says. "And I was influenced by the work of [Swiss surrealist artist] H. R. Giger."

When you're working on *Star Trek*, Wood notes, cause and effect guide design. "You have to think in terms of '*why* they look that way,' in addition to 'how they look.' With the Borg, the idea was that the drones lived for centuries, and that their body parts would wear out and be replaced with mechanical body parts. I wanted to show that they didn't wear out uniformly, so some of them had eye patches, and some had fake legs or arms. I spent a *lot* of time in the hardware store," she says with a laugh, "and got a lot of parts there—plastic tubing and odds and ends, little pieces that we could paint and put together. And I found a company that had molds of various body parts, like torso and leg pieces, which they could produce very quickly."

Even though the drones shared a uniform look, Wood created a separate sketch for each one, "because they each had different artificial body parts," she explains. "I developed a system around a fabric called 'popcorn spandex' that Velcro adhered to. We backed the tubes and hardware parts with Velcro so they would stick to the suit. That was great," she says, "but all the little pieces were separate, so every time we put the costumes together, they had to be reassembled."

Opposite: Wood's Borg costume sketch, and her hands-on assessment of its realization.

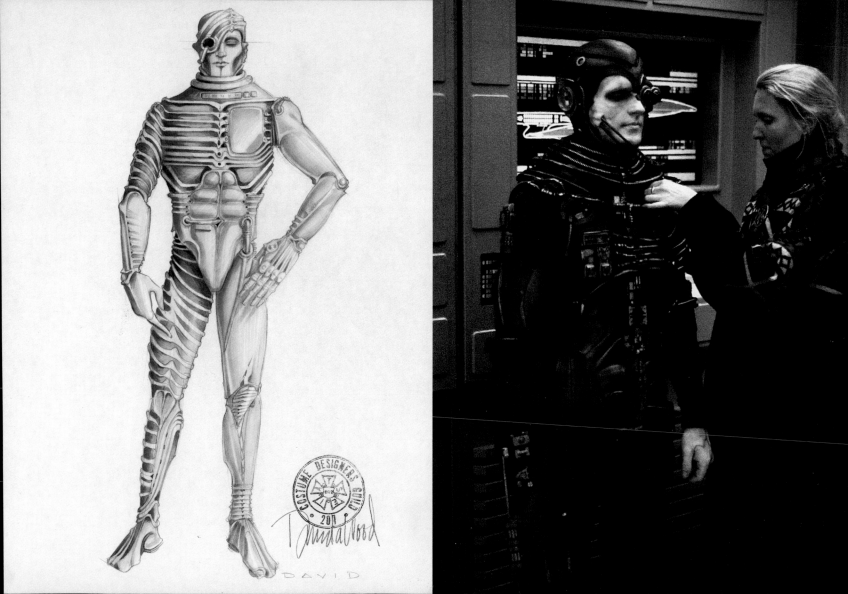

Designing the Borg in "Q Who?" required close interaction between *TNG*'s makeup and costume departments, with Durinda Wood responsible for most of the drone's body, and Michael Westmore covering its exposed body areas—primarily head, neck, and hands. "Durinda came up with a rough sketch that showed a man in a suit with tubes running around and attached to it," Westmore recalls. "The head area she kept deliberately vague."

Once Wood selected the materials for the costume, Westmore had to integrate the headgear with the rest of the bodysuit. "I built the original helmets in the wardrobe department while they were working on the suits, so we could communicate with each other and make sure that our respective designs were meshing properly," he says. "I made the headpieces out of foam rubber that would be comfortable for the actors, and colored it to match the costume." The headpieces included little clamps so the tubing that Wood incorporated into the suits could easily attach. Westmore studded the helmet with little pieces of machinery—urethane parts cast from model kits and bits of disemboweled electronics equipment.

"If we had a large exposed area of skin on the face or arm, I ran a tube directly into it," he continues. "I created a latex appliance that looks like a bullet hole that glues onto the skin, and the tube glued right into the hole in the appliance."

Westmore gave the Borg a zombie-like pallor "so the viewers would know that they were seeing a creature that couldn't be reasoned or negotiated with," he explains. The white makeup base that he used blocked out all of the natural skin tones, making them look as though "the life has been leached out of them."

To create headgear for the episode's "baby Borg" (played by the son of Carol Eisner, assistant to line producer David Livingston), Westmore created a plaster cast from a similarly sized doll's head, then fashioned a tiny Borg headpiece. A black cord ran from the headpiece to the tot's chest, where it was attached with two-sided tape. They had to do several takes because the teething baby became fixated with the cord and kept chewing on it . . . which the filmmakers deemed way too adorable for a baby Borg.

on a drone while David Livingston and Rick Berman observe.

Right: Borg facial concept by Rick Sternbach.
Opposite: Westmore puts the finishing touches

"The script said that the interior of the Borg ship was endless, as far as you could see," production designer Richard James says. "We didn't have that much space, so I raised my hand in the production meeting and said, 'Uhhh, how far is endless?' To accomplish it, I thought, 'I've got to make this like a hall of mirrors.'"

James's concept, seen in this preproduction sketch, looked as if it could do the trick—almost. Notes James, "The only area that was a problem for Gene Roddenberry was the structure I'd created in the center," which, Roddenberry pointed out, conflicted with the desired "endless" vista. So out it went, resulting in an image that looked as if it had "no top or bottom, nor up or down." Ultimately, most of it would be represented in a matte painting rendered by Illusion Arts' Syd Dutton. "You'd be surprised how little there was of an actual physical set," James adds with a chuckle.

That matte painting, recalls Dan Curry, "was large, at least six feet by six feet, done in oils on Masonite. It actually had a small hole in it, cut out so that the actors' live action could be inserted via rear projection." Curry's team combined the elements by making two camera passes. "We used a

motion-control camera system and shot only the painting on the first pass. On the second pass, all the lights were turned off so that only the projected live action would be photographed," he explains. "We put some high-tech-looking structures in the foreground—taken from a Legions of Power toy construction set—to provide some scale and create multi-planing and a sense of three-dimensionality for the camera pullback."

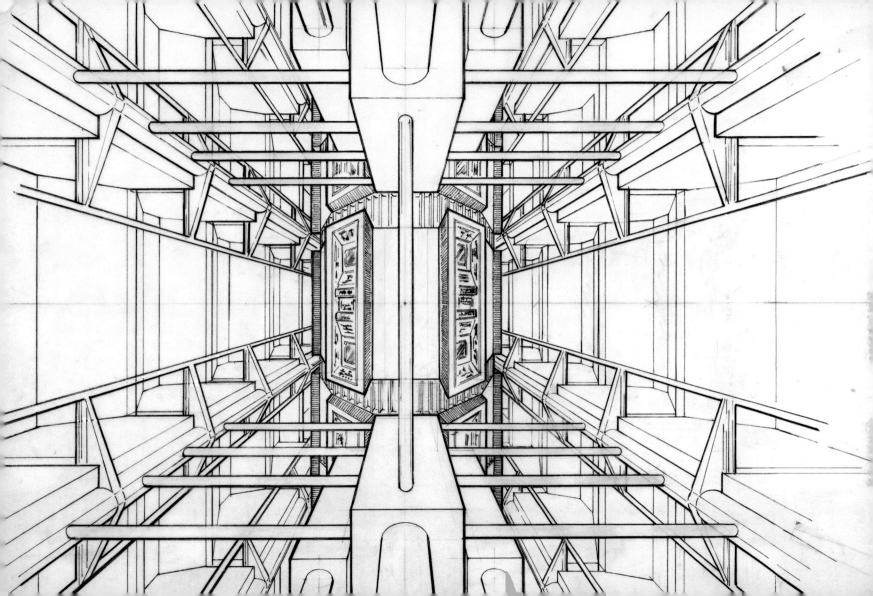

> **Grebnedlog:** *"We are Pakleds. Our ship is the Mondor. It is broken. We are far from home. We need help."*
>
> **La Forge:** *"Let me guess. Their rubber band broke, right?"*

Captain Picard accompanies Wesley Crusher on a long shuttle ride to Starbase 515, where Wesley will take exams for admission to Starfleet Academy and Picard will undergo an artificial heart replacement procedure. Back on the *Enterprise*, Commander Riker underestimates a slow-witted crew of Pakleds who ask for help repairing their vessel. After Geordi La Forge completes the repairs, the Pakleds take the engineer hostage and demand all of the data in the *Enterprise*'s computer. As Riker considers a show of force, he receives word that complications in Picard's surgery have left him near death, leaving Riker with a dilemma: head immediately for Starbase 515 or rescue La Forge?

Who's more stupid—the Pakleds or the people who are fooled by the Pakleds?

"Samaritan Snare" is an entertaining example of an "idiot plot." That is, a plot that is kept in motion solely by virtue of the fact that everybody involved is an idiot.

Some attribute the definition of this term to film critic Roger Ebert, others to author and editor Damon Knight. And Knight, for his part, credited author and critic James Blish. Unfortunately, although two of those three men were science fiction writers—and one of them had written a *Star Trek* novel and numerous episode adaptations—none of them were asked to parse this script before it went into production.

Actually, there's only one idiot in "Samaritan Snare," and surprisingly, it's not one of the Pakleds, who prove to be rather clever at playing (slightly) dumber than they actually are. No, it's Commander Riker who receives the distinction of playing the episode's idiot (although it might look better on his record to say that his decision to send Geordi to the Pakleds represents an uncustomary lapse in judgment). To their credit, the rest of the crew do what they can to balance things out. Worf—whose primary responsibility as chief of security is to voice paranoid concerns about strangers—fulfills his job function by asking, "Do we really need to send our chief engineer over to them?" Riker shrugs off this pertinent observation, along with Worf's subsequent suggestion that they simply give the Pakleds the *information* they need to make repairs. Not long after, Troi pops onto the bridge to warn Riker that the Pakleds are not what they seem and that *Geordi is in great danger*. Riker doesn't quite believe it—after all, everything *looks* fine over there. Alas, as was often the case during the first two seasons, Troi's abilities are not well defined. As a result, her warning is too vague to be of any help. Data tries to help her out, noting: "Our Betazoid counselor is often aware of things beyond our perceptive abilities." But Riker, unable to believe that these fat, potato-like individuals are capable of subterfuge, simply gives Geordi an "everything okay over there?" and leaves things at that—until it becomes hit-you-over-the-head obvious that *Geordi is in great danger*.

The episode's salvation comes in the form of the "crimson force field" subterfuge that Riker, Data, and the engineering team create to confuse the Pakleds. It's a worthy successor to James T. Kirk's "corbomite" charade, and it may just save Riker from an official reprimand by the captain. But considering that the captain, too, suffers from the collateral damage of an idiot plot thread in the episode (a starbase facility full of highly trained medical specialists has to send for Dr. Pulaski to deal with an unforeseen hitch in Picard's cardiac replacement surgery?), he might just overlook it.

"Send in the clones." —Danilo Odell

The *Enterprise* sets out to rescue two separate groups of Earth expatriates whose colonies are on the verge of extinction. The Bringloidi are a simple people who favor a nontechnological lifestyle; their world is about to be destroyed by solar flares. In contrast, the Mariposans have become so dependent on technology that their entire populace is made up of clones derived from the five original inhabitants. They need fresh DNA if their colony is to continue. Picard feels that the salvation for both groups could lie in a rather unorthodox solution.

Initially inspired by her negative feelings about the closed-door U.S. immigration policies she saw developing in the 1980s, Melinda Snodgrass's "Ladder" story evolved into a more generic cultural clash during the rewrite process. Nevertheless, the episode drew flack from different quarters for aspects of the script that rubbed some viewers the wrong way.

The first complaint concerned an alleged stereotypical portrayal of the Irish. The Bringloidi (derived from the Irish word for "dream": *brionglóid*) are humans of Irish descent who, centuries earlier, rejected advanced technology in favor of an agrarian lifestyle. They farm, make their own clothes, and raise animals for food. Unfortunately, their main on-camera representative is Danilo Odell, whose primary interest appears to be making sure there's an ample supply of alcohol on-hand. But the perceived slight may have merely been rushed rewriting; per Snodgrass, Maurice Hurley, who is of proud Irish descent, had a loving hand in the depiction of the Bringloidi.

The other complaint came from viewers with strong pro-life sentiments, who viewed Riker's impulsive decision to destroy clones created from his genetic material as a pro-abortion stance. While Snodgrass apparently didn't set out to make that kind of statement, in subsequent interviews she allowed that she is pro-choice, and that Riker's statement about exercising "control over our own bodies" is a reflection of those views.

Less commented upon but equally relevant from the perspective of the philosophy behind the Prime Directive: Was it really Picard's prerogative to force an acknowledged "shotgun wedding" upon the inhabitants of two disparate Earth colonies? He informs the Mariposans that they must change their established cloning culture and get into bed—literally—with the down-to-earth Bringloidi, who need a new place to live.

Hmm. Providing a home in exchange for services rendered. Well, it's not the first time a Starfleet captain has advised a culture that engaging in good old-fashioned S-E-X might be just the thing to put their civilization on the right path. (See *The Original Series* episode "The Apple.")

As the *Enterprise* ferries a group of delegates to a Federation conference, the crew learns that one of their passengers is Counselor Troi's mother, Lwaxana. Lwaxana is a handful at the best of times, and Picard is dismayed to discover that she's in the throes of "the Phase"—a time of life that quadruples a Betazoid woman's sex drive. To escape her advances, the captain flees to the holodeck to pass time as his favorite gumshoe, Dixon Hill. Meanwhile, Dr. Pulaski watches over a pair of comatose Antedean delegates.

Makeup man Allan Apone was in the right place at the right time.

"It was my very first day working on *The Next Generation*," he says. "I had just finished doing *Miami Vice*, and when I got back to town, Michael Westmore asked me to come in. The Mick Fleetwood makeup was first up."

Mick Fleetwood, drummer for the iconic rock 'n' roll band Fleetwood Mac (their 1977 album, *Rumours*, held the number one position on the American music charts for thirty-one weeks), wanted to be on the show, and it didn't bother him that the Antedean mask would render him unidentifiable. "He's a huge *Star Trek* fan," Apone says. "He just wanted to be a part of it."

The Antedean "fish-head" look started as a sketch by Rick Sternbach. "Mick had come in about a week earlier to have an alginate head cast made," Apone notes. "Then Michael had the mask molded and sculpted in his little lab setup." Before fitting the mask over Fleetwood's head, Apone applied dark makeup around the drummer's eyes. "The mask had to be easily removable," Apone says, "so I only partially glued it on his face, and didn't glue it around his eyes at all. I put the makeup around his eyes so it

would blend it in and hide the seams." He also placed strips of foam tape on Fleetwood's cheeks and nose. "Those are pressure point places," he explains. "The mask was tight, and they gave his face a little relief."

Apone, founder of Makeup & Effects Laboratories (MEL), which made the "Conspiracy" creatures in season one, worked on and off with *The Next Generation*'s makeup department throughout the show's seven-year run. And in between his responsibilities on numerous feature films, he often returned to Paramount, to work on *Deep Space Nine*, *Voyager*, and *Enterprise*. "Every time I came back from doing a feature, Michael would call me."

Despite all those faces he worked on over the years, he never forgot that day with the drumming Antedean. Apparently, neither did Mick Fleetwood. "I ran into Mick only a couple of years ago," Apone reports today. "So I reintroduced myself as his *Star Trek* makeup man, and he said, 'Oh my God, was that not the most fun time?' He was just so excited about having done it."

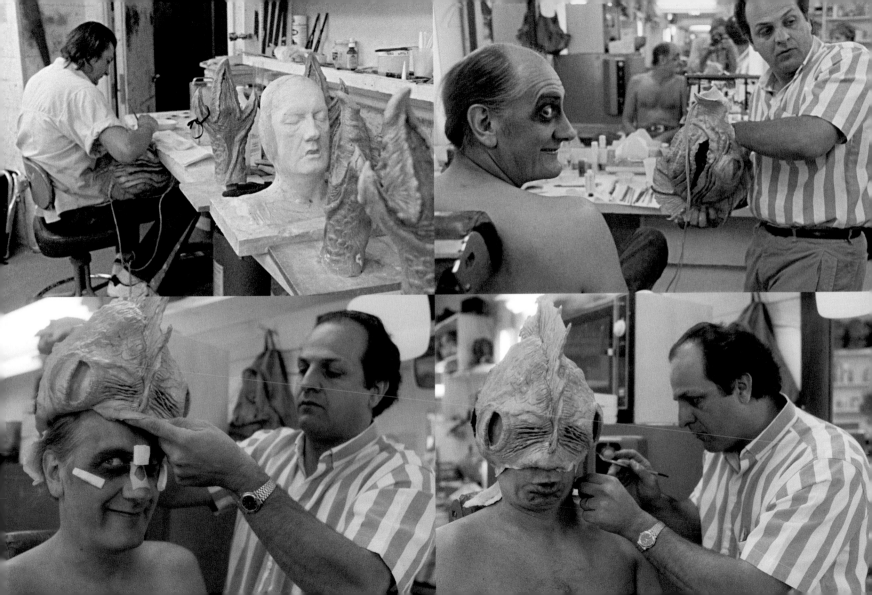

Worf is unsettled at the arrival of K'Ehleyr, a special envoy from the Klingon Empire. She's on the *Enterprise* to assist in intercepting a Klingon sleeper ship launched when the Federation was still at war with the Empire. If the *T'Ong*'s Klingon crew awakens before the *Enterprise* reaches it, they are likely to begin attacking Federation outposts. Half-Klingon, half-human K'Ehleyr is an untraditional member of the warrior race—which is one of the reasons the passionate relationship between her and Worf soured years earlier. As the *Enterprise* speeds toward the *T'Ong*, relations between Worf and K'Ehleyr seem as icy as they once were between the Federation and the Empire. But beneath the ice, the fire still burns.

Although she's played four different alien characters (the Vulcan Selar, the half-Klingon K'Ehleyr, a female Q, and the Andorian Tarah) in three different *Star Trek* series (*TNG*, *Voyager*, and *Enterprise*), actress Suzie Plakson would be the last to call herself a "sci-fi person." She loves science fiction fans, however, and is a frequent guest at *Star Trek* conventions. "I feel like an honored guest at an ongoing global party," she explains. "I'm always treated really nicely."

And how does she feel about being immortalized in plastic?

"The action figure is flattering," she responds, "but I'm a little annoyed that they didn't put her in the *better* outfit—the maroon one with the gold belt. To be incredibly shallow about it!" she adds with a deep-throated chuckle.

Following a well-received performance as Dr. Selar in "The Schizoid Man" early in season two, Plakson was invited to read for the role of K'Ehleyr. "There was a line—'Sorry, I had to make myself beautiful'—and I thought this was riotous, because I had this big old wrinkly forehead on," she recalls. "Anyway, it's not like I played it for huge laughs, but I've done a lot of parlor comedies and that was the kind of attitude I gave it. The people who were listening to me didn't bat an eyelash, but after I got the role, someone came up to me and said, 'Suzie, there is no *winking* in the twenty-fourth century.'"

Her take on K'Ehleyr may have been a bit broad for some on the set, but, she insists, it's the way the character was written. "When you're a guest on someone's show, you have to behave like a guest in someone's home," Plakson says. "But they say, 'If it ain't on the page, it ain't on the stage,' and I would say that about K'Ehleyr." The character's sense of humor is part of why she is so popular with the fans. The Klingons of *Star Trek* are a notoriously serious lot, and K'Ehleyr, with her sense of wry, self-deprecating humor that Plakson played to the hilt, was like a breath of fresh alien air.

Opposite: Durinda Wood's sketch of K'Ehleyr in her "better," more glamorous outfit, and in the fighting garb chosen for the action figure.

Realizing that the recently encountered Borg represent a dire threat to the Federation, Picard asks Starfleet to send an expert to oversee a battle simulation exercise between the *Enterprise* and the *Hathaway*, a derelict starship that will be under Riker's command. But in the midst of their war games, a Ferengi ship fires on the *Enterprise*, rendering its weapons system inoperative. The Ferengi have misinterpreted Picard's attack on the *Hathaway*, inferring that Riker's ship holds something of great value that the *Enterprise* covets. And unless Picard surrenders the *Hathaway* and its valuable booty, the Ferengi promise to destroy both Starfleet vessels.

Sometimes a script calls for a guest star to be a very specific physical type. Actors who play Cardassians, for instance, generally are tall with little body fat; Ferengi actors are short; Klingons tend to be built like football players. But if a script or story point doesn't specify a look, some departments stay on hold until the casting department makes a decision. Such was the case of the Zakdorn.

"There was nothing in the 'Peak Performance'

script telling me what the character would look like," Michael Westmore recalls. And so he waited until veteran actor Roy Brocksmith came in to sit and have his head cast in alginate. "It wasn't until I started sculpting over the cast of Roy's head that I was able to come up with an idea for his character, Sirna Kolrami," says Westmore. "Roy has a full, round face, and I designed a set of appliances that would work with his features. We made a piece that went over his nose and upper lip, two pieces for the cheeks, and an appliance for his forehead." Westmore notes that he didn't want to do anything with the character's hair, so he instructed the stylist to slick it back. "That exposed more of his face," he says. "I also left his hands alone, because I knew there would be several scenes of him playing a game, and he would need his hands free." Brocksmith's physical type set the standard for Zakdorn characters to come. "Once we had established what they look like, I used the same makeup for the Zakdorn quartermaster in 'Unification.' It was just a matter of adjusting and making a new set of appliances to fit the actor."

For seven seasons, *Star Trek: The Next Generation*'s audience was treated to high-quality, highly "realistic" imagery—such as this tense standoff between the *Hathaway*, the *Enterprise*, and the Ferengi attack vessel *Kreechta* ("Peak Performance"). Yet these striking images seldom have appeared in books or magazines. There's a reason for that—and an interesting story as well.

Back in the 1960s, if a *Star Trek: The Original Series* script called for a fantastic image, the people charged with creating the effect worked with traditional film and optical techniques. "Everything had to be shot optically back then," says Gary Hutzel, one of several visual effects coordinators who worked on *The Next Generation*. "So even though many *TOS* episodes had only ten or fifteen of what today we would consider 'simple' visual effects shots, literally every effects house in town had to be booked to work on them. That was a big deal on the budget and schedule they had."

"*The Original Series* had a lot of problems delivering effects on film," confirms Robert Legato, one of *TNG*'s alternating visual effects supervisors. So while they were developing *The Next Generation*, Legato notes, "Bob Justman, Peter Lauritson, and

Rick Berman said, 'Come up with a faster system.'"

The *TNG* team decided to use a videotape format, then combine the various "elements" electronically (for instance, a star field as a background layer, a planet as a middle layer, and the *Enterprise* as the front layer). "We still shot the separate elements on film," Hutzel says, "but we transferred the film to videotape and combined the images in the digital realm. It was faster, and we used about one-tenth the number of people to do the same amount of work. It saved a massive amount of money."

For the first three seasons, the *TNG* staff worked in one-inch analog tape format, the prevailing technology at the time. In the fourth season, they switched to a brand-new digital format called computer graphic imaging, or CGI—even though some of the hardware was still considered "research and development," and came without operating manuals. "It was a whole different world," Hutzel notes. "We regularly did thirty or forty shots per show and had twenty days to deliver them."

In most cases, the process eliminated the use of film altogether—and therein lies the problem. While videotape and CGI saved both time and money, the technologies had one unfortunate shortcoming:

there were no photographic images of the *final* effects shots. Thus, the only way to reproduce one of *TNG*'s visual effects in a book—such as this one—is by doing a "frame grab" directly off the video image. And frame grabs, unfortunately, always look a bit "soft" on the printed page.

Troi and Pulaski force Riker to relive his most primitive memories of survival in the hopes that it will eradicate a deadly microorganism that has invaded his brain.

Picture a crowded freeway. A driver sees something and steps on his brakes, causing his brake lights to flash. The driver behind him, seeing those lights, taps his own brakes. And so on, and so on, down the line—a chain reaction. Traffic slows until, a minute later and a mile back, it comes to a near standstill. Then, hopefully, movement picks up.

Picture "Shades of Gray," the last "car" of the season, slowing, coming to a full stop—and stalling. So what prompted *those* brake lights?

There were four obstacles in the road:

Time: The writers' strike early in the season led to a slow start . . .

Material: . . . and, struggling to catch up, the producers never managed to bank some scripts for the future.

Money: The Borg episode, "Q Who?" assimilated a large portion of the year's budget . . .

Time: . . . which left the underfunded final episode only three ultra-thrifty shooting days.

But, as they say, the show must go on.

"They didn't have a final script," then-script coordinator Eric Stillwell recalls. "So Maurice Hurley put together this really rough framework for a story and said to me, 'We need you to watch every episode we've done so far and write down the time codes for scenes that would fit into these Riker dream sequences.' I spent eighty hours that week scanning through the episodes, finding clips so the producers could pick which ones to plug in."

That's the genesis of this money-saving "clip show." In the end, the producers utilized clips from nineteen episodes. But that wasn't their only cost-cutting calculation. Surrounding the clips was a bottle show using only the regular cast and a few extras (with no expensive guest stars) and placed primarily on two sets: the transporter room and sickbay (ensuring minimal setup time and camera moves during the rushed shooting schedule).

By their very nature, bottle shows and clip shows are prone to certain pitfalls, and with its wafer-thin plot, "Shades of Gray" was unable to steer clear. The director and editor had to stretch the new footage to fill out the broadcast hour, inserting an inordinate number of unnecessary shots, like repeatedly showing O'Brien at the transporter controls. Superfluous takes—Picard entering and exiting sickbay—go on for longer than usual. Such pacing—which absorbs precious slices of time—would, in other episodes, be unthinkable.

The average *TNG* episode traditionally shot for seven days. "Shades of Gray" was a three-day shoot—and one wonders whether Riker's joking statement may not have been a scripted commentary about the process. "My grandfather once got bit by a rattlesnake," he says. "After three days of intense pain, the snake died."

Much like this season finale.

Postscript: For his stalwart efforts behind the scenes, Eric Stillwell received his first on-screen credit: "Researcher."

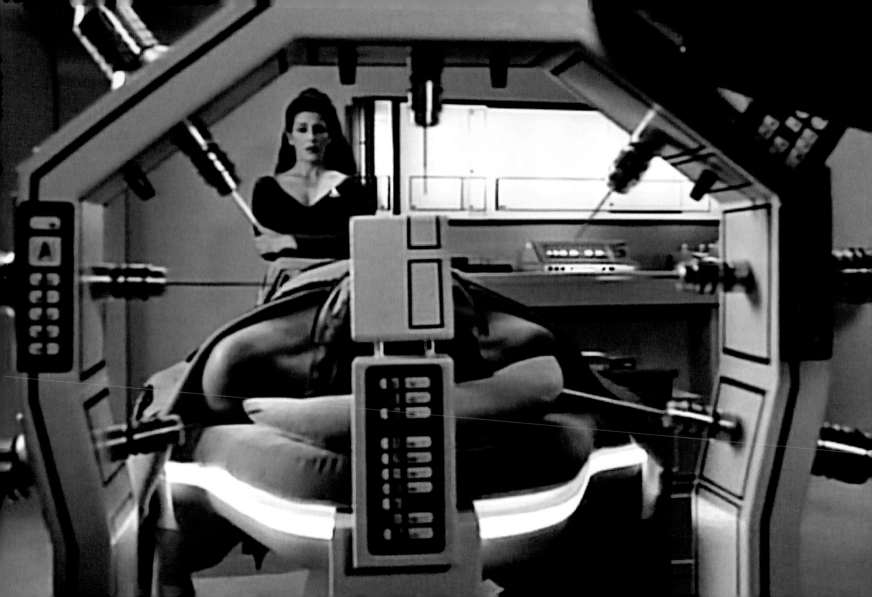

In season three, with ratings skyrocketing, the studio felt it was time for some upgrades, such as enhancing the main title sequence. Dan Curry's visual effects team shot additional star field backgrounds to add to the originals created by Rob Legato, then added new astronomical phenomena, including a "solar nebula."

In concept, notes Michael Okuda, "It was a solar system in formation, before the planets coalesce from the gas and dust." In actuality, it was a length of yarn that Okuda had coiled and glued around an eight-inch hole cut in a piece of black Formica-laminated plywood. Okuda dribbled bits of plaster and acrylic modeling paste on the coil, then handed the four-foot by four-foot item to Rick Sternbach, who airbrushed several colors onto it before passing it to Curry.

"We mounted it on the motion control rig used for photographing model spaceships and did various passes on it, all using the same move," Curry says. "For one pass, we placed a large lightbulb in the center hole and used heavy diffusion to create the illusion of the glowing core of the galaxy. Then we blended it with a star field in the compositing bay."

Right: The composited shot.
Opposite: The model.

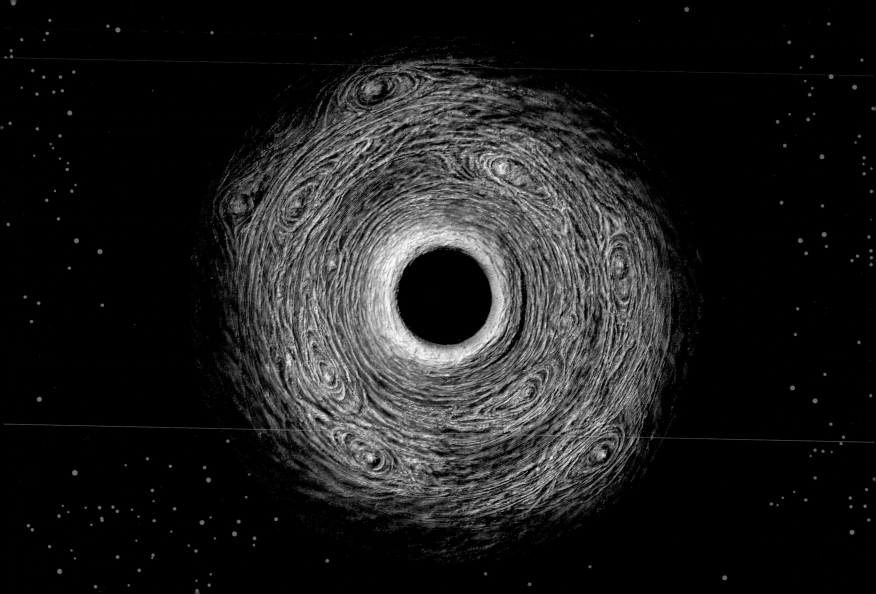

Although filmed after "The Ensigns of Command," "Evolution" aired as *TNG*'s season three premiere, and, as such, served to bring viewers up to speed on some of the changes that had taken place over the show's hiatus. These included:

• A new face: Actually, it was the return of a familiar, much missed face. Gates McFadden returned as Doctor Beverly Crusher, following what had been, ostensibly, "a year's service at Starfleet Medical." *TNG*'s fans had missed Beverly and expressed their feelings. Once again, a letter campaign made an impact on the course of *Star Trek*.

• A new costume designer—and new threads for the crew: "The uniforms we'd been wearing were designed to be very formfitting," Patrick Stewart said in a BBC interview. "But they put strain on you everywhere, so you would be continually having to push against the pressure of the spandex."

"Rick Berman didn't want to see any wrinkles," notes Durinda Rice Wood, the show's costume designer for season two, "so the uniforms had elastic straps that ran from the shoulders to underneath the

actor's heels. I was *dying* to redesign them, but they wouldn't let me." In fact, they didn't permit a change until after Wood left the series. "The actors wore Rick down," she says, chuckling. "And Bob . . . *Bob!* got to redesign them."

"Bob" is costume designer Robert Blackman (opposite), whom Wood had recommended as her replacement. His first task at the beginning of season three: turning the familiar jumpsuits into two-piece uniforms. "We ended up with Eisenhower-esque mandarin collars," Blackman comments. "It made them more formal, gave them more dignity." Well, that's true of the men's costumes, at any rate. The producers (notably all male) still felt that the female officers' uniforms should maintain a sleek design line, so Troi and Crusher would continue in spandex jumpsuits, as would (temporarily) background crew members under the rank of ensign. Blackman himself fit right in, becoming an integral member of the *Star Trek* staff.

But by far, the most important changes were the ones that took place behind the scenes, in the writers'/producers' offices on the west end of the Paramount lot. . . .

As the season began, Michael Wagner, an Emmy Award–winning veteran of *Hill Street Blues* who'd most recently developed the science fiction series *Probe*, took Maurice Hurley's position heading up the writing staff. It was, to say the least, a tumultuous time. Hurley had left behind nothing that was ready to shoot. While the holdovers on the writing staff—Hans Beimler, Richard Manning, and Melinda Snodgrass—were working on new material, Wagner needed to hit the ground running. He had a story idea in his head, but he needed someone to help flesh it out. On impulse, he called Michael Piller, with whom he'd worked on *Probe*.

Primarily a writing producer, with shows like *Simon & Simon* and *Miami Vice* to his credit, Piller hadn't worked as a freelance writer for some time, but he liked Wagner's story idea and agreed to turn it into a script.

But change was in the air.

It didn't take Wagner long to realize that he wasn't a good fit for *TNG*. He got two other stories started ("The Survivors" and "Booby Trap") and then bowed out. "Wagner only stayed a few weeks," Eric Stillwell recalls. "And for a brief period, there was *no* head writer." Piller's script, "Evolution," was very well received by *TNG*'s producers. Given his experience in the business, it made sense for Roddenberry and Berman to offer Piller the job as head writer—which Piller accepted.

It turned out that Piller was exactly the frontline officer the show needed. *TNG*'s third season is looked upon by most as the year *TNG* found its sea legs, producing stories that not only entertained, but also made its audience care about the characters.

Piller was a hard worker who believed in pushing himself just as hard as he pushed his staff. But that didn't mean every day was "wine and roses," confesses Ronald D. Moore, who was plucked from obscurity after Piller read his *TNG* spec script. "Michael's hallmarks were his earnestness and his complete lack of guile," explains Moore. "He didn't have a deceptive bone in his body, and he had a big heart. However"—Moore pauses—"he used to be a 'suit' and a network censor, and there also were *those* aspects to his personality, which sometimes drove the writers crazy."

"Michael had a tremendous work ethic," recalls Ira Steven Behr, who ran the writers' room for much of the third season. "He refused to let the show get away from us. He wouldn't throw up his hands and say, 'This is undoable.' He supported good ideas, even if ultimately those ideas were shot down further up the line. And he wanted the show to be interesting. He disagreed with people, but they knew that it was nothing personal. It was business."

"It was *family* business," Moore adds. "And Michael was one of us. He wasn't one of '*them*.' We had an 'us' and 'them' sort of mentality, and everybody *out there*," Moore says, laughing, "was trying to screw us. Michael was our head writer, and we respected him."

"I want the seals of power and place,
The ensigns of command . . ."
—John Quincy Adams

The *Enterprise* heads for Tau Cygna V, a world ceded by Federation treaty to a reclusive species known as the Sheliak Corporate. The Sheliak want a group of long-forgotten Federation colonists to be evacuated from the planet within three days, and the *Enterprise* has been assigned to ferry those colonists to a new home. Unfortunately, there are far more of them than Captain Picard was expecting. There's no way he can remove fifteen thousand settlers in three days. To compound matters, the leader of the colony has no intention of moving his people. Lieutenant Commander Data must convince him otherwise, as Picard attempts to negotiate more reasonable terms with the Sheliak.

The Sheliak Corporate. It seems an odd name, doesn't it? Brings to mind a boardroom full of cigar-smoking businessmen with type A personalities. It certainly doesn't ring familiar to the ear like the usual stellar subjects: Vega, Deneb, Rigel . . .

But Sheliak is indeed a celestial object, perhaps better known as Beta Lyrae. The name Sheliak derives from the Arabic word for harp or lyre, hence Lyra, the constellation in which this star lies. Or make that *stars*. Sheliak is an eclipsing binary, two stars in such close orbit that they appear to observers on Earth as a single point of light.

Melinda Snodgrass, who, beyond her *Star Trek* efforts, also authors well-researched science fiction novels, wrote the episode. "Melinda was always good about using real astronomy in her episodes," observes scenic artist supervisor Michael Okuda, who (along with senior illustrator Rick Sternbach) also served as one of the show's science technical consultants.

As for the rather bizarre appearance of the Sheliak people (if one can call them that) . . . well, there were no scientific references for *that*, so Rick Sternbach was able to wing it with his concept art.

"I didn't do any preliminary drawings for the Sheliak before doing this illustration," Sternbach recalls. "We often had to get stuff done really fast and send it over to the producers. I had a description that was partly from the script and partly from wardrobe and makeup, and I knew the set was going to be a dark, drippy, sparkly, shiny sort of interior with alien-looking controls. So I just launched into some color pencils and gouache on a piece of blackboard."

"And then," he says with a chuckle, "it turned up on film pretty much the way it looked on the illo."

TREK³

"ENSIGNS..." Alien Set   Sternbach 7·89

Stubbs: "Do you know baseball?"
Wesley: "Yes, my father taught it to me when I was young."
Stubbs: "Once, centuries ago, it was the beloved national pastime of the Americas, Wesley. Abandoned by a society that prized fast food and faster games. Lost to impatience."

Following Beverly Crusher's return to the *Enterprise*, son Wesley discovers that his science project involving microscopic "nanites"—robots so tiny they can enter living cells—has gotten out of hand. The rapidly multiplying miniscule machines have entered the starship's computer core, causing system malfunctions throughout the ship. An impatient scientist determines that the machines threaten the success of his lifelong effort to study the explosion of a neutron star, and tries to destroy them. But the nanites, which have evolved to the point of sentience, strike back, endangering not only the scientist, but the entire crew of the *Enterprise*.

"Michael Piller loved baseball," states Ira Steven Behr. "It's the thing that most defined the complicated personality that he had. The first thing that Michael and I bonded over was movies—we were both fans of Errol Flynn—and the second thing was baseball."

That Piller followed America's pastime should surprise no one; he inherited his love of the sport from his mother, the late Ruth Roberts, a songwriter. Among the songs she wrote were "I Love Mickey," a 1956 tribute to New York Yankee slugger Mickey Mantle (who, incidentally, sang on the recording), and "It's a Beautiful Day for a Ballgame," which was played for many years at Los Angeles Dodgers home games. Perhaps most significant was her 1961 composition (with Bill Katz) "Meet the Mets," for fifty years the official theme song of the New York Mets. Clearly, young Michael grew up in a household with more than passing awareness of the game.

All of which brings up a very odd question. "The first thing Michael did in the first *Star Trek* episode he wrote was to say that *baseball no longer existed in the twenty-fourth century*," Behr notes. "And I was like, 'Wow, Michael, you just killed the thing you love. *Why?*' And he always just laughed. I told him, 'Michael, that is the strangest thing I ever heard.'

But he never gave me an answer as to why he did it," Behr says with a sigh. "Michael and I, over many years, went to many baseball games together. *Most* of the socializing we did consisted of going to baseball games. But he could never articulate why he killed baseball. That is part of his mystery."

Piller passed away in 2005, the mystery unsolved.

The crew discovers that all but two of the eleven thousand inhabitants of Delta Rana IV have been destroyed by a warlike race known as the Husnock. Kevin and Rishon Uxbridge, an elderly pair of bota-nists, are the only survivors. They claim to have no idea why their lives were spared, but they refuse to evacuate, even when a Husnock ship returns to the area. The heavily armed vessel fires on the *Enterprise*, damaging its weapons systems, and later obliterates the Uxbridges' home. But Picard suspects that somehow the Uxbridges—or at least one of them—are responsible for the Husnock war-ship's actions, and he won't leave the area until he learns the truth.

Opposite: Dan Curry's storyboards for one of the episode's attack sequences reveal some penciled-in last-minute changes to the visuals.

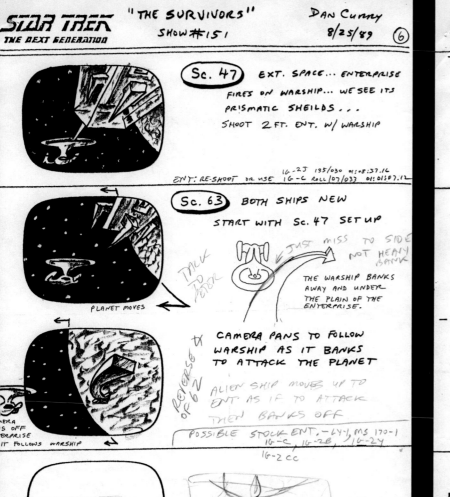

Sc. 47 EXT. SPACE... ENTERPRISE FIRES ON WARSHIP... WE SEE ITS PRISMATIC SHEILDS... SHOOT 2 FT. ENT. W/ WARSHIP

ENT: RE-SHOOT OR USE 16-2J 135/030 01:08:37.16
16-C ROLL 107/033 01:01:07.12

Sc. 63 BOTH SHIPS NEW

START WITH Sc. 47 SET UP

TALK TO PETER

JUST MISS TO SIDE NOT HEAVY BANK

THE WARSHIP BANKS AWAY AND UNDER THE PLAIN OF THE ENTERPRISE.

PLANET MOVES

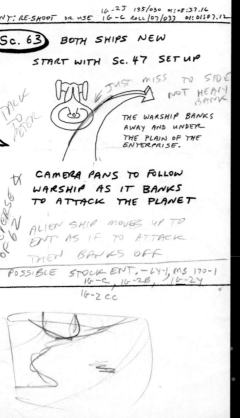

CAMERA PANS TO FOLLOW WARSHIP AS IT BANKS TO ATTACK THE PLANET

REVERSE OF 6

ALIEN SHIP MOVES UP TO ENT. AS IF TO ATTACK THEN BANKS OFF

POSSIBLE STOCK ENT. — LY-1, MS 170-1
16-C, 16-2B, 16-2Y
16-2 CC

CAMERA S OFF ELPRISE IT FOLLOWS WARSHIP

Sc. 64 ON MAIN VIEWER... WARSHIP FIRES ON PLANET CAUSING AN EXPLOSION.

D.O

Sc. 65

CUT 1 EXTREME CLOSE UP OF ENTERPRISE.-- (MATTE PAINTING FROM "WHERE SILENCE HAS LEASE")... FIRE PHOTON TORPEDO

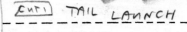

CUT 1 TAIL LAUNCH

CUT 2 USE PRE-COMP FROM **Sc. 64**... PHOTON TORPEDO HITS WARSHIP... IT EXPLODES.

THIS ✗

64, 65

CAN FLOP FOR 27, 28 ?

No. They don't do their own stunts.

For the first five seasons of *TNG*, Jonathan Frakes's primary stunt double was Dan Koko, seen at right hanging from a rig that represents the snare set by Kevin Uxbridge in "The Survivors." While the position doesn't look particularly comfortable, Koko's assignment that day was a piece of cake compared to some of the stunts for which he is best known. Just three years prior to working on *The Next Generation*, he set the world "high fall" record for a leap from a ninety-foot platform set atop the twenty-five-story Vegas World hotel in (where else?) Las Vegas, plummeting 326 feet at ninety-eight miles per hour.

But then, Koko always was a high achiever. He set a California record in 120-yard high hurdles while in high school, and won thirty-two medals in track meets throughout the United States between 1972 and 1974. Still, it never occurred to him that he could make a living doing things that other people didn't have enough nerve to try, at least not until a friend

Opposite: Jonathan Frakes extends his leg and prepares to fall backward onto a conveniently placed air mattress. The movement will be matched by Koko—except that his leg (right) will be pulled upward by the snare, allowing him to complete the action portion of the stunt.

Liko: "I believe I have seen the Overseer. He is called the Picard."
Riker: "Uh-oh."

After the natives of Mintaka III discover a team of Federation anthropologists on their planet, a chain of events threatens to push the Mintakans' evolving culture back to more primitive beliefs. As the *Enterprise* crew attempts to retrieve the anthropologists, a Mintakan named Liko is injured, and Doctor Crusher takes it upon herself to bring him to the ship for treatment. Crusher tries to erase his short-term memory, but the recovered Liko soon spreads tales of the "gods" he has encountered. At Liko's urging, the Mintakans capture Troi and consider sacrificing her in order to gain favor with "the Picard," whom they believe is the overseer of the gods.

The script for "Who Watches the Watchers?" said that the inhabitants of Mintaka III were "proto-Vulcan humanoids at the Bronze Age level." This informed Michael Westmore that it was time to break out the traditional pointy ears, which, in most viewers' eyes, make Vulcans Vulcans. Beyond the ears, however, he improvised. Because the Mintakans were at a somewhat primitive stage in their evolution, the makeup designer opted for heavier eyebrows than those sported by traditional Vulcans, and he also gave them a slightly pronounced browridge—more of a tip of the hat to Neanderthal man than to the big-browed look that he gave to *TNG*-era Romulans. Per the story line, Riker and Troi visit the planet disguised as a pair of Mintakans, so Jonathan Frakes and Marina Sirtis received the same treatment as the episode's guest stars—right down to the yellowish skin tones and banged wigs.

The location chosen for filming would have been familiar to Captain Kirk's traditional Vulcan first officer. "Who Watches the Watchers?" was shot at Vasquez Rocks, home to footage that has shown up in dozens of films and television shows, including four episodes of *The Original Series*: "Arena," "Shore Leave," "The Alternative Factor," and "Friday's Child."

It's a Hollywood truism: everyone—every waiter, bartender, and grandmother—has written a screenplay. Which is why there's a codified process for submitting screenplays to the studios—beginning with Rule #1: "You gotta have an agent." There are reasons. First, few nonprofessional screenplays are "good." Agents seek out the more worthy screenplays, and by extension, writers. Second, and perhaps more important, agents, most of whom are attorneys, protect both the writer and the producer from claims of plagiarism. Which is why, unless your uncle owns the studio, you can't submit a screenplay without an agent.

With one exception. During the last decade of the twentieth century, *anyone* could submit a script directly to the producers of *Star Trek*. That was Michael Piller's idea.

"There were no scripts when Michael started," says Eric Stillwell, script coordinator at the time. "He had to turn things around really fast."

Piller quickly beefed up the writing staff—and took one more step. "He told Rick Berman, 'I need to open this up to freelancers,'" Stillwell recalls. "So we started allowing anyone who was interested to submit a *Star Trek* script, so long as they signed a re-

lease form. We came up with a list of guidelines, like, 'Don't write a Q story,' 'Don't use Kirk and Spock,' all the things Rick and Michael didn't want. The fans had been sending us unsolicited scripts anyway," Stillwell notes, "so we started returning what they'd sent, along with release forms and guidelines so they could resubmit it with the proper paperwork." The tactic worked—too well. "We weren't even active on the Internet yet, but the news spread though fan circles. We received about five thousand scripts a season," he says with a laugh.

Some of the freelance hopefuls were more creatively competitive than others. "Writers would do weird things to stand out," Stillwell says. "They'd send boxes of cookies with their submission. People on staff used to joke, 'Don't eat that—it could be poisoned.'"

Regardless of the detailed rules, some of the public just never understood the process. "The guidelines were very specific," Stillwell says. "'Submissions must be on eight-and-one-half by eleven-inch three-hole-punched paper, fastened with two brass brads.' But this was back in the day when people still had dot matrix printers, which used paper that came out in one long connected strip. And they

would send in scripts on one, long, connected page. We'd send them back," he says with a sigh, "with a note saying, 'You'll have to resubmit this. . . .'"

The Story -- What Doesn't Work

1. First, do NOT write a story which does not principally involve our continuing characters.

   Yes, we do like to see interesting new characters -- but only when used in *addition* to an interesting story line centering on our Starship crew regulars.

2. We do not do stories about psi-forces or mysterious psychic powers.

   No matter how fantastic the events in a story, the explanation must be extrapolated from a generally accepted science theory. (We have accepted the telepathy of Counselor Deanna Troi because many reputable scientists acknowledge the possibility of such abilities, but you will note that we have limited Troi to "reading" only emotions.)

3. We are not buying stories which cast our people and our vessel in the role of "galaxy police".

   Nor is our mission that of spreading 20th Century Euro-American cultural values through the galaxy. Stay true to the Prime Directive. We are not in the business of toppling cultures that we do not approve of. We are not "space meddlers."

4. We are not buying stories about the original "Star Trek" characters: Kirk, Spock, McCoy, Uhura, Chekov, Scotty and Sulu. Or their descendants.

   As much as we love our original cast (they are our children, after all), we want our audience's attention centered now on our new characters.

---

5. We do not accept stories which are FANTASY instead of SCIENCE FICTION.

   The difference between the two is profound. Despite the fact that both science fiction and fantasy can deal with unusual events, a science fiction story is based on an extrapolation of a generally accepted scientific fact or theory. Fantasy, which our format does not permit, need have no basis in reality.

6. We're not interested in "SWORDS AND SORCERY."

   Knights and princesses, stalwart yeomen and dragons are not science fiction for our purposes.

7. Don't treat deep space as a local neighborhood.

   Too often, script ideas show characters bouncing from solar system to solar system, planet to planet, without the slightest comprehension of the distances involved or the technologies required to support such travel. Fine (and even *fun*) on SPACE RANGERS but not on *Star Trek* (see page 3).

8. "Star Trek" is not melodrama.

   Melodrama is a writing style which does not require believable people. Believable people are at the heart of good *Star Trek* scripts.

9. Do not consider Klingons, Romulans, or Ferengi the only villains in space.

   We are determined not to copy ourselves. If, as dramatists say, "villains make the story," how about the other fascinating aliens to be found in a galaxy filled with billions of stars and planets.

---

10. Beware of spaceship battles.

    They cost enormous amounts of money and are not really as interesting as people conflicts.

11. Plots involving an entire civilization rarely work.

    What does work is to deal with specific characters from another culture and their interactions with our Starship characters.

12. No mad scientists, or stories in which technology is considered the villain.

    It doesn't make sense for a group of 24th Century interstellar travelers (whose lives depend on the successful workings of their technology) to be Luddites.

13. Avoid Storms in Space.

    It is best to seek expert technical advice before using or describing "space storms." Such not only rarely happen but also have nothing in common with Earth ocean storms.

After Marla Aster, the ship's archaeologist, is killed on an away mission, Captain Picard and Counselor Troi convey the sad news to Aster's young son, Jeremy, who is surprisingly stoic. Not long after, the crew discovers that an energy being from the planet that Aster was exploring has come aboard the ship and is masquerading as Jeremy's mother so the boy will not suffer her loss—a situation that Captain Picard fears will do the boy more harm than good.

It wasn't what Ronald D. Moore originally planned to do with his life. He had gone to Cornell on a Navy ROTC scholarship, studied government, and even contemplated becoming a lawyer. But all that fell apart in Moore's senior year when he dropped out of Cornell.

So maybe he wasn't cut out to be a lawyer. Maybe what he really wanted to do was earn a living *writing*. Maybe the place to do that was . . .

Hollywood.

Contrary to myth, success was *not* right around the corner, despite the change of zip code. In fact, it was several years down the road. In the introduc-

tion to this book, Moore provides the fascinating details of just what led to the sale of his first script, "The Bonding."

"The Bonding" was one of the very first script purchases made under Michael Piller's newly instituted open submission policy. "[It] was very rough," Piller recalled in a 2002 interview, "but it had a great idea at the core, about a kid who created a duplicate of his dead mother in the holodeck. I took the story to Gene [Roddenberry], who said, 'This won't work, because in the twenty-fourth century, children don't mourn the death of their parents. Death is considered a part of life.'"

Roddenberry's increasingly utopian view of the future (particularly edicts that nixed any kind of conflict between the central characters) stymied a lot of writers, but thankfully, Piller's conversation with the Great Bird yielded an approach to the story that both pleased Roddenberry and retained much of Moore's core concept.

Moore chalks up the entire experience to luck, a *lot* of luck. "I was very fortunate to be in the right place at the right time," he reflects. "I normally don't do things like walk onto sets with a script and try to sell it. That was pretty atypical for me. The fact that

Michael found it and read it and bought it and then *made* it was extraordinary."

18   KODAK 5063 TX

18   ▷ 18A

"If we resist, we die. If we don't resist, we die." —Riker

Captain Picard is excited when the *Enterprise* comes across an ancient relic from a long forgotten war: an old Promellian battle cruiser that has been floating in space, untouched, for a thousand years. The crew soon discovers that the dead Promellians aboard fell victim to a booby trap set by their enemies—and the booby trap is still active. With only hours to spare before his own comrades meet equally untimely deaths, Chief Engineer Geordi La Forge consults with an interactive facsimile of Dr. Leah Brahms, designer of the *Enterprise*'s engines, to find a way to extricate the ship from the trap.

How far we've come. Sort of.

Back when *The Original Series* first aired, interracial relations were a Very Big Deal. The scripted kiss between Kirk and Uhura in "Plato's Stepchildren" reportedly made NBC program executives so squeamish that they pressured filmmakers to shoot it so that viewers at home couldn't *quite* tell whether the couple's lips actually touched.

Skip ahead two decades to 1989. The specter of black/white relations had lost the potential to shock and inflame the viewing audience. No one thought twice when the casting department hired a white actress (Susan Gibney) to play the brilliant (and, coincidentally, very attractive) female engineer who ignites the romantic fantasies of Geordi La Forge in "Booby Trap."

But they should have. Ironically, the folks in the casting department made a rare mistake. The female engineer, identified in an early draft of the script as "Navid Daystrom," was the implied descendent of the brilliant scientist Richard Daystrom, memorably played by African American actor William Marshall in *TOS*'s "The Ultimate Computer." Oops. Well, not *everyone* associated with *Star Trek* gets all of the subtle continuity references to earlier incarnations.

When script coordinator Eric Stillwell suggested that a name change might be in order, the character was rechristened "Leah Brahms," a graduate of the Daystrom Institute.

"Booby Trap" offered Captain Picard the rare opportunity to man the *Enterprise*'s helm. Patrick Stewart prepared for the task with a bit of method acting—drawing on a memory from shooting the series' pilot. He'd seen Brent Spiner crack his knuckles and stretch his fingers at the ops controls, so Stewart mimed the same exercise as he sat down at the helm console. "It was a little homage to Brent," recalls background player Guy Vardaman, explaining that Stewart emulated the action to make it appear that "all Starfleet people do this to warm up their fingers."

They don't, of course (with the rare exception of Scotty, typing in the formula for transparent aluminum in *Star Trek IV: The Voyage Home*). Stewart's playful hand jive wouldn't appear in the episode, as he no doubt knew. But that didn't stop him from commenting to Spiner, post-scene, "Did you see what I did for you?"

After finding the remains of a Romulan vessel on a world plagued by fierce magnetic storms, La Forge is separated from the rest of the away team and captured by an injured Romulan. While the engineer tries to convince the Romulan that they must work together if they wish to survive, Picard engages in some politically charged brinkmanship with Romulan commander Tomalak, in the hopes of avoiding war.

Paramount calls it "Stage 16." The *TNG* call sheets called it "the cave set." But to the show's cast and crew, it was . . . "Planet Hell."

"I hated Planet Hell with a passion," Jonathan Frakes says. "It was dirty. It was limiting. It was a horrifying place to work."

"There was the smell of a tomb about it," Dan Curry comments. "People would be wheezing by the end of the day."

"It kept us on schedule because we could pretend we were on other planets, instead of traveling to outside locations," Frakes adds. "So, although dreadful, it was convenient."

Most importantly, it was *available* when con-struction of *TNG*'s sets got underway in 1987. "We needed a ravine for 'Encounter at Farpoint,'" Herman Zimmerman recalls. "There was an old swimming pool from a previous movie under the floor of Stage 16, so I cut a big hole over that area. At the time, we couldn't afford to use fiberglass, so we used tinfoil to line the pool." Zimmerman later expanded this "cave set," by continuing the "rock" walls upward from the stage floor level. "We cobbled the walls together with every grip platform we could find, and sheathed it with lathe and plaster," he says.

When Richard James replaced Zimmerman in season two, he made some changes. "I did away with the walls on the stage level, because that was my turnaround area [for temporary sets] and I needed the room," James says. "But we kept the tallest portion standing, over in the corner where it was out of the way."

Zimmerman's ravine worked fine for "The Enemy," although . . . "The crew *hated* to shoot down in that pit," James comments. "They had no room to set up the camera or anything. Most of the time we'd go down there only for a tight shot, and then work on the stage level."

No one today remembers which early produc-tion was responsible for the swimming pool, but, Michael Okuda notes, "Years before *TNG*, the area was featured as a cavern on the surface of the moon for the miniseries *Space*."

Perhaps that's why the crew found so little breathable air in there.

Troi: "It's ridiculous, and wonderful. I feel completely out of control. Happy. Terrified. But there's nothing rational about this."
Crusher: "Who needs rational when your toes curl up?"

The *Enterprise* plays host to a group of dignitaries who have gathered to negotiate for the rights to an apparently stable wormhole located near the planet Barzan II. If the initial report from a Barzan probe is accurate, the wormhole could provide an invaluable shortcut to a distant part of the galaxy. But even as an underhanded empath attempts to manipulate the bidders, and some conniving Ferengi threaten to destroy the wormhole, La Forge and Data discover that the passage isn't what everyone thinks.

Another hot-button issue during *The Original Series* era was S-E-X. Yes, the sixties was the decade of free love and the birth control pill and crazy young kids living together without benefit of holy matrimony—but television censors weren't about to allow audiences to view such things in prime time. Thus,

when the ever-lustful Captain Kirk made his move on the femme of the week, the camera angle would shift from him and her kissing to something like an oil lamp, merrily burning away. Nudge, nudge, wink, wink—it was a metaphor—get it? Or they'd go to commercial mid-kiss and come back later to show Kirk sitting on the edge of the bed, zipping up his boot.

By the late 1980s, however, S-E-X was all over television. Married couples in sitcoms were allowed to sleep together in double beds. Series regulars were allowed to (discretely) make love to opposite-sex partners, even if they weren't married.

So Deanna Troi was free to get it on with the smooth-talking quarter-Betazoid negotiator she'd met the day before. Not that she was "easy," of course. Her suitor still had to do the old "hair seduction" routine (*you're too uptight—it must be your hair—let's loosen that bun—ah, that's better*), practiced by on-screen males since time immemorial. Even the supremely charismatic Khan had to use that old chestnut on Marla McGivers to raise her thermostat ("Space Seed").

It's unclear whether Deanna or Devinoni Ral brought the massage oil to their little party, but they both seemed to enjoy the benefits.

Captain Picard attempts to reconcile the inhabitants of Acamar III with the Gatherers, a group of renegades that broke off from Acamarian society a century earlier. Although both sides express tentative interest in reuniting, the peace talks grow complicated when Riker discovers that the Acamarian woman he's fallen in love with is actually an assassin who lives only for revenge against a faction within the Gatherers.

In Hollywood, the infamous "six degrees of separation" is shorter yet.

"The Vengeance Factor" was written by Sam Rolfe, who cocreated the popular television series *Have Gun, Will Travel* in 1957. That series helped to establish the reputation of an up-and-coming writer named Gene Roddenberry, who wrote twenty-four episodes. In 1964, Rolfe developed *The Man from U.N.C.L.E.* for MGM, created the show's bible, and wrote the series' pilot. The tongue-in-cheek spy show was extremely successful, but Rolfe, feeling he'd given it what he could, opted to leave after one season. Not long after, Herbert Solow, vice president of

Desilu Studios, hired Rolfe to write a pilot script. In a return to his roots, Rolfe created a western: *The Long Hunt of April Savage*. The project looked promising —ABC agreed to finance the pilot—but Rolfe, who had already made plans to spend the next year in London, couldn't stick around to produce it. That job went to an associate of Solow's who, coincidentally, Rolfe knew quite well: Gene Roddenberry. The pilot never went to series, but Roddenberry went on to create *Star Trek,* and Rolfe, after he returned from London, created a few more series. By the time *The Next Generation* hit the airwaves, Rolfe was in his sixties and working only when he felt like it. Invited to contribute a script to the series created by his old friend, Rolfe delivered "The Vengeance Factor"—a story set in the twenty-fourth century that feels like it might have worked equally well as a western. Four years later, Rolfe responded to a request from another former colleague now associated with *Star Trek: U.N.C.L.E.* veteran Peter Allan Fields. Rolfe soon delivered what would be his final script: the *Star Trek: Deep Space Nine* episode "Vortex."

Opposite: The eerie backdrop seen behind the plundered Federation science outpost was originally

painted for the classic 1956 movie *Forbidden Planet*. How did it wind up on the *TNG* set? "We rented it," explains Michael Okuda. "I saw it in a catalog and I'd been lobbying [production designer] Richard James to use it on the show for some time. He was perfectly willing to go along, so long as we used it for an appropriate episode/setting."

"'Now, if these men do not die well, it will be a black matter for the king that led them to it.'"
—Picard (quoting William Shakespeare)

A Romulan defector attempts to convince Picard that an invasion of Federation space by the Romulan Empire is imminent. Unfortunately, the only way to prove or disprove the Romulan's claim is to take the *Enterprise* across the Romulan Neutral Zone, an act that in itself could trigger war between the Federation and the Empire. Despite warnings from the Klingons, who have a deep distrust of the Romulans, Picard opts to cross into Romulan territory—only to run into his nemesis, Commander Tomalak.

Right: Rick Sternbach's preproduction sketch of the Romulan scout ship.
Opposite: The scout model as seen in the episode.

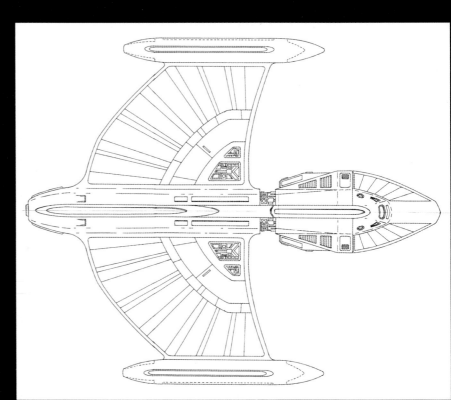

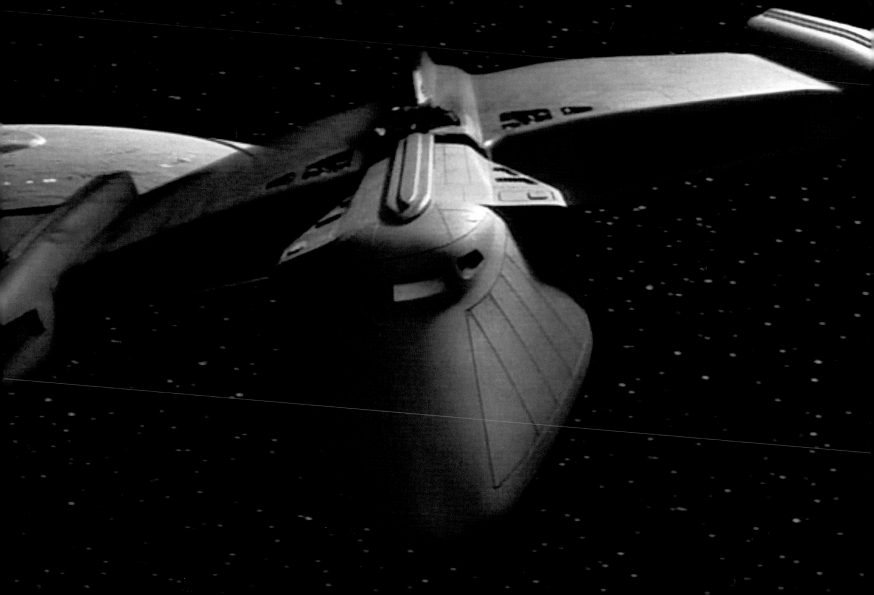

"Basically, we threw out my first draft of 'The Defector,' and 'gangbanged' the second draft," Ron Moore says. "That's a very un-PC phrase that means the entire staff worked on the script together." But he has no regrets. "Other scripts of mine went through varying degrees of rewrites," he notes, "and they almost always were improved in the process."

In the first draft, Data returned, via the holodeck, to 221B Baker Street as Sherlock Holmes. Unfortunately, following the airing of "Elementary, Dear Data," a "misunderstanding" of the legal sort arose between the estate of Sir Arthur Conan Doyle and Paramount Pictures. The matter ultimately was resolved (thus allowing the sixth-season Holmes episode, "Ship in a Bottle"), but Moore's teaser for "The Defector" had to be jettisoned only two days before filming was to begin. Resident Shakespearean Patrick Stewart suggested a sequence from *Henry V* as a replacement. As a result, Stewart appeared in the teaser in two different roles: as Picard, enjoying Data's portrayal of King Henry, and (under heavy makeup) as Michael Williams, a holographic

watching 'The Bonding' being shot, and they introduced me to him," he says. "He was very gracious and asked me what I was writing next. I said, 'Oh, it's called "The Defector,"' and I explained that it's about this Romulan who comes across the Neutral Zone to warn the Federation about an impending attack. And Patrick's response was, 'Oh, lovely. Well, just remember this—the captain doesn't do nearly enough screwing and shooting on this show!'"

What the captain wants, the captain gets. Soon he would receive more opportunities to engage in both activities.

Right: Soon-to-be story editor Ron Moore with the new four-foot shooting model of the *Enterprise*-D, which was introduced in "The Defector."
Opposite: King Henry and Michael Williams indulge a pair of groundlings on the Paramount lot.

Emerging from a lengthy period of war, Angosia III applies for membership to the Federation. During a perfunctory visit from the *Enterprise*, a prisoner escapes from Angosia's lunar penal colony, and Picard's crew helps to capture him. But once the captain learns that the colony's prisoners are actually former war veterans who are now too violent to live among Angosia's civilians, he formulates an entirely different opinion about Angosia's potential as a Federation member.

Some people get a leisurely first day on a new job. Others work on *Star Trek* productions.

"I went into the office," says Ira Steven Behr. "I said hello to Hans [Beimler] and Ricky [Manning], both of whom I knew, got introduced to Richard Danus and Melinda Snodgrass, walked into Michael [Piller's] office, and he threw a script at me and said, 'Rewrite act three!' It was 'The Hunted,' as I recall. I went, '*Huh*?' and he said, 'Just rewrite it and have it on my desk this evening.' So I ran around, asking for help. I mean, it was my *very first day*. And everyone else was too busy to really help."

Behr was hardly a neophyte. He was a veteran writer/producer (*Fame*, *The Bronx Zoo*), and he certainly knew his way around a production office. But *TNG* was . . . different. "It was a mess," Behr says frankly. "They were behind. They had nothing in the hopper. The writing staff was miserable. Eventually, everything just cooled out and the show got some stability.

"Luckily, act three of 'The Hunted' was basically a giant chase scene through the Jefferies tubes, big action without much character stuff. I was able to write it with no idea what I was doing. I gave it to Michael and he said, 'Fine. Great. Terrific.' And then he threw another script at me and said, 'Rewrite act three.'"

Opposite: Just as guest actors are sometimes recast, so are ship models. "The Hunted" features a small Angosian transport vessel. Carrying minimal weaponry and lacking warp capability, "it's not very cherry" (as Jan and Dean might have sung—had "Surf City" been on Angosia) . . . but it still gets prisoner Roga Danar where he wants to go. This little workhorse vessel started out as a Straleb security ship, designed by Rick Sternbach for "The Outra-

geous Okona." With a nip here and a tuck there, it was an economical choice for the vessel hijacked by Danar.

The Angosian model sold at the 2006 Christie's auction for $4,000.

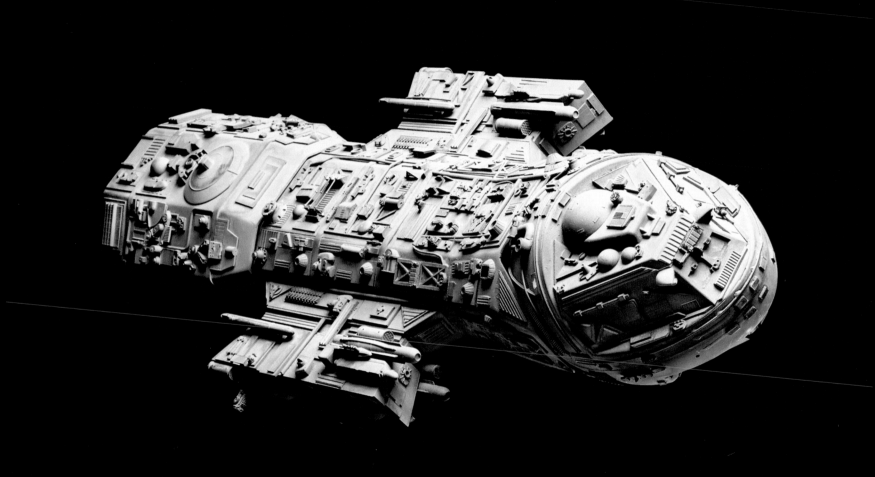

Data: *"I have been reviewing the history of armed rebellion and it appears that terrorism is an effective way to promote political change."*

Picard: *"Yes, it can be, but I have never subscribed to the theory that political power flows from the barrel of a gun."*

Data: *"Yet there are numerous examples where it was successful. The independence of the Mexican State from Spain, the Irish Unification of 2024, and the Kenzie Rebellion . . . Would it be accurate to say that terrorism is acceptable when all options for peaceful settlement have been foreclosed?"*

Picard: *"Data, these are questions that mankind has been struggling with throughout history. Your confusion is only human."*

While delivering aid to the inhabitants of a planet torn by civil war, Doctor Crusher is taken hostage by terrorists who have the ability to transport via the dangerous technology of "dimensional shifting." Although sympathetic to the rebels' cause, Captain Picard begins to realize that this is a planet where the Federation cannot take a stand, not even to save Crusher's life—or his own.

Thematically similar to the episode that preceded it—a man of violence earns a certain amount of sympathy from *Enterprise* crew members, although his destructive behavior is deplored—"The High Ground" was far more controversial. In fact, it didn't air on the BBC until 2007 (seventeen years after airing in the United States), and has never been shown on the RTÉ (the official broadcaster of the Republic of Ireland). Initial airings on Sky One were edited. The episode was, however, released uncut on video and DVD in the UK and Ireland, and was featured at Belfast's Cathedral Quarter Arts Festival in 2007.

The episode was selected for the Belfast event "because of the issues it raises in relation to censorship," festival director Sean Kelly explained at the time. "It dates from 1990, a time when songs were being banned and [Irish] republican politicians' voices being dubbed by actors."

The regional sensitivity regarding the episode's implicit suggestion that terrorism would help to bring about "the Irish Unification of 2024" is understandable. The Good Friday Agreement of 1998— which signified an end to the war in Ireland against British Rule and British presence in the country— was several years away, and the sentiments that led to the discussions that brought it about were virtually unspoken at the time. Nearly a decade after the agreement, Kelly scheduled the episode in hopes that attendees would "see the funny side of an occasion on which the powers-that-be decided to censor an episode of a popular science fiction series because of what was happening politically at the time."

Opposite: Post–terrorist mayhem, the actors discuss their next scene with Gabrielle Beaumont, *Star Trek*'s first woman director.

Stripped of his powers and evicted from the Continuum, the now mortal Q seeks refuge aboard the *Enterprise*. While Picard isn't sure he can believe Q's story, he *is* certain that Q's presence will complicate the *Enterprise*'s mission to prevent the Bre'elian moon from crashing into the inhabited planet it orbits. Unfortunately, it may also threaten the safety of the entire crew; the Calamarain, a gaseous lifeform with a grudge against Q, have decided that this would be the perfect time to take revenge.

The "Deja Q" opening sequence called for Q to appear—floating horizontally—on the *Enterprise* bridge. To accomplish this feat, visual effects supervisor Dan Curry used a technique that wasn't difficult or even unique, he admits, although it *looked* great on-camera. "It's one of the few shots we've done that came out looking *exactly* like the storyboard. I'd picked the spot for the camera in advance, and the scene played out just as I drew it.

"The script said, 'Q appears nude,'" Curry explains. "We planned to have John de Lancie lay on a wooden board that couldn't be seen due to Patrick Stewart's position in the shot. As we were prepping the shot, John showed up on the set with his bathrobe on. When we were ready to go, he dropped his bathrobe and he was stark naked. That caused . . . ummm . . . a bit of a stir." In fact, de Lancie had been provided with a G-string for modesty's sake, but it was ultimately determined that the shot just wouldn't work unless he was au naturel.

Doug Drexler, who'd recently won an Oscar for his work as part of the makeup team on the feature *Dick Tracy*, was the lucky artist who got to apply de Lancie's body makeup for that shot. He'd already applied a coat of Max Factor Pan-Cake while in de Lancie's dressing trailer, then accompanied the actor to the set for touch-ups. That's when director Les Landau, an old hand at working with this cast and crew, saw an opportunity to milk the situation for its comedic opportunities. When de Lancie, sans clothing, took his mark on the stage, the director cried out: "*Makeup!*" Drexler stepped forward, and Landau pointed at de Lancie's gluteus maximus. "I think you missed a spot!" As the makeup artist obediently stroked a little more Pan-Cake onto the posterior area in question, Landau drew the attention of every crew member present by shouting: "*Ladies and gentlemen—Academy Award–winning makeup artist Doug Drexler!*"

"It's something I'll never forget," says Drexler, although it's unclear if he means that in a good or bad way.

Below: Patrick Stewart chats up Brent Spiner while Michael Westmore double-checks Data's blinkies.

Opposite: Curry's preliminary sketch for Q's surprise appearance. He and his team shared an Emmy nomination for Outstanding Achievement in Special Visual Effects for the episode.

DAN CURRY

"Second officer's log, Stardate 43611.6. Programming of the holodeck has taken eighteen hours, eleven minutes, and is now complete. All participants have entered their depositions. Technical schematics and complete records from the lab's ground computers, as well as Dr. Apgar's personal logs, have been included. The re-creations will have a nominal eight-point-seven percent margin of error." —Data

During a stopover at a Starfleet research station, Riker is accused of murdering Dr. Apgar, a scientist who was developing a new source of energy. With two witnesses claiming that Riker's actions seem to support the accusation, and with scientific evidence pointing to the same conclusion, Picard attempts to defend his first officer by using the holodeck to re-create the events leading up to Apgar's death.

"My first assignment on staff [as story editor] was to help gangbang the freelance script 'A Matter of Perspective,' and none of us took credit on it," recalls Ronald D. Moore. "There was a philosophy on the show that I carry forward to this day: you don't put your name on other people's scripts. So there was a lot of rewriting of other people's material that we generally never took credit for. Ira [Steven Behr] always said, 'We're writers and producers on the staff. We're paid a lot more than the freelancers, and we have all the power. The freelancer writes his script and has no power after that, and we can do anything we want [with his material], so we should give him the dignity of having full credit on it. We don't need to take that from him and take away his residuals.'"

Freelancer Ed Zuckerman's script for "A Matter of Perspective" offered an intriguing variation on Kurosawa's film *Rashomon*, where a crime witnessed by four individuals is described in four mutually contradictory ways, thanks to the subjectivity of perception. Rather than use flashbacks, as is traditional in cinema, the unique *Trek* variation substituted interpretations of the pertinent data by the *Enterprise*'s holodeck.

One additional person contributed to the episode: David Krieger, who served as a scientific consultant during *TNG*'s third and fourth seasons. Krieger provided the rationale behind why the holodeck—which, per the series bible, cannot create anything that represents a danger to the ship or the crew—suddenly began generating harmful bursts of radiation. Krieger's solution: while the holodeck's reconstruction of the dead scientist's lab was not in itself inherently dangerous, when combined with an external radiation source (a "harmless lambda field generator" on the nearby planet's surface), the holographic device's geometry made it as effective as the scientist's real wave converter in creating the destructive phenomenon he had been studying.

Although Krieger was compensated for every episode he consulted on, he never received screen credit. That week he got a "bonus"; the writers dubbed the dead scientist's radiation field "Krieger waves," terminology now permanently enshrined within *Star Trek* canon.

Although it's said that too many cooks spoil the soup, every now and then a room full of talented cooks manage to serve up an exceptionally tasty offering. That's the case with "Yesterday's *Enterprise*."

Here's the recipe, starting with the raw ingredients:

- A spec script, submitted by Trent Ganino, in which the *Enterprise*-C appears from the past. If Picard sends the starship back, its crew will die; telling them that will change history. The script languished on the freelance pile for a year.

- A story pitch from Eric Stillwell about Spock's father, Sarek, who returns from the Guardian of Forever to find that the universe has changed. Sarek must convince Picard that the timeline has been altered and help put the universe back on track. Michael Piller rejected the story because it contained too many *TOS* "gimmicks."

- A comment from Denise Crosby, suggesting her desire to guest on *TNG*.

Michael Piller suggested that Ganino and Stillwell blend their two stories together, Stillwell recalls, "using Trent's *Enterprise* from the past, and my alternate universe, making Guinan the character who realizes that everything has changed." Piller bought the resulting draft, then sent it to the writing staff for seasoning—along with one caveat that presented a serious challenge to the creative process.

"The only time Denise and Whoopi Goldberg would *both* be available for filming was the first week of December," Stillwell relates. "And it was already November. So Michael told the staff they had to write it over Thanksgiving weekend. They were all moaning and groaning."

Now it was time to bring the script to a boil and serve it up. Overseeing the process was Ira Steven Behr. "It was all written in the white heat of a couple days," he recalls. "I brought in Hans Beimler, Ricky Manning, and Ron Moore to break the story with me. And I got everybody excited by talking about killing the characters in this alternate universe and giving them all death scenes. I said, 'It's like the old World War Two movie *Bataan*, where the de-fenders are killed off, one by one. The movie ends with the last man standing at his machine gun with the enemy coming at him until the smoke from his gun obscures the screen.' I told them, 'At the end, we'll have Picard alone, firing phasers in the smoke of the burning bridge, and that's how we'll go out.' Everyone said, 'Okay, we're unhappy, and we can't kill the episode—but *we can kill the characters*.' So we wrote these great death scenes—and then of course, we weren't able to do them because of production time and cost," he says with a sigh.

In the end, "Yesterday's *Enterprise*" earned accolades as a fan favorite, right behind Piller's "The Best of Both Worlds." "I had a friendly rivalry with Michael about whose episode was more popular," Stillwell says, chuckling. "I'd say, 'Yours was a two-parter, but mine was the most popular *single* installment.' And Michael would just roll his eyes."

"It was a nice little challenge to go back and work up the *Enterprise*-C as a melding of Picard's *Galaxy*-class ship and the *Excelsior* (the *Enterprise*-B)," Rick Sternbach says. "Andy Probert had previously done a sketch that was a blend of those two ships, and I fleshed out the design work and Greg Jein built the miniature. You could really see the evolution from B to C to D."

Jein did more than build the miniature. He also had the task of altering the pristine model to make it look like it had been in a major battle at Narendra III. "To simulate the damage on the *Enterprise*-C, we used a lot of leftover pyro that we had from the Fourth of July," Jein confesses, "like firecrackers and smoke pots. We actually scorched the surface of the ship rather than painting it on."

Opposite: The scorched model being prepared for its close-up. Ship models often were mounted upside down during filming to accommodate certain camera angles.

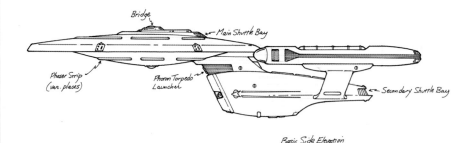

Trek³

NCC-1701-C *Ambassador Class*
U.S.S. *Enterprise*
Var. 1

Bridge

Main Shuttle Bay

Phaser Strip
(var. places)

Phaser Torpedo
Launcher

Secondary Shuttle Bay

Basic Side Elevation

sternbach 11·89

Data: "What do you feel, Lal?"
Lal: "I love you, Father."
Data: "I wish I could feel it with you."
Lal: "I will feel it for both of us. Thank you for my life. Flirting. Laughter. Painting. Family. Female. Human . . ."

Data's creation of an android "daughter," whom he names Lal, sparks a fierce debate with Starfleet over whether the female android should be studied in a lab or allowed to remain with Data on the *Enterprise*. When Admiral Haftel insists on coming to the starship to observe Lal's behavior and determine her fate, the visit triggers an unanticipated response in Lal's programming.

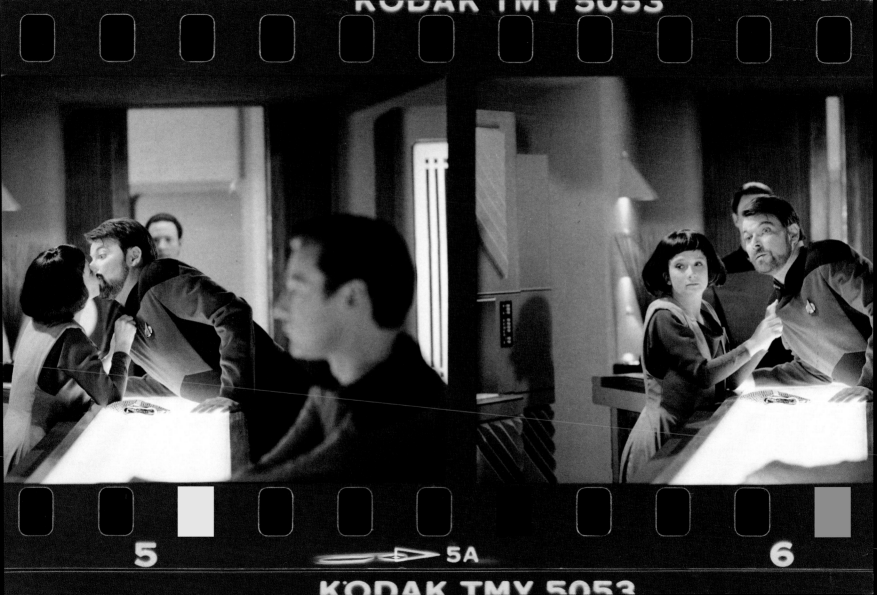

Actors generally aren't needed on-set for long portions of their workday, so being a featured player in any production can mean a lot of downtime. If they're "on call," they have to be "available," but they aren't required to stand around in the sound-stage. Typically, when an actor isn't delivering his lines, he'll retreat to his trailer to make a few phone calls, catch up on the news, or take a nap.

And by *TNG*'s second season, says Jonathan Frakes, "I'd had enough naps." What he really wanted to do—forgive the cliché—was direct.

"The opportunity was staring me in the face," he explains. "As I looked around the set, I really sensed that the director was in charge of the storytelling. I liked the thought of having that control, and I liked the idea of being involved in all aspects of making the product."

So Frakes approached Rick Berman. "Rick initially was reluctant to get involved in what traditionally is seen as a 'perk' for series regulars," Frakes says. "But what he did—and it wound up being a real gift—was tell me, 'You really need to prepare for this.' So I started shadowing all the other directors through the process, watching Rick Kolbe and Cliff Bole and Bob Scheerer, and then I spent like three hundred hours in the editing room with Bob Lederman and the other guys. I spent preproduction time with Junie Lowry, who allowed me to attend the casting sessions, and in post with Rob Legato and Dan Curry, creating those amazing effects. Rick and I laughingly referred to it as 'going to Paramount University,'" the "student" says with a chuckle. "I'd go to the studio even when I wasn't on call, just to do all this 'class work,' if you will."

A year passed before Frakes finally got a chance to step behind the camera. "Rick wouldn't roll, and he wouldn't roll," Frakes says. "My wife, Genie, God bless her, told me, 'If you really want to do this, *stick with it* until he finally gives you one.' And finally the stars lined up with this great script by René Echevarria, 'The Offspring.' By then, the whole crew was behind me, because it was a real tight family, and it ended up that I was totally *over*-prepared. The script was a great Brent [Spiner] story—which is a plus in itself—with a wonderful guest cast." It went so well that Berman put Frakes into "the rotation" of recurring directors.

As the seasons passed, most of *TNG*'s main actors got a chance to direct—after attending the same "university." The effect even spilled over to sister shows *Deep Space Nine* and *Voyager*. Today Frakes is an in-demand director on a variety of television series, and fellow *Trek* actors LeVar Burton, Roxann Dawson, and Robert Duncan McNeill are equally successful—all because Frakes was tired of naps.

"I can't take credit for any of that," Frakes says. "Once that door was open . . ."

It wasn't actress Hallie Todd beneath all that gold in the sequence where Data introduced Lal to Geordi and Troi. It was actor/dancer Leonard Crowfoot, who had previously appeared (sans prosthetic makeup) in "Angel One."

"Only one actor in a thousand would have agreed to endure what Leonard endured," Michael Westmore says. "We made a full head appliance that covered his nose and ears, and dropped the mouth hole down to his chin. So he couldn't hear well, or breathe through his nose, and in order to breathe at all, he had to stick his finger in the mouth hole. That meant he could only breathe between scenes when the camera wasn't running. Plus, since he was wearing silverized contact lenses, his vision was severely impaired."

Because Lal, at this point, was supposed to appear androgynous, Westmore designed a square pectoral covering for Crowfoot's chest, thus removing the nipples. His team also built a foam gender-hiding "diaper" that was glued to the actor's crotch.

"Just putting on the makeup was brutal for Leonard," recalls makeup man Doug Drexler. "Luckily, he was one of the most Zen guys I've ever met. He stopped eating the day before and got his entire system cleared out so that he wouldn't have to pee during the day. He knew it would be a disaster if we had to get him out of that thing before he was done shooting."

But surprisingly, that wasn't the worst Crowfoot had to endure.

"Mike gave me some gold makeup paint that he said would wash off with soap and water. I thought, 'Really?' I had my doubts.

"But I began applying it at two A.M.," Drexler says. "It took about four and a half hours. Then he faced that long shooting day. Finally, long after dark, the crew went home, and I started taking him out of the gold makeup. Mike had an early call for the next morning, so it was only me. I started putting makeup remover on his arm and, well, forget it," Drexler snorts. "That makeup paint was bulletproof! After hours and hours of rubbing, I called Mike and asked if he could get somebody to open the studio gym, which he did. That's when I got into the shower with Lenny Crowfoot and a loofah sponge. I scrubbed him down like I was giving my dog a bath. It was . . . uh . . . memorable," Drexler says with a chuckle. "I'd never taken a shower with a man before."

And Crowfoot still had two more days of shooting ahead of him!

"We worked on different combinations of makeup remover," Westmore notes, "and by the final night, we were able to get him cleaned up in only an hour and twenty minutes."

"I remember the day I met René Echevarria," relates Ira Steven Behr. "I *still* make fun of him—*so* nervous, and *so pretentious,* from New *Yawk,* where the theat-*ah* is *every*thing. But he wrote a damn good script."

"I made a *terrible* impression on the writing staff," Echevarria confesses. "I had no idea how hard they'd been working, or the trenches they'd been in. I came in thinking I was going to show them how to do *Star Trek*. Because I didn't think the show was as good as it could be."

Pretty cocky for a guy who was working odd jobs to support himself while he wrote and directed plays that were (by his own admission) "appropriate for a young, pretentious, beret-wearing denizen of the East Village."

But he had a yen to do something else. "I was a fan of the original show, and when *TNG* started, I began noodling ideas and sending them to Paramount," Echevarria explains. "I had no idea that wasn't really done in the business. The first couple scripts I sent were epic, big scale, but I hadn't heard back. So I decided, 'Well, this is the last one.' And I thought: Data is a character that wants, more than *anything,* to be human. What if he decided to have

a child? That's the *most* human thing he could try to experience. So I wrote that script and sent it. I didn't hear back for months."

Then he got a call from Michael Piller.

"I'd never heard his name," explains Echevarria. "So I said, 'What do you do on the show?' He said, 'I'm executive producer.' I said, 'How come I've never seen your name in the credits?' And he said, 'I'm new here.' *That* was the beginning of my great relationship with *Star Trek*," Echevarria says with a laugh. "And *then* he said, 'I read your script. I really like it. We want to produce it. And we want to bring you to L.A. next week.' I was like, 'Wow!'

"We broke the story," he continues. "It changed considerably. Initially, Data was the father and the ship's computer was the mother. There was some comedy—Data argued with the computer about how to raise Lal. It had some jeopardy with a Ferengi. But what made Michael excited was that it took place entirely on the *Enterprise*. They needed a money-saver, and this was just the ticket.

"They gave me ten days to write a new script," he recalls. "After I sent it in, Michael called. He said, very straightforward, 'I'm really disappointed. You didn't capture what we're looking for.' I was crushed.

He said, 'It's your first time writing something professionally, and you kind of choked. Your spec script was one of the best I've ever read. Anyway, we're taking it over from here.' And he hung up.

"I thought, 'Oh my God, my first break in the business and I *blew* it,'" Echevarria exclaims with a groan. "I thought I'd never hear from them again."

Fortunately, he was wrong.

Kurn, a Klingon exchange officer who arrives to serve on the *Enterprise*, turns out to be Worf's long-lost brother; but the reunion is less than sweet. Kurn brings bad news: their dead father, Mogh, has been branded a traitor, supposedly responsible for the deaths of four thousand Klingons at the hands of the Romulans. For Worf, there is only one choice; he must go to the Klingon homeworld and face the High Council in order to challenge the accusations. But after Kurn is injured, Worf turns to the only other person he would trust to act as his defender before the Council: Captain Picard.

Opposite: Richard James's Emmy Award–winning design for the Klingon Great Hall.

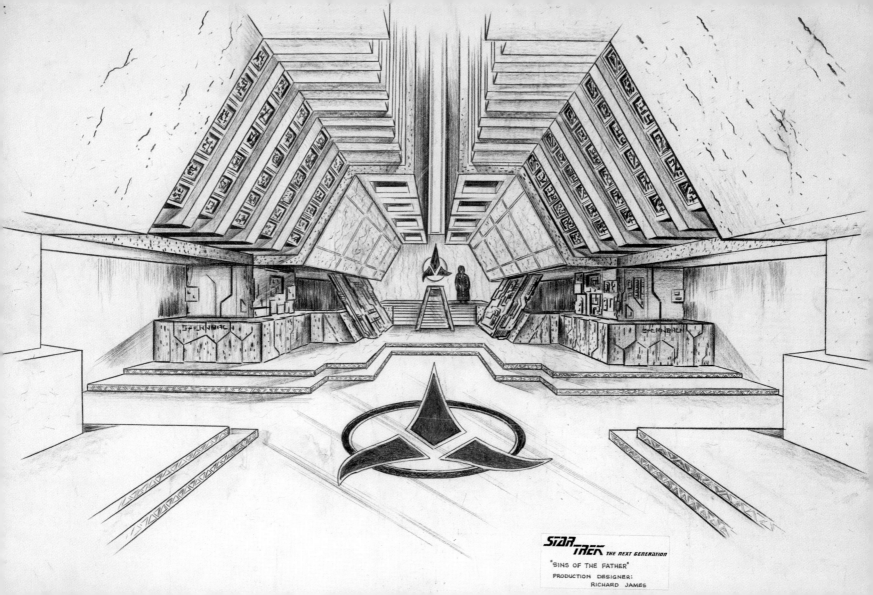

STAR TREK THE NEXT GENERATION
"SINS OF THE FATHER"
PRODUCTION DESIGNER:
RICHARD JAMES

"When Michael Piller came in, he made a creative decision to shift the focus of the show from being about the planet and the aliens of the week to our characters aboard the *Enterprise* and how our characters are affected by the story," Ronald D. Moore says. "It really was that fundamental character shift in focus that provided our biggest change in course."

"Michael and I talked a lot about how hard it was to get *characterization* into *The Next Generation*," recalls Ira Steven Behr, "because Gene Roddenberry had dictates that he was just rigid about. That everyone in the twenty-fourth century was free of psychological problems. That there was no conflict among people. The thing that made *The Original Series* work—that continued to be entertaining even after the special effects were outdated and the social problems it addressed began to feel a little simplistic—was the relationship between Kirk, Spock, and McCoy. *That's* what makes *The Original Series* sing. So we found ways, throughout the episodes, to make the characters alive and to explore them as much as possible. It was very difficult to get to that place, but ultimately that's what made *TNG* credible."

"Sins of the Father" served as a transitional episode, subtly shifting from the old focus to the new.

Certainly, it was about "the planet and the aliens of the week," specifically Klingons and the Klingon homeworld. But more specifically, it explored the character—in both senses of that word—of Worf. Against an intricate and corrupt political backdrop, viewers learn, along with Worf, that he has a brother, that honor is more important to him than life, and that despite having been raised among humans, Worf is a warrior among warriors.

In creating a continuing story line for Worf, *TNG* actually moved beyond the dynamic that made *The Original Series* so successful. In the first *Star Trek*, only "the big three" characters showed any sign of character change or growth. Worf's leading role in "Sins of the Father" broke through the "glass ceiling" between the upper and lower tiers of characters. It became possible for any of the main characters to carry an entire episode, to have a continuing story line. In that sense, *TNG* proved to be far more egalitarian than its predecessor, and set the course for future *Star Trek* series.

Not long after Ronald D. Moore joined the *TNG* writing staff, he gained a reputation among producers and viewers alike as "a Klingon expert." But he hadn't planned things that way.

"It was the luck of the draw," Moore says, "something that happened literally in that first week when I joined the writers' staff. Michael Piller asked me if I was a fan of *The Original Series*. Well, I knew a lot about *Star Trek*, and, unlike most people around the show," he says with a chuckle, "I wore my fandom on my sleeve. So Michael asked me to write a memo explaining how I saw the Klingon and Romulan races. I wrote a memo on what I thought were the defining characteristics of the two species."

The memo impressed Piller enough that he decided to give his new writer an assignment. "After he read my memo, Michael handed me two freelance scripts to work on," Moore says. "I believe that one involved the backstory with Worf's father and Khitomer. And the other one dealt with going to the Klingon homeworld. And Kurn, Worf's brother, was involved with one of them. These eventually became the basis for 'Sins of the Father.' The episode represented the first time in the series—in the franchise, actually—that the show went to the Klingon homeworld, and it es-

tablished a lot about Klingon culture, traditions, and societal stuff.

"And 'Sins' definitely left the door open for a follow-up," notes Moore. "All the Worf stories spring from that episode. Suddenly Worf had this dangling thing about his honor. And that became a springboard to the 'Redemption' two-parter, following up on all the political machinations we'd set into motion.

"It was my first experience in creating a world and a culture, and I really enjoyed making up things about the Klingons' history and traditions," Moore continues. "I got handed a lot of Worf stuff, so I became very fond of him. I took him from this one place to another place. But actually, whoever I was writing for that week was my favorite character, because as a writer, you're just trying to invest yourself and do something with them, and they become your favorite for that episode."

Picard 2: *"There's a danger in becoming too detached, of never permitting ourselves to get closer."*
Crusher: *"Is that what you want, Jean-Luc? To get closer?"*
Picard 2: *"You're a very attractive woman."*

Picard is kidnapped and imprisoned by a race of beings that wants to study his behavior and also that of his crew, who are unknowingly serving under a Picard double. As the *Enterprise* crew begins to worry about their captain's increasingly unorthodox behavior, the real Picard and his eclectic cellmates plan an escape. But someone in that group may actually be their captor.

In each of *TNG*'s seven seasons, Michael Westmore and his team received at least one Emmy nomination for Outstanding Achievement in Makeup. In fact, during some seasons, they were nominated for multiple episodes (as were the show's visual effects teams). In 1990, their work on "Allegiance" received a nod—not surprising, considering that

Westmore had to create three new alien species for the episode. As always, Westmore enjoyed the challenge, crafting a fierce, multiple-tusked, warthog-like Chalnoth; a wrinkly-faced Mizarian bearing more than a passing resemblance to *Dick Tracy*'s Pruneface; and the lumpy-headed, unnamed race of aliens that kidnaps Picard to observe the "unfamiliar concepts" of authority and leadership. Because the script indicated that the captor aliens were identical, a pair of twins was cast, which saved a bit of time (the latex appliances that were tailor-made for one alien perfectly fit the other, so the team could use the same molds to create pieces for both). Westmore also developed a feminine version of the Bolian makeup that he'd previously created for a male character in the episode "Conspiracy."

As for the Emmys, this wasn't Westmore's year. "Allegiance" lost to tied episodes of *Alien Nation* and *The Tracey Ullman Show*.

03 | 147 "CAPTAIN'S HOLIDAY"

While reluctantly vacationing on the pleasure planet Risa, Picard finds romance and adventure with Vash, an attractive female archaeologist who'll do just about anything to beat a Ferengi and several time-traveling Vorgons in a hunt for the *Tox Uthat*, a dangerous superweapon from the twenty-seventh century. The Vorgons tell Picard that he's destined to find the weapon and give it to them so that they can return it to its appropriate place in time, but after spending some time around the seductive Vash, the captain isn't sure whom to trust.

"Captain's Holiday" is a lighthearted escapade that pleased just about everyone . . . except for the man who wrote it.

"I had an idea for a show about the captain going to this pleasure planet," Ira Steven Behr begins with a sigh. "And there he steps into something like a holodeck—you go in to face your greatest fear. Picard steps in and discovers his biggest fear is not that he's going to fight some big alien something, or face a dozen Romulan warbirds. No, it's that he's going to be made an *admiral* and Riker will be given command of the *Enterprise*. It's the idea that *the ship will go on without him*. They have one last mission together, and then he has to accept that he's no longer captain and will have to find his own identity. I was very excited about it, and everyone on staff seemed to like it."

Well, not quite everyone.

"I went to meet with Gene Roddenberry," Behr continues. "And Gene said, 'There's no way we're going to do this episode. Jean-Luc Picard is John Wayne, and John Wayne has no fears about growing old.' I told him that I was quite familiar with John Wayne movies, and in some of the best, he *does* have fears, and he *does* have doubts, and he *is* conflicted.

"But Gene said, 'No, this is the twenty-fourth century. This wouldn't be a problem for him. If he had to give up the *Enterprise*—I'm not saying he'd like it, but it wouldn't even cause a ripple in his mind. But, you know, I *like* the idea of the pleasure planet! *That's* what you should do. Send him to a pleasure planet where everyone is having sex. That's why they come to the planet! And give Picard an adventure!'

"And I'm thinking, *'Really?'* So while I'm digesting this, Patrick Stewart asks me to have lunch in the commissary. He's an absolute gentleman, as pleasant as pleasant can be. But eventually he says, 'You know, there's a rumor floating around that there's an episode under consideration where the captain has fears of growing old. . . .'"

Stewart, as it turns out, didn't relish that idea, either. And he was eager to share his thoughts about a preferable direction for his character. "The captain doesn't fight and screw enough," Stewart explained, echoing earlier comments he'd made to new writer Ron Moore. "Write me a show like that."

"So I went back and came up with the show as it now exists," Behr says, "with the *Horga'hn* and the MacGuffin of the *Tox Uthat*. Which now sits in my library."

Behr is philosophical about his trip down the literary rabbit hole. "If someone initially had told me, 'Come up with an episode where *this* is the main idea,' I could have gotten behind it," he confesses. "But the fact that it *started* with this dramatic look deep behind a character's psyche, and wound up getting the captain laid . . ."

That, as they say, is showbiz.

Data: *"I witnessed something remarkable. In-dividually they were both so . . ."*
Troi: *"Wounded? Isolated?"*
Data: *"Yes. But no longer. Through joining, they have been healed. Grief has been transmuted to joy. Loneliness to belonging."*

The *Enterprise* risks a confrontation with hostile Romulans and destruction by an impending super-nova in order to help a Federation emissary establish relations with Tin Man, a sentient life-form that resembles an organic spaceship. The emissary, Tam Elbrun, is a Betazoid like Troi, but he's never developed the ability to block the thoughts of other individuals. His psyche is fragile, possibly even un-stable. After Picard learns that Elbrun has developed an empathic bond with Tin Man, he begins to ques-tion the Betazoid's loyalties. When the Romulans attack, will he put the life of the strange alien being above that of the *Enterprise* crew?

In 1977, Dennis Bailey and David Bischoff were nominated for a Nebula Award for a short story called "Tin Woodman," which appeared in an issue of *Amazing Stories* magazine. Although they lost (to Harlan Ellison's story "Jeffty Is Five"), they expanded "Woodman" into a novel, which was published by Doubleday in 1979. And ten years later, they suc-cessfully sold a spec script based on "Woodman" to the producers of *TNG*. The original story concerned a young boy with psychic abilities who is sent into space by the government, which considers him a dangerous misfit. The crew of the spaceship on which he's traveling is charged with finding a sen-tient starship and bringing it back to Earth. However, the boy, via his abilities, winds up making contact with the alien vessel first, and takes matters into his own hands. The titles "Tin Woodman" and "Tin Man" are, of course, derived from the beloved character in L. Frank Baum's classic children's novel *The Wonderful Wizard of Oz.* Like the Woodman, the alien—code-named "Tin Man"—desperately longs to have its heart restored.

The Next Generation stories rarely focused on out-side characters, but every now and then an episode like this would win over the producers. Various *En-terprise* crew members alternately view Tam Elbrun with suspicion, compassion, or, in Data's case, sim-ple curiosity. The regulars, particularly Data, spend as much time on-camera as Elbrun, but ultimately, it is Tam's story. Bailey and Bischoff would make one additional contribution to *TNG*. They wrote one of several drafts used to create the fourth season episode "First Contact" . . . which also focused on non-regulars.

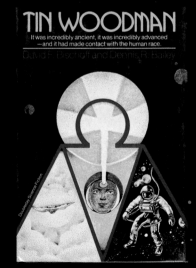

TIN WOODMAN

It was incredibly ancient, it was incredibly advanced —and it had made contact with the human race.

David F. Bischoff and Dennis R. Bailey

Herman Zimmerman, on the *Enterprise* bridge railing:

"There was one prop maker, a fellow named Jim Woods, who personally built that railing, and I'm afraid he was so passionate about doing it that, in a sense, he gave his life for it. He was in a motorcycle accident a couple of days before he was to finish it, and he didn't want anybody else to touch it. So he came in against his doctor's orders and finished it. About a week later he had an aneurysm in his brain and died. I don't know whether he would have lived if he hadn't finished it, but for the first couple of seasons we had a little dedication plaque under the part of the railing that you couldn't see that mentioned Jim.

"Jim was a consummate mechanic, and he made the railing in a way that probably nobody else could have figured out. It was a compound ellipse—which is a very difficult thing to fabricate. First, he drew an ellipse on the floor and then he built a wall to that ellipse. Then he drew another ellipse on that now elliptical vertical wall. And to those lines, he built another wall that became the support for the railing all the way around. On to that, he lightly tacked the first layer of eighth-inch bender board, which is a flexible wood. And then, piece by piece, he laminated eighth-inch bender board until he reached the right thickness—which is somewhere between six and nine inches, depending on which part of the railing you're looking at. And while doing this he managed to create all the voids necessary for the lights and the running of wires inside it. It was really a work of genius. I don't know of anybody else who was working at Paramount at the time who could have figured it out. That's one of the reasons that railing is so important to me."

Right: The railing, nicknamed "the horseshoe" by the crew.

Opposite: Prop maker Jim Woods at work during *TNG*'s preproduction phase.

"Pardon me, but why is Lieutenant Barclay being referred to clandestinely as a vegetable?"
—Data

Nervous, insecure Reginald Barclay, one of La Forge's engineers, compensates for his inability to cope with his real life by living out elaborate fantasies in the ship's holodeck, to the point where Troi and the rest of the crew worry that he has developed a holo-addiction. But when a runaway acceleration problem threatens to destroy the *Enterprise*, La Forge is forced to seek a solution from the man least likely to be able to solve anyone's problems.

"Being afraid all the time, of forgetting some-body's name, not knowing what to do with your hands. I mean, I'm the guy who writes down things to remember to say when there's a party. A▮▮en when he finally gets there, he winds up al▮▮e in the corner trying to look comfortable ex-amining a potted plant." —Barclay

Contrary to Gene Roddenberry's oft-stated vision of the future, not every person who serves on a twenty-fourth-century starship is perfect. Everyone may *look* polished and trim—they'd have to be to fit into the uniforms—but, just like today, most humanoids still carry around a little psychological "baggage."

How else to explain Barclay? He can't simply be an aberration. If he were *that* unusual, he'd never have made it through Starfleet Academy. The *Enter-prise* is loaded with the best and the brightest. We see the adventures of those people on-screen every week. But even Starfleet's flagship needs its share of "everymen" doing their jobs on the lower decks.

Every twenty-first-century high school has its share of kids who don't readily blend in with the cool crowd▮ Rather than mixing with the cheerleaders and the football stars at hot weekend dance clubs, those kids are more likely to spend their time at home reading a little sci-fi, or playing games online, or attending a *Star Trek* convention.

Barclay's a nerd who's good at solving engineer-ing puzzles, but not at making conversation. He works in a world where sci-fi is reality, online games are life and death, and conventions—like baseball—are a thing of the past. So he finds something even better. He finds the holodeck.

The shooting script for "Hollow Pursuits" de-scribes the setting for Barclay's favorite fantasy in this way:

"A picnic setting, as exquisite as a Gainsborough canvas . . . a swing suspended from a tree branch on which the image of a woman is swinging in flowing petticoats, a silent garment draped on the grass and spread with delicacies . . . a boy dressed as 'Blue Boy' eating messily with his hands . . ."

Production designer Richard James took the script's directives to heart, and made Barclay's self-esteem program into a lush landscape, resplendent in golden sunlight filtering through the greenery. "I wanted it to feel slightly unreal, and Marvin Rush did a great job of lighting it," James says. "With Gates McFadden on that swing, it was so pretty, one of our more elaborate holodeck sets, and really fun to do."

Data: "Your collection has been confiscated. All of your stolen possessions are being returned to their rightful owners. You have lost everything you value."

Fajo: "It must give you great pleasure."

Data: "No, sir, it does not. I do not feel pleasure. I am only an android."

Data is captured and held against his will by Kivas Fajo, an unethical collector of one-of-a-kind artifacts who thinks that Data will be the jewel of his collection. Although initially unwilling to "perform" for his captor, Data succumbs to Fajo's demands when Fajo threatens to harm his own innocent assistant if the android refuses to comply. But after the assistant attempts to help Data escape, Fajo kills her, pushing Data to the brink of behavior that—theoretically, at least—contradicts his programming.

Right: Brent Spiner and veteran actor Nehemiah Persoff demonstrate that fans aren't the only ones who like to pose with famous actors.

Ira Steven Behr has no problem remembering what happened during the production of "The Most Toys." Two distinct memories stand out: a sad reflection on a life cut tragically short, and a sweet reminiscence about the late Michael Piller.

The sad memory is common knowledge to everyone who worked on *The Next Generation* in 1990. British actor David Rappaport—perhaps best known to American audiences for his role in Terry Gilliam's *Time Bandits*, and for a recurring role on *L.A. Law*—originally was cast as the unscrupulous Kivas Fajo. But Rappaport did not appear in the final version of the episode.

"He was so *good* in the role," Behr recalls. "He filmed for two days and the dailies were phenomenal. He was compelling to watch—a little person with a lot of talent, like Peter Dinklage now, and Michael Dunn before him. But he was an unhappy man."

After shooting for two days, the production shut down for the weekend. But before filming started up again on Monday, the producers received shocking news: Rappaport was in the hospital, the result of a failed suicide attempt. Two months later, Rappaport again tried to take his own life. Sadly, this time he was successful.

The role was hastily recast with Canadian actor Saul Rubinek, a school chum of the episode's director, Timothy Bond. Although filling in at the last minute had to be difficult for Rubinek, he gave a chilling performance and made the role his own.

Behr's happy memory is far more personal. "It's what I think about most when I remember that show," Behr says. The script dictated that one of the items in Kivas Fajo's collection was a baseball card—but didn't indicate which one. Knowing that Michael Piller was, perhaps, the number one fan of the sport in the L.A. region, Behr consulted with him. Together, the pair decided on Roger Maris's 1962 card, which, Behr relates, "would have had all his stuff from the year before, when he hit those sixty-one homers and beat Babe Ruth's record.

"At the end of the episode, Michael came up to me and whispered in a very un-Michael-like way, 'Hey Ira, do you think they'd let me keep that card? Do you think they'd give it to me?' Because it was an original card, not a mock-up. It wasn't worth that much, but it *was* real. I said, 'Michael, you're *the executive producer*. Of course they'll give it to you if you ask them.' And that's what started his mania for collecting baseball cards. He wound up with an incredible collection, and it all started with this one card. He was a guy who usually kept his emotions in check—but this made him *so* happy."

Opposite, left: A production still of Rappaport as Fajo.

Opposite, right: Piller on the set of a later creation, *Star Trek: Voyager*.

Fajo: *"Why don't you accept your fate? You will return to your chair and you will sit there. You will entertain me and you will entertain my guests. And if you do not, I will simply kill somebody else. Their blood will be on your hands, too, just like poor Varria's. Your only alternative, Data, is to fire. Murder me. That's all you have to do. Go ahead. Fire. If only you could feel rage over Varria's death. If only you could feel the need for revenge, then maybe you could fire. But you're just an android. You can't feel anything, can you? It's just another interesting intellectual puzzle for you. Another of life's curiosities."*

Data: *"I cannot permit this to continue."*

Fajo: *"Wait! Your program won't allow you to fire. You cannot fire. No—"*

Is Data capable of murder? We know that his "brother," Lore, certainly was. Dr. Soong created Data without emotions so that he wouldn't be subject to the abject cruelty that emotional beings are capable of. But it doesn't take emotions to kill. When the appropriate circumstances are in play, Data can defend himself and others—and even fire a phaser set to kill.

Did Data try to kill Fajo? "The Most Toys" writer Shari Goodhartz shared her opinion with award-winning comic book author Marv Wolfman on Wolfman's blog:

"On the set, I asked Brent Spiner whether he thought Data purposefully pulled the trigger or not, and he was adamant that Data did fire the weapon, which was my intent as well. But the powers-that-be wanted that kept ambiguous, so it was. If I had a chance to do it over, with all the experience I have behind me now, I would argue passionately for Data's actions and their consequences to have been clearer, and hopefully more provocative."

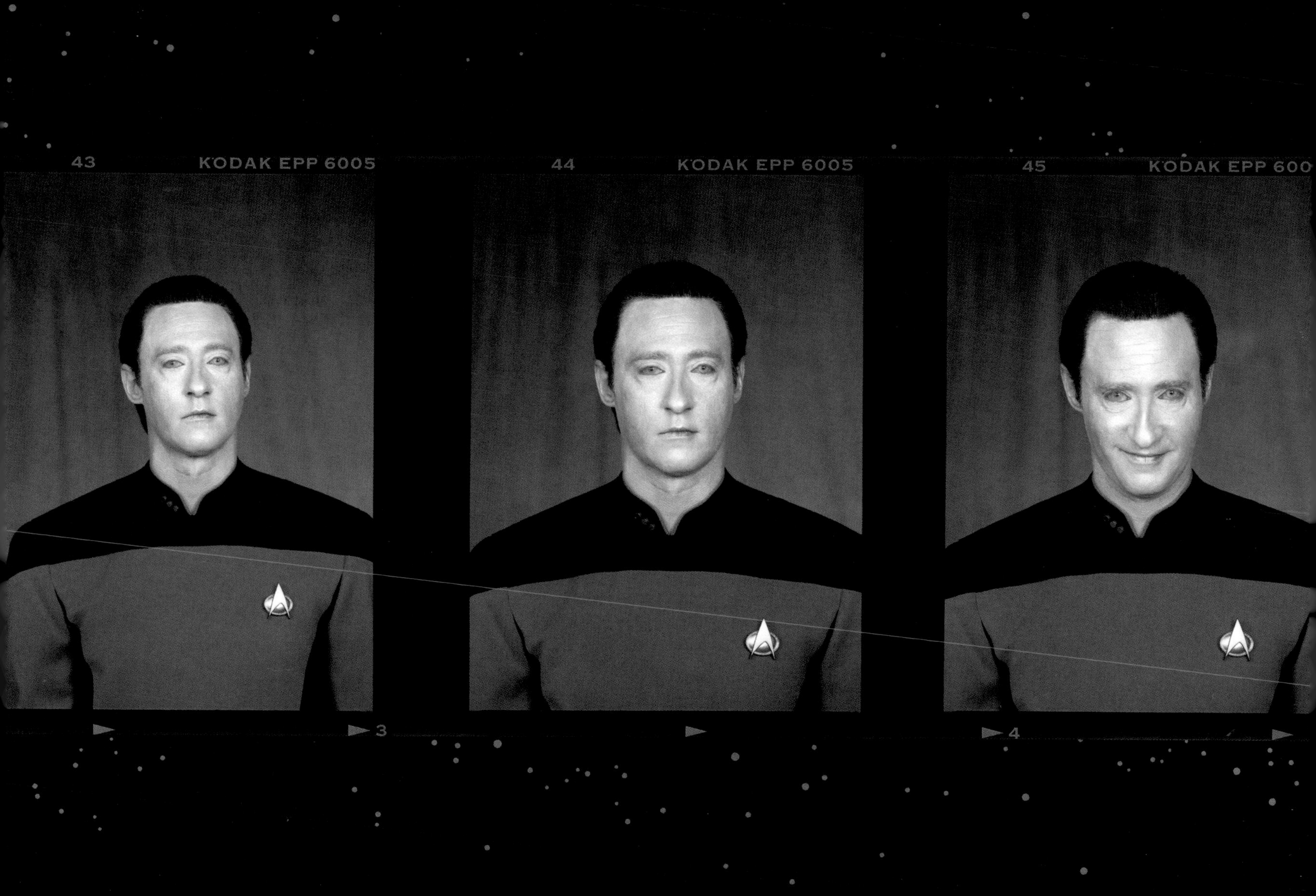
43
KODAK EPP 6005
44
KODAK EPP 6005
45
KODAK EPP 600
3
4

The success of a mission to establish diplomatic negotiations between the Federation and the Legarans is thrown into doubt after Captain Picard learns that Sarek, the esteemed Vulcan ambassador who was to conduct the negotiations, is suffering from an incurable disease that causes a loss of emotional control. The Legarans will speak only to Sarek, who clearly is unfit to deal with them. For the sake of the mission, and the salvation of the Vulcan's pride, Picard offers Sarek the loan of something very precious: the captain's own mental stability.

Gene Roddenberry had made it clear since *TNG's* inception that he didn't want to bring in baggage from the first *Star Trek*. In the seasons that followed, the prohibition against using Klingons and Romulans had gone by the wayside, but there was still sensitivity regarding familiar characters. "Gene was the idea man, but a lot of the things that made *Star Trek* work were brought in by others," actor Mark Lenard said in 1994. "When he created *The Next Generation*, I believe he moved it ahead in time so there would be no doubt that none of the old characters would still be around." That way, Lenard suggested, he could demonstrate that the new show rested on its *own* laurels.

But times, and minds, change. Including Roddenberry's. "One day I was in Gene's office," Lenard recalled, "and he said, 'You know, it's about time that Sarek comes back. After all, Vulcans age very slowly.' I thought that was a good way to put it, not that they live a long time, but that they age very slowly. And I'm *glad* they age slowly—because it took a year and a half before they found a script for me to play."

Sarek indeed had aged—by a hundred years— since Lenard last played him. Yet the actor didn't feel a need to study the ways of the elderly. "I left that to the script and the makeup man," he said. "In this one I was so old that even my ears had wrinkles!

"The script dealt with a Vulcan with a very rare disease, kind of a version of Alzheimer's," Lenard continued. "I knew something about that. We used to call it 'senility' when I was a kid. So I didn't consciously do a lot of stuff. Part of it was what the script demanded and the other part was instinct."

"Sarek" marked Lenard's first opportunity to work with Patrick Stewart, and he enjoyed their collaboration. "Patrick was young and professional, and his acting was simple, pure, and clean," he said. "There's a great confidence in Patrick that's very important for an actor. When he had that emotional scene, he did it with great skill. And when he was just behaving himself, he did that with great skill, too."

"Sarek" is lauded as one of *TNG*'s finest hours, but the script was not completed without a battle or two, the most hard fought concerning the use of one word. The Battle of Helm's Deep had nothing on The Battle to Use Spock's Name.

"Oh, my God," groans Ira Steven Behr. "I couldn't believe it. I mean, they'd used McCoy in the *pilot*. And despite Rick's pronouncement that 'We *never* reference the old series—never, ever'—he'd agreed to do this show about Sarek, which is *already* referencing it. So Ron [Moore] and I were working on the rewrite and the long mind-meld scene, and we wrote that, at one point, Picard/Sarek yells, 'Spock!' And Rick said, 'Take it out.' It was a two-week battle. We kept losing. Then finally one day I was in his office talking about a different episode. We were having fun, joking around, and out of nowhere I said, 'Rick, tell me again why we can't just say the word "Spock"?' His body stretched backward in his chair, and his body language was like, *'Goddammit, not that again!'* Then he leaned forward and said, very simply, 'I don't know.' So I asked again, 'Can we just say "*Spock*"?' And finally he said, 'Yeah. But it's the only time we're ever going to do it.' 'Fine,' I said. He just didn't want to argue about it again."

While Berman clearly had high regard for the man who'd brought him into the franchise, there was a palpable feeling around the office that Gene Roddenberry's involvement in *TNG* was waning. In an interview several years later, Michael Piller recalled that the portrayal of Sarek reminded him of the reality of Roddenberry's deteriorating physical state. "It was clear that [Gene] was not the same man that he had been," Piller said. "We all respected him so much, and he'd been such an important, strong leader of the franchise and everything it stood for. But here was this great man going into decline. I immediately felt a very strong connection to the premise of 'Sarek,' because I could see that it really was about the universe we lived in on a daily basis."

Star Trek's barriers to its beginnings were breached with that episode. "The mention of Spock was the breakthrough that allowed us to open the doors, that allowed us to embrace our past," Piller said. From that point forward, *Star Trek* adventures would be played out over a much broader canvas.

Right: He Who Must Not Be Named . . .

Riker, Deanna, and Lwaxana Troi are kidnapped by a Ferengi bent on making Lwaxana his mate and exploiting her telepathic skills for profit. Riker attempts to signal the *Enterprise* for assistance, but Wesley Crusher, the one person aboard who might be able to understand the strange transmission, is about to leave the ship to take his Starfleet Academy oral exams, meaning the trio may just be out of luck.

Gene Roddenberry's assistant Susan Sackett and her writing partner Fred Bronson submitted "Ménage à Troi" as a vehicle for Majel Barrett's yearly appearance on *TNG* as Lwaxana Troi. Conceived as a riff on O. Henry's short story "The Ransom of Red Chief"—with over-the-top Lwaxana taking the place of the obnoxious kidnapped child—the episode evolved into a more textured piece with input from members of the show's regular writing staff, and from Roddenberry himself. "Gene wasn't doing much writing by that point," recalls Ron Moore, "and I think this was the last episode he actually did a pass on."

The episode primarily serves as a broad comedy, with its emphasis on crude Ferengi shtick, and Picard's memorable mashup of several Shakespeare sonnets as he attempts to convince DaiMon Tog of his "ardor" for Mrs. Troi.

There is a serious moment, however, when Picard, recognizing that Wesley has sacrificed a personal opportunity in order to rescue Riker, Deanna, and Lwaxana, offers the boy a field promotion to ensign. That story beat resonated with Gene Roddenberry, who'd created the character of Wesley and was genuinely fond of actor Wil Wheaton. Roddenberry commemorated Wesley's promotion by coming to the set and shutting down production long enough to present Wheaton with a gift: the actual bars he'd received when he himself was field-promoted in the Army Air Corps.

Wheaton never forgot Roddenberry's generosity, and years later he found a way to repay it. In 2007, during a ceremony in which Gene Roddenberry was posthumously inducted into the Science Fiction Hall of Fame, Wheaton presented the bars to the Great Bird's son, Eugene Roddenberry Jr. In a moving speech, Wheaton stated: "To commemorate *this* occasion, I would like to present Eugene Roddenberry with his father's ensign's bars, because he has done more to earn these bars than I ever could have. More than anyone else today, he continues to honor the legacy his father created, and I know that Gene would want him to have them."

Below: Writers Sackett and Bronson with Tog and Mr. Homn.

Opposite: Two of Roddenberry's favorite characters: Wesley Crusher (in full ensign's garb) and a Ferengi.

The *Enterprise* rescues an injured amnesiac with strange healing powers, then learns he's being pursued by representatives of the Zalkonian government. The Zalkonians claim this alien "John Doe" is an escaped prisoner who's been sentenced to death for his heinous behavior, but Beverly Crusher suspects that something far stranger is behind their desire to see "John" exterminated.

Although *Star Trek*'s open submissions policy allowed many neophyte screenwriters to see their ideas produced, a staff writer was invariably involved in polishing and revising their best efforts. After that, it went back to head writer Michael Piller for additional polish. But Piller had so much confidence in Ira Steven Behr that he opted to share responsibility for bringing a script all the way to fruition. "He would be in charge of one episode, and I'd be in charge of the next," Behr says. "We'd alternate."

"Transfigurations," René Echevarria's second script for *TNG*, was one of Behr's. "That's the last thing I did on *TNG*," Behr recalls. "That's how I went out on the show, doing that rewrite. I remember as

I finished it, I thought, 'Okay, that's it. My *Star Trek* adventure has ended.'"

But only for a while. Behr was eager to move on to his other projects, which included a movie idea he'd sold to super-producer Joel Silver (*Die Hard*, *Lethal Weapon*, *The Matrix*, *Sherlock Holmes*). When Paramount called and offered him a generous two-year play-or-pay deal to come back to *TNG*, he turned it down. But Piller refused to give up on him. "We were friends," says Behr. "For the next two years we'd go to baseball games, or he'd call and say, 'How's the movie coming? What else are you doing?' And then one day we went to a game and he said, 'Look, we're doing a new show. It's going to have more humor and conflict and it's going to reflect your sensibilities a lot more than *TNG*. I want you to read the bible. . . .'"

Which explains, shorthand, why Behr returned to the *Star Trek* franchise to spend seven years as the showrunner for *Deep Space Nine*. "I remember talking to my sister while I was making up my mind," he muses. "She said, 'Look, you had such a miserable experience that year, and it left you kind of sad that it didn't work out, so maybe this is a chance . . .'"

Behr suddenly chuckles. "She was a big *TOS* fan. She just wanted me to work on *Star Trek*."

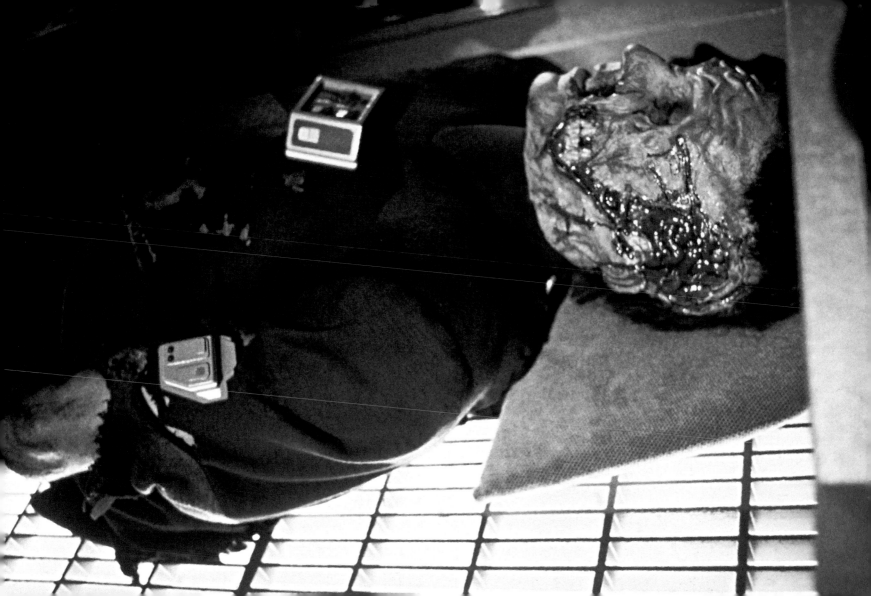

He'd blown his big break in showbiz screenwriting—or so he thought. Months after René Echevarria turned in that "disappointing" script for "The Offspring," he received another fateful phone call.

"It was from Michael [Piller], and he told me, 'Hey, I meant what I said. I thought your spec script was one of the best I've ever read, and that you choked on the rewrite. But I'm going to give you a shot at something. We've got a story no one seems to be able to crack. There's not much to it. It's just a notion. We want to do a medical show. We want it to be about Beverly. They find a guy on an asteroid, or a planet, or a crashed spaceship. Half his body's gone. There's no way he's going to survive. And she saves him. That's all we've got.'

"And I said, 'Okay.'

"And Michael said, 'If you can crack that, I'll give you another shot.'

"It was an *extraordinary* opportunity," Echevarria relates, "and a rare thing for somebody to remember how they felt about a first draft. So few people are willing to say, 'I like this,' or 'I believe in this person.' It's so much easier to go along with whatever other people are saying. So Michael Piller didn't just give me my first opportunity. He gave me my *second* opportunity when I botched my first.

"I took my time and I came up with what became 'Transfigurations,'" Echevarria continues, "with the idea that it would turn into a love story, and this guy was transitioning. *Star Trek* has done a lot of episodes over the years about beings that exist as just pure energy. Well, at some point these beings have evolved from being humanoid to this new state—so what's *that* like?

"And Michael liked it well enough that I got a chance to do a second draft. And then they worked on it in-house as well, and it turned into a nice little episode."

Echevarria's favorite memories of this second trip to Hollywood include a chance meeting with Gene Roddenberry in the hallway of the production offices. "Someone introduced me and said, 'This is the kid who wrote the "Data's Daughter" episode.' And Gene said, 'Aw, kid, you made me cry. It brought a tear to my eye.'"

When a Federation colony disappears, Starfleet suspects that the Borg threat previously encountered by Picard has finally reached their turf. Lieutenant Commander Shelby, a Borg specialist, is assigned to assist in the *Enterprise*'s investigation. Although Shelby's strategies clash with Commander Riker's, the two realize that they must find a way to work together after the Borg collective captures and "assimilates" Captain Picard. But an attempt to retrieve Picard ends in failure, pushing the crew to the grim conclusion that they may have to kill the captain in order to save Earth.

For all of *TNG*'s high watermarks during the third season—and there were quite a few—it was "The Best of Both Worlds" that elevated *The Next Generation* from *Star Trek* Little League to the majors. Consistently voted the all-time favorite *TNG* episode in fan polls, this episode ranks right up there with *TOS*'s "The City on the Edge of Forever."

And, according to Ira Steven Behr, it had everything to do with Michael Piller.

"Michael came to me while I was working on 'Transfigurations,'" Behr recalls, "and said that he wanted to write the two-parter with the Borg. A show about Picard being 'Borgified.' I said, 'Okay, we'll get everyone together and we'll break the story.'

"At that point, Michael's relationship with the writing staff was not good, to say the least. He'd distanced himself from them. He wanted me to deal with them and keep things going through the pipeline, so he could be in his room polishing the scripts. He knew that most of the staff was going to jump ship at the end of the season.

"So he said to me, 'You know what, I'm going to do this one on my own. I'll give you the story to read, but I just don't want to go into the room with the staff. I think I can do this one. I think I have a feel for it.' That's what he said. 'I think I have a feel for this one.' And off he went.

"And what he did was brilliant. By Borgifying Picard, Michael tapped into Picard's humanity. Because at the time, the fans were bitching about Picard. They'd say, 'He's too cold.' And, 'He isn't Kirk.' But by Borgifying Picard—which is something that Michael really related to, because there was a little bit of Borg in *him*—it led the way to 'Family,' and all the episodes that really made the series step up.

"And he did it himself. He *imagined* it himself. He *got it* himself. And I don't think he gets the credit he deserves," Behr says, "for single-handedly validating the series. It's what kept the franchise alive."

After "The Best of Both Worlds, Part I" aired, the fan community went crazy. Not only was it the first *Star Trek* two-parter since *TOS*'s "The Menagerie" (twenty-three years earlier), but it was the first *Star Trek* cliff-hanger *ever*.

Which meant that the show's audience was doomed to chew its collective fingernails for *three months* until they found out what happened.

Although Ira Behr loved the episode, he didn't really understand the tension. "When I gave Michael Piller my notes on the script—all pretty minor, by the way—I said, 'Michael, that's a *terrible* cliff-hanger. The last line is "Fire," and *no one's* going to think that Borg ship's going to explode.' But Michael just said, 'Don't worry about it.' Then when I watched the episode I *still* felt that it didn't work, because I knew the tension of the cliff-hanger would end just thirty seconds into the beginning of the next season."

From the standpoint of logic and sheer craft, Behr was right on. Of *course* the cube carrying Picard wouldn't blow up under fire from the *Enterprise*. But somehow, that wasn't the point. The scene was taut, Ron Jones's musical sting was sharp—and that TO BE CONTINUED card after the screen went to black was as brutal as the impact of a photon torpedo.

And there was another factor at work, ratcheting up the tension. The fans had heard a rumor—one that, in fact, was also drifting around the Paramount lot—that Patrick Stewart's contract discussions with the studio had stalled. Concerned members of the audience feverishly debated on computer bulletin boards whether or not this meant Picard *was* going to get blown to smithereens in the first episode of season four.

In a less public forum, Michael Piller had his own cliff-hanger going. Believing his tenure on the series to be a good experience but *not* the way he wanted to spend the rest of his career, he'd only agreed to do *TNG* for a year. But by the end of the season, Piller explained in a 2002 interview, "I was struggling with whether or not to stay. And this came out in the screenplay for Part I, as Riker addressed similar issues." It wasn't until Piller had a chat with Gene Roddenberry that he made up his mind. "Gene came in at the end of the season and said, 'Look, this show needs one more year to really catch fire, and it would mean a lot to me if you came back one more year to see it through.'

"To have the man come to me and ask me to do that," reflected Piller, "how could I say no?"

But it did put Piller in a real jam.

"I'd had no intention of coming back when I wrote Part I," he said with a sheepish smile. "I had *no idea* how to beat the Borg. I figured it would be somebody else's problem!"

TO BE CONTINUED...

Where's Waldo?

Actually, no one with that name is known to have worked on *The Next Generation*. The more pertinent question is, "Where's Patrick, Brent, Michael, Marina, and Wil?" They're not here either, nor is Rick Berman, proving that a "class photo" for a television production is a very difficult thing to engineer; in fact, a full gathering was rarely attempted—and never accomplished—on *TNG*.

The problem is that not every member of a production team is on the set at any given time. Some are off-site at looping sessions, or at the local hardware store, shopping for alien paraphernalia. One or two are confined to makeup chairs, having a latex appliance glued to his or her forehead. Others are setting up camera equipment for a crucial scene during a week when the schedule is too tight to interrupt. It's all in the nature of the beast. And, of course, the beast (of the week, that is) isn't there, either.

This memorable attempt, set up at Gene Roddenberry's request during the final shooting days on "The Best of Both Worlds, Part I" at the end of season three, is as good as it ever got. Sharp eyes can pick out Jonathan Frakes, Gates McFadden, Michael Piller, Ronald D. Moore, Rick Sternbach,

Michael Okuda, director Cliff Bole, writing intern Hilary Bader, Susan Sackett, and the Great Bird himself, along with some of the best behind-the-scenes talent in Hollywood.

Even sharper eyes will recognize that they're standing in the middle of "Planet Hell," a.k.a. Stage 16, dressed up this particular day as Jouret IV, former home to the New Providence colony wiped out by the Borg.

The third season marked a transitional period for *The Next Generation*; the fourth was when the series began to reap the benefits of the massive effort that had gone into it. In October 1990, its eightieth episode aired, demonstrating not that this second outing was better than its predecessor (which left the airwaves in 1969 after only seventy-nine episodes), but that it clearly was going to live longer . . . and prosper, too. Soon Paramount's licensing operation, once an ancillary of motion picture marketing, would become a stand-alone entity, a testament to the impressive revenues that *Star Trek* merchandise was earning. Braced by an endorsement from Viewers for Quality Television—the first ever to be given to a non-network show—and two technical Emmys, the series' popularity continued to build.

Behind the scenes at *The Next Generation*, the writers' room saw a few more "comings and goings," but stability would be at hand by season's end. In a personnel shift that was curiously parallel to one the previous year, Lee Sheldon, *TNG*'s newest writing producer, brought in Jeri Taylor to rewrite a problematic script; then Sheldon bowed out after eight episodes and Taylor stayed on.

Although Taylor was a veteran producer of *Quincy, M.E.*; *Magnum, P.I.*; and *In the Heat of the Night*, she briefly wondered if she'd gotten in over her head. "Suddenly Human," the script that served as her entry point to the show, played to her charac-

ter skills. But while she knew how to write about people, she knew very little about *Star Trek* or its history. She quickly immersed herself in a self-prescribed *Star Trek* crash course, watching tapes of all of the *TNG* episodes to date, followed by *The Original Series*. She studied *TNG*'s in-house tech manuals, the show's writers' guides, and *The Making of Star Trek* (by Stephen Whitfield). By the end of the process, she was more versed in *Star Trek* than many of her predecessors. Of course, it would take some time to assimilate all that knowledge, but, as it turned out, she would have plenty of time. Originally contracted as a supervising producer, Taylor would rise in the *TNG* ranks to eventually share the executive producer title with Michael Piller and Rick Berman. The trio joined forces to create *Star Trek: Voyager*, which debuted in 1995, eight months after *The Next Generation*'s departure from the airwaves.

Opposite: Jeri Taylor's script for "Suddenly Human" won her a seat in the *TNG* writers' room.

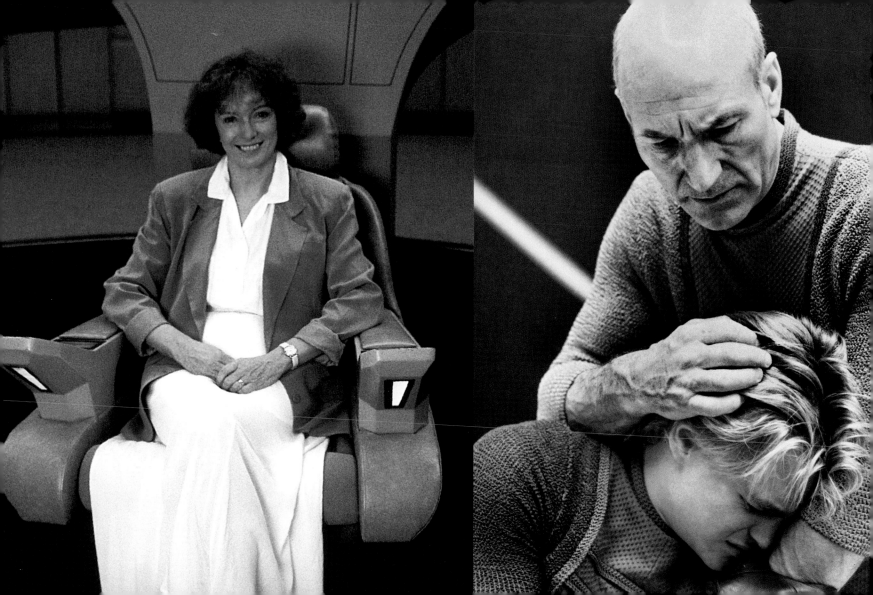

Riker: "How much do you remember?"
Picard: "Everything. Including some brilliantly unorthodox strategy from a former first officer of mine."

Following a failed attempt to destroy the Borg cube, Riker struggles to devise an effective strategy to stop the cybernetic invaders from assimilating the populace of Earth. Realizing that the Collective is using Picard's knowledge to defeat the humans, Riker sends an away team to the Borg cube to recapture the *Enterprise*'s assimilated captain. His goal: turn the tables on the Borg by using Picard's connection to the hive mind to destroy *them*.

"The first time I met Michael Piller," Brannon Braga recalls, "was in the summer of 1990. I showed up at his office on the Paramount lot to introduce myself as the new intern on the writing staff. I remember walking in and seeing him sitting at his computer, wearing one of his baseball hats, and he was saying, 'Beat the Borg. *Beat the Borg. How* do we beat the Borg?' He was still figuring it out."

"I had created an unsolvable problem," Piller confessed in 2002. "And to be honest, as I started writing the second part of the cliff-hanger that was supposed to resolve the story, I just didn't know what was ultimately going to beat them."

The idea of turning one of the Borg's main strengths into their collective Achilles' heel did not occur to Piller until two days before filming was set to begin. "I didn't discover it until the characters did," Piller explained. "I like to stand back as a writer and let the characters speak and [I] listen to them and sort of take notes."

Piller called the process "Zen writing"—and whether it involved channeling, osmosis, or clairvoyance, it seems to have worked. The personalities of the *TNG* characters were, by this time, so well established in his mind, that he was able to let go . . . and allow *them* to do the heavy lifting. *He* may have gotten them into this fix, but per Piller, it was the *crew*—including the Borgified Picard—that got themselves out.

Right: Locutus assimilates the following week's script.

In "The Best of Both Worlds," Michael Piller not only succeeded in getting under the skin of the previously unflappable Picard, but also influenced the future course of *Star Trek*. *TNG* had already dabbled in elements of continuity—with recurring themes, returning guest characters, and Worf's ongoing family problems—but the *Star Trek* franchise had never before dealt with the lingering pain of deep trauma. If Captain Kirk had been violated by the Borg during *The Original Series*, it's unlikely that he would have dwelled on the ordeal in later episodes. But the *TNG* writers refused to shy away from the personal fallout of this episode. Rather, they explored it, deepening the audience's understanding of just who Picard was. His experience with the Borg had torn a hole in his soul. Viewers saw hints of his internal agony in that single tear that trickled from his eye as the Borg tinkered with his brain, and in that somber, undecipherable look on his face as he stared out into space at the conclusion of the episode. Although produced after "Suddenly Human" and "Brothers," "Family" was pushed up to air one week after "The Best of Both Worlds, Part II." "Family" would press home the point that Picard, although once again physically whole, was

not yet healed. And other episodes, such as "The Drumhead," "I, Borg," and the *Deep Space Nine* pilot "Emissary," would verbally touch upon the scar tissue of his assimilation, as if to determine whether the wound was still tender. It was—and nothing made that clearer than the second *TNG* film, *Star Trek: First Contact*, where Picard's simmering feelings of angst and anger would at last boil over, nearly overwhelming the rational strategist so respected in Starfleet.

Inner conflict, the stuff of true drama! It took assimilation by the Borg for the *TNG* writers to transform Jean-Luc Picard into a fully realized human being.

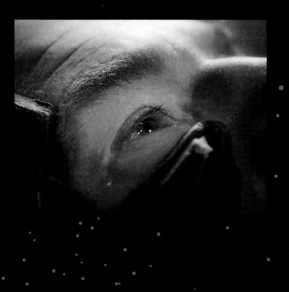

Rob Legato fought the battle of Wolf 359 twice . . . and lost both times.

As much as everyone on the *TNG* staff wanted to depict the infamous Battle of Wolf 359, shooting it was deemed prohibitively expensive. Thus, only the aftermath of the devastating battle was presented to the audience in "The Best of Both Worlds, Part II." But just a few years later, visual effects supervisor Rob Legato—who'd created the graveyard of ships for the *TNG* episode—was given the opportunity to re-create the conflict for the pilot episode of *Deep Space Nine*. Benjamin Sisko, the lead in that series, was one of the few Starfleet survivors of Wolf 359; it made sense to show his perception of the attack.

Legato, instructed to shoot the effects sequence weeks before the live-action photography on the *DS9* episode commenced, felt a bit like a kid in a candy store. "It was fun to do because I was allowed to make it up from scratch," he says. "There was no backlog of stock footage for it. The script said that they were right in the middle of this big, fierce, ugly battle, so I included tons of debris in all the shots. Ships that were burning, on fire, flying past the camera. I made sure that all of the debris had the correct names on it, the names of the ships

that were mentioned in 'The Best of Both Worlds' (*Tolstoy*, *Kyushu*, *Melbourne*, and *Saratoga*), so the episodes would tie together."

Alas, the producers ultimately decided to shoot the live action as if the Starfleet ships were *about* to enter into battle with the Borg, rather than joining them mid-fray. Which meant that Legato had to go back and *remove* all the extraneous ships and debris from his footage. "It was a heartbreaker," he says, "because it was a ton of work and very good-looking stuff—much bigger than anything seen on a *TNG* show."

Picard must decide what to do with a boy whose parents were killed by Talarians when he was an infant. Jono's grandmother is a Starfleet admiral who wants Picard to bring the boy home. But his adoptive Talarian father threatens war against the Federation if Picard doesn't turn him over. Although Picard's solution to the dilemma—let the boy make the decision—seems logical, he's unprepared for the consequences.

Like its predecessor, *TNG* has the reputation for producing shows that deal with "social problems." "Suddenly Human" reaches into that creative pot— but although it stirs the contents, the results are not what you'd expect.

Initially, the story follows a custody dispute, as Picard debates taking a young human boy from the Talarian warrior who killed his parents, and sending him back to his human grandmother. Were this *The Searchers* rather than *Star Trek*, the decision would be obvious. John Wayne had no compunctions about taking Natalie Wood away from the "savages" who'd killed her parents. As bigoted as Wayne's

character was in that film, returning a child to her blood kin seemed appropriate. Here, an additional element is thrown into the mix: unlike Wood's character, Jono will be allowed to choose which path he wishes to take.

Along the way, there's a thematic side trip into possible child abuse when Doctor Crusher notes that injuries Jono has sustained seem "unnatural." But that's a red herring. Ultimately, the important details in this story can't be determined with the naked eye—or a medical tricorder.

As the story plays out, Picard, long alarmed by the prospect of spending time around children, feels empathy for the troubled youth, and Jono learns he can enjoy being with humans. This seems to set up the audience for a group hug and a shuttle leaving for Earth as Jono's tough foster parent, Endar, silently gnashes his teeth.

But then something unexpected happens: Jono drives a dagger into the captain's chest! Why? Because he's a savage? No, the emphasis on external social issues has distracted us from the real crucible. This episode isn't about rights of adoptive parents, or child abuse, or the elite majority versus the noble savage. It's about what goes on within a child's mind

when he teeters on the brink of decision. Jono is so torn that he commits a heinous crime in the hopes that he'll be executed—thus eliminating the need to make a mature choice.

The solution presented by Picard is not cut and dry. It may even be wrong. But that's the way it is with "social problems." Even those channeled through *Star Trek*.

Opposite: Director Gabrielle Beaumont shows the gentlemen how it's done.

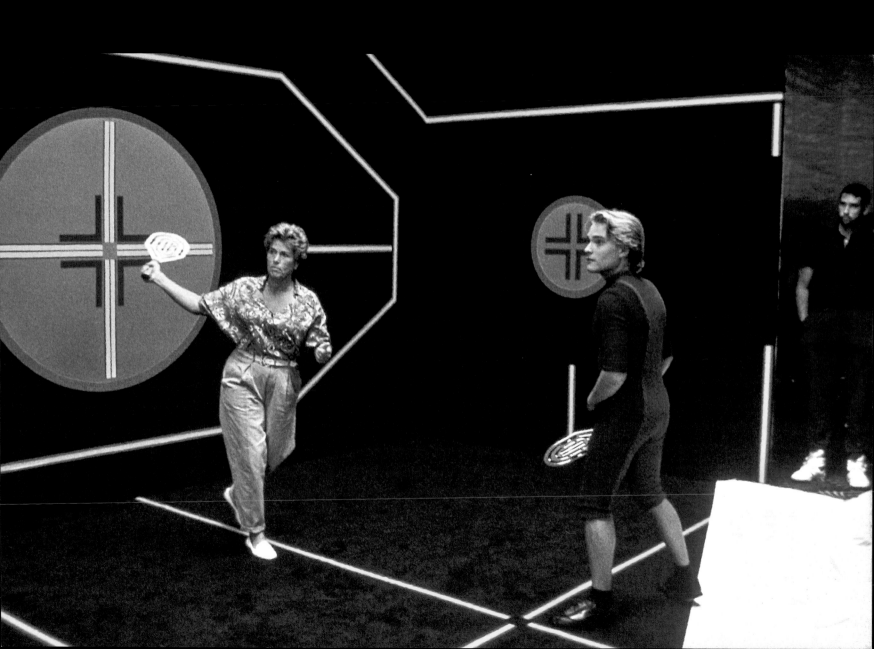

"They're brothers, Data. Brothers forgive."
—Crusher

An apparent malfunction in Data's programming causes the android to alter the course of the *Enterprise*, endangering the life of a desperately ill boy on the starship. Upon reaching the mysterious planet to which he's been drawn, Data abandons the ship and beams down to a laboratory, where he finds his creator, Dr. Soong. Soong explains that Data's behavior was triggered by a homing signal he sent out. He's summoned his creation because he's perfected a chip that will allow Data to experience human emotions for the first time. But before he can install it, Data's android "brother," Lore—who was also summoned by Soong's signal—arrives, and the specter of sibling rivalry rears its ugly head.

"When I had to play the character of Dr. Soong in 'Brothers,' I didn't have a clue as to who the character was," Brent Spiner says. "He was just a generic old man. It wasn't until I saw the makeup on my face that I knew what to do. At least seventy-five per- cent of that performance was due to Michael West- more. He put the idea onto my face, and I suddenly understood."

"The first thing I did in creating Brent's makeup for Dr. Soong was build up his cranial structure to suggest that he had more brain cells than a normal human being," Westmore explains. "We then did a full four-hour aging makeup on him. We had special contacts made for his eyes to simulate cataracts. I made an old-looking set of teeth to cover his real teeth. We covered his entire face with a thin layer of appliances. And we made pieces to cover the backs of his hands. For a scene where Dr. Soong touches Data's face, we had to apply Brent's makeup to the back of somebody else's hand so it could appear in the same frame."

"People started treating me like I was old, even though I had worked with them for three years at that point," Spiner adds. "Everybody was treating me with so much more respect, because I was a man who had lived a long life. And the older I acted between scenes, the nicer people treated me. It was incredible."

It only took a homing beacon and a shuttle to get Data, Lore, and Dr. Soong into a room together. But filming their meeting proved more difficult, given that the very singular Brent Spiner played all three characters. It required a bit of trickery that the hard-working visual effects teams would continue to improve upon over the course of the various *Star Trek* series. Under department heads Rob Legato and Dan Curry, they applied the techniques established here onto multiple Rikers, multiple Worfs, multiple Kiras (on *DS9*), et cetera.

Such trickery generally starts with a "locked-down" camera, with the tilt and pan releases screwed tightly in place, and the tripod "nailed" to the floor. This guarantees that there will be no camera movement *whatsoever*. "With the camera locked down, we determine which of the characters drives the shot, who's in the foreground, and who's in the background," Dan Curry explains. "Then we shoot the background character live in the scene, and shoot the foreground character against blue screen so we can composite him in.

"If circumstances allow," Curry continues, "we roll in a little portable blue screen so the characters are all in the same lighting setup. Otherwise we have

to take careful note of the lighting, because shooting the blue screen element later makes it harder to re-create the camera height, tilt, and focal distance.

"When the actor has to change costume, or go to makeup or hair, the changes can be very time-consuming," Curry says. "That determines whether we can shoot the blue screen at the same moment on the set, or whether we have to shoot it on another day, or even another stage."

These techniques work fine when the character in question is standing still. But that's not always what the director wants. "If one character walks around another," Curry explains, "we'll shoot a reference using a stand-in, in order to see where his shadow falls. Because if the shadow of one character falls on the other, we have to re-create it on the blue screen element. You can use a human being to cast the shadow, or, depending on the nature of the shot, it may be as simple as just waving a flag."

And then there are the times when a locked-down camera just won't do at all. "When directors design shots where the camera moves around the actor, we'll rent a motion control camera, along with an operator, and bring them in," says Curry. "The reason is simple. The camera has to repeat exactly the

same thing with each character; otherwise, the elements won't composite together properly. The motion control camera has a 'memory head.'"

In which case, it's the actor that has to be "locked down"—metaphorically speaking, that is.

Below: A difficult shot: Brent Spiner portrays both actors, courtesy of blue screen magic—but when Soong touches Data's face, the hand belongs to a photo double.

Opposite: An easier shot: Brent Spiner as Lore, and two photo doubles as Data and Soong.

With the *Enterprise* in dry dock for repairs, following its encounter with the Borg, Picard beams down to Earth to visit the family he hasn't seen in twenty years. The reunion is less than pleasant for the captain, who is still coming to grips with his recent brutalization by the Borg. As he considers abandoning Starfleet for a safer life on his homeworld, he must also deal with the long-simmering hostilities of his older brother, who resents Picard for abandoning his family responsibilities years earlier. In the meantime, Worf's human foster parents visit him on the ship, and Doctor Crusher shares a holotape of her late husband with their son, Wesley.

Coming near the middle of *The Next Generation*'s run, it's odd that one of the most popular episodes, "Family," is a drama served straight up, sans most of the usual "science fiction" elements. Sure, Wesley's father shows up in a holo-letter, but his message could as easily have been delivered in an envelope from a postman's canvas bag. And Worf's parents arrive by shuttle, but a Greyhound bus would have been as efficient. The delivery methods act only as interesting, but not really necessary, sci-fi affectations.

Rather than neutrino streams and nebulas, the episode concentrates on the emotional status of three characters. Worf's discomfort over the presence of his Russian parents is laced with humor, while Wesley's reaction to the message from his deceased father weighs in at the other end of the emotional spectrum. Picard's story, meanwhile, stands in the center, extending in all conceivable emotional directions. It also stands at the script's structural center; it's the reason the episode exists. And the reason that it almost didn't.

Following Picard's journey into Borg purgatory, the captain needs a vacation. He's been violated and traumatized. His journey home to reexplore his roots is *necessary*, as is the audience's desire to accompany him and share in the experience.

But not everyone felt that way.

"Gene [Roddenberry] didn't really like 'Family,'" relates screenwriter Ron Moore. "He felt that it was too much 'art,' and there wasn't any adventure. And he didn't like the conflict between Picard and his brother. I remember having a meeting in Gene's office where he pretty much wanted to throw out the story and the script, because he didn't buy the premise. At that time, Gene was still advocating the idea that in the future, humanity had solved most of its problems. That people in the twenty-fourth century didn't have personal conflicts.

"I walked out of that meeting thinking, 'Oh, my god, what are we going to do?'" Moore recalls. "Michael [Piller] just looked at me and said, 'Go and write it anyway, I'll deal with Gene.' And he did. I don't know what went on behind the scenes, but the story went through, and the script went through, and we did the episode."

"We spent a lot of time looking for Picard's country home in France," production designer Richard James says. "Finally, we found the exterior of a suitable house in Sherman Oaks, north of Los Angeles, but then we had to find the vineyard. In the script, the house and the vineyard are right together, but, of course, the locations weren't that way. We found the vineyard somewhere else, way out in the valley.

"While we were looking, I told [director] Les Landau, 'The house has to have a row of trees, and the vineyard has to have a row of trees.' And Les said, 'Why?' And I explained, 'Because the fight is going to bring Picard and his brother to the trees, and when they fall through, they'll be on the other side. They'll fight until they fall into the mud in the vineyard.' Les said, 'How are we going to do that?' and I said, 'It's going to depend on the location.'

"Well, the house we found had a driveway. We poured dirt onto it to make it look like a country road, and then we poured similar dirt at the vineyard to make the ground match the dirt on the driveway. And fortunately, the driveway had a row of cypress trees, which I enhanced with our own shrubbery. Then, of course, I took that same shrubbery out to the vineyard and enhanced the trees there.

"So in the episode, the guys start fighting on one side of the trees and shrubbery, and when they get pushed through, we cut. After they fall through, they're rolling around in the dirt in the vineyard," James says with a chuckle, "which is some sixty miles away."

Right: A Chateau Picard wine label, created for the wedding scene in *Star Trek Nemesis*. We're told it was a very good year.

After a warp field experiment conducted by her son Wesley is aborted, Doctor Crusher finds that her familiar universe has been radically altered. One by one, her friends and colleagues seem to be vanishing, while the crew members that remain insist that the missing people never existed at all. Soon Crusher is alone on the *Enterprise*, unaware that the threatening vortex that's appeared on the ship is her only chance to return to the normal universe.

The *Enterprise* crew refers to it as "the master systems display console"; the *Star Trek* production crew just calls it "the pool table," because . . . well, that's what it looks like. Repurposed from the video display table seen at Starfleet Command in *Star Trek IV: The Voyage Home*, the master systems display console allows engineering personnel to quickly gauge the overall status of the *Enterprise*-D. Whether or not it can sustain a static warp field bubble *without* hazardous side effects (i.e., trapping some innocent bystander in an alternate reality) remains to be seen, but if you want to try it, make sure you have the Traveler on speed dial.

The *Enterprise* crew is caught in the midst of a civil war on Turkana IV, Tasha Yar's homeworld, when they try to rescue Federation engineers being held by one of the clashing factions. Although Picard doesn't trust either side, he accepts assistance from an opposing faction, in order to retrieve the engineers. The faction's representative proves to be Tasha Yar's younger sister, Ishara. Influenced by his friendship with the *Enterprise*'s former security chief, Data feels an immediate kinship with Ishara. Unfortunately, trustworthiness is not a familial trait.

"Data was far and away my *TNG* favorite," writer Joe Menosky says. "A great character, and a great actor, to write for. And probably the closest in spirit to *TOS*-type characters. The pleasure with Data was walking the line between android and human, and hinting at moments when a deeply vulnerable true humanity would be glimpsed beneath the machine. True humanity? Or was it just our imagination? That was the line. In 'Legacy,' that moment came through with the look on Brent's face in the last second before we cut to black. It was just wonderful."

Superficially, "Legacy" resembles earlier *TNG* episodes "The Hunted" and "The High Ground"; each dealt with fractious factions contributing mayhem to non-Federation planets. But some notable elements make "Legacy" stand out from the pack.

Tasha Yar's sister, Ishara, provides an emotional backdrop to what might otherwise be a cut-and-dry tale of "extract the Federation engineers from the turf wars below." Tasha's former companions aboard the *Enterprise* see in Ishara what they hope to see—a woman worthy of their trust and friendship, the brave bearer of their dead friend's "legacy." Even Data, who has no emotions, allows himself to be misled by Ishara—a nice contrast to his behavior at the poker game in the teaser, where Riker compliments the android on having become very difficult to bluff.

Another noteworthy aspect is symbolic. "Legacy" was the eightieth episode of *Star Trek: The Next Generation*. The final episode of *The Original Series* was "Turnabout Intruder"—episode 79. Accordingly, *TNG*'s cast and crew took note of this milestone by holding a small onstage party when they wrapped production, hoisting glasses to the future of *Star Trek*'s thriving "offspring." Even the

"Legacy" script marked the occasion—with a tongue-in-cheek inside joke. In his opening log, Picard notes that the *Enterprise* is bypassing its "scheduled archaeological survey of Camus II." The Camus II archaeological dig was the setting for "Turnabout Intruder."

Below: Director Robert Scheerer demonstrates positioning for a critical scene.

"Mr. Worf . . . A reprimand will appear on your record." —Picard

K'Ehleyr travels to the *Enterprise* to inform Worf of two vital facts: that Klingon leader K'mpec has been poisoned by one of the two contenders for leadership of the Klingon Council, and that Worf is the father of her young son, Alexander, who has accompanied her to the ship. Before he dies, K'mpec asks Picard to arbitrate the power struggle between Gowron and Duras, the two Klingons vying to become his successor. K'Ehleyr learns that one of the two men has a duplicitous connection to the Romulans, but she's unable to identify the traitor until she learns the truth behind Worf's discommendation a year earlier—a delay that will imperil her life.

Perhaps Worf carries a GET OUT OF JAIL FREE card in his wallet. When he kills Duras in "Reunion," he defends his actions with a simple, "I have acted within the boundaries of Klingon law and tradition." Picard lets him off with a reprimand, even though Worf is a Starfleet officer who carried out that act within the boundaries of a Starfleet vessel.

What makes the *Enterprise*'s resident Klingon immune to punishment?

"Worf is a character who operates more from the heart than the head," explains Ron Moore. "There are times when his emotions and his sense of honor and his sense of right and wrong override what Starfleet might consider the proper way to go."

Not that this excuses his behavior. It's just hard to hold him to the same standards as his crewmates when doing so would gut the essence of his core personality.

But as a rule, Moore notes, he does feel that the central characters of a series should "pay consequences for their actions." Thus, he would be harder on Worf a few years later, when the Klingon committed another serious infraction in *Deep Space Nine*'s "Change of Heart," which Moore wrote. There, Worf defies orders by turning his back on an assignment that may save millions of lives, in order to save only one: his wife Jadzia.

Worf's commander, Captain Benjamin Sisko, takes the matter very seriously, but once again special circumstances keep the Klingon out of the brig, as Sisko explains:

"I don't think Starfleet will file any formal charges. Even a secret court martial would run the risk of revealing too much about their intelligence operations. But this will go into your service record. . . ."

Great. Right next to the one filed by Picard.

Opposite: Director Jonathan Frakes plans Worf's next move.

"The script to 'Reunion' called for a special Klingon bladed weapon," visual effects producer Dan Curry recalls. "I'd always been irritated by weapons in movies that were designed to *look* cool but in reality couldn't be handled practically. I'd been imagining a curved weapon partially influenced by Himalayan weapons like the kukri [the wickedly curved knife of the Gurkhas of Nepal, arguably the most renowned fighting knife in the world]. I was also thinking about the Chinese double ax, Chinese fighting crescents, and the Tai Chi sword. I combined elements of all those things in order to come up with an ergonomically sound weapon."

Curry made a foam core version of his design, an admittedly flimsy prototype of what would come to be known as the *bat'leth*, and showed it to Rick Berman. "And Rick liked it," Curry notes. No one knew at the time that the weapon would become a kind of symbol for the species. "Now you seldom see a picture of a Klingon without a *bat'leth* in his hands," Curry adds with a smile.

Curry then began to work with Michael Dorn, developing a fighting style to go with the weapon. "We didn't want the Klingons simply to be vicious," he says, "so I thought it would be an interesting dichot-

omy if they had a very subtle internal quality, as well as being incredible fighters—like the samurai during Japan's Tokugawa period, who were dedicated to poetry as well as sword-fighting. We started primarily with Tai Chi, so we could practice in 'slow motion' and have that meditative quality, but I made the style more clawlike and scary-looking by combining it with Hung Ga, a very aggressive Chinese style, and Tae Kwon Do, which is a Korean style." The result: *Mok'bara*, the ritual Klingon martial art.

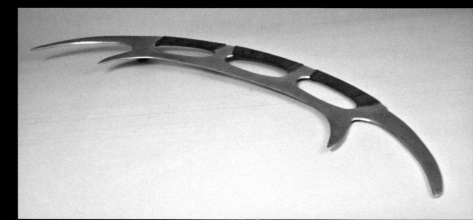

Sometimes the past comes back to haunt—or humor—you. Particularly when a part of that past was hidden under Klingon makeup. A case in point:

In 2010, as executive producer on the television series *Caprica*, Ron Moore hired a writer whose credits included the screenplay to the feature *Lara Croft: Tomb Raider* and numerous episodes of TV's *Friday Night Lights*. The writer's name was Patrick Massett.

"We were in a writing session," Moore recalls, "and at some point Patrick said, 'You worked on *Star Trek*, right?'

"And I said, 'Yeah, I worked there for many, many years.'

"And he said, 'Well, I actually played a Klingon.'

"And I said, 'Are you serious?'

"And he said, 'Yeah. I played this character that Worf killed with a sword.'

"'*Duras?* You played *Duras*?'

"'Yeah, that's the character.'

"And I looked at him and said, 'Are you insane? I *wrote* that episode. In fact, I *created* your character in "Sins of the Father."'

"We were just astonished," Moore says. "The currents had brought us together after all these years in such an unexpected way."

During an away mission on Alpha Onias II, Riker falls unconscious and awakens to discover that sixteen years have passed. He's told that he's now captain of the *Enterprise*, and that Picard is a Starfleet admiral who travels in a Romulan warbird. Doctor Crusher explains that a long dormant virus in Riker's system recently became activated and destroyed his memories of everything that transpired in his life during the past decade and a half. Riker has difficulty accepting this bizarre revelation, and becomes increasingly convinced that he is the victim of a diabolical Romulan charade designed to make him reveal classified information. The truth, however, is even stranger than that.

Opposite: Creating a successful aging effect does not necessarily mean covering an actor's face with rubber. "Future Imperfect" called for more subtlety. "Each member of the *TNG* cast was supposed to have aged sixteen years," explains Michael Westmore. "The producers decided that rather than having each actor sit in a makeup chair for two or three hours, it would be a better idea to suggest their age by changing the hairstyles, and maybe doing a little rubber stretching around the eyes. I thought it was a sensible approach, because most of the actors were in their thirties, and even aging them sixteen years would only put them somewhere in their forties. Most people don't look dramatically different at that age, and it would have been a waste of time and energy using prosthetics to achieve that effect."

Two decades plus. That's a heck of a long time. Talk to someone who worked on *The Next Generation* and some things come back as if they happened yesterday. Others . . .

"Didn't I have a kid on the show?" asks Jonathan Frakes.

Frakes has been talking about the *TNG* episodes that he directed. "Reunion" brings to mind a little boy who played Alexander. . . . But then Frakes recalls another young boy from another episode, one that he *didn't* direct. Did he have a son? he wonders, unsure.

Not quite, he's told. There was, however, a little alien boy who pretends to be your son. Barash, a.k.a. "Jean-Luc Riker," a.k.a. "Ethan."

It all comes back. "Ah," he says. "'Future Imperfect.' I saw a little piece of that the other day. The show is on *everywhere* now." He laughs.

Forget a detail and it's bound to come back to you in reruns. Barash/Jean-Luc/Ethan. One child actor (Chris Demetral) who bore a lot of aliases on his young shoulders. One part of a fond memory frozen in time.

Opposite: "Father" and "son" visit with Gene Roddenberry on one of the Great Bird's rare set visits.

After learning that he finally has been accepted into Starfleet Academy, Wesley welcomes Picard's invitation to accompany him on an away mission that could resolve a mining dispute on an arid world. But following a shuttle crash and a near disastrous search for water that leaves the captain near death, Wesley finds himself charged with the weighty responsibility of keeping both himself and Picard alive until a rescue team can locate them.

Right: Director Corey Allen works with Wil Wheaton and veteran character actor Nick Tate. Once a promising actor (*Rebel Without a Cause*, *Sweet Bird of Youth*), Corey Allen veered from his thespian aspirations to focus on directing in 1970 and never looked back. By the time he received the call to direct the pilot for *TNG* in 1987, he'd helmed multiple episodes of forty-seven different television series, and a slew of TV movies. In total, Allen directed five episodes of *The Next Generation*, including two of Wheaton's episodes as a guest star ("The Game," "Journey's End").

No one can be in two places at once.

Which is why Wil Wheaton quit his job on a hit TV show.

Wheaton had enjoyed a successful acting career before signing aboard Starfleet's flagship. Starting with his first break in a Jell-O Pudding Pops commercial with Bill Cosby, he worked regularly, starring or costarring in dozens of movies and TV series, including his leading role in the hit feature film *Stand by Me*. Then he joined the crew of the *Enterprise*. It took warp drive to slow him down.

"I was constantly having to pass on really good movie roles because I was on the series," Wheaton has explained on his blog site, WilWheaton.net. "I had been cast by Milos Forman to be in *Valmont*. . . . We were going to shoot it during the hiatus and the shooting schedule for *Valmont* would have carried me over about a week into the regular season schedule into *Star Trek*. So I would have had to sit out the first episode of the year. . . . So I said, 'I need to be written out of this particular episode because I'm going to do this movie. . . .' They said, 'We can't write you out because the first episode of the season is all about you.' . . . So I had to pass on the movie. And a couple of days before the season was to premiere,

they wrote me out of the episode entirely."

At that point, Wheaton says he knew it was time to leave *TNG*. Like former costar Denise Crosby, he left on good terms, and with his character heading off to the Academy, the producers left the shuttle bay doors wide open for return visits as a guest star. The plot of Wheaton's final episode as a regular cast member primarily focused on his character, and the writers gave him a great speech in the last act:

"In the past three years, I've lived more than most people do in a lifetime. I think I'm very lucky, no matter what happens. How many people get to serve with Jean-Luc Picard? Sir, you don't know this. No one knows this, because I never told anyone. All of the things I've worked for, school, my science projects, getting into the Academy, I've done it all because I want you to be proud of me. If there is one thing that I've learned from you, it's that you don't quit. And I'm not going to quit now. I've seen you think yourself out of worse problems than this, and I'm going to think us out of this. You're not going to die. I'm not going to let you die."

Opposite: Following the wrap of "Final Mission," cast and crew attend Wheaton's farewell party on the soundstage.

Following the *Enterprise*'s encounter with a cluster of two-dimensional life-forms, the crew discovers they're unable to resume course, and Troi finds she's lost her empathic powers. The ship's situation is dire; it's being dragged toward a spatial phenomenon that almost certainly will destroy it. Troi's situation is devastating only on a personal level. Unable to sense the emotions around her, she feels useless as the ship's counselor. Could the two events be interrelated?

As "The Loss" opens, Troi is conducting a therapy session with Ensign Brooks, who lost her husband five months earlier. Brooks expresses the belief that she's coping quite well, but Troi knows better. She suggests that Brooks is trying to avoid the pain of her loss, and with a few guided questions, she gets Brooks to bawl like a baby.

Which is good. It's all part of Troi's grief therapy model, apparently based on the teachings of Elisabeth Kübler-Ross, the twentieth-century psychiatrist who wrote *On Death and Dying*. Brooks has been stuck at the "denial" stage for months; her

"breakthrough" in Troi's office suggests that she may be ready to move on to a new stage.

But let's leave Brooks and turn our attention to the real patient in this story—Counselor Troi.

Troi loses her empathic abilities seconds after Brooks leaves her office, her powers overwhelmed by the giddy emotions of some two-dimensional life-forms that are clustered around the *Enterprise*. They're playing havoc with the ship's systems, and as the crew struggles to get the starship under control, Troi goes through Kübler-Ross's "five stages of grief":

1. Denial—*"The Betazoid brain has a remarkable ability to heal itself. This condition could just reverse itself in time. . . . I may be perfectly fine by tomorrow."*

2. Anger—*"If our positions were reversed, I wouldn't have been in here treating skinned elbows while you were lying passed out on your office floor. I'd have been there a lot sooner. Perhaps in time to prevent this from ever happening!"*

3. Bargaining—Because she quickly decides the situation is hopeless, Troi skips right past this stage to leap into the wallow of depression. Seeing as she's the one with the degree, who are we to stand in her way and tell her to play by the rules?

4. Depression—*"It's time I accept the truth, Captain, and resign as ship's counselor. I can no longer fulfill my obligations. What other option is there?"*

5. Acceptance—*"I never fully appreciated how difficult and how rewarding it is to be human. . . . There is something to be learned when you're not in control of every situation."*

Interestingly, Troi reaches the "acceptance" stage only *after* she has regained her empathic abilities. Well, it's easy to be gracious and say nice things about being human when you're so much *more* than human, isn't it? Would she have reached acceptance *without* regaining her powers? Quite possibly—so long as her human friends kept her plied with chocolate.

"Second Officer's personal log, stardate 44390.1. Record entry for transmission to Commander Bruce Maddox, Cybernetics Division, Daystrom Institute. Dear Commander Maddox, in reference to your most recent letter, I agree that your study lacks sufficient primary source information on my programming and operation. Therefore, in response to your request, this correspondence will include a complete record of my activities during a normal day, with particular emphasis on my perceptions of friendship . . ."
—*Data*

As Data contemplates the impending marriage of his friend Keiko Ishikawa to Transporter Chief Miles O'Brien, he learns about the peculiar minutiae—such as last-minute jitters and ballroom dancing—that surround human nuptials. At the same time, he investigates the apparent death of the Vulcan ambassador whom the *Enterprise* was ferrying to the Neutral Zone in order to conduct treaty negotiations with the Romulans.

Two separate ideas were floating around the *TNG* writers' offices: follow a single character throughout an entire day aboard the *Enterprise* (a pitch submitted by freelancer Harold Apter), and celebrate a wedding on the ship. After someone suggested marrying the two plots, the show moved into active status.

Delegating Data as the character to follow was a no-brainer; as the only crewman who didn't sleep, viewers would be able to observe his activities around the clock. Choosing Miles O'Brien and Keiko Ishikawa—the latter a character who'd never been introduced to viewers—as the happy couple was less of a sure thing. After all, O'Brien hadn't even possessed a first name until the episode "Family." But he did have his supporters; throughout season three, Ira Steven Behr voiced the opinion that O'Brien, as portrayed by Colm Meaney, was the series' best onboard representative of an "everyman," and Behr's interest influenced the character's development. When the writing staff conceived the wedding to enhance Data's day, O'Brien was standing in the right place, at the right time.

Writer Ron Moore was particularly taken with the minutiae surrounding life aboard a Starfleet vessel. "I liked establishing all the little rituals that would make up a day on the *Enterprise*," Moore says. "I remember reading in Stephen Whitfield's book *The Making of Star Trek*, that, per Gene Roddenberry, certain lights on the ship were dimmed at times, to simulate day and night. Gene felt that human beings were accustomed to diurnal cycles, with darkness and light triggering certain biorhythms. I wanted that to be a part of the episode. That's why when Data takes over in the morning, he turns the lights up, and at the end of the day, the lights on the bridge go down. I also liked the formality of somebody relieving somebody else on the bridge. That stuff contributed to what turned out to be a great, fun episode."

The ballroom dancing subplot came from Apter, who was given the first crack at the teleplay. "In Apter's version, there was a scene on the holodeck where Data literally does John Travolta's big disco number from *Saturday Night Fever*," Moore recalls with a chuckle. "Complete with the white suit. It was *hysterical*! Everybody knew we were never going to do that, but the idea of including some dancing was then in the air. And given the fact that Brent Spiner is a bit of a hoofer, well, it was a natural opportunity to have Data dance."

That, and the fact that Gates McFadden was an accomplished choreographer—with three Jim Henson theatrical productions under that section of her résumé—ensured that someone would be cutting the rug while others were cutting the cake.

Despite Keiko's transient case of cold feet prior to the ceremony, the O'Brien-Ishikawa union apparently was a success. Keiko would show up in seven additional episodes of *TNG*, including one in which she gives birth to daughter Molly, and then figure prominently in the plots of nineteen episodes of *Star Trek: Deep Space Nine*.

"It's not you I hate, Cardassian. I hate what I became because of you." —O'Brien

Picard is shocked when a highly respected starship captain apparently turns renegade and begins destroying Cardassian vessels. Captain Maxwell claims that the Cardassians, who recently signed a treaty with the Federation, are secretly rearming for war. Unfortunately, he has no proof. Picard demands that Maxwell—Transporter Chief O'Brien's former commanding officer—surrender his ship, but Maxwell refuses. Reluctant to fire on a fellow officer, Picard asks O'Brien to convince his old comrade to surrender peacefully.

Heart of Darkness, Joseph Conrad's novella about the search for an official who's gone rogue, has served as the jumping-off point for numerous creative efforts, perhaps most famously the film *Apocalypse Now*. As she wove threads from Conrad's story into the teleplay for "The Wounded," Jeri Taylor also presented another theme: that former enemies don't necessarily become fast friends just because a war has ended. That premise demanded a new "enemy," and so were born the Cardassians.

TNG had, by this point, tested several new adversaries for its intrepid heroes. The producers discovered that the avaricious Ferengi didn't offer much threat, while the Borg were entirely *too* threatening to use on a regular basis.

But the Cardassians clicked: a powerful, intelligent race that speaks calmly, yet seems quite sinister. Their appearance plays into an innate human distrust of cold-blooded creatures, making them a perfect species upon which to build enmity. And build the *Star Trek* writers would, not only in future *TNG* episodes, but also in *Deep Space Nine*, where the Cardassians would be featured as the main "bad guys."

Taylor's teleplay establishes many details about the Cardassians, but the most memorable thing about them is their reptilian look, devised by Michael Westmore. "I created a twin row of bony ridges, which started from the peak of the eyebrows and ran all the way back into the hairline," he says. "Then ridges went down the sides of the neck and flared out to the shoulder tips, giving the Cardassians a strange, menacing appearance, like a praying mantis, or a king cobra." Perhaps the most distinctive Cardassian facial feature is the spoonlike indentation in their foreheads, inspired by a painting Westmore saw that portrayed a woman with—you guessed it—a spoon in the middle of her forehead.

The makeup influenced Robert Blackman's Cardassian costume designs, which had to accommodate the pronounced neck ridges. And in subsequent episodes, it also influenced casting. "A long neck and sharp, angular face lent itself to the makeup," Westmore notes. "So it was important to find actors with the proper physical characteristics." Marc Alaimo, who plays Gul Macet in "The Wounded" and who would appear on *DS9* as Gul Dukat, is said to have the perfect Cardassian physique.

Opposite: O'Brien sizes up a Cardassian in Ten-Forward. Note that the stars that typically appear outside of the window ports need to be added in postproduction.

The inhabitants of Ventax II are in a panic. A thousand years ago, they made a pact with the devil, Ardra. She granted them a millennium of peace and prosperity in exchange for their later enslavement. Time's up—and Ardra has arrived for her "due." Picard offers to arbitrate against the contract on behalf of the Ventaxians. But if he loses, Ardra warns, the Ventaxians won't be the only ones to lose their souls.

If "Devil's Due," with its hints of humor and "magical" threats, seems reminiscent of an original *Star Trek* episode, perhaps it's because it almost was.

Reportedly, the story was on Gene Roddenberry's wish list when he made his initial pitch to Desilu in the 1960s—but it didn't make the cut.

An updated version made it to script stage a decade later, when Roddenberry was devising the proposed television series *Star Trek: Phase II*. The *Enterprise* comes upon a planet where an old man named Zxolar lays dying. A thousand years earlier, Zxolar had entered into a contract with the energy creature Komether to bring his world "a thousand years of

joy." Now Komether has reappeared, prepared to claim the planet when Zxolar dies. Kirk proposes a trial to determine the validity of the contract, and Komether agrees; if Kirk loses, the creature will get the *Enterprise* as a bonus. Kirk eventually discovers that Komether's power stems from Zxolar's will, and manages to employ the old man's own willpower to exorcise Komether.

The episode *might* have been made—if not for a blockbuster called *Star Wars*. That prompted Paramount execs to pull the plug on *Phase II* and refocus on producing a more lucrative *Star Trek* movie instead.

Twelve years later, *TNG* producers realized that a writer's strike would leave them short of scripts. They dug into the old files and came up with two *Phase II* scripts they liked. One became "The Child," and was produced in season two. The other was "Devil's Due." Michael Piller ordered a full rewrite of William Douglas's script from Philip LaZebnik, then a writer on *Wings*. Among LaZebnik's most important changes was transforming the genderless energy being into Ardra, a sexy female foil for Picard.

Still, one can't help but wonder how Kirk would have responded if Ardra had appeared in *his* cabin and murmured, *"I could give you a night that would*

light fire in your dreams until you die." Or how Ardra might have responded if he'd taken her up on it.

Opposite: Director Tom Benko and Michael Westmore discuss character motivation with the Fek'lhr.

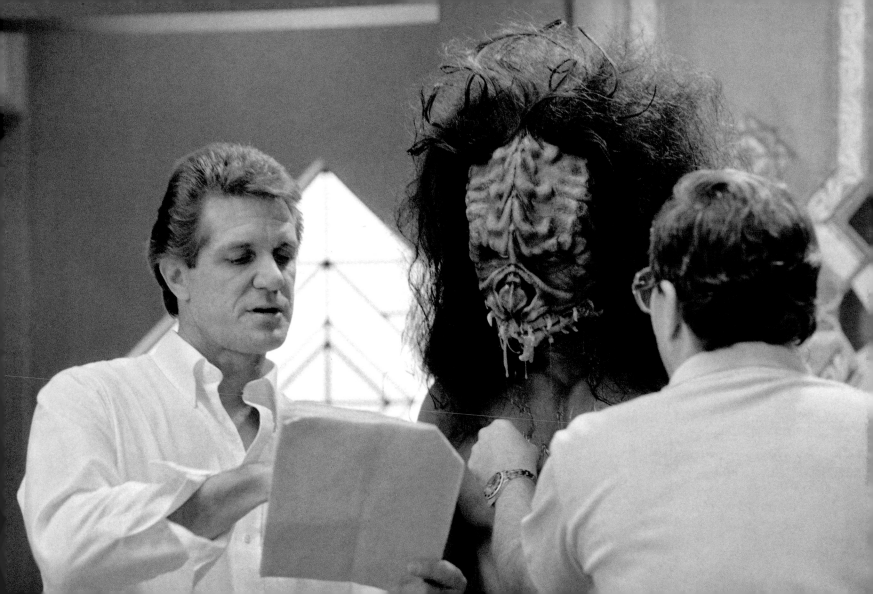

"The mirror . . . I came in here . . . I looked into the mirror. It wasn't me, Worf! It wasn't me! It was my face, but it wasn't me inside." —Troi

While en route to investigate a mysterious planet, the entire crew—with the exception of Data—is rendered unconscious by a wormhole that appears out of nowhere. After they revive, Data explains that they were unconscious for only thirty seconds—but a variety of clues discovered around the ship seem to indicate that he's lying. The android's subsequent attempts to prevent them from investigating that mysterious planet raise further suspicions. When Picard confronts him, Data finally admits that he was ordered to keep them from the planet *and* to lie . . . by Captain Picard himself.

They say that possession is nine-tenths of the law. But when it comes to *alien* possession—wherein a *TNG* script dictates that some *Enterprise* crew member will undergo mental hijacking—viewers can reasonably predict (about nine-tenths of the time) that the possessee will be Counselor Deanna Troi.

It's not that she's naïve or weak-minded, but as an empath with latent telepathic abilities, Troi apparently is unusually vulnerable to mental violation. You might say she's something of a parasitic psychic magnet.

"Clues" is the most clear-cut example of this vulnerability, with similar advantage being taken of the counselor in "Eye of the Beholder" (in which she gets swept up in an "empathic echo" of an earlier tragedy), "Man of the People" (she becomes the "receptacle" for the negative emotions of an amoral Lumerian), and "Power Play" (she's host to a malevolent disembodied prisoner of a penal colony . . . although, to be fair, O'Brien and Data are also possessed in this scenario). There are also more subtle inhabitations: a Douwd, who doesn't want her poking around in his business, fills her mind with music, in "The Survivors"; and a benevolent life-force—presumably attracted by their psychic similarities—actually implants itself within her body in order to experience life as a human, in "The Child."

Whether Troi's proclivity for possession is an asset or a problem for the crew is debatable, but one thing is clear: while she's on board, it's unlikely that anyone else will be cohabited by unwelcome guests

. . . at least nine-tenths of the time.

Below: Dixon Hill invites Guinan to the holodeck—giving Whoopi Goldberg an opportunity to ditch her Guinan duds for an episode.

Lanel: "I've always wanted to make love with an alien."
Riker: "Listen, Miss—"
Lanel: "Lanel."
Riker: "Lanel, I really have to get going. All the other aliens are waiting for me."
Lanel: "Oh, it's not so much to ask, and then I'll help you escape."
Riker: "It's not that easy. There are differences in the way that my people make love."
Lanel: "I can't wait to learn."

During an away mission to observe a pre-warp civilization, Riker is injured and brought to a hospital, where the locals quickly realize he is not from their world. Despite the attempted intervention of the planet's sympathetic science minister, Picard and Troi's efforts to retrieve the first officer are stymied by the government's concern about the social crisis that a widespread revelation of Riker's presence could trigger.

"First Contact" was probably more fun to film than

it was to write. You see hints of that in the number of writers' names attached to the final credits. There are five names associated with the teleplay: two different sets of writers working as teams (Dennis Russell Bailey and David Bischoff; Joe Menosky and Ronald D. Moore), and one additional writer—the show's head writer, Michael Piller—who eventually completed the final draft. A sixth name attached to the credits belongs to Marc Scott Zicree, who pitched the original story concept.

With all of that activity, it's easy to assume that the script for "First Contact" went through many changes, which Ron Moore confirms. "It was a particularly difficult story break," admits Moore. "I remember that the first go-round on that story had to do with Riker and a bunch of other people on a shuttlecraft. It went down on that planet and that sort of jump-started the whole 'first contact' thing. And I remember sitting in the writers' room, breaking that story over and over and over again, to the point where we realized it just wasn't working. We had to throw the whole thing out and start all over again. It was a difficult story to bring into focus."

It was likely Michael Piller's fondness for the basic premise—how *does* the Federation handle first-

contact situations?—that kept it alive, and his willingness to go toe-to-toe with the powers-that-be to temporarily remove an in-house roadblock that resulted in a viable script. Early versions of the script—the ones that didn't work—had been written from the point of view of the regular *TNG* characters. Piller realized that the story would be much more interesting if told from the perspective of the natives—but that went against the show's established format. He finally managed to convince Gene Roddenberry and Rick Berman to let him break format for this one episode, with the promise that he and the other writers wouldn't attempt to bend or break that rule again.

04 ‖ 192 "GALAXY'S CHILD"

"We're out here to explore, to make contact with other life-forms, to establish peaceful relations, but not to interfere. And absolutely not to destroy. And yet look what we have just done."
—*Picard*

Chief Engineer Geordi La Forge is thrilled when Dr. Leah Brahms comes aboard the *Enterprise*. Unfortunately, Brahms is nothing like the idealized holographic version La Forge fell for a year earlier. She's cold and humorless, not to mention married. To make matters worse, after she inadvertently discovers La Forge's holodeck program, he's the *last* person she wants to associate with. But when the *Enterprise* becomes the reluctant nursemaid to a newborn alien life-form that's draining the ship of its energy, Brahms and La Forge must work together in order to save both the baby and the ship.

Opposite: Dan Curry's storyboards for "Galaxy's Child" convey the *Enterprise*'s initial meeting with the mother creature—a fascinating first-contact sequence that abruptly turns tragic—and the ship's attempt to reunite the baby with others of its own kind.

STAR TREK
THE NEXT GENERATION
"GALAXY'S CHILD"
SHOW #190
DAN CURRY
1/21/91
②

Sc. 15 B ON MAIN VIEWER...
GENTLE PROBE CONTINUES
... CREATURE STARTS
TURNING.... USE TWICE?
SPECIAL BEHAVIOR

Sc. 16 CUT 1 EXT. SPACE...
CREATURE CONTINUES TO
ROTATE AS IT EMITS A
POWERFUL ENERGY BOLT...
ZAP CONTINUES AROUND
MANTLE
*SHOOT FROM BEST ANGLE
TO FEATURE LIFE FORM*

ROTATION
CONTINUES

Sc. 18 CUT 2 CONTINUATION OF
ACTION FROM ABOVE...
CREATURE IS HIT BY PHASER
... SPECIAL BEHAVIOR AS IT
REACTS TO HIT... LIGHTS
START TO FADE

Sc. 16 CUT 2 EXT. SPACE...
SHIP IS HIT BY ENERGY BOLT
NO SHIELDS
Sc. 18 CUT 1 SHIP FIRES PHASER

SHIP: 1G - 3Y DAN & RON 4.1 SHIPS
TC: 07:04:27.00

STAR TREK
THE NEXT GENERATION
"GALAXY'S CHILD"
SHOW #190
DAN CURRY
1/11/91
④

Sc. 60, 62 ON MAIN VIEWER
SEVERAL ADULT CREATURES
APPROACH OUT OF ASTEROIDS
Sc. 71 CREATURES ARE CLOSER...
CHANGE COLOR
Sc. 71B VERY CLOSE
Sc. 73 BABY JOINS THEM

Sc. 64A, 65A CREATURES
APPROACH ENTERPRISE...
CAMERA FOLLOWS CREATURES
MOVING OVER ASTEROIDS
REVERSE ANGLE OF ABOVE

10 SEC

CREATURES

Sc. 65B 74B RE COMP WITH BIGGER
ENTERPRISE AND <u>NO</u> ASTEROIDS
... CREATURES IN SLIGHTLY
DIFFERENT SYNC
(65A)
4 SEC

Dan Curry's concept renderings for the unnamed creatures—seen here in a charcoal sketch (for Junior) and in delicate pastels (for Mama)—would be realized in two formats. Model maker Tony Meininger built versions in fiberglass, while effects house Rhythm & Hues created the CG creatures, marking one of *Star Trek*'s earliest uses of the developing technology. While an early design for the space-being appears to have been based on a squid, the final version clearly resembles a horseshoe crab. Note that the baby, like many young'uns, has a proportionately larger head than Mama. Of course . . . assuming that *is* the baby's head.

GALAXY'S CHILD
BABY CREATURE

TOP VIEW

SIDE VIEW

12/17/90

DAN CURRY

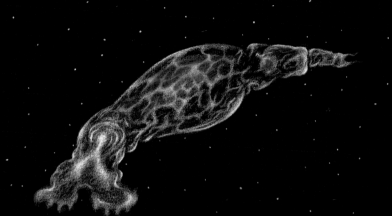

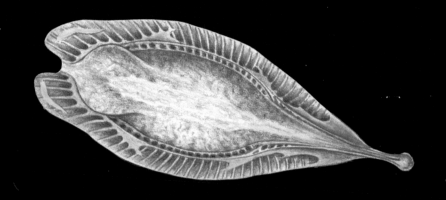

MOTHER CREATURE
DORSAL SIDE

MOTHER CREATURE

ABDOMINAL SIDE

DAN CURRY

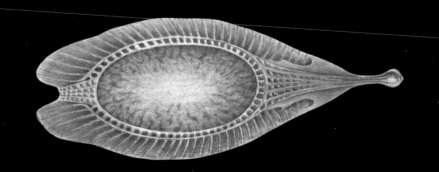

"Eyes in the dark. One moon circles."
—unidentified telepathic voice from the other
side of Tyken's Rift

The *Enterprise* finds the *Starship Brattain* drifting in space, all but one of its crew dead. The survivor, a catatonic Betazoid, offers no clues as to what happened—at least, none that make any sense. Soon, most of the *Enterprise* crew begins to exhibit the same symptoms noted by the *Brattain*'s captain in his logs: they have lost the ability to dream and are becoming mentally unstable. Troi, on the other hand, is suffering from bizarre nightmares that seem to match those of the injured Betazoid. Crusher recommends they leave the area, but the warning comes too late; the *Enterprise*'s engines no longer function and the ship is trapped in a spatial rift.

Opposite: Unable to experience REM sleep, crew members aboard the *Enterprise* experience increasingly frightening hallucinations. Only Troi possesses the key to freeing the ship; by using directed dreaming, she successfully gets a message to the inhabitants of a second ship trapped in the rift.

Rick Sternbach's orthographic drawings, which convey the shape and size of the *U.S.S. Brattain* through related two-dimensional views, served as the basis for the backlit graphics displayed on that ship's bridge (right). "I inked a top view and a side view," Sternbach says, "and then numerical callouts were added with bits of xeroxed typography and little pieces of black tape. After the black-on-white graphic art master was finished, we sent it out to be shot on high contrast Kodalith photonegative film. That film was then colored with bits of gel. That, by the way, is the way we did it in the old days, before ink-jet printing was available," Sternbach adds with a chuckle.

The *Brattain* model was a modified re-use of the *Miranda*-class *U.S.S. Reliant*, seen in the feature film *Star Trek II: The Wrath of Khan*.

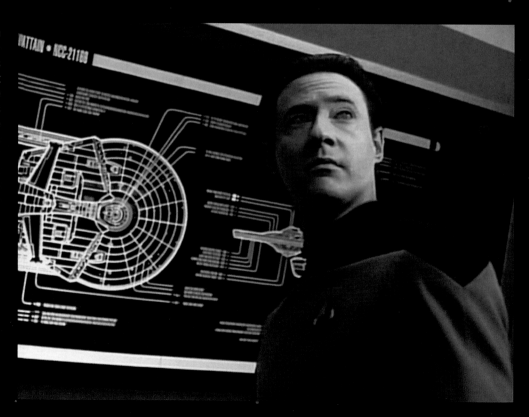

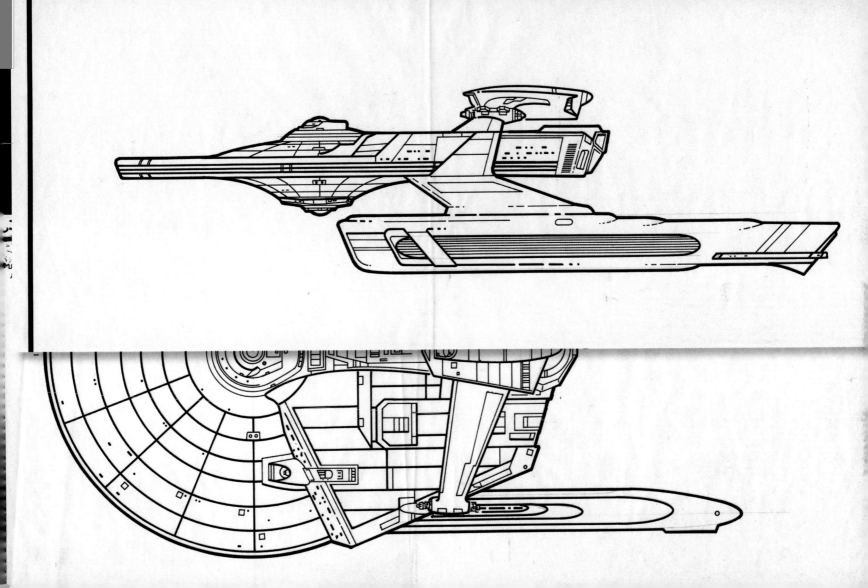

As La Forge and former shipmate Susanna Leitjen investigate the recent disappearance of colleagues who accompanied them to Tarchannen III five years earlier, Leitjen falls ill, her body infested by a parasite that is rewriting her DNA and turning her into an alien form. Crusher speculates that the same fate may have befallen their former crewmates, whose abandoned shuttles have been found in orbit around Tarchannen III. With Crusher working to save Leitjen, La Forge attempts to solve the mystery on his own . . . until he falls prey to the parasite and finds himself compelled to beam down to the surface of the planet.

Opposite: Rick Sternbach's rendering of the Tarchannen outpost. Note the helpful reminder on the exterior doormat.

Trek⁴ "Identity Crisis"
STARFLEET OUTPOST

PLEASE WIPE FEET

During his final year at the University of California, Santa Cruz, Brannon Braga won a scriptwriting internship offered through the Academy of Television Arts & Sciences. The prize: eight weeks with *Star Trek: The Next Generation*. "I applied for the internship out of curiosity, and I was amazed by the experience," Braga says. "I didn't realize that TV shows had 'writing staffs' and that they were written by groups of people under a 'showrunner.' It was magical. And towards the end of my stint, Michael Piller gave me a script to rewrite."

That script was "Reunion," and it paired him with Ron Moore, "the second youngest writer on staff after me," Braga notes. "It launched a long and fruitful partnership." The well-received joint effort resulted in Braga's being offered the opportunity to write a script on his own: "Identity Crisis." "I wanted to do a Geordi story because I really liked LeVar Burton as an actor, and I didn't think his character got enough screen time," he explains. "There was an old spec story about him laying around the office, and they gave it to me to develop."

It didn't take long for the novice writer's creativity to emerge. "I decided to do an homage to the movie *Blow-Up* using the holodeck. Michael and Jeri [Taylor] really liked that idea." *Blow-Up* is, of course, the classic 1966 film by Italian director Michelangelo Antonioni, in which a photographer attempts to prove that he's captured images of a murder by creating grainy oversize enlargements of his negatives. Braga enjoyed crafting the sequence in which Geordi attempts to extrapolate the presence of the peculiar Tarchannen life-forms using the holodeck, but claims his script wasn't a classic. "I wrote a couple of drafts and took it as far as I could," he says. "For a solo effort, I guess it was okay. Let me put it this way: I did a good enough job to get hired on staff."

How is it that Braga won the internship in the first place? "What impressed Michael Piller was that my transcripts showed that I got a D in a course on human sexuality," Braga recalls. "Michael thought, 'This guy must be interesting—how do you almost fail that class?'"

From small beginnings come great things. The future executive producer was on his way.

Right: The eager young intern gets a turn at the helm.
Opposite: Under the watchful eye of director Winrich Kolbe, Data hunts for beings that cannot be seen.

At first glance, it may *look* a bit like a wet suit covered in spaghetti, but rest assured, the transformation from human to Tarchannen "lizard person" involved *far* more effort than that. In fact, it took the makeup crew six hours to complete LeVar Burton's full metamorphosis—the longest makeup session ever done on *TNG*, according to Michael Westmore.

"In the first stages of the transformation from the parasitic virus, little blue veins began to appear on the victim's neck and face, and the fingers started to grow together," Westmore explains. "Each vein was a tiny appliance that had to be glued on, and the more the disease advanced, the more veins had to be added. We also created appliances for the hands and feet, to simulate the fingers and toes fusing together."

The further the transformation went, Westmore continues, the more complicated the makeup became. "We changed the nose and muzzle area, adding an appliance to make it look like a reptilian snout, and continued to add more blue veins. For the final stage, LeVar had appliances on his head, hands, and feet, and his entire body was covered with tiny blue veins. He had to stand there for six hours as five makeup artists glued on the veins, which then had to be hand-painted with fluorescent paint to make them glow."

Burton's makeup included contact lenses that were treated by an on-set ophthalmologist. "The doctor wiped LeVar's eyes with a special stick normally used for glaucoma testing, which makes the eyes glow when exposed to ultraviolet light," explains Westmore.

Although Burton's makeup was the most intense, Westmore's team also had to transform guest star Maryann Plunkett, and Los Angeles radio personalities Mark (Thompson) and Brian (Phelps), who were eager to work on the series. "Mark and Brian were too busy for fittings, so we made them suits that could be slipped on in pieces," Westmore notes. Unlike the transformed Burton, who had a prominent close-up on the transporter pad, the disc jockeys' scene was filmed under ultraviolet light on a darkened set, so the difference in appearance wasn't noticeable to viewers. But preparing them still took time. "Even with the prepainted suits, it took two hours to glue everything on them," he adds. "On the day they were filmed, the two of them actually conducted their daily radio show from our studio."

The crew discovers an alien probe near the malfunctioning Argus Array telescope. As La Forge and Reg Barclay attempt to examine the probe from a shuttle, it emits an energy surge, knocking Barclay unconscious. He recovers quickly, but it's soon clear that Barclay is a changed man, a super-genius who knows how to fix the telescope in a fraction of the time it would normally take. As the crew struggles to adjust to Barclay's amazing new abilities, he surprises them all by connecting his brain to the ship's computer and putting the *Enterprise* on course for an unknown destination thirty thousand light-years away.

Joe Menosky wrote "The Nth Degree" as an homage to the classic science fiction short story (and later novel) "Flowers for Algernon," Daniel Keyes's award-winning tale of a mentally challenged man who undergoes experimental brain surgery to increase his intelligence. The surgery works—but only temporarily. Barclay's transformation is also temporary, the result of alien intervention. "Writing for Barclay was a bit like writing for Data—you just knew you couldn't lose," relates Menosky. "And

it's the only episode I managed to do during my two years on staff where I pitched the idea, wrote it, and turned in a first draft that was basically shot as is. So it was a pure and clean experience for me."

Of course, one person's pure and clean experience is inevitably someone else's problem.

"The problem was with the last act," explains Rob Legato, who directed "The Nth Degree," his second such assignment for *TNG*. "In the original draft, the explanation for why Barclay had become what he had become wasn't very satisfying. We didn't know how to play the creature at the end. Benevolent? Godlike?

"And we needed more magic. In the original version, the alien was going to board the ship, and no one really liked that—too normal. A character just standing there on the bridge is flat and not so amazing to look at. Appearing on a viewscreen, that's kind of flat too. What, we go all this way to see a guy *on the screen*?"

Legato, who also oversaw visual effects for the episode, eventually opted to create a 3-D effect wherein the Cytherian's huge head would appear to pop out of the screen. That, in turn, would allow him to have a literal face-to-face conversation with Picard.

At the same time, Menosky dialed back the alien creature's behavior from menacing to inquisitive and friendly. "We've done many shows where ship members were taken somewhere against their will and then released," Legato explains. "We wanted to find a different way to play this encounter."

Below: The director of the episode compares notes with the director of the play in the episode.

The captain and Vash are reunited when the *Enterprise* hosts an archaeology symposium, but their disparate personalities soon have them sparring instead of spooning. Enter Q, who offers to do Picard a favor by getting him and his ladylove back together again. When Picard rejects the notion, Q transforms the captain into Robin Hood and sends him, Vash, and several members of Picard's senior staff to Sherwood Forest for a less than idyllic romp.

Opposite: Picard's Robin Hood duds—sans tights—and Vash's medieval-style Maid Marian gown from "QPid."

When we last saw Ira Steven Behr, he had left the frenetic world of television production for the more glamorous lifestyle of "feature film writer" . . .

"Michael [Piller] called me up and said, 'Someone pitched a story about King Arthur and Guinevere, where Picard would be Arthur on the holodeck—and it's not working,'" Behr says. "'Would you like to come in and talk it over?'

"I felt kind of bad that I had jumped ship on Michael, and I was waiting for the rewrite notes on this feature I did for Warner Bros., so I said, 'Yeah, I'll come in.' But then I started thinking about it: If we make Picard King Arthur, he's going to be the guy who does the whole Camelot thing of 'Might does not necessarily make right; let's govern peacefully.' Well, every episode of the show is about trying to make peace in the galaxy, so that just sounds boring. So I said, 'What about Robin Hood? Why don't we try that?' I knew that Michael was a fan of the old Errol Flynn movie and so was I. And Michael said, 'Yeah, absolutely—let's do that.' So I wrote it, g   atch them do the sword fight scene on the set and all that. I wrote a whole script and they shot it while I was *still* waiting for my notes from the studio. That's the difference between TV and mov-

ies. That, and the fact that after a year and a half of working with them, they never made the movie."

On the other hand, few television shows have more impact on American culture than *Star Trek*. Months later, says Behr, he was in a bookstore and his eye fell upon a display of greeting cards. "I saw a picture of Worf as Will Scarlet, so I picked up the card and he's saying, 'I am *not* a merry man.' I thought, 'Wow.' I mean, what a strange world. I wrote an episode for Michael and here it is on a greeting card."

Right: The aforementioned card, part of Hallmark's popular line of licensed *Star Trek* products.

I PROTEST!

I AM **NOT** A MERRY MAN!

About that scene where Worf smashes Geordi's mandolin—was that a takeoff on the famous scene in . . . ?

"Yeah, it was," admits Ira Steven Behr. "Obviously it was a little nod to John Belushi in *National Lampoon's Animal House*. But it was also a little nod in my mind to the fact that at times I was not the biggest fan of the characterization on *TNG*. Geordi was a very sweet character who was kind of underused. He didn't have much of a dark side to him. He's the kind of human that Klingons would have devoured. And Worf—you know, from a Klingon perspective—I was sure that Worf would lie in bed at night thinking, 'Can't they at least let me kill *Geordi*?' So taking the mandolin and smashing it was the Klingon view of the Federation and the 'perfect society' the show portrayed."

Opposite: Note that props typically are not destroyed during rehearsals, so the mandolin remains intact during this run-through.

"You know, there are some words I've known since I was a schoolboy. 'With the first link, the chain is forged. The first speech censured, the first thought forbidden, the first freedom denied, chains us all irrevocably.' Those words were uttered by Judge Aaron Satie, as wisdom and warning. The first time any man's freedom is trodden on, we're all damaged." —Picard

An explosion aboard the *Enterprise* leads to a high-level investigation headed by Admiral Norah Satie, a retired officer renowned for her skill at exposing conspiracies. Satie quickly determines that a visiting Klingon officer was attempting to smuggle diagrams off the ship, but the Klingon denies any involvement in the explosion. Satie refuses to give up on her investigation, even after the explosion is proven to be an accident, and she accuses Picard of treason when he challenges her charges against an innocent crewman.

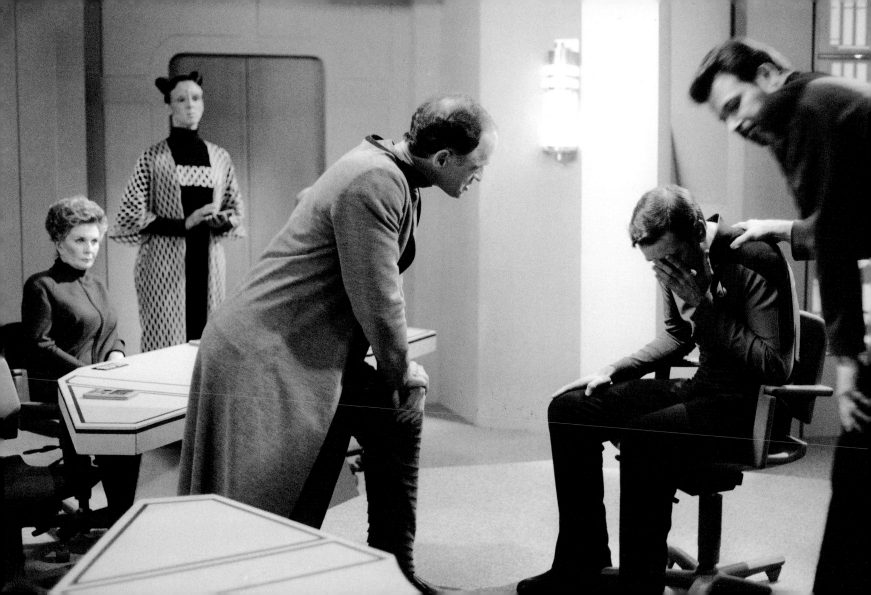

"We think we've come so far. Torture of heretics, burning of witches, it's all ancient history. And then, before you can blink an eye, suddenly it threatens to start all over again. . . . Villains who twirl their mustaches are easy to spot. Those who clothe themselves in good deeds are well-camouflaged." —Picard

The notoriety of the 1692 Salem Witch Trials, in which twenty innocent men and women were executed as "witches," is matched in America only by the 1954 Army-McCarthy Hearings held by the United States Senate's Subcommittee on Investigations. In the hearings, Senator Joseph McCarthy, under the guise of "anticommunism," accused his perceived opponents, and a long list of others seemingly picked out of the Hollywood phone book, of political disloyalty. The televised spectacle, which "blacklisted" many innocent people, remains a low point in American history. And it served as background material for "The Drumhead."

"God bless Jeri Taylor for writing that script," says Jonathan Frakes, who was assigned to the episode for his third time behind the camera. The script, of course, was exceptional, but it was a challenge, because essentially it all takes place in one room. "With courtroom dramas, there are only so many good camera angles," he explains. "It's kind of like being on the *Enterprise*'s bridge. There are only so many good shots—so you've got to hope the acting is good."

That wasn't a problem with "The Drumhead." Getting Golden Globe and Emmy Award–winning British actress Jean Simmons to play tightly wound Admiral Norah Satie was a dream come true for Frakes. "I cast her," he states enthusiastically. "I had the privilege of spending a year with her when I was in *North and South*. She played my wife's [actress Genie Francis] mom. I remembered Jean from *Guys and Dolls*, and from *Hamlet*. I've always thought she was arguably the classiest, most significant actor we had on the series," he says. "She was wonderful in the scenes with Patrick [Stewart]. And she was still so gorgeous."

That she was a classy doll goes without saying. But Frakes also discovered that Simmons was something else. "Jean was a monstrous Trekkie," he says with a laugh. "The show used to air on Wednesdays, I think, and on Thursdays she had a group of people who would get together to talk about the episode from the previous night. That thoroughly surprised me!"

Opposite: Great Bird meets Great Trekkie.

"I made a mistake in 'The Drumhead,' one that I have vowed *never* to make again," director Jonathan Frakes confesses. "Michael Dorn had to go somewhere. And he said, 'Is there any way you can shoot me out?' And I said, 'Oh, sure, man, don't worry.'

"I thought I had finished with his shots, and I turned to the first assistant director Brad Yacobian and told him, 'Dorn can go.' Brad's number one rule is: 'Never release anyone who's in the scene *until the scene is absolutely completed*.' Because," Frakes continues with a chuckle, "you never know if some *crazy* director's going to want to do a turnaround shot or pick something up.

"So an hour later—by which time Dorn's obviously ripped off his turtlehead and is in the wind—we set up a shot that was *pointing exactly* at the place where Dorn had been! There was absolutely *no way* to pretend that he shouldn't be there.

"Well, the great Marvin Rush was the director of photography on the show at that time, and Marvin looked at me, and I looked at him, and I said, 'We're screwed.' It was really a challenge. We had to design a shot where the camera pushed in on someone who would have been standing *next* to where Dorn had been, and when we came back out, we were on

the *other* side of where Dorn was.

"It was a very nasty lesson," Frakes says, laughing, "because it caused a totally unmotivated camera move based on friendship. I've always remembered that moment—the 'oh, shit' moment—and I want to send a message to other directors:

"'*Never release your friends*.'"

Timicin: *"I want very much for you to understand. Fifteen or twenty centuries ago, we had no Resolution. We had no such concern for our elders. As people aged, their health failed, they became invalids. Those whose families could no longer care for them were put away in death-watch facilities, where they waited in loneliness for the end to come, sometimes for years. They had meant something, and they were forced to live beyond that, into a time of meaning nothing, of knowing they could now only be the beneficiaries of younger people's patience. We are no longer that cruel, Lwaxana."*

Lwaxana: *"No, no, you're not cruel to them. You just kill them."*

Lwaxana Troi falls in love with Timicin, a scientist who is participating in an experiment to test his theories of stellar ignition. Timicin hopes to use the technique to save his world's dying star, but the experiment fails. Although Lwaxana encourages Timicin to continue his research, the scientist reveals that he can't. It's time for him to go home for "Resolution"—a ritual suicide invoked at the age of sixty to save children from the burden of a parent's aging.

⟡

She's daughter of the Fifth House, holder of the Sacred Chalice of Rixx, and heir to the Holy Rings of Betazed, but the "larger-than-life" persona of Lwaxana Troi often rubs people the wrong way, and verges, at times, on sheer caricature.

But not here. This time she actually seems to have fallen in love. She's found a man who appreciates her vibrancy, her wisdom, and her sense of humor—a man who's fallen in love with *her*.

But the relationship is not to be. Time's up for Timicin, who must fulfill his commitment to society by ending his life. Talk of "death panels" that urge granny toward euthanization may be political chicanery in our twenty-first-century society, but on Timicin's twenty-fourth-century planet, social mores dictate it.

This isn't the first time *Star Trek* has spotlighted forced euthanasia. Back in 1967, Captain Kirk faced death booths on Eminiar VII ("A Taste of Armageddon"). He put an end to the enforced suicides that were the by-product of a lengthy war. Picard doesn't approve of enforced suicides any more than Kirk did—but the situation here is different. The Prime Directive must stand.

"Half a Life" aired in 1991, just a year after Dr. Jack Kevorkian carried out his first public assisted suicide. While Peter Allan Fields's teleplay can be interpreted as a strong statement about the ethics of euthanasia, one can also view it as a simple statement that someone will always fight against the concept of unnaturally taking a life.

In the end, however, what viewers are left with is a feeling of compassion for Lwaxana, who accepts Timicin's beliefs even though they don't reflect her own, and who chooses to stand by her man at his Resolution. It's the bravest thing we've ever seen her do, and it goes a long way in proving she may not be a caricature after all.

Doctor Crusher falls in love with Odan, a Trill mediator who has been assigned to settle a bitter dispute between the inhabitants of two moons. But after Odan is mortally injured, she discovers that "Odan" is actually a symbiotic worm that lives inside a humanoid host body. He will survive if he's quickly transplanted into the body of another humanoid from Trill, but the *Enterprise* is a long way from that world. With the dispute between the moons reaching a crisis and Odan weakening, Crusher does the only thing possible. She transfers the symbiont into a human volunteer: Commander Riker.

Right: Crusher introduces Riker to his symbiont.
Opposite: Michael Westmore had to create a design for the Trill host's face *and* his abdomen for "The Host." "I built a rubber stomach area for Odan, adding hair to it so that it would blend into actor Franc Luz's own torso," Westmore says. "There were three bladders underneath the false skin, so that when his stomach pulsated, indicating the presence of a creature underneath, we blew into a series of air tubes, which expanded the bladders. The surrounding rubber was very soft, and we were able to make the bladders swell quite a bit."

Several years later, he'd wind up reconceiving Trill facial makeup for *Deep Space Nine*, although the pouch design for that series' Trill, Jadzia Dax, would be similar to Odan's.

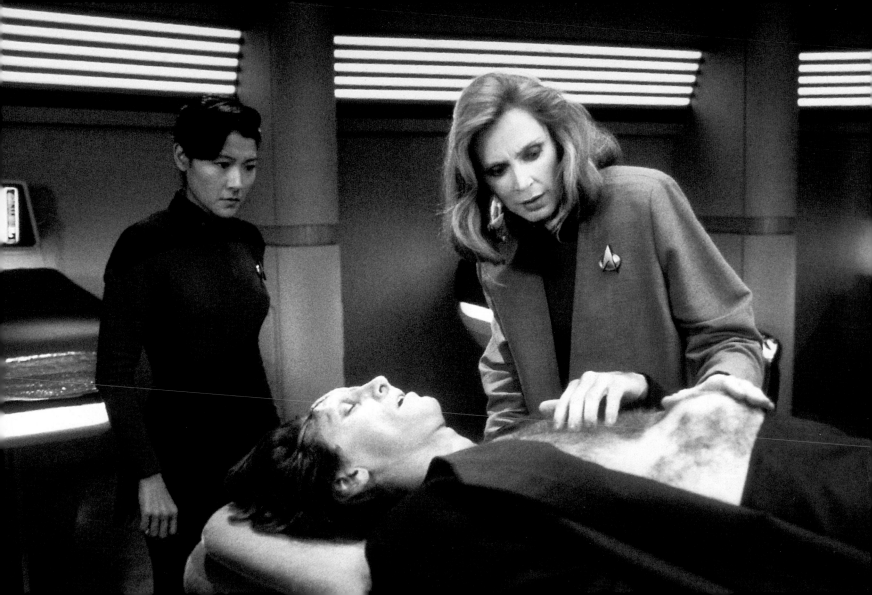

"Perhaps it is a human failing, but we are not accustomed to these kinds of changes. I can't keep up. How long will you have this host? What would the next one be? I can't live with that kind of uncertainty. Perhaps, someday, our ability to love won't be so limited." —Crusher

In a 1976 lecture about *Star Trek* in New York City, Gene Roddenberry stated, "The whole show was an attempt to say that humanity will reach maturity and wisdom on the day that it begins not just to tolerate, but to take a special delight in differences in ideas, and differences in life-forms."

Let it not be said that Beverly Crusher didn't give Gene's philosophy about life-forms a fighting chance in "The Host."

As the episode starts, viewers learn that the good doctor has fallen in love with Odan, a Trill ambassador who is traveling aboard the *Enterprise*. But after he is fatally injured, Beverly finds she's been deceived. It wasn't the ambassador's manly form (now expired) that won her heart—it was the not-so-attractive slug (still alive) *inside* his belly that was responsible for those sweet nothings whispered into her ear.

"The Host" is about the nature of love. The Trill are a "joined" species: humanoid bodies occupied by symbiotic organisms in a mutually beneficial arrangement. Odan, as it turns out, is the name of the *slug*. Like Cyrano de Bergerac, Odan, who possesses all the charm and charisma, has romanced Beverly via a more attractive stand-in. Then Odan is temporarily transferred into the body of Beverly's good friend Will Riker. The doctor bravely rises to Roddenberry's challenge and accepts that love is indeed a spiritual quality, independent of, and undiminished by, physical form. But later, when Odan receives a new permanent home in the body of a Trill female, Beverly, explaining she can't take all the changes, gives up on the relationship. And so Roddenberry's philosophy is put on hold.

But not for long. The series' producers liked the concept of the Trill. When they picked a pantheon of alien heroes and heroines for *Deep Space Nine*, they included the joined Trill Jadzia Dax. The writers tweaked and improved upon some details related to the Trill, but they left intact the notion that the symbionts have emotions that travel with them from joining to joining. The Dax symbiont—which would fall in love while hosted within both male and female bodies—never bothered to question the appropriateness of its feelings for men, women, or even hotheaded Klingon life-forms.

Opposite: A lab coat, blocking, and careful camera angles helped camouflage the fact that actress Gates McFadden was seven months pregnant with son James Cleveland McFadden-Talbot during filming.

La Forge sets out for a vacation on Risa, but his shuttle is apprehended by Romulans who hope to use him in a plot to drive a wedge between the Federation and its Klingon allies. La Forge returns to the *Enterprise* with no memory of the encounter—nor of the fact that he's just been exposed to days of mind-control techniques that have turned him into the perfect assassin.

Recycling isn't a modern invention—particularly not *literary* recycling. Shakespeare found fodder for his plays in previously published materials; his sources for *Romeo and Juliet* include a poem written by Arthur Brooke in 1562—a poem Brooke is said to have derived from stories published in 1530 and 1544.

Which only goes to show: *If a story works once, it'll work again.*

A more recent (and pertinent) example:

In 1934, Robert Graves wrote *I, Claudius*, which included, among other themes, an assassination plot. The novel inspired a 1937 film and then seemed largely forgotten by the entertainment industry until it was remade, forty years on, as a British miniseries.

In 1959, novelist Richard Condon wrote *The Manchurian Candidate,* a novel in which American POWs are brainwashed by Communist agents to become political assassins. Passages from Condon's novel closely resemble passages from the earlier Graves work, although the similarity wasn't noticed until after both authors' deaths.

In 1965, a few years after the film adaptation of *The Manchurian Candidate* wowed the public, the television series *Voyage to the Bottom of the Sea* aired "The Saboteur," an episode in which one of the series' lead characters is kidnapped and brainwashed by enemy agents who intend to use him to subvert a strategic mission and assassinate his commander.

Next came the *TNG* episode "The Mind's Eye." Geordi La Forge is mentally conditioned to assassinate a Klingon governor as part of a complex Romulan plot to implicate the Federation as enemies of the Klingon Empire.

How did that story make it into René Echevarria's purview? "It was a pitch by a freelancer," recalls Echevarria, who wrote the script. "It was sold as *The Manchurian Candidate* with Geordi, as I recall."

TNG producer David Livingston, the latest graduate of "Paramount University," directed. As a fan of the 1962 movie helmed by John Frankenheimer, Livingston consciously emulated Frankenheimer's style, setting up shots similar to those in the movie and echoing Frankenheimer's choice of camera lenses.

So whose story is it? It's hard to say.

But Shakespeare undoubtedly would have understood.

Below: Special lighting enhances a scene in which Geordi's POV is elicited by a steadicam operator holding a phaser.

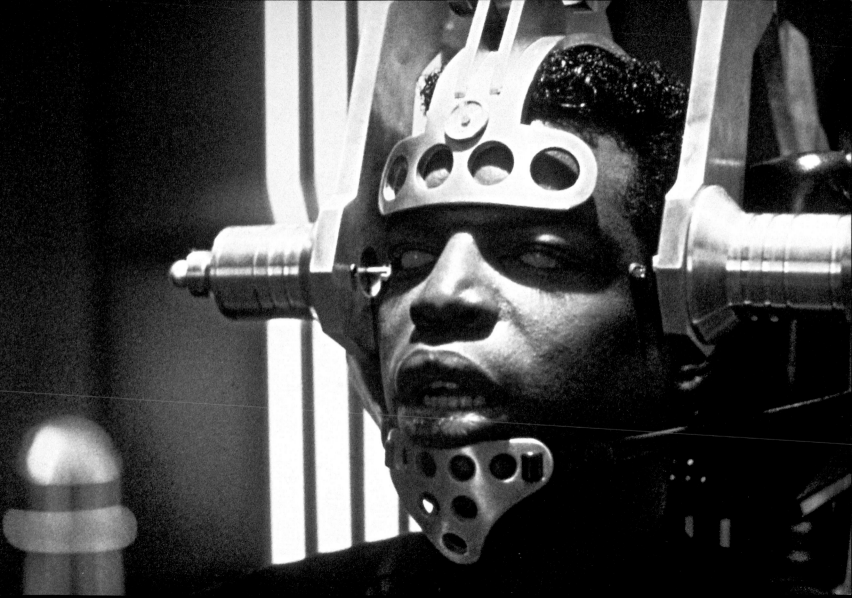

"Darling, you remain as aesthetically pleasing as the first day we met. I believe I am the most fortunate sentient in this sector of the galaxy."
—Data

In his never-ending quest to learn more about the nature of humanity, Data accepts the affections of shipmate Jenna D'Sora and pursues a romantic relationship with her. However, Jenna soon comprehends the downside of a "programmed" relationship. As the couple attempts to work out its problems, the *Enterprise* moves into an area of space rendered deadly by a nebula that is creating small gaps in the fabric of space, deforming any matter that comes into contact with them.

Patrick Stewart made his directorial bow in this episode. Stewart is humble about his skills, particularly when he compares them to those of Jonathan Frakes, his predecessor at "Paramount University." "Jonathan was completely prepared," Stewart acknowledges. "He walked onto the set that first morning a director. Not like me—an actor who was

going to have a go at it. But that's what paved the way for me, and the directing actually became the most important part of the work for me over the next few years. To know that there would be a couple of episodes each season that I would be allowed to direct—those moments became landmarks for me."

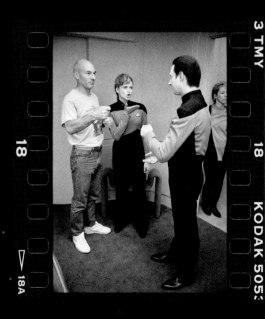

Data: *"Jenna, are we no longer a couple?"*
Jenna: *"No, we're not."*
Data: *"Then I will delete the appropriate program."*

"This was another chance to walk the line between Data's hardwiring and his programmed 'heart'—to explore whether there really is a ghost in the machine," Joe Menosky recalls. "And it was the first episode where Ron [Moore] and I collaborated. We split the work between us and then showed each other what we had done. Later, on *Voyager*, when Brannon Braga and I collaborated, we would typically sit in a room and write each word together. Each method has its pluses and minuses."

"I loved the notion of Data involved with a woman who fell in love with him, because it was a sort of callback to when *The Original Series* was on," says Ron Moore. "There were so many women who were *in love* with Spock. So much of Leonard Nimoy's fan mail was from women, women who were falling in love with this remote, inaccessible character with the idea that *'I could touch his heart—I could get to Spock like no one else.'* I was fascinated by that aspect of fandom. So I thought, well, what if

we did that with Data and there was a woman who fell in love with a man who *literally* doesn't have a heart, who could not give her something emotional. I wanted to see that relationship crash on the rocks. I wanted to see the moment when she realizes that he really can't give back to her what she wants."

It *is* an intriguing idea, and one that's filled with humor until we reach the predestined moment when the relationship smashes into that unavoidable rocky shoal. Relationships end, even make-believe relationships. But how much harder would it be to hear your formerly significant other tell you that he was going to delete the program that made you a couple? Jenna is a bit of a mess, inside and out—she's clingy and, despite her good looks, more than a little insecure. But unlike Data, she does have a heart, and the audience can't help empathizing with her when she walks out of Data's quarters—and is instantly replaced by the other female in the android's life: Spot, the cat.

As Picard heads for the Klingon homeworld to oversee Gowron's installation as leader of the High Council, the *Enterprise* is intercepted by a ship bearing the future leader himself. Gowron reveals he has learned that the surviving members of the vengeful Duras family are plotting to incite civil war within the Empire. Not long after, Gowron's installation ceremony is interrupted by the arrival of the Duras sisters, Lursa and B'Etor, who announce that Toral, son of their dead brother Duras, will challenge Gowron for leadership. Worf, taking a leave of absence from Starfleet, meets with Gowron and offers him the support of an alliance of Klingon warships led by his brother Kurn, *if* Gowron will restore his family's honor. Gowron would prefer Federation help, but when the Duras faction attacks his ship, it seems that Worf is the only ally at hand. . . .

✦

"Makeup has a magic going back to the days of primitive people painting their faces and making masks for themselves to commune with spirits," explains Doug Drexler. "It has a psychological effect on the human brain. There were actors who came in to play Klingons who had never seen the show. So it was part of the job, as the makeup artist is applying their makeup, to help the actor find the proper mindset. I was there the first time Robert O'Reilly was made up as Gowron. As he did his scenes, every once in a while he would bug his eyes. He looked like a thermometer about to pop! So when he came off the stage, I told him, 'You should do that all the time!' He may have been planning to do it anyway, but he did keep doing it. In fact, it became his trademark."

STAR TREK: THE NEXT GENERATION

100th EPISODE

"Redemption"

Broadcast date: week of June 17, 1991

Those darned Durases. They just keep going and going and . . .

In this go-round, we get Duras times three—two Duras sisters and one bastard son, more bad apples from a bad family tree—and learn that the Duras clan is attempting to foment a civil war within the Klingon Empire. Against this backdrop, there's Gowron attempting to take his seat as the new leader of the Empire's High Council, Worf still trying to restore his family's honor, and the revelation of a mysterious, pointy-eared character who's been skulking around in the shadows throughout the season. All of which adds up to . . .

"A very big epic tale," says writer Ron Moore. "It was the first time we ever did a war story, even though it was with the Klingons. Gene wasn't a big fan of going in that direction, nor of placing such a big emphasis on Worf. Gene did not feel that Worf was a primary character—the show was about Picard. We had to fight a bit to get there."

However, as Worf might have said, it was a *worthy* fight, one that gave rise to plot elements that would prove invaluable for future storytelling. It was also . . . fun.

"It *was* fun to write things for Worf," Moore ac-

knowledges. "He was the one guy in a Starfleet uniform who could do bad things. He could beat people up! He could get upset! He could have problems! And the Klingon guest stars were *always* fun to write for. I really enjoyed writing for the Duras sisters."

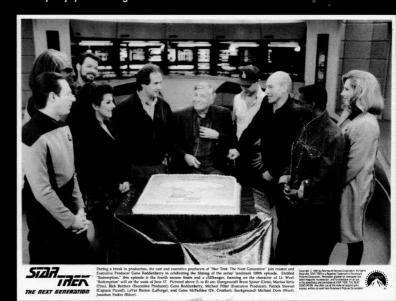

During a break in production, the cast and executive producers of "Star Trek: The Next Generation" join creator and Executive Producer Gene Roddenberry in celebrating the filming of the series' landmark 100th episode. Entitled "Redemption," this episode is the fourth season finale and a cliffhanger, focusing on the character of Lt. Worf. Pictured above (l. to R) are: (foreground) Brent Spiner (Data), Marina Sirtis (Troi), Rick Berman (Executive Producer), Gene Roddenberry, Michael Piller (Executive Producer), Patrick Stewart (Captain Picard), LeVar Burton (LaForge), and Gates McFadden (Dr. Crusher); (background) Michael Dorn (Worf), Jonathan Frakes (Riker).

STAR TREK
THE NEXT GENERATION

Gene Roddenberry's words to Michael Piller a year earlier had been prophetic. By the end of the fourth season, *The Next Generation* had caught fire. Ratings continued to rise, breaking its own all-time-high records. Although it was a non-network series airing on different days of the week in different markets, *TNG* had become, for its burgeoning audience, "must-see TV."

If the eightieth episode had provided a good excuse for a small on-set party, the completion of "Redemption," the hundredth episode, was cause for a full-out celebration. A large sheet cake delivered to the bridge set became a "photo op" for the cast and crew (see image on spread 213), with Paramount proudly notifying the media of this important landmark.

The show's increasing popularity continued to draw famous personalities to the soundstages, some to appear in episodes, others just to tour the set. But none was more famous than the gentleman who popped by during filming of "Redemption"—a former Hollywood actor who now resided on the opposite end of the country.

"We all got to meet Ronald Reagan," recalls Ron Moore. "We were told to wait on the set. The Secret Service came in, and then President Reagan. Gene was sitting in a director's chair; he walked with a cane at that point. And as the president entered, Gene got up from his chair and dropped his cane. Ronald Reagan bent over to pick up the cane and hand it to Gene. It was such an odd, beautiful moment, Reagan bowing before Gene and handing him his cane. It was really sweet."

Right and opposite: President Ronald Reagan gets the VIP tour of the Klingon High Council chamber. Pictured with Reagan are actors Patrick Stewart and Brent Spiner; producers Gene Roddenberry, Rick Berman, and Michael Piller; and A. C. Lyles, an employee of Paramount Pictures since 1928. During the 1950s and '60s, Lyles was a prolific producer of profitable low-budget westerns for the studio. He remains active at the studio to this day, a living link to Old Hollywood who serves as the studio's unofficial "ambassador of good will." A longtime friend of Ronald Reagan (the two arrived in Hollywood around the same time), Lyles functioned as a Hollywood liaison during the Reagan administration, enlisting celebrities to entertain at presidential functions.

As *Star Trek*'s twenty-fifth anniversary loomed on the horizon, Paramount Pictures prepared for the festivities by green-lighting a sixth movie featuring the cast of *The Original Series*. *Star Trek VI: The Undiscovered Country* would debut in December 1991. It was a film that acknowledged the passage of time, something that Kirk himself had noted as far back as the second *Star Trek* film ("*Galloping about the cosmos is a game for the young, Doctor.*"). In fact, the signatures of the series' seven main actors would appear in the end credits of the film, as if they were signing off on their involvement in the franchise, and leaving it to their successors at *The Next Generation*.

The studio recognized that it could generate a bit more press coverage for the anniversary by focusing on the creator of the extremely lucrative franchise. But Roddenberry's involvement with the film side of *Star Trek* was, by this time, minimal.

What do you give someone for his twenty-fifth anniversary?

Gene Roddenberry already had the adulation of fans around the globe. He had a star on Hollywood's Walk of Fame—the first ever given to a television writer. His financial situation was quite comfortable. And with the obvious success of *The Next Generation*, Roddenberry had at last earned the respect of the studio "suits," who had once dismissed *Star Trek* as a mere flash in the pan.

But the one thing Roddenberry *didn't* have was a building named after him. And there on the Paramount lot was a newly completed office building, set to house personnel of its television division. The building rested comfortably beside the studio's famous "B-tank," a sunken parking lot where Moses parted the Red Sea and Kirk crash-landed a Klingon bird-of-prey.

Could there possibly be a more perfect match?

On June 6, 1991, a dedication ceremony was held in front of the Gene Roddenberry Building. For this momentous occasion, the casts of *The Undiscovered Country* and *The Next Generation* stood at either side of the Great Bird. Roddenberry stepped up to the microphone and spoke to a commingled crowd of Paramount employees and reporters. The speech was classic Roddenberry, grateful for the honor . . . but not lacking in a humorous barb toward his benefactors:

"All I've done in *Star Trek* is have fun, daydream—and Paramount has graciously given me an office to do that in, has paid me more money than I really feel I deserve—and they earned more for themselves than I really feel they deserve."

Although previously opposed to getting the Federation involved in the Klingon civil war, Picard decides that he must help expose a disturbing fact: Romulans are supporting the disruptive Klingon faction led by the conniving Duras sisters. In the meantime, Worf is kidnapped and delivered to Lursa and B'Etor, who want Worf to join their side. And Picard is unnerved when he's approached by Sela, a mysterious Romulan officer who bears an uncanny resemblance to Tasha Yar, the *Enterprise*'s dead security chief.

The Borg cliff-hanger at the end of season three had really piqued the *TNG* viewing audience's appetite for a new season of episodes. Given the opportunity to kindle a similar level of enthusiasm from the fans at the end of season four, Ron Moore scripted a two-part tale of Klingon/Romulan political intrigue that would, coincidentally, formally introduce a character whose existence wouldn't have been possible but for a queer twist in time and space, courtesy of "Yesterday's *Enterprise*."

Just as Denise Crosby's desire to guest on *TNG* had led to the presence of Tasha Yar in that episode,

Crosby's pitch to Rick Berman about a child born within that alternate timeline led to the creation of Sela. Crosby pictured Sela as a human, perhaps the daughter of Yar and Christopher McDonald's Castillo, but the *TNG* writers modified Sela's backstory, making her the offspring of a Romulan general who became enamored with the time-marooned Tasha. The result: a deadly enemy with a familiar face.

Lursa and B'Etor, the Duras sisters, were fierce, forthright, ruthless . . . and sensual as all get-out. Which certainly begs the question: when writing for characters like these, was there a line that the writers dared not cross—perhaps a sort of tease limit?

"Not per se," Ron Moore says with a laugh. "I was always trying to find out how far over the line I could go with that stuff. But the Duras sisters actually came from Michael Piller. I think Michael was really intrigued with them, so I just played to that in my scripts."

Perhaps the most titillating thing about Lursa and B'Etor was their amazing attire, created by Robert Blackman. Guy Vardaman, a Klingon extra in both parts of "Redemption," recalls the day he first saw their costumes. "I was sitting on the soundstage and Bob Blackman brought in Gwynyth Walsh (B'Etor) and Barbara March (Lursa), dressed as the characters. These outfits were tailored for women that are very curvaceous, but tough as nails. They've got an opening in the chest that really pushed the cleavage aspect of the costumes *and* the actresses. Gene was on the set that day, and that was a happy surprise for Bob, who was glad that Gene could take a look at his latest creation.

"So Bob says, 'What do you think?' Gene looks at the costumes and gets a huge smile on his face. It's as though Bill Theiss [known for his very revealing *TOS* costumes] had come back and designed these. Gene looks up and down and stops to squint at that opening in the chest, and you can see the gears working in his head, that he's decided this is a prosthetic that's part of the costume. The prosthetics had gotten so good by then, some of them blended in so you couldn't tell where they ended and the actor began. So he stuck out his index finger and poked what he thought was the prosthetic. And immediately realized that it was *not* a prosthetic. And turned bright red. And the actress—I think it was Gwynyth—says, 'Yup, that's all me.' And she started laughing."

Vardaman, who periodically served in Roddenberry's office as a research consultant, notes, "I'd never seen Gene embarrassed by anything before, but he was clearly surprised by this. I think this was the biggest surprise he'd had in years."

"Enkidu fell to the ground, struck down by the gods. And Gilgamesh wept bitter tears, saying, 'He who was my companion through adventure and hardship, is gone forever.'" —Picard (at El-Adrel)

Captain Picard's attempts to communicate with an alien race known as the "Children of Tama" are interrupted when Dathon, the captain of the Tamarian ship, kidnaps Picard and beams him to a nearby planet. After Dathon joins him there, Picard realizes that the alien is well intentioned, and is determined to bridge the communications gap between them. But can Picard master Captain Dathon's bewildering language before he falls victim to the predatory crea-

standard-duty uniform, and represented a more casual dress option for Picard, similar to Captain Kirk's green V-neck wraparound tunic in *The Original Series*. Designed by Robert Blackman to make Picard stand out from the rest of the crew, the variant was created at the suggestion of Patrick Stewart.

"For the first year that I worked at *TNG*," reveals writer Joe Menosky, "'Darmok' was considered *the* 'unfixable' script. But Michael Piller was unwilling to abandon it."

"Darmok" is considered one of *TNG*'s finest episodes. However, it didn't seem very promising at the outset. Here's the essence of Philip LaZebnik's original story, as recapped by Menosky:

"An *Enterprise* away team lands on a planet and splits up. Each member encounters in turn a mysterious little alien boy drawing in the dirt, who greets them with one word: 'Darmok?' No matter what the crew member's response might be, the result is that he or she is mysteriously catapulted into orbit, wrapped in some mummification cocoon. It felt very much like that Bridge of Death sequence in *Monty Python and the Holy Grail*, where the Bridge Keeper asks a question and if the knight's answer is wrong, he gets flung into the volcano. Finally, Picard arrives, and when the boy again says 'Darmok?' Picard sits down in the dirt to play with the kid—because 'Darmok,' he realizes, means 'play.' The riddle solved, the away team is released from their cocoons and all's well that ends well.

"None of this worked within the context of our se-ries," Menosky explains. "But one day Michael announced we were going to meet on 'Darmok.' We all went in to talk about a rewrite, and he assigned it to *me*. When we walked out of the meeting, Ron Moore shook my hand and said, 'Nice knowing you, Joe,' as if this assignment was my death sentence—gallows humor in recognition of two other writers that Michael had recently let go when they failed to live up to his expectations.

"I worked on the assignment for several days and had zero to show for it—and no thoughts that I could even propose," he continues. "So when Michael reconvened the staff to talk about it, I truly thought that I might be fired. But Michael was really excited. He'd just seen *Dances with Wolves* and was completely blown away by the scene with Kevin Costner's character and the Native American warrior around the campfire, who don't speak a word of each other's language, but finally make themselves understood. Michael announced, 'That's it: one man, one alien, alone on a planet, around a fire. They don't know each other's languages, they struggle to overcome their differences, and finally break through to communication. And maybe there's a big monster.'

"And I said, 'I can do that,'" Menosky reveals. "So I went off for the weekend and wrote a story memo that solved the 'language problem,' in other words, 'How to get past the universal translator.' I laid out a plot and included the big themes of language, communication, and mythology. Michael was absolutely thrilled. It was a true 'page one rewrite'—I kept only the title 'Darmok,' from the original script, because I liked the sound of the word."

Opposite: Cast and crew gather around director Rick Kolbe, with Menosky's script.

As he immersed himself in the script for "Darmok," Joe Menosky faced a challenge: find a reason that the universal translator can't properly decipher the Tamarian language. The solution he found is both simple and complicated: the language would be based entirely on metaphor.

"That way," Menosky explains, "even when you translate the words, you don't get the meaning. To illustrate how this works, I used 'Juliet on the balcony,' from *Romeo and Juliet*. It's an image of romantic longing, but only because we all *know* that particular story. You need to know the source tale being referenced."

Armed with this plan, the writer set out to create a language—on a very tight schedule. "This was before the Internet," Menosky explains, "so I couldn't just Google 'metaphorical languages' and come up with a list. I used what I knew right then, off the top of my head."

He drew on three sources: the work of psychologist James Hillman, a quote by Dante translator John Ciardi, and Chinese historical aphorisms. "Hillman's emphasis on 'All is metaphor' was the first thing I thought of," Menosky says. "That brought to mind a great quote from Ciardi, 'Every word is a poem,'

which led me to think that metaphor could be the basis of the language. Then I remembered the extremely dense, 'historical' metaphors present in medieval Chinese poetry and philosophical works like the *I Ching*."

The *I Ching* contains ancient oracular statements represented by sixty-four sets of hexagrams. One, identified as "Darkening of the Light," stood out in Menosky's memory. It describes the life of Prince Chi, forced to live at the court of the evil tyrant Chou Hsin. "'Chi at the court of Chou' was the first sentence I wrote for the Tamarian language," Menosky notes. "But I didn't use it in the episode, or I'd have revealed my source."

Instead, Menosky created tales of Tamarian mythology. "For example, I wrote, 'Shaka when the walls fell,' adding just enough imagery to hint at 'a complete failure, a major collapse of an endeavor,'" he explains. "Although less concise than the Chinese prototype, it would be comprehensible for viewers.

A final image came to Menosky late in the writing. "When I reached the scene where Picard was to reciprocate Dathon's gift of a story with one of his own," he says, "I thought of *Gilgamesh*, which so defines Western archetypes that I wound up

there almost unconsciously. The fact that *Gilgamesh* is about two warriors who are enemies, become friends, and one of them dies, was a combination of 'writer's luck' and inevitability.

"Gene Roddenberry died not long after 'Darmok' aired," Menosky recalls. "At the funeral service, Patrick Stewart mentioned 'Darmok' in his memorial speech, saying we had just done an episode that referenced the Homeric Hymns and the root metaphors of our culture. He used it as a way to validate and praise Gene's creation.

"That moment might have been the proudest I've ever been about anything I've written for *Star Trek*."

The crew is unsettled by the arrival of Ensign Ro, a disgraced Starfleet officer of Bajoran origin. Although Ro was previously court-martialed for disobeying orders on an away mission, resulting in the deaths of eight crew members, Starfleet admiral Kennelly has pardoned and assigned her to the *Enterprise.* Her ostensible mission is to persuade Bajoran rebels to stop attacking and raiding Federation colonies. But Picard soon learns that the rebels, displaced from their homeworld by the Cardassians some forty years ago, were not to blame for the attacks—and that Kennelly's orders to Ro are very different than those he conveyed to Picard.

While Rick Berman seldom spilled the beans to the press about upcoming story arcs for *The Next Generation,* he regularly allowed Dan Madsen, the president of Star Trek: The Official Fan Club, to interview him for the fan club's magazine. It was a goodwill gesture that typically paid off both in fan enthusiasm and, of course, ratings. As season five approached, Berman dropped some interesting hints about a brand-new character whose debut was

in the wings. "We have an episode coming up that focuses on a character who might very well recur," Berman told Madsen. "This is an alien woman who was in Starfleet but got into a whole lot of trouble a number of years ago, and was court-martialed, booted out of Starfleet, and sent to prison. She is now brought back for one specific mission. So she's a woman with somewhat of an attitude. She develops a special rapport with Guinan. She's a very interesting character, played by actress Michelle Forbes, the same actress who played Dara in last season's episode 'Half a Life.'"

Thus, weeks before the episode aired, the fans were primed to welcome Ensign Ro—although they had yet to learn her character's name.

Would you be surprised to find out that the guys in the *Star Trek* writers' room weren't given access to any more information about the future of the *Star Trek* franchise than the fans were? "We knew that a new show called *Deep Space Nine* was going to be starting up, and that the producers wanted to create a character they could spin off into it," says writer Naren Shankar, then the show's in-house science consultant. "But we weren't privy to a lot of their plans at that point."

"There was a lot of discussion of Ensign Ro, and where that character was going," concurs Ron Moore. "We heard that Michael [Piller] had plans for the character, but we didn't know too much about that show, just the basic concept. But clearly it was heading in a direction with the Bajorans and the backstory that was developed in 'Ensign Ro.'"

"It was a weird time, in a way," continues Shankar. "We were the established show, but this new one was starting up, and you couldn't help thinking, 'We wanna be on the shiny new thing.'"

Behind the producers' backs, the "young guns," as Shankar jokingly refers to the group of writers (all primarily in their mid- to late twenties) mocked the mysterious new series. "When they first revealed that it was going to be set on a space station," Shankar notes, "we said, 'A *space station*? *What*? Are they going to wait for adventure to come to them?' One day Brannon [Braga] was ranting about that and he said, 'Wait, I can see it now. Episode 13—' And zooming his hand through the air as if it were a spaceship, he knocks over this cup filled with pencils and goes, 'ARRRGGGHHHHHHHH! Dah, dah, DAHHHH!'"

Shankar chuckles at the memory. "Filter that through the prism of jealousy, and I think you'll be somewhere around the truth," he says.

Ironically, while the writers were curious about where fate would take Ro Laren, Michelle Forbes was not. She reportedly enjoyed her periodic visits (six in all) to the *Enterprise* over the next few years, and was well liked by cast and crew. But she eventually declined the offer to join the cast of *Deep Space Nine*, opting to leave her career plans open-ended.

Thus was born an opportunity for actress Nana Visitor, who would soon fill the boots of an equally strong-willed, but ultimately very different, Bajoran character on *Deep Space Nine*: former freedom fighter Major Kira Nerys.

Picard: "Doctor, the sperm whale on Earth devours millions of cuttlefish as it roams the oceans. It is not evil. It is feeding. The same may be true of the Crystalline Entity."

Dr. Marr: "That would be small comfort for those who have died to feed it. We're not talking about cuttlefish; we're talking about people."

Picard: "I would argue that the Crystalline Entity has as much right to be here as we do. Now, Commander Data has some theories on how we might communicate. Please confer with him."

After the Crystalline Entity—which years earlier killed the colonists of Omicron Theta—attacks another colony, Picard joins forces with scientist Kila Marr to hunt it down. Marr has been searching for the entity for years, ever since it destroyed her son. But Picard's determination to find a peaceful way to stop the creature's onslaught of humanity is at odds with Marr's obsession with revenge.

Is the good captain passing the buck when he instructs Marr to plead her case with Data? Perhaps, but there's a reason for that: Picard really isn't the focus of this particular tale. It's Data who, by all rights, should be front and center in "Silicon Avatar." Four seasons earlier, in "Datalore," it was Data's "brother," Lore, who drew the Crystalline Entity to Omicron Theta. The death of those 411 colonists, including Marr's son, Renny, is a part of Data's family history. So by redirecting Marr's attention to Data, the captain is simply keeping the story's trajectory on track.

In this version of *Moby-Dick*, Marr stands in for Ahab, bent for revenge against that huge, crystalline space whale. And who could blame her? "Losing a child has to be the worst possible thing any parent can go through," teleplay writer Jeri Taylor says. "'Silicon Avatar' was a hard episode to write because I was trying to imagine and live those feelings. It was very distressing." It's understandable for viewers to feel empathy with Marr; her sense of loss is timeless and universal.

But at the same time, a point of view favoring the Prime Directive can be similarly understood. If the entity *is* sentient, if it *can* communicate, then the *Enterprise* can't just destroy it. But Marr—who feels no compunction to follow Starfleet's moral code—

kills it anyway. Was she wrong? By destroying it, uncountable lives likely *are* saved. And as no less a philosopher than Spock once said, "Logic clearly dictates that the needs of the many outweigh the needs of the few."

Or the one.

Marr will be punished for her transgression—if not by Picard or Federation authority, then by her own conscience after Data dispassionately informs her that her son, Renny, would be saddened by her actions. She will, no doubt, live with that for the rest of her days.

Is it any wonder that Picard passed the buck?

A catastrophe leaves the *Enterprise* severely damaged, with Troi in charge on the bridge, an injured Picard trapped in a turbolift with three frightened children, and a pregnant Keiko O'Brien about to give birth in Ten-Forward with only Worf to assist. With an explosion of the ship's antimatter pods likely at any moment, Troi must decide whether or not to separate the saucer section from the stardrive section, a decision that would spell doom for anyone still alive in engineering.

Right: Two really big *Star Trek* fans: Guy Vardaman, and the piece of equipment used to simulate the vacuum of space sucking the atmosphere out of the cargo bay.

Opposite: Ron Moore's love letter to *The Towering Inferno* and *The Poseidon Adventure* gave unusually juicy parts to each of the *TNG* regulars, allowing them to exercise their dramatic "chops." Between takes, Stewart and Sirtis discuss which is the greater challenge for their characters: taking command of the ship during a harrowing disaster . . . or babysitting.

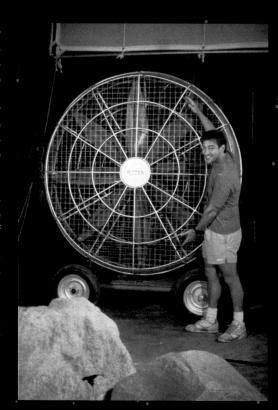

"Congratulations, you are fully dilated to ten centimeters. You may now give birth." —Worf

In this homage to big-screen disaster epics, viewers found Picard trapped in a turbolift shaft with (*horrors!*) children, Troi forced into making life-and-death command decisions on the bridge, and, most frightening of all, Worf delivering a baby in Ten-Forward.

"The idea," recalls teleplay writer Ron Moore, "was to trap the characters in different areas of the ship and follow their individual story lines. The Worf plot came out of our constant search for things to cut against his fierce, hyper-masculine Klingon nature. We all fell in love with the idea of him being the guy who delivers the baby. And Michael Dorn liked doing comedic stuff. I think he got tired of us beating him up all the time. Typically, we took him to some planet with a tough alien culture, and then we'd fall back on the stereotypical *'these guys were so tough that they kicked Worf's ass!'* Delivering a baby was much more fun for him."

For the trials of Troi, Moore decided to put her to a command test and put all the big decisions on her shoulders. However, he admits that wasn't exactly fair. "It's like the navy," he explains. "She wouldn't be in the chain of command to be in charge of the bridge in a situation like this. A medical officer on a U.S. Navy ship wouldn't technically be the next one in line. You never saw McCoy command the *Enterprise*, although he outranks Sulu. But I wanted to bend the rules because it made for an interesting character piece." Moore would make it up to Troi in the seventh season's "Thine Own Self," where her command potential would play out more fairly.

But it was the captain's predicament that he most looked forward to writing. "I put Picard in the turboshaft because I wanted to make it *rain* in there," Moore says. "I'd been reading about NASA's gigantic Vehicle Assembly Building at the Kennedy Space Center—the one they used to assemble the Apollo and Saturn rockets, and the Space Shuttle. At the time they built it, it was the largest interior space that had ever been enclosed, in terms of volume. And they'd had a problem with clouds forming near the ceiling, and rain actually would come down! The engineers had to figure out how to deal with that.

"I had this notion that in a really tall turboshaft—an enclosed space—that when all the power went out, it might start to rain," Moore says. "The danger would be with lightning lancing through the tube.

Unfortunately," he says with a sigh, "anything that has to do with water on a set is just an enormous pain in the ass. It's too cost prohibitive and takes forever. So we couldn't do it. But that's the only reason Picard's in the turboshaft."

Opposite: Director Gabrielle Beaumont provides Michael Dorn with an on-set demonstration of how to deliver a baby.

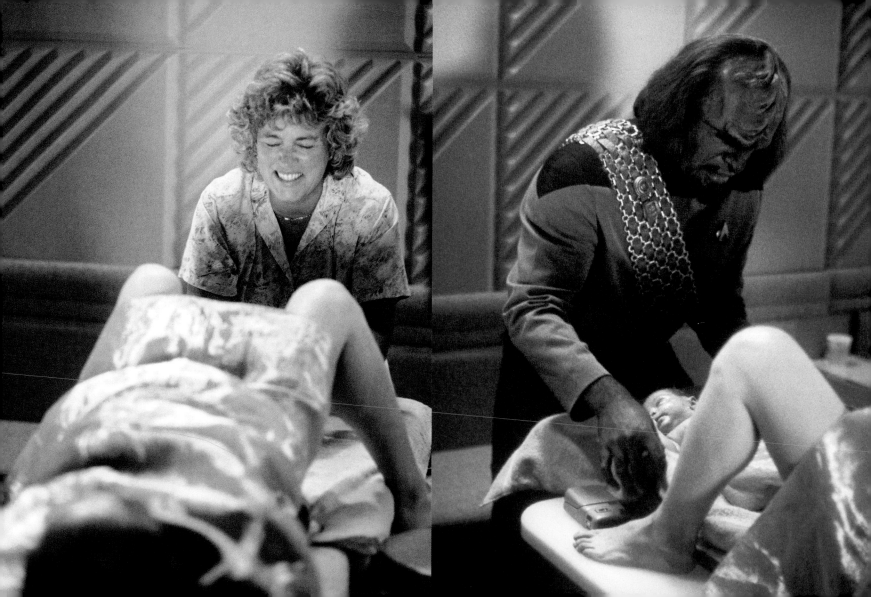

Troi: "Chocolate is a serious thing."
Riker: "I brought something back from Risa. Better than chocolate."
Troi: "Oh? What is it?"
Riker: "Just a game."

Riker returns from a vacation on Risa with a game that he's eager to share with the crew. Unfortunately, the game is psychologically addictive, and it quickly turns virtually every member of the *Enterprise*'s crew into a mind-controlled pawn of the Ktarians, who are using the devices to gain control of Starfleet. After Data—who, as an android, is unaffected by the game—inexplicably is "incapacitated," only visiting Starfleet Academy cadet Wesley Crusher and young engineering ensign Robin Lefler stand in the way of the insidious scheme.

Opposite: The titular "game," created from a telephone headset by property master Alan Sims.

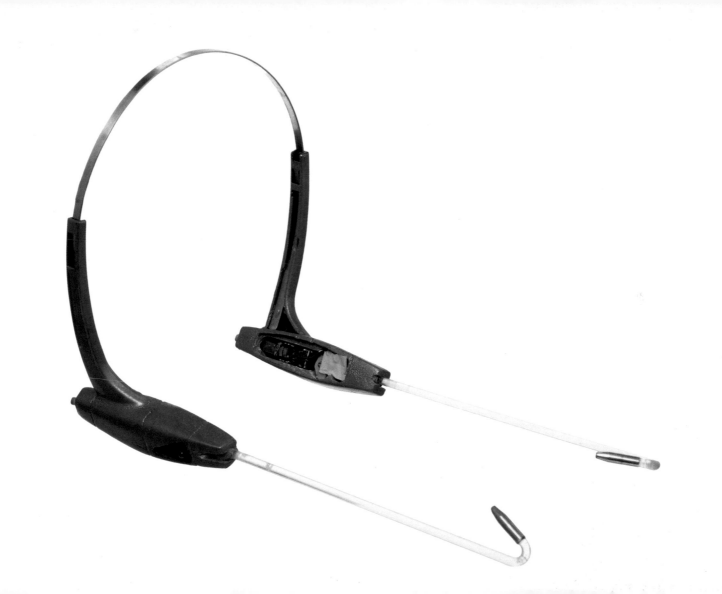

"I liked Wesley," Brannon Braga says. "But it always was a challenge to make him a little hipper. He came across as so wholesome. I wanted to keep his brightness, but also give his character an edge. Now that he was at the Academy, I wanted to mention that he was getting into mischief and was a little more savvy. And I made him aggressively interested in Robin Lefler. I think Wil Wheaton appreciated that."

One suspects Braga is correct; the episode provided Wheaton with a once-in-a-lifetime opportunity to give future film star Ashley Judd her first on-screen kiss. According to Braga, it was an opportunity he pondered for himself, albeit unsuccessfully. "I hit on Ashley on the set," he admits twenty-five years later, "and was dutifully ignored."

"The Game" marked Braga's first script as an official staff member. The story had been around the office longer than he had. "Susan Sackett and her writing partner Fred Bronson had a cool idea about a game that could be used to take over the minds of the crew," he recalls. "Apparently they never figured out what the game was, so Michael [Piller] handed me the concept to work out. I came up with this little visor-like thing that would stimulate the pleasure center of your brain. For all intents and purposes, it would give you an orgasm when you reached a certain level, although that wasn't mentioned on-camera."

Reaching the pleasure center of Troi's brain meant revisiting a character note established two seasons earlier: her love of chocolate. In "The Price," Troi finds the food replicator incapable of serving up a real chocolate ice-cream sundae; this time, however, there's no such trouble, and Troi finds her dessert quite satisfactory. Maybe a little *too* satisfactory. "People were very split over whether they loved or hated the chocolate scene," Braga recalls. "There were some who felt uncomfortable with the sexual innuendo, but I thought it was good to see our characters in a fresh situation."

Braga cops to a certain thematic resemblance to *Invasion of the Body Snatchers*. "It was corny, even at the time," he admits. "But I enjoyed writing it. It was fun to realize that Picard had been seduced by the game, and it was fun to watch Beverly Crusher attempt to entice her son. The script was produced exactly as I wrote it, so it was an extremely positive experience for me."

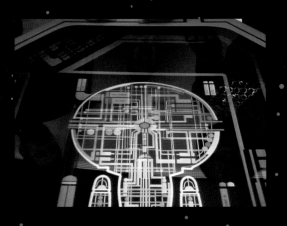

Spock: "In your own way, you are as stubborn as another captain of the Enterprise I once knew." Picard: "Then I'm in good company, sir."

Hearing that legendary Starfleet officer Spock may have defected to the Romulan Empire, Captain Picard travels to Vulcan to talk to Spock's father, former ambassador Sarek, who is near death from the ravages of Bendii Syndrome. In a rare lucid moment, Sarek discloses that Spock has long harbored hopes of peacefully reuniting the Vulcan and Romulan peoples, who once were part of the same civilization. Rather than committing treason, Spock actually may be initiating steps to achieve that peaceful goal. Determined to find the truth, Picard and Data, disguised as Romulans, set out for the Romulan homeworld.

Upon finding Spock, Picard learns that the Vulcan is indeed on an unauthorized mission to reunify his people with their sundered brethren. Spock counts among his allies a Romulan senator named Pardek and the Romulan proconsul Neral. But if Neral is actually on the up-and-up, why is he secretly meeting with Commander Sela, the Romulan who recently helped to incite the Klingon civil war? And why

have the Romulans recently stolen a small convoy of Vulcan ships from a space salvage yard?

When "Unification, Part I" aired the week of November 4, 1991, a somber title card appeared at the start of the show: GENE RODDENBERRY—1921–1991. The Great Bird had passed away on October 24. Just two days earlier, he had attended a screening of the upcoming feature *Star Trek VI: The Undiscovered Country*. And now, two weeks after Roddenberry's death, the most recognized character from his first *Star Trek* series was scheduled to appear alongside the cast of the second.

Like the estranged children of a first and second marriage, these "siblings" had mingled very little during *TNG*'s early years. McCoy and Sarek had managed to bridge the divide, but the mere mention of Spock's name had been strenuously resisted. But in 1991, such resistance seemed, if not futile, then certainly inconsequential. This was *Star Trek*'s twenty-fifth anniversary, and it was shaping up to be the year of one big *Star Trek* family. Michael Dorn, cast as Worf's grandfather, was seen in *Star Trek VI*, while Spock's *TNG* appearance represented the Vulcan's first new small-screen adventure in over two decades.

Roddenberry's death cast a pall over some of the festivities, but nothing could hold back the cultural juggernaut that his creation had become. A new *Star Trek* series—*Deep Space Nine*—was already in development, and there were whispers about moving *The Next Generation* to the features side of the Paramount lot. More new incarnations of *Star Trek* would follow, all conceived without benefit of the creator's touch. Would he have minded? It seemed unlikely. In a 1988 interview, Roddenberry stated: "I would hope that there are bright young people growing up over time who will bring to [*Star Trek*] levels and areas that were beyond me. And I won't feel jealous about that at all. . . . It'll go on without any of us, and get better and better and better. That really is the human condition—to improve."

Right: A mere five months after the festive dedication ceremony, a commemorative wreath was placed at the entrance to the Gene Roddenberry Building on the Paramount lot.

Opposite: The memorial service at Forest Lawn brought out studio personnel, crew members, and celebrities from past and present eras—not to mention dozens of fans that had figured out where the service was to take place.

****

Memorial Service

GENE RODDENBERRY

Service held
November 1, 1991 - 2:00 p.m.

at the
Hall of Liberty

****

Vocalist
Ms. Nichelle Nichols

Pianist
Mr. Nathan Wong

Speakers
Mr. Ray Bradbury - Ms. Whoopi Goldberg
Mr. Christopher Knopf - Mr. E. Jack Neuman
Mr. Patrick Stewart

Scottish Pipers
Mr. Eric Rigler - Mr. Scott Ruscoe

Service conducted by
Forest Lawn Mortuary, Hollywood Hills

Spock: *"Perhaps you are aware of the small role I played in the overture to peace with the Klingons."*

Picard: *"History is aware of the role you played, Ambassador."*

Spock: *"Not entirely. It was I who committed Captain Kirk to that peace mission, and I who had to bear the responsibility for the consequences to him and his crew."*

Of the thousands of story pitches submitted to the *Star Trek* producers after Michael Piller instituted the "spec script program" in 1989, the most eminent undoubtedly was the one for "Unification," offered up by one of *Star Trek*'s most esteemed players: Leonard Nimoy. How did that come about?

"It had to do with a matter of timing, as well as my interest in the show," Nimoy said in an interview with *Star Trek: The Official Fan Club* magazine in 1994. "I was interested in *The Next Generation*, and at the same time, we were just finishing up [principal photography on] *The Undiscovered Country*. I thought that if we could do a *TNG* episode in which we hinted at the beginnings of a crossover between *The Original Series* and *The Next Genera-*

tion through the Spock character and through the backstory of Spock's character, it would be helpful to both. I thought it would be interesting to the fans to see the connection between the two stories. It just seemed that it made sense for me to make an appearance at that point.

"So I went to Rick Berman and Michael Piller and said, 'How about it?'"

The timing, as it turned out, was useful in several ways. Postproduction on the movie took longer to complete than the entire production cycle for the episode, so "Unification" wound up airing a full month before the release of *The Undiscovered Country*. In hindsight, cynical fans might interpret Spock's appearance on the TV show—and a tantalizing bit of dialogue in the teleplay that hinted at the film's central plot—as an obvious example of marketing for the upcoming release.

But Rick Berman, who cowrote the story for the episode with Piller, would disagree. "It's a validation of *our* series from *The Original Series*," Berman said at the time the episode aired. "There has been so much talk about the two series, in a competitive way. This is a union, a joining of the two. And that's very positive for the fans."

Mark Lenard relished resurrecting the character of Sarek for "Unification." "They only sent me part of the script," Lenard noted in a 1994 interview with the authors of this book. "I read it and thought, 'Well, I'm only in one scene, but it's a *good* scene—a bit like King Lear.' So I did it."

Sometime later, he was at a *Star Trek* convention—"Albany, or Springfield, or wherever," he said, with the smile of a man who'd participated in more than a few conventions over his lifetime. "They showed both parts of the episode, and I saw them there for the first time. But I hadn't known that Sarek died!"

How did he feel about the death of his character?

"I thought it was kind of chintzy," he admitted. "I didn't think it was respectful of the character. I got all kinds of letters about it."

Although he was touched by the influx of concern from fans, the actor believed that there was no reason why he *couldn't* appear as Sarek in films that took place in an earlier era, or even as another character (he had, after all, also played a Romulan and a Klingon within the *Star Trek* franchise). As Spock once said, there are always possibilities.

"Jimmy Doohan, who was at that same convention, said to me, 'Well, did anybody see Sarek die? Was anybody there?'" recalled Lenard. "I said, 'No.' 'Well,' Jimmy told me, 'then you're all right.'"

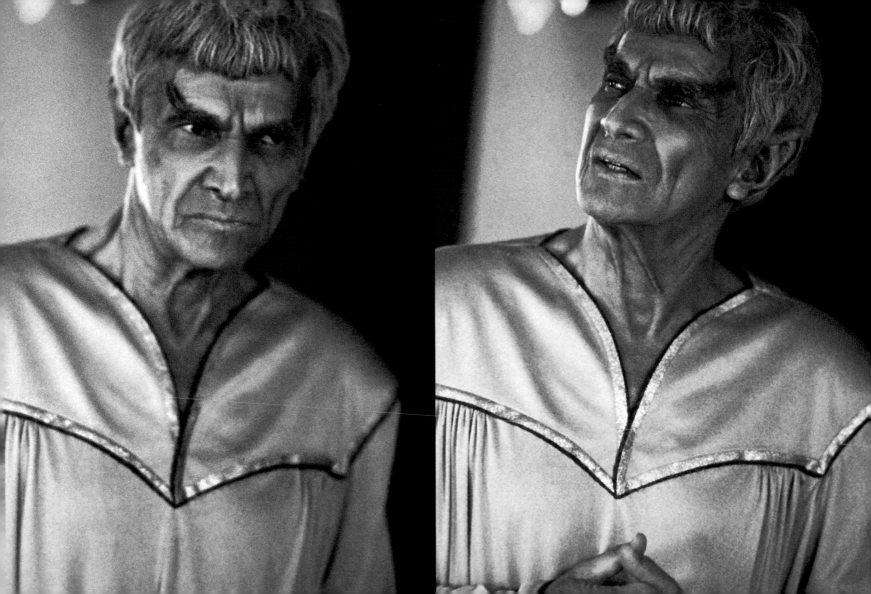

05 | 232 "A MATTER OF TIME"

The crew's attempts to save the inhabitants of Penthara IV from the devastating aftereffects of a massive asteroid strike are interrupted by the arrival of Berlinghoff Rasmussen, a purported historian from the twenty-sixth century, who claims to be studying their era. But the rather curious nature of Rasmussen's questions about the twenty-fourth century, and his interest in gathering—and stealing—technological "artifacts" from the *Enterprise*, make Troi and the others increasingly suspicious of his origins.

"A Matter of Time" marks the second of Rick Berman's two scripts for *TNG* (he also wrote "Brothers" in season four, and shared a story credit with Michael Piller for three other episodes). "I had done a lot of writing when I was working on documentaries," he explains. "On *Big Blue Marble*, I pretty much wrote the entire show. And I was dying to get back into writing. It was a little intimidating because I was working with a whole bunch of really good writers [on *The Next Generation*]." Berman went through the script process like everyone else—he pitched the concept, then broke and developed the story with

Michael Piller and the other writers—and made the changes they suggested, too. "It worked out nicely," Berman comments. Reportedly, Berman had in mind Robin Williams (yet another celebrity *Star Trek* fan) for the role of Rasmussen, but the comedic actor was busy doing the film *Hook*. *Max Headroom*'s Matt Frewer, known for performances similarly colored by his off-the-wall sense of humor, won the role.

Opposite: The exterior of Rasmussen's stolen time pod is a redress of the shuttle *Nenebek* from "Final Mission." It would be seen once more in *TNG*—portraying a Klingon shuttle in the seventh season's "Gambit."

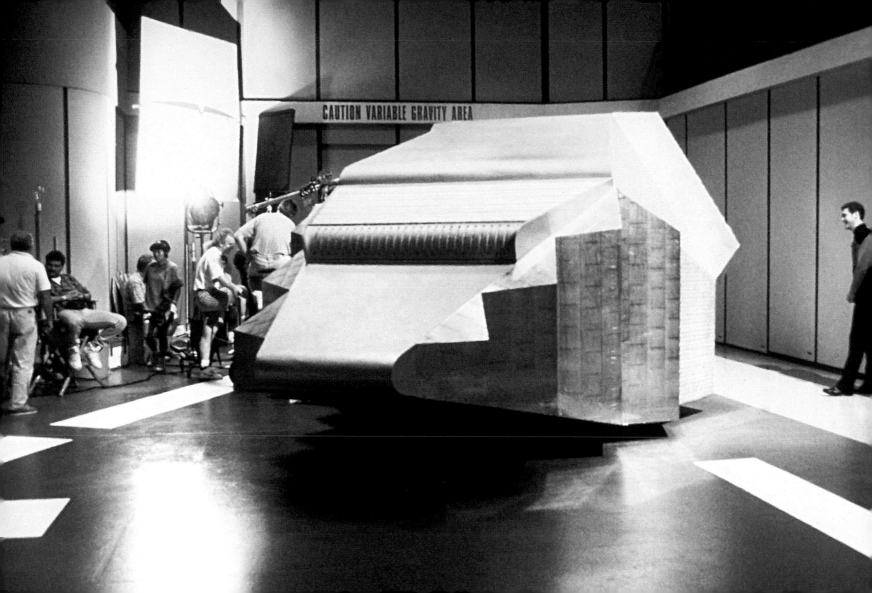

Picard: "You can't expect me to believe that the layout of my ready room can possibly be of interest to future historians."

Rasmussen: "No less so than your legendary modesty, Captain. If I could describe to you what a thrill it is to be here. [He gestures at the painting.] **This** *is the original."*

Rasmussen's awe of the painting over Picard's sofa was faked, but plenty of viewers experienced the real thing whenever they saw that work of art on camera. But how did it come to be there? For the answer, you'd need to step back in time to 1987. . . .

As *TNG*'s sets were being built, Andrew Probert and Rick Sternbach felt inspired.

"There was a large blank wall over the couch in Picard's ready room," Sternbach recalls. "So Andy and I approached John Dwyer, our wonderful set decorator, and said, 'Something needs to be put over that couch.' Then we volunteered to do a painting."

"Typically, captains' offices have *some* sort of ship painting," Probert says. "We thought it'd be fun for Picard to have a picture of his *own* ship. I did the layout, and then Rick painted this killer background,

because he's an award-winning astronomical artist. After he completed it, I painted the *Enterprise*."

"Andy did a wonderful rendering of the ship," Sternbach comments. "This was while the model still was being built up at Industrial Light & Magic."

"We did it on our own time," Probert adds. "Each of us took it home to work on. When it was ready, we loaned it to John to put in the captain's office."

"This was before we had any sort of computers in the office," says Sternbach, "so we did it in traditional media: acrylics, on eighth-inch Masonite."

After the series ended, several companies sold licensed prints of the painting, and General Mills even did a poster to accompany a cereal campaign. "The painting got around," Sternbach says. "But I don't believe it's ever been published in a book."

Until now, that is.

Right: Viewers occasionally caught a glimpse of the painting over actors' shoulders, but this is the only episode where a character actually mentions it.

Berlinghoff Rasmussen took note of another item in Picard's ready room: a saltwater aquarium, home to only one resident. Picard never called the Australian lionfish swimming there by name, yet everyone working behind the scenes on *TNG* knew it: "Livingston," named for producer David Livingston.

Reportedly, actor Patrick Stewart was not fond of Livingston's presence in the ready room, feeling that using a captive creature as a set prop was antithetical to a series that promoted the dignity of all species. Nevertheless, he spoke of it fondly—if a bit cheekily—on the BBC's Cult website:

"I came to feel very, very sentimental about the [*Enterprise*] sets and the things that went with them," Stewart commented. "Whenever, as it did from time to time, the lionfish in the fish tank in the captain's ready room died, it was always a sad moment."

Livingston didn't start his long swim in outer space. Like many others aboard the *Enterprise*, the lionfish first flexed his fins on Earth—at Mark's Tropical Fish in Studio City, California. Similarly, Mark Weitz, the store's owner and designer of Livingston's abode in the ready room, didn't start out as a "fish wrangler to the stars." During the late 1960s, when Captain Kirk was exploring the galaxy in the original *Enter-*

prise, Weitz was touring America as keyboardist of the rock band the Strawberry Alarm Clock. Although uncredited, Weitz co-composed their popular psychedelic standard "Incense and Peppermints," which reached number one on the pop charts in 1967. In his present life, beyond the work he did for *TNG*, Weitz has designed aquariums for such shows as *CSI: NY* and *Hell's Kitchen*.

Rock on, Livingston.

It started as a happy coincidence. "In 1991, I went to a New Year's Eve party in Pasadena near where the Rose Parade floats were parked for the pre-parade judging," recalls Neil Newman, then Paramount Licensing Group's vice president of marketing. "The floats were remarkable, and I immediately thought that the parade would be a great venue for *Star Trek*'s twenty-fifth anniversary. So I contacted float builder Festival Artists and did a pitch. As it turned out, the theme for the following year was 'Voyages of Discovery,' which obviously fit well, so the owner of Festival Artists presented it to Nestlé, their largest corporate sponsor, who immediately agreed to sponsor the concept."

Which is why a massive version of the *Starship Enterprise*-D was a featured float in the 1992 Tournament of Roses Parade in Pasadena, California. Nestlé and Paramount agreed on a hundred-foot float, to be titled "Space . . . The Final Frontier," which would depict the *Enterprise* soaring above the solar system, thus celebrating the year's parade theme as well as International Space Year. "The biggest technical challenge was being able to make the *Enterprise* fit under a low bridge that is a permanent part of the parade route," Newman notes. The

solution awaited only blocks away—at Pasadena's Jet Propulsion Laboratory. Using the studio's blueprints of the starship and shuttlecraft, JPL engineer Michael Johnson determined how to keep the five-thousand-pound *Enterprise* suspended forty-three feet in the air. Johnson designed a massive arm that moved the ship up and down. He cantilevered the forty-five-foot-long starship out over the front of the float, which also exhibited two shuttles sailing among meteors above a vivid red and orange planet.

"All kinds of clubs came to decorate the float," Newman says, "including *Star Trek* crews from all over the West Coast." The volunteers decorated the *Enterprise* surface with tens of thousands of silver-tree leaves, adding accents of sweet rice and shiny black, pressed seaweed. Pumpkins were used to fashion the comets, with thousands of stems of Oncidium orchids illuminating their shimmering tails. And the planets were decorated with a variety of plant materials: lotus pods, yarrow, powdered yams, coxcomb, mosses, and button mums.

"It was pouring down rain the weekend before the parade when we took Majel Roddenberry to Azusa [California] to see the progress," Newman says.

"But as always, it was crystal clear on New Year's morning. The *Enterprise* flew down Colorado Boulevard without a hitch."

The float was dedicated to the memory of *Star Trek* creator Gene Roddenberry, who had passed away only two months earlier.

Worf is less than thrilled when his foster mother, Helena, arrives with Alexander in tow. Although Helena and Worf's foster father, Sergey, had agreed to raise the boy after K'Ehleyr's death, Helena now reports that Alexander is having a difficult time adjusting to his new life; he needs to be raised by his father on the *Enterprise*. Predictably, Worf and Alexander have a difficult time adjusting to one another—a situation aggravated by a ship-based experiment that becomes life threatening.

The thing that director Robert Scheerer liked best about "New Ground" was that it presented a touching story between two characters that just happened to be *alien*s. "It didn't matter what they looked like," Scheerer says. "It was simply people dealing with people."

Scheerer also got a kick out of working with the actors behind those alien facades, particularly the shorter one. "Brian Bonsall *loved* playing Alexander," he says. "That boy had more fun, just putting on and wearing the Klingon makeup. On the first day, he was a little nervous, but from the second day on, he was a real pro."

Scheerer gives credit for the change in Bonsall's performance to the taller actor, Michael Dorn. "Michael is big and hulking," Scheerer says, "but he's also a very sensitive guy. I talked to him about the basis of a father's love, all the frustrations a father has to deal with, and he understood it." It was, Scheerer notes, a unique place for Dorn's character. "Quite often, Worf's position on the ship, particularly the bridge, is to feed lines to others. It was a pleasure that he had something to do with some *body* in it."

"New Ground" marked Bonsall's first appearance as Alexander; the character had debuted a season earlier in "Reunion," played, at that time, by young actor Jon Steuer. Although the director of "Reunion," Jonathan Frakes, managed to develop a close rapport with Steuer, the little boy was deemed too shy for subsequent appearances. Thus Bonsall, whose tenure on *Family Ties* proved that he could handle a recurring role on a television series, got his chance to visit the makeup chair— and the twenty-fourth century.

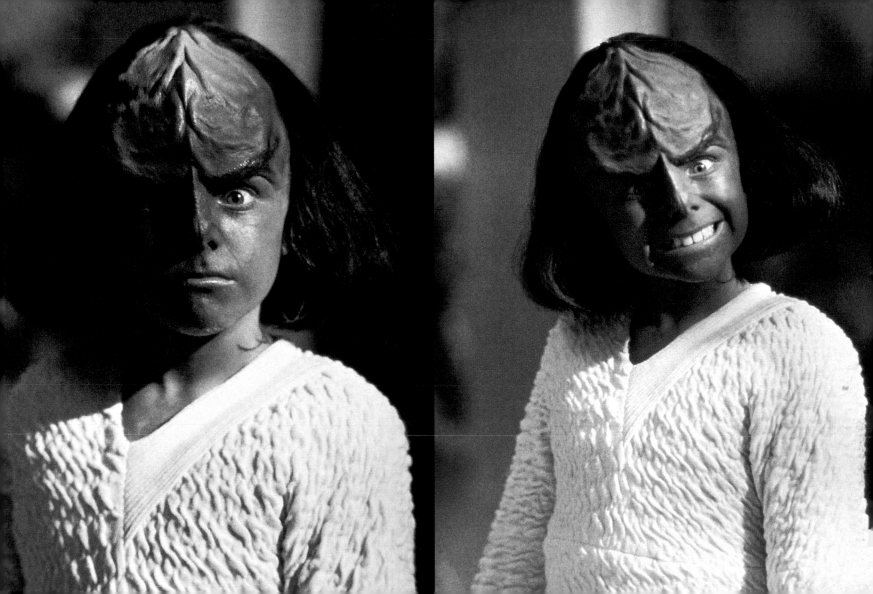

Fans of country music likely think they know everything about singer Eddie Rabbitt. But are they aware that the Nashville superstar was a major *Star Trek* fan?

By *The Next Generation*'s fifth season, the cast and crew were so used to celebrity visitors on the Paramount set that Rabbitt's impromptu appearance during the filming of "New Ground" didn't faze them in the least. In fact, it seems like they gave his presence a big "thumbs-up."

Rabbitt began his singing and songwriting career in his native Brooklyn, but it was a move to Nashville and the sale of the song "Kentucky Rain" to Elvis Presley that jump-started his career. And what a career it was: between the years 1976 and 1989, he scored twenty-six number one hits on the country charts, and eight Top 40 hits on the pop charts. Rabbitt was no stranger to Hollywood; his song "Every Which Way But Loose" served as the theme for the Clint Eastwood movie of that name, and one of his biggest hits, "Drivin' My Life Away," was written for the film *Roadie*.

Sadly, Eddie Rabbitt succumbed to lung cancer in 1998 at the age of fifty-six, just six years after his tour of the *Enterprise*.

The *Enterprise* comes upon the wreckage of a research vessel whose crew was investigating the interior of a Black Cluster, a region marked by intense gravitational tidal waves. The only survivor of the ship is Timothy, a traumatized young boy who fabricates an implausible story about what damaged the *Vico* and killed his parents. Timothy forms an attachment to Data, who rescued him from the vessel, and soon begins to emulate the android. But when the *Enterprise*'s investigation into the disaster sets the starship on course for a similarly tragic outcome, the crew's lives depend on Timothy's revelation of what *really* happened on board the *Vico*.

"Hero Worship" focuses on the pairing of Data, the android with an enduring wish to become human, and a young boy who, as a result of his recent trauma, would rather be an emotionless android. But there was a third partner in the relationship: Counselor Troi. And that was not to writer Joe Menosky's liking.

"It was a Troi-heavy episode, and I had a love/hate relationship with Troi," he explains. "Loved the actress, but hated the character. I used to say that having a full-time therapist on board the *Enterprise*—in a command position no less—would date our series more than any other story element. And in retrospect, that was true. In the 1980s, America was the 'Therapeutic Culture.' Therapy-speak and thinking infected pretty much everything. Unfortunately," Menosky continues, "Gene Roddenberry felt the need to include it as something essential in terms of updating the 'new' *Star Trek*. But look around now [in 2012]. All that stuff is virtually gone. Drugs took over, things like Prozac, which is not necessarily an improvement.

"But maybe," the writer wryly observes, "the NEXT *Next Generation* will have a full-time pharmacist on board."

Opposite: Director Patrick Stewart provides young Joshua Harris with some artistic tips for the upcoming sequence.

Everyone knows that Data is a consummate Renaissance android who excels at music, art, and poetry (which is, admittedly, not to *everyone's* taste). Brent Spiner, however, is not *quite* as talented as his alter ego. He can play guitar (as he demonstrates briefly in "Silicon Avatar"), and he can sing (as he's demonstrated in several Broadway musicals and two of the *Star Trek* movies). But it's unlikely that he paints at Data's masterful level.

Most of the paintings seen on *The Next Generation* were created by members of the show's art department. However, the lovely landscape that Data is seen working on in "Hero Worship" actually was rendered by Dan Curry, who also supervised the episode's visual effects. "I thought it would be fun if Brent was painting one of my own works," explains Curry. "So I brought in a landscape I'd done in Central California. The art department made a print on canvas that looked slightly unfinished so Brent could dab paint on it." The name of the original piece, which hangs in the Curry home, is *Golden Hills Near Hollister, CA.*

4 ▷ 24A 25

Tarmin: "You, Mister Worf? I would love to explore Klingon memories."
Worf: "Klingons do not allow themselves to be . . . probed."

After a delegation of Ullians, a race of telepathic historians who conduct research by probing subjects' long-forgotten memories, comes aboard the *Enterprise*, Counselor Troi experiences a peculiar twist on an otherwise pleasant memory, then lapses into a coma. As Riker and Crusher attempt to figure out if there is a connection between the presence of the Ullians and Troi's condition, the commander, too, falls into a coma, followed by the doctor, leading Picard to suspect that one of the Ullians is a "memory rapist."

"'Violations' was a tough story to do," Jeri Taylor says. "But it was an immediately attractive idea: the idea of rape being a mental thing as opposed to a physical thing. Even though it's mental, not physical, the violation is no less profound."

"Violations" is not the first *Star Trek* episode to deal with "mind rape," nor would it be the last. In 1967's "Mirror, Mirror," an alternate-universe version of Spock forced his way into McCoy's mind to access the knowledge he desperately needed. A quarter of a century later, our own universe's Spock did the same to the treacherous Valeris in *The Undiscovered Country*. His motivation was similar, and was here rationalized as being necessary under the urgent circumstances—but one suspects that Spock wasn't proud of his actions. In a science fiction setting, as Taylor notes, mental violation is as vicious a crime as physical rape.

And poor Troi, so often the victim of mental predators, would no doubt experience déjà vu when Shinzon attempts to have his telepathic way with her years later in *Star Trek Nemesis*. It's a shame she never learned the Betazoid equivalent of "occlumency," the magical defense of the mind against external penetration, as taught at J. K. Rowling's fanciful Hogwarts school.

Opposite: The term "controlled chaos" doesn't quite describe the activity that takes place between shots on a show, which is why "Quiet on the set!" is shouted regularly by one of the assistant directors lurking about like hall monitors. The minute the director calls "Cut" on a shot, dozens of crew members spring into action, retouching hair and makeup, adjusting collars on costumes, or changing the angle of a light, while actors reach for their scripts and eyeglasses, or leave the set altogether for a quick trip to the trailer or the telephone. Here director Robert Wiemer discusses the dining scene with his cast, while hairdressers and others do those things that they do.

Picard is frustrated when Aaron, the leader of a human colony on Moab IV, resists the *Enterprise*'s efforts to save his world from impact by the rapidly approaching fragment of a stellar core. Because the inhabitants of the colony have been genetically engineered to constitute a "perfect" society, Aaron refuses to allow them to evacuate—nor is he happy about the "corruption" factor involved in allowing Picard's crew to mix with his society as they work together to prevent the disaster. Complicating matters is Aaron's attraction to Counselor Troi, and another colonist's desire to leave her manufactured utopia.

Writer James Kahn's single contribution to *Star Trek: The Next Generation* was a story treatment titled "The Perfect Human." Soon after, he set out on a career writing for such series as *TekWar, Xena: Warrior Princess*, and *Melrose Place*, all of which led him to a supervising producer position on *Star Trek: Voyager*.

Writer Adam Belanoff's career followed a similar trajectory. Working from Kahn's treatment, he

drafted his only *TNG* teleplay, giving it the new title "The Masterpiece Society." Belanoff then moved on, as a writer and producer on *Murphy Brown* and *Cosby*, and then into a long tenure as co-supervising producer on *The Closer*.

And so the episode proved a fine beginning for their impressive careers.

"Not many elements from 'The Perfect Human' ended up in 'The Masterpiece Society,'" Belanoff noted in 1993, "but one of the things that did make it was the genetically engineered society. In Kahn's conception, it was an idyllic community that contained, essentially, a hundred Dolph Lundgrens and Paulina Porizkovas, romping around semi-clothed, Adam and Eve–like. It was a beautiful *Blue Lagoon* colony."

Michael Piller was about to discard the concept when Belanoff arrived in his office, courtesy of a USC graduate screenwriting fellowship. "I asked Michael, if you were designing such a community, would you design a place where everybody had beautiful blond hair and large biceps? Wouldn't it be more interesting to have one Mozart, one Picasso, one Einstein, and so on, creating this masterpiece society where each person was in and of himself a masterpiece?"

Piller liked the idea and gave the writing assign-

ment for Kahn's treatment to Belanoff, who incorporated Joe Menosky's suggestion that the society was contained within a controlled ecosystem, à la Tucson's Biosphere 2. Belanoff added one additional twist. "People need obstacles," he explained. "In a place where *everyone* is an Einstein or a Mozart, there's nobody to perform for, everything is provided for, and life is quite easy. Things would tend to stagnate. So we created a biosphere where everything was so finely balanced that even one person's departure could harm it."

The teleplay was generally well received— except by one particular viewer who wasn't easily impressed. "My genetics teacher watched the episode and thought the drama was great, but the genetics part was terrible," Belanoff said.

The entire crew suffers complete memory loss after an unknown alien ship scans the *Enterprise*. Although unable to recall their names or duties, they quickly realize that somehow they still know how to operate the starship. In the confusion, no one notices that Kieran MacDuff, identified by the ship's computer as the *Enterprise*'s executive officer, is someone they've never seen before. The computer also provides evidence that they are on a mission to cross into Lysian space and destroy that species' central computer, as well as any Lysian vessel that attempts to stop them. Somehow, it all feels wrong to Picard, but his new first officer insists he must follow his orders.

"Clues," "Conundrum," and the upcoming "Cause and Effect" all cover similar territory: the crew of the *Enterprise* encounters . . . *something*, and then lose their memories—either of the encounter, or of their own identities. Yet each, in its own way, stands out as a unique episode, with the fourth season's "Clues" evolving into an old-fashioned mystery (*Why did Data lie?*), "Cause and Effect" into a high-con-

cept-driven adventure (*The* Enterprise *is caught in a time loop*), and "Conundrum" into a tale most akin to cold war subterfuge (*Win a war by convincing powerful strangers that your enemy is* their *enemy*). Of the three, only "Conundrum" attempts to play out the humor of the situation, with Worf staking a claim on the captain's chair, Data being mistaken for a bartender, and Riker bedding Ro Laren, a woman with whom he normally can't have a civil conversation.

Right: A scene from "Conundrum" as captured by Robbie Robinson, one of the show's unit photographers.

Opposite: Besides being an award-winning make-up artist, Doug Drexler is also a talented graphic artist. He often carried a drawing pad with him to the *TNG* soundstages in order to occupy his time while waiting to do touch-ups on the actors. "I did a number of on-the-spot sketches while I was sitting on my makeup kit," he says. The sketch at hand captures the action during the filming of "Conundrum." Seated next to Picard, in what would normally be Riker's position, is the faux first officer MacDuff, or, as Drexler describes him, "the naughty alien messing with our gang."

05 || 243 "POWER PLAY"

Data: *"Lieutenant, I must apologize for my in-*
advertent misconduct toward you."
Worf: *"No apology necessary."*
Data: *"Your restraint was most remarkable."*
Worf: *"You have no idea."*

While investigating a distress call from what they believe to be an uninhabited moon, Troi, Data, and O'Brien are possessed by alien entities that hijack their bodies and use them to take hostages aboard the *Enterprise*. Their ultimate goal: to free the non-corporeal spirits of condemned criminals from the moon's penal colony and take command of Picard's ship.

"Working on 'Power Play' wasn't much fun at all," confesses writer Brannon Braga. "The story went through a lot of writers' hands, and had been written and rewritten and rewritten again. Finally, it fell into my lap and I did the best I could with the concept. But it was just a basic hostage drama with aliens, another body-snatcher story."

The budget-minded producers didn't have much

fun with it either. Although it originally was intended to be a money-saving bottle show filmed primarily on the *Enterprise*, efforts to make the episode more interesting resulted in some major action scenes and a sequence shot on Stage 16 involving wind, blowing sand, atmospheric fog, and lightning. The costs ballooned accordingly.

"The episode benefitted from two things," Braga says. "Our regular line producer, David Livingston, directed the episode and he really elevated the material. Top-notch directing. And also, the show at the time was at the top of its game—incredibly popular—and it just seemed like Patrick Stewart and the others could just do no wrong in the audience's eyes. So even though it was a mediocre script in my opinion, it turned out okay. At least we got to see our characters being different without a lick of pretension. No themes, no issues, no metaphors. Just a good, solid action show."

Right: Director David Livingston demonstrates the abject terror that he wants Rosalind Chao to evince.
Opposite: Ro and Geordi experience the ship's "easy access" conduits.

No. They don't do their own stunts (redux). And here's one example why.

"Marina [Sirtis] was always very active, like the rest of the cast—very physical," says stunt coordinator Dennis Madalone. "She always wanted to do her own stunts, but I always brought in a stunt double."

The stunt required during the shooting of "Power Play" was a basic foot fall. All Sirtis had to do was fall over. Simple. So director David Livingston offered her the opportunity to do it herself. "And I said, 'Sure, I can do that,'" recalls the actress.

The first take went fine, with Sirtis rolling her body slightly to one side, "as I'd been taught to do in drama school, because there are no important bits on your side," she says. For the next take, the director suggested she fall straight back, so the camera could see her face. "Well, my brain stopped and I said, 'Sure,' and on take two I fell straight back—and was laying there, immobilized. I couldn't get up. I had hurt my back."

"She hit the ground like a stuntwoman," says Madalone. "She was great. Her feet were up in the air, her hair went flying. I was proud of her. But when she got up, she got up real slow."

Reportedly, the injury took several weeks to heal, but Sirtis gamely continued filming, successfully concealing any discomfort she may have been experiencing.

"The capper to the story is that when I saw the episode, they never came in for a close-up," laments Sirtis. "It was a big wide shot that covered all of us. It could have been Michael Dorn in my wig and costume and no one would have known! After that I became *much* more careful about stunts!"

Opposite: Dan Curry's storyboard for the lightning strike sequence precisely guided Livingston's direction.

STAR TREK
THE NEXT GENERATION

"POWER PLAY"
SHOW # 215

Dan Curry
1/14/92

Sc. 19
CUT 1
LIGHTNING BOLT STRIKES AS O'BRIEN ATTEMPTS TO ACTIVATE ENHANCER ROD.

LIGHTNING CROSSES FOREGROUND OF FRAME... WHITE OUT

Sc. 19
CUT 1
CUT 2
⑥ Sc. 24
HIGH ANGLE... LIGHTNING ZAP CONCLUDES BEASTIES FLY IN FROM ABOVE CAMERA
TRIANGLE OF ENHANCING BEAM IS ON ... AWAY TEAM BEAMS OUT

Sc. 23
BEASTIES ENTER TROI, O'BRIEN, & DATA... BUT NOT RIKER

Sc. 24
RIKER ACTIVATES ENHANCEMENT BEAMS

"When a Klingon can no longer stand and face his enemies as a warrior, when he becomes a burden to his friends and family, it is time for the Hegh'bat. Time for him to die." —Worf

Paralyzed after an accident, Worf would prefer to commit ritual suicide than to live with only partial mobility. But when he realizes that Klingon customs dictate that his young son must assist in the ceremony, Worf chooses to accept the dangerous surgical option offered by a neuro-specialist whom Doctor Crusher considers to be unethical—despite the very real chance that the untried technique might kill him.

"I hated working on 'Ethics,'" growls writer Ron Moore. "Hated everything about it. I wasn't a big fan of doing medical shows to begin with, and that particular one had a ton of medical jargon and technology and medical ethics. The only thing I found interesting was that Worf wanted to die, but there was a whole internal fight about euthanasia and what the show was saying, and how it could be interpreted that it's not honorable to live with a dis-

ability. And I said, 'That wouldn't matter to Worf. He wouldn't want to *live* like that. He's a *Klingon*, and a Klingon would want to be killed.'"

But while Moore couldn't wait to move on to the next episode, visual effects supervisor Dan Curry was inspired by it.

With a fine arts degree from Middlebury College, Curry worked for a time as a biomedical illustrator before breaking into the entertainment industry. During his lengthy career on the various *Star Trek* series, Curry enjoyed the ever-deepening analysis of Klingon culture and anthropology conducted by the franchise's writers. "There were frequent references about Klingon anatomy in the scripts, such as the number of ribs—which I concluded would have to be in a lattice design to fit them all in, and provide strong protection for internal organs," he explains. "I also considered a more protective clavicle, redundant bones in the upper arms and legs, and so forth. These alien anatomical features had to fit within a human body."

Recalling his earlier career as an illustrator, Curry created a unique Klingon portrait. "I was thinking John Singer Sargent [an American artist of the late nineteenth to early twentieth century, known

for his realistic portraits] meets Andreas Vesalius [the fourteenth-century anatomist/physician considered the founder of human anatomy]," explains Curry. The result was his painting, *The Visible Klingon*, an eighteen- by twenty-four-inch piece done in oil on Gatorboard. After some discussions with Michael Westmore, Curry added a horn to the foot, explaining, he says, "why Klingons never developed soccer."

"I have had those feelings, those longings, all of my life. It is not unnatural. I am not sick because I feel this way. I do not need to be helped. I do not need to be cured." —Soren

When the androgynous J'naii species ask for the *Enterprise*'s aid in locating a missing shuttle, Riker finds himself working with Soren, a J'naii pilot. The pair pass the time by comparing their respective cultures. Soren explains that the J'naii are forbidden to engage in gender-specific relationships, and never publicly identify themselves as either male or female. Those that do express sexual preference are captured and brainwashed into "healthy" attitudes. But Soren admits that "she" has always felt female, and is, in fact, attracted to Riker.

"'The Outcast' allowed us to examine the issue of sexual intolerance in a unique, offbeat way," Jeri Taylor says. "I identify with the disenfranchised and the powerless of our world. So I really wanted to make a statement for tolerance, broad-mindedness, and acceptance of those who are disenfranchised."

Not everyone in the audience shared Taylor's feelings—which didn't really surprise the producers. The episode was crafted to demonstrate the injustice of certain social-sexual attitudes prevalent in twentieth-century society. They figured that was likely to irk viewers who liked their social-sexual attitudes the way they were, thank you. But while they did get some complaints from social conservatives, they got many more from members of the gay community, who complained that the episode hadn't gone far enough, and that it couched the question of sexual orientation in a way that heterosexuals easily could think was about heterosexuality.

According to a 2001 Salon.com article titled "Gay Trek," the most contentious issue was Soren's statement that on J'anii, "Some have strong inclinations for maleness. Some have urges to be female. In our world, those feelings are forbidden." There was no mention of those with "urges to be female" being attracted to other females, or the "male-inclined" being drawn to males. There was no mention of homosexuality at all. And although Soren's speech goes on to describe the need to "lead secret and guarded lives," gay viewers thought the producers felt the need to slink around the allegory.

While it's easy to understand the controversy, it's impossible to address it twenty years on. The series attempted, in the typically broad way that *Star Trek* has utilized since its very beginnings, to address a social injustice by putting it in alien drag (so to speak).

"When we deal with an issue, we have to find an oblique way of addressing it, incorporating a science fiction element that turns it on its ear," explains Taylor. "'The Outcast' succeeded in that way for most of the audience. It is still the episode of which I am most proud."

Opposite: Sometimes a kiss is romantic. Sometimes a kiss is controversial. And sometimes, particularly when there's a beard involved, a kiss makes your nose itch—but you can't deal with it till the director calls "Cut!"

To a film production studio like Paramount, space is money. Not "outer" space (although creating stories about that can be quite lucrative), but "rental" space. In a very real sense, the major Hollywood studios are, as much as anything else, rental landlords. They rent space such as soundstages, makeup and wardrobe trailers, and the carpentry mill, charging even their own productions for every square inch of real estate occupied. It's called show *business* after all, with the accounting department keeping a close eye on the bottom line.

Thus, one of the tasks assigned a producer is to make maximum use of every inch of the space being rented. It didn't take long for the producers of *Star Trek: The Next Generation* to realize that the shuttlebay set took up an inordinate amount of space for the small amount of time it was used for filming. And so it was assigned an additional duty: as waiting area and lunchroom for the background actors, or "extras."

While the cast and visiting costars were assigned private trailers to relax during their downtime between scenes, and the filmmaking staff had their offices scattered about the lot, the extras had only the waiting area. There they could read, knit, play cards, converse—or, if they were so inclined, close their eyes and contemplate climbing aboard the shuttlecraft for a quick trip to Risa, the pleasure planet.

Historical note: The full-scale version of the shuttlecraft type 6 (pictured) was introduced in the episode "The Outcast." A miniature of the vessel had appeared earlier in the season, in "Darmok."

It's déjà vu all over again . . . and again . . . and again, when a mission to chart a region known as the Typhon Expanse leads the *Enterprise* to repeated disaster. The ship's propulsion system fails, and the crew finds itself on a collision course with a ship that seems to appear out of nowhere. Offered differing advice from Data and Riker, Picard makes a decision and pays the price as the *Enterprise* strikes the other vessel and explodes—and then pops back into existence a short time later as the crew repeats the same routine, thanks to a time loop that has snared them like flypaper.

Right: Director Jonathan Frakes prepares actor Kelsey Grammer for his transition from Dr. Frasier Crane to Captain Morgan Bateson. Grammer's scenes on the *Bozeman* were filmed on the bridge of the *Enterprise*-A, recently retired from service in the film franchise following the events of *Star Trek VI: The Undiscovered Country.*

"When I got the script to 'Cause and Effect,' I thought it was a joke from Brannon Braga," director Jonathan Frakes says. "I read act one. I read act two. I read act three. I read act four. I read act five. And I said, 'You guys are screwing with me! C'mon!'"

"I remember Jonathan saying that," Braga relates with a chuckle. "And he wasn't alone. When the episode aired, people thought there was something wrong with their TV sets, or that the station was airing the same act again."

The confusion arose from a story device apparently new to some of the viewers: a time loop. "We were trying things on the show that had never been done before," Braga notes. "Time loops were common in science fiction literature, but this was pretty daring for television. And remember, this was before the movie *Groundhog Day*.

"The idea came from kind of a challenge that had been laid down," Braga says. "Gene Roddenberry didn't want us to do certain things on the show. 'No time travel' was one of those things. To me, that was a direct challenge, because that's my favorite kind of story. So I decided to do time travel in a way that hadn't been seen before. Usually, time travel stories have someone going back to stop something from happening. It seemed to me that you could do *anything* with time. You could be caught in the same day over and over again. And that's where it started.

"It was hard to write," Braga continues, "because each act is subtly different. I remember sitting in the room with Michael [Piller] and the staff breaking that story, wondering, 'How are we gonna break them *out* of the time loop?' It took us several days before we came up with using the poker game and sending a message through Data. Then Jonathan did a *brilliant* job in filming each repeated scene a little different."

"The same scene had to be shot *five* different ways!" Frakes recalls. "Man! It was a real challenge. In a weird way, planning all those different courtroom shots in 'The Drumhead' had prepared me for it, because a lot of it takes place on the bridge. I decided to have the actors do it exactly the same way each time, but to show it from a different point of view. I'd watched a lot of directors by then, and directed a few episodes, so I knew all the possible bridge angles—and I think I used *all* of them."

"At the time, the episode felt like this funky experiment," Braga comments. "Now, twenty years later, it's considered a 'classic.' I'm friends with Seth MacFarlane, the guy who created *Family Guy*. He loves *The Next Generation*, watched it when he was growing up. He told me 'Cause and Effect' was his favorite episode—and then he said, 'I was eleven years old when I saw it.'

"Which makes me feel old!"

Eric Alba was one of many young visual effects associates who worked behind the scenes on *Star Trek* during the early 1990s. "I held a swing position in postproduction," Alba notes. "At the time, we were shooting *The Next Generation* and *Deep Space Nine,* and I worked for both series.

"*Star Trek* was my first TV show and my first visual effects job, so I always say that *TNG* and *DS9* were my film school, since I never actually went to one. The things I learned there I still carry with me today. I learned a lot about teamwork and what a collaborative art form filmmaking is, even at the TV level. My mentors Dan Curry and Rob Legato and Gary Hutzel were all very generous with their time and willing to teach me. I was in a unique situation—a very young kid who was allowed to learn all of this stuff at the beginning, before computer graphic imaging was everywhere."

Alba was—and still is—an avid photographer, and he kept his camera with him on the job, just in case something interesting caught his eye. The photo opposite is of Alba with one of the saucer sections that were blown apart in "Cause and Effect." "They blew up four or five models, all built by Greg Jein. Greg always kept the molds—what we called the

negative—for the ships he built, so he could create new pieces if he had to repair something. Greg had to paint them and put all the details on, but he didn't have to include lights. You can see in the picture that the models were pre-scored so they would break apart easily during pyro."

Right: Just a few of the extremely talented people who worked on *TNG* and *DS9* effects, circa 1993. Left to right, foreground: visual effects supervisors Joe Bauer, Glenn Neufeld, David Stipes, and Gary Hutzel. Behind the desk: visual effects producer Dan Curry, and (on the floor) model maker Greg Jein.

"The first duty of every Starfleet officer is to the truth. Whether it's scientific truth, or historical truth, or personal truth. It is the guiding principle upon which Starfleet is based. If you can't find it within yourself to stand up and tell the truth about what happened, you don't deserve to wear that uniform." **—Picard**

A member of Wesley Crusher's five-person flight squadron at Starfleet Academy has been killed during a complicated in-flight maneuver. Wesley and the other members of the team say that the youth panicked during the maneuver, inadvertently triggering the accident. As Starfleet conducts an investigation, Picard suspects that the four survivors are hiding something, and he pressures Wesley to come forward with the truth. But the truth could cost Wesley more than the friendship of his teammates; it could end his career in Starfleet.

For a show that initially tried to dodge continuing story lines for supporting characters, "The First Duty" did a lot to set that precedent on its ear. Shan-non Fill, as Cadet Sito, would reprise her role (and redeem her character) in the seventh season episode "Lower Decks." Boothby, played by veteran character actor Ray Walston, would appear twice in *Voyager* (although in both cases, he was a faux Boothby). And Robert Duncan McNeill soon would become a regular cast member on *Voyager*, playing someone who was *almost* (but not quite) Nick Locarno. That show's executive producers—Rick Berman, Michael Piller, and Jeri Taylor—had been so impressed with McNeill's performance in "The First Duty" that they created a role for him: Tom Paris, a character patterned after Locarno, but with a difference. "Locarno seemed like a nice guy, but deep down he was a bad guy," McNeill told *Star Trek: The Official Fan Club* magazine in a 1997 interview. "Tom Paris is an opposite premise. Deep down he's a good guy. He's just made some mistakes."

While not a character per se, the Japanese gardens at the Tillman Water Reclamation Plant in Los Angeles, first seen in the episode "Justice," made such a positive impression as the setting for Starfleet Academy and nearby Starfleet Headquarters in "The First Duty," that it became the permanent go-to location shoot for all future *Star Trek* episodes set in the fictional facility. Tillman would be seen in one additional *TNG* episode, and nine subsequent episodes of *Deep Space Nine*, *Voyager*, and *Star Trek: Enterprise*.

Like Ron Moore, Naren Shankar attended college at Cornell. In fact, they met as members of the same fraternity, and became good friends. When Moore left town to try to make it as a writer in Los Angeles, Shankar toiled on at Cornell, obtaining an engineering degree. A few years later, he says, "I was finishing up my doctoral dissertation, but by then I'd already decided I didn't want to be an engineer anymore." At that point, all it took was a bit of encouragement from Moore, who'd recently begun working on *The Next Generation*, to motivate him westward.

"I wrote a spec *Star Trek* script, Ron showed it to the guys on the show, and they liked it enough to hire me on as a Writers' Guild intern," Shankar relates. After his internship ended, his engineering background won him a spot as the show's in-house science consultant. "But they also let me pitch stories," he says. "My first credit was 'The First Duty,' which Ron and I wrote together. Ron had been in ROTC in college and we were both into military history. We wanted to do a show set at Starfleet Academy and pick up where Wesley was with his life. Our focus was on the notion of choosing between your friends and your duty. And the script actually caused a fair amount of tension between us and Michael Piller."

"There were *always* fights in the writers' room," explains Ron Moore. "A lot of arguing. But the writers were not muzzled there—Michael [Piller], Ira [Behr], and Jeri [Taylor] put up with a lot from us."

The fight, in this case, was over Wesley's moral dilemma. "Naren and I took the position that Wesley shouldn't be ratting out his friends," Moore continues. "He should go down with them. And Michael took this parental position: 'As the father of teenagers, I can tell you that it's just wrong, and telling the truth is more important than anything else.' But *we* felt that your word to your friends is more important on some levels than your obligation to the rules. Naren and I weren't that far removed from being that age in college, and being in those kinds of circumstances. Wesley had given his *word* to hold the secret about what they had done and what led to this kid's death. He had to stand by that with his buddies. But Michael felt that sent a bad message, and that telling the truth is what *Star Trek* is about."

Moore laughs. "It could get pretty passionate in that room. You could take an argument as far as you possibly could, and there was no penalty. Sometimes you convinced them and sometimes you didn't. Michael would finally say, 'Enough. No.' But no one ever held a grudge."

One wonders whether, years later, and with more perspective, Moore and Shankar ever came to see Piller's point of view on this particular episode.

Shankar chuckles as he sums it up concisely: "Nope."

"Life's true gift is the capacity to enjoy enjoyment." —**Lwaxana**

As if the presence of Lwaxana Troi—who has arrived with the startling news that she plans to marry a man she has never met—isn't bad enough, the *Enterprise* begins to experience a bizarre number of system malfunctions that gradually increase in severity. Geordi and Data trace the problem to metallic parasites that infested the ship as it passed through an asteroid field—but with the life-support system failing and the crew's oxygen supply running out, it's obviously too late to call in the exterminators.

Michael Westmore's second *TNG* Emmy win, for Outstanding Individual Achievement in Makeup for a Series, was for his fanciful holodeck creations in "Cost of Living." "Thanks to the holodeck, I never knew what sort of characters I'd be called upon to create," Westmore says. For "Cost of Living," he devised the strange group of characters on the opposite page, all of whom inhabited the Parallax Colony of Shiralea VI, a favorite destination, apparently, for Lwaxana Troi. "There was a fire sculptor, who had an elaborate set of head appliances; the dancer, whose entire body had to be painted; and the poet, whose wig and beard were made of rope," the makeup designer elaborates. "We literally used dyed hemp for his hair, hand-laying each strand. And we had a lot of fun doing the juggler, who wore a nosepiece, and had ears that wrapped around his head—an idea I'd had for a long time. For a more whimsical look, we added spiked hair and eyebrows that grew up in the center of his forehead."

Robert Blackman also received an Emmy that year, for Outstanding Individual Achievement in Costume Design for a Series—although most likely *not* for the "ensemble" that Lwaxana wore to her wedding ceremony (right).

A leopard never changes her spots—but occasionally she loans them out.

Former Dutch model Famke Janssen's charismatic performance in "The Perfect Mate" made as big an impression on the *Star Trek* producers as her counterpart Kamala did on the *Enterprise*'s male crew members. The episode's production coincided with casting on *Deep Space Nine*, where Piller and Berman were having a tough time finding the right actress to play Jadzia Dax, their Trill science officer. Suddenly, with Janssen, they thought they'd found the answer to their prayers.

But Janssen turned them down. "I wanted some kind of guarantee that I could do feature films on the side," Janssen recalls. "And while I felt [*Deep Space Nine*] was a great opportunity, I felt I would get lazy as an actor if I didn't keep challenging myself with different parts."

Janssen went on to appear in a variety of films, including a memorable turn as sexy villainess Xenia Onatopp in the James Bond thriller *GoldenEye*, and three turns in the *X-Men* franchise (once again opposite Patrick Stewart). Months later, Terry Farrell would win the role of Jadzia, but Janssen's imprint on the role still would be felt—via her sexy spots.

When *TNG* viewers were introduced to the Trill in "The Host," the species sported a pronounced browridge, courtesy of Michael Westmore. But the studio didn't like the idea of hiding a beautiful new female character behind a lumpy forehead. Eventually, the footage of Dax in the prosthetic was scrapped, and Westmore substituted spots reminiscent of Kamala's in "The Perfect Mate." They worked so well that all Trill characters subsequently introduced bore the spots, consigning the look of Odan in "The Host" to the mysterious realm of "it never happened."

Also in that "never happened" vein: a fantasy sequence at the end of "The Perfect Mate," in which Picard imagines "rescuing" Kamala from the boring life that awaits her on Valt Minor.

MOVING WITH PICARD'S EYES - EXTREME CLOSEUP

62 HER FACE

as Alrik removes the veil.

> KAMALA
> *I am for you Alrik of Valt.*

And as Alrik leans forward to kiss her . . .

> PICARD
> *I'm sorry. I cannot allow this to proceed.*

Alrik turns sharply to Picard . . .

> ALRIK
> *What did you say?*

> PICARD
> *Kamala will be remaining aboard the Enterprise . . . with me . . .*

Kamala reacts, looks to Picard . . .

> ALRIK
> (flabbergasted)
> *With you?*

> PICARD
> *Chancellor, the trade agreements will be satisfactory . . . you yourself told me that was your priority. She is mine. Let us begin the real work here of establishing a long and just peace . . .*

Alrik takes a moment to regain his composure . . .

> ALRIK
> *Very well, let us begin . . .*

As she smiles with an expression of love for her captain . . .

Although both Piller and Patrick Stewart liked the sequence—which was shot at the same time as the scene that actually appears in the final episode—Rick Berman ultimately nixed it.

Opposite: Kamala and Alrik react as Picard intervenes.

As Captain Picard attempts to figure out how and why the *Enterprise* is being drained of power, Troi tries to figure out why sweet Clara Sutter has recently become such a naughty little girl. Clara keeps blaming all of her misbehavior on an imaginary friend named Isabella, but no one believes her—until Isabella attacks Troi and tells Clara that her people are going to kill every person aboard the *Enterprise*. Realizing that Isabella's "people" are behind the starship's power drain, Picard tries to reason with Isabella, only to discover that naughty alien entities are no easier to reason with than naughty little girls.

It's 2011 and his new series, *Terra Nova*, will premier in about a week, yet Brannon Braga still enjoys going through a list of his *TNG* episodes. When he comes to "Imaginary Friend," he starts to chuckle, but it's an ironic, self-deprecating kind of chuckle. "You can see the pattern here, can't you?" he asks. "I go from writing a good one—"

Like "Cause and Effect"—

"Like 'Cause and Effect,'" he confirms. "And then 'Imaginary Friend' falls into my lap for a rewrite. It's like I would be rewarded for doing a good episode by being given one of *these*."

"One of these" would be a story that already had been through the hands of several freelancers before it got to him. Still, "Imaginary Friend" isn't a bad story—it's just one in which Braga didn't have much room to maneuver.

"I think it's one that people don't like very much," Braga admits. "It was a cute little story, maybe a little predictable. The concept might have been better as a half-hour *Twilight Zone* episode than an hour of *The Next Generation*.

"I actually *enjoy* writing for children," he says. "Let me put it this way: it's a lot easier to write a young girl's dialogue than Captain Picard's. Picard is *brilliant*. He's articulate. He solves problems in the *right way*. He's thoughtful, presidential. I'm *none* of those things. So the hardest character for me to write for, in my entire career to date, is Captain Picard," he says.

"He's still at the top of the list. Writing a seven-year-old girl? No problem."

Tracking a distress signal to a distant world, the crew of the *Enterprise* finds the wreckage of a Borg cube and one surviving drone. Although Picard initially wants no part in assisting the injured Borg, Doctor Crusher convinces him to allow her to treat it aboard the ship. Separated from the Borg collective, the drone begins to regain a sense of individuality, and members of the crew who were initially skeptical about its presence begin to feel empathy for the lost soul, who takes the name "Hugh." Picard, however, remains convinced that Hugh cannot be redeemed, and he instructs La Forge and Crusher to find a way to utilize his mental connection with the Borg to destroy the entire species.

By *TNG*'s fifth season, René Echevarria had pitched and sold several stories to the show's producers. He'd also been given the opportunity to work on other freelancers' scripts, including "The Perfect Mate." Yet he'd remained in New York City, not quite ready to trade life on the fringes of Broadway for a more promising future in Hollywood. "I, Borg" would change all that.

Like "The Offspring," it was a story that sprang from one of Echevarria's "ruminations" on keynote elements of the series, in this case, the Borg. "They were such successful characters," Echevarria says, "and yet the producers hadn't touched upon them since the big two-parter. They didn't think they could top themselves in terms of scale and scope. So I had this flash of inspiration: What if you reversed the way you look at the Borg? What if this was an intimate story about *one* of them? What would just *one* Borg be like—by himself? What if we found a crashed ship with one living Borg inside?"

The producers loved his pitch. But it was only after Echevarria flew out to L.A. to develop the script that they realized how much he had grown as a writer. "I came in and I said, 'Here's how the story lays out,' and they said, 'Yeah, that works. Do that.'

I made some patient discoveries along the way as I was actually writing it. And from my perspective today, as somebody who now *hires* writers to work on projects that *I* oversee, I realize that this is something a producer looks for—somebody who brings more to the material than you sent them off with. Something that surprises you. And I think I sort of surprised Michael [Piller] because on my own, in the writing of it, I came up with the whole gag that Hugh only uses the word 'we'—doesn't understand the word 'I.' And I came up with the idea of Picard acting like Locutus, and trying to push Hugh to the point where Hugh says, 'No, *I* will not do that.' And that's the moment when Picard realizes that something has changed about this little Borg.

"And that's when they asked me to come and be on staff. That's when I moved from New York and started getting serious about writing for television instead of trying to do groundbreaking plays in basements!"

With production number 223, *TNG* film editor Robert Lederman became the latest in the line of "first-timers" allowed to direct. By luck of the draw, he was assigned to "I, Borg," an episode destined to tug at the audience's collective heartstrings. Part of its quality was inherent in the compelling script written by René Echevarria. But casting, too, contributed to the episode's emotional impact, and Lederman joined supervising producer Jeri Taylor in that process, looking at almost thirty actors before picking Jonathan Del Arco to play Hugh. "This character would be different than the Borg we've had on previous shows, simply because he was going to obtain an aspect of individuality," Lederman explains. "I believe it was Jeri Taylor who first thought of him as 'Edward Scissorhands.' Not only did that give us the 'hook' we were looking for, but it was also helpful in terms of my direction of Jonathan."

Lederman worked with the young actor—who, with his white Borg makeup, large eyes, and wistful expression, actually *did* resemble Johnny Depp's Scissorhands character—to establish what they referred to as "the Borg meter." This allowed them to pinpoint where Hugh's inner evolution was at any given point, with "one" being all Borg and "ten" be-

ing nearly human. "In every scene, we had a number for where he was on the scale," Lederman says. "During rehearsal, if I said, 'Jonathan, you're at six—we need you to be at eight,' he immediately knew what I meant."

Once again, Michael Westmore Jr.'s talent with electronics enhanced a character's makeup. Westmore Sr. had decided to use a hologram for one of Hugh's prosthetic eyes, and in one of the scenes, Geordi asked Hugh if he could take a look at it. "Hugh reaches up, pulls off the piece, and hands it to him," recalls Westmore Sr. "And the question I asked myself was, what do you see when a Borg pulls his eye out?" Westmore designed the eyepiece with magnets built into both sides of the appliance, so that it would click together. His son created what was revealed in the prosthetic beneath. "He built a four-colored LED, so when Hugh pulls off his eyepiece, a series of red, green, yellow, and orange lights started blinking," Westmore Sr. says. "We hooked the LEDs to a battery pack on the actor's back, and ran the wires inside the headpiece." Westmore Jr. was also responsible for creating the electronics in Hugh's Borg hand.

Opposite: Lederman and Del Arco compare readings on the Borg meter; between scenes, Del Arco peeks out from beneath the prosthetic.

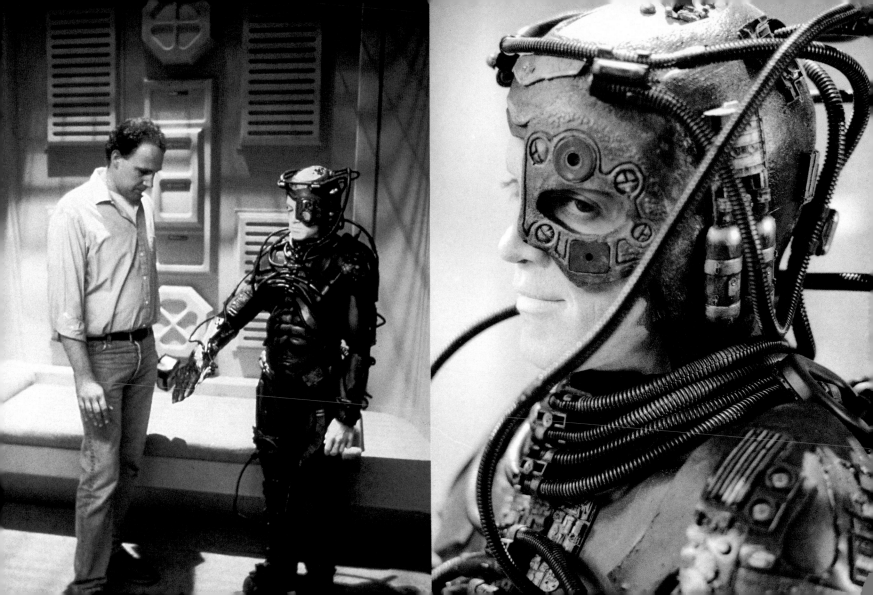

Picard responds to a distress signal from a Romulan science vessel by assigning Geordi and Ro to assist its crew. But when the pair attempts to beam back to the *Enterprise*, something goes wrong and they never arrive. Reluctantly, Picard declares them dead, and the crew plans a memorial service. There's only one thing wrong with that plan: Ro and La Forge are alive and well. They're just "out of phase," thanks to the ill-fated—and illicit—test of a new cloaking field by the Romulans. As the Romulans, worried that Picard and company will figure out what they were doing, quietly plot to sabotage the *Enterprise*, Geordi and Ro try to find a way to communicate with their friends before it's too late.

"We were always trying to find ways to work Ro into our scripts," Ron Moore shares. "She was someone you could count on to bring spark into any scene and stir up conflict with the other characters. That's the kind of thing a writer is always looking for."

No surprise, then, that Ro played such a prominent role in "The Next Phase." "The episode was a kick," says Moore. "I really enjoyed the ghost story aspect of it. You know: getting to go to your own funeral, walking around on the *Enterprise* with people mourning you, watching Riker play his trombone at your wake."

Fun to write and fun to watch—but maybe not such fun to shoot. Walking through walls is not as simple as it looks. Michelle Forbes and LeVar Burton spent two extremely long days on a separate Paramount soundstage, filming the necessary blue screen sequences, doing take after take for director David Carson and visual effects supervisor Rob Legato.

The "interphase cloak" being developed by the Romulans was too good an idea to waste on one episode. Moore would bring back a similar device—one developed by some amoral Starfleet types—in his episode "The *Pegasus*."

Right: Susanna Thompson played the female Romulan officer Varel, the first of several *Star Trek* roles the actress would inhabit. She'd return to *TNG* the following season as a mental patient in "Frame of Mind," then beam over to *Deep Space Nine* to play Jadzia Dax's lover in "Rejoined." She also guest-starred as the Borg queen in three episodes of *Star Trek: Voyager*.

"If you remember what we were, and how we lived, then we'll have found life again. . . . Now we live in you. Tell them of us, my darling." —Eline

After being struck by an energy beam from an ancient probe, Picard finds himself on the drought-stricken world of Kataan. Although the captain retains all of his memories of life aboard the *Enterprise*, the people of Kataan insist that he has always lived on their world. To them, he is a simple laborer named Kamin, the beloved of a young wife named Eline. It's a reality that Picard initially rejects, but with no sign of the *Enterprise*, he comes to realize that he may as well make the best of his new life.

Opposite: The sentimental value of the prop for Kamin's Ressikan flute, offered by Christie's in 2006, was greatly underestimated by the auction house. Its initial estimated value was $300. The final selling price: *$40,000*.

"To me, 'The Inner Light' has always represented the serendipitous nature of storytelling," Joe Menosky relates.

"Michael Piller wanted to do an episode about 'Picard's Unlived Life,' and the staff tried for over a year to come up with a story. Brannon Braga and I worked out at least a half dozen concepts ourselves—and they all failed. The whole staff had a huge desire to see this theme happen in some form or another.

"Morgan Gendel had been the network rep on *Hunter,* the first television series I worked for. One day, he asked if he could pitch to *TNG,* and he pitched an idea to me about a probe that shot all of this information into Picard's head. As soon as I heard it, I told Brannon, and he agreed that Morgan had cracked it and provided the mechanism for a story about Picard's unlived life. But the story was very raw. There was too much of a chance that if we let Morgan tell it to Michael right away, Michael would say no. So we gave Morgan some ideas, and he went off to work on it. He re-pitched it to us several times over the next few weeks. At some point, Ron Moore came into the process, and he was just as excited about it as we were.

"When Morgan was ready, we scheduled a meeting for him with Michael, and after the pitch, Ron, Brannon, and I jumped in like it was the first time we'd heard it. 'Isn't that GREAT!' 'This is it!' 'Fantastic!' Michael just sat there and let us rave for a bit. And then he said, 'I love it.'

"After that, the break session for 'Inner Light' was amazing. Everybody was in love with the result. Each of us would have *killed* to write the script, because we knew how great it was going to be, that it was destined to become a part of *Star Trek* history. Peter Allan Fields's number was next in the rotation, so he got assigned to work behind Morgan on the script. Morgan was a very solid writer, and Pete certainly was top-notch—underrated in my opinion—just a really fine stylist. And by then, Michael had developed a very personal attachment to the episode, so he did a significant, uncredited rewrite on the dialogue himself.

"This great story almost didn't happen. Morgan's probe was such a simple idea. Anybody could've thought of it, but nobody else did. It makes me wonder how many other 'untold' stories were out there that we missed.

"A massive amount of work went into the 'development' of the pitch," Menosky continues with a chuckle, "and Michael never knew it was happening. It wasn't until many years later that he learned how hard the junior staff had 'worked him' on this."

Opposite: Coproducer Peter Lauritson had the good fortune to draw "The Inner Light" for his first directing assignment.

It's hard to pinpoint just what makes "The Inner Light" one of *The Next Generation*'s most popular episodes. It's a very simple story: zapped by a mysterious space probe, Picard is forced to live out the rest of his days on a dying alien world. Being *Star Trek*, of course, "the rest of his days" adds up to only twenty-five minutes of Picard's normal existence aboard the *Enterprise*. The probe turns off its beam and Picard finds himself back home. The End.

It could have been an old *Twilight Zone* episode—intellectually stimulating but emotionally uninvolving, because it happens to one of those anonymous characters who inhabit anthology shows. Viewers find it difficult to invest their emotions in a character they've only known for half an hour.

But viewers can and do invest their emotions in Picard. They *know* this man. They've traveled across the galaxy with him for 125 hours. They've come to understand his likes and dislikes, and even his deepest fears. So they experience this disorienting situation along with him. And thanks to an incredible performance by Patrick Stewart, they *feel* it as well.

What would it be like, to be torn from your everyday existence, and tossed into another life—one that you've spent many years avoiding? After you re-alize that this, now, *is* your life, that this *is* your beautiful house, this *is* your beautiful wife—you yield to the situation. And commit to it, because you are a person who commits, no matter where you are or what name they call you. You commit to loving your wife. You commit to loving your children. You commit to your friends and your community.

It's as if the episode's broadcast *is* the mysterious probe, forcing the viewers at home to live Picard's "unlived life" along with him. And when that "life" ends, when the episode is over, we are as emotionally upended as he is. We understand his loss, because it's ours, too.

The experience apparently affected Patrick Stewart as well. In an interview shortly after the episode aired, he noted, "The most affecting sequence [in 'The Inner Light'] was the one scene where I was with the actress who was playing my wife, late one warm evening, sitting on a bench outside. I remember looking at her and thinking, 'This is what it feels like to be elderly: sitting on a bench with someone you know so well, and this is what lies ahead.' That was the one time I had a sense of, God willing, what was waiting for me."

"The Inner Light" won the World Science Fiction Society's Hugo Award for Best Dramatic Presentation in 1993.

An unusual 500-year-old artifact—Data's head—found at an excavation site beneath San Francisco leads scientists to summon the crew of the *Enterprise* to the scene. Picard learns the excavation was initiated following the discovery of triolic wave traces in the cavern. Because no one on Earth could have produced those waves during the nineteenth century, the finding suggests evidence of alien visitors in Earth's past. The *Enterprise* travels to Devidia II, home to a species that uses the rays, and encounters both a time rift and beings that the crew can't see because they are slightly out of phase. Picard is hesitant to send Data into a situation that could lead to his eventual decapitation, but the android is the only one capable of manipulating the equipment that will shift the aliens' time frame and render them visible. Data succeeds, but before he can report back, another time rift opens, sending the android back to the nineteenth century, where he meets writer Mark Twain and Guinan, the *Enterprise*'s long-lived alien bartender.

Opposite: "Time's Arrow" made good use of the ship's transporter pattern enhancers first seen in "Power Play." Note that Rick Sternbach's sketch

(right) included a "possible packaging scheme" that the folks at Makeup & Effects Laboratories (MEL) picked up on when they created the prop. "We look at each piece individually and determine the best way to manufacture it," says MEL's prop fabrication supervisor Don Coleman. "The emitters themselves are polished aluminum, and the case is black ABS [acrylonitrile butadiene styrene], a tough, impact-resistant plastic. I built the case and Paul Elliott [MEL's chief operating officer, as well as its electronic and mechanical designer] created the emitters."

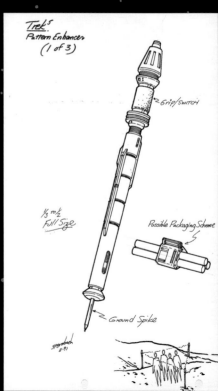

Trek 5
Pattern Enhancer
(1 of 3)

Grip/Switch

1/3 to 1/2
Full Size

Possible Packaging Scheme

Ground Spike

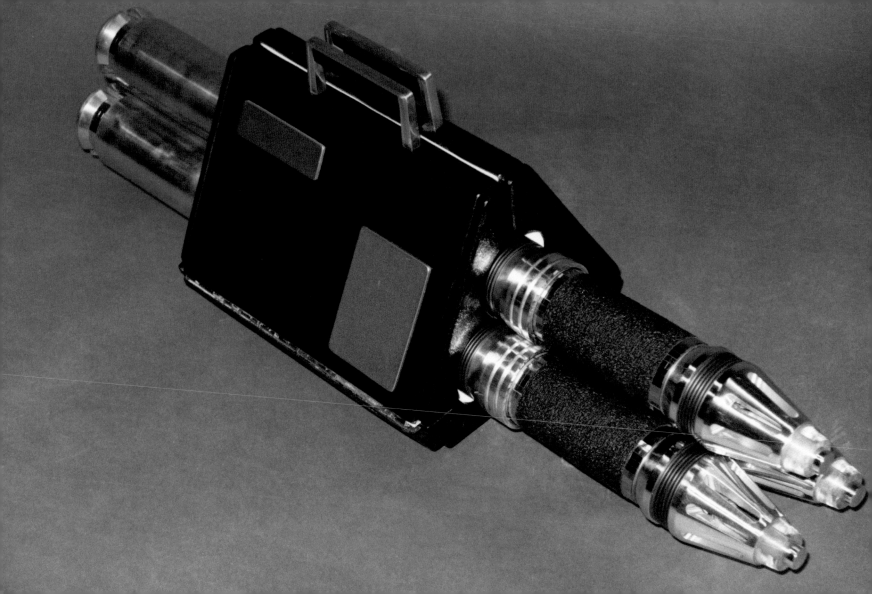

"'Time's Arrow' was a bit of a mess, but I was happy with the Mark Twain stuff," notes writer Joe Menosky. "I'd immersed myself in Twain's writings, especially his essays and lectures, so I felt that I really hit his 'voice.' People thought I actually was quoting him, but I was just writing in the way I thought he would speak. 'Part One' was the last full *TNG* episode I did before leaving the series to go live in Italy for three years."

Although Menosky's tenure on *TNG*'s staff lasted less than two seasons, his relationship with *Star Trek* was much more entrenched. "I was obsessed with it *before The Original Series* even aired," he says, laughing. "I was nine years old and my head was filled with Clarke, Asimov, and Bradbury, and all the Silver Age Marvel comics. So when I heard the radio promo for something called *Star Trek*, the name itself was enough to send me over the moon. When the show premiered, all my anticipation was rewarded a thousand times over. It was a completely solitary obsession," he adds. "I used to 'write' and act out *Trek* stories in my living room, just for me."

Years later, Menosky moved to Hollywood and landed a job on the popular cop drama *Hunter*. "My agent set up a pitch meeting with Michael Piller on *The Next Generation*," he recalls. "Michael didn't like my pitches, but he liked my background, so *he* pitched an idea to *me*. That story became 'Legacy.' And on the basis of that script, I was hired on staff."

Menosky's sabbatical in 1992 didn't mark the end of his *Star Trek* career. He consulted long-distance from Italy on five more *TNG* episodes. "Michael tried to coax me back to the U.S. by telling me he'd never imagined doing *Deep Space Nine* without me—an incredibly nice thing to say. When I finally did get back, *DS9* was locked in, so I went over to *Voyager*."

And after *Voyager* came to a close, Menosky again yielded to Piller's siren song. "He hired me as a consulting producer on *Stephen King's The Dead Zone*. It was a different experience," he says. "I think I went into the office only once. We did everything by e-mail. It was a blast to work with Michael in a non-*Trek* format. It actually increased my respect for him as a writer and a showrunner."

Right: Expatriate Joe Menosky in Italy, 1993.

AT THE
EDGE OF
THE FINAL
FRONTIER

SEASON 06

267

In season six, the long-rumored *TNG* spin-off, *Star Trek: Deep Space Nine*, became an inescapable fact. With its premiere locked in for January 1993, last-minute adjustments went on behind the scenes. Jeri Taylor became *TNG*'s co-executive producer, allowing Michael Piller to pay more attention to the "new baby." Colm Meaney and Rosalind Chao agreed to transfer over to the space station, as did writer Peter Allan Fields and visual effects producer Robert Legato (Dan Curry became the sole visual effects producer on *TNG*). Brannon Braga, however, turned down a similar opportunity.

"It was incredibly enticing," Braga relates now. "Michael, my mentor, was the one who offered me the job. But I turned him down. I was so entrenched and so in love with *The Next Generation* characters that I wanted to stay with the show for *however* long it lasted. I'm really glad I did, because I wound up having the opportunity to write the final episode with Ron Moore—and a couple movies, too."

Robert Hewitt Wolfe, a young freelancer whose *TNG* script for "A Fistful of Datas" had impressed the producers, was summarily assigned to do a test script for *DS9*. The result—"Q-Less"—passed muster with returning producer Ira Steven Behr, and Wolfe joined the *DS9* staff.

Although Joe Menosky had departed for Europe, the "young guns"—the core group of twentysomething writers on *TNG*—remained intact.

"It was Ron, René Echevarria, Brannon, and myself," says Naren Shankar. "*TNG* represented our first job in the business. That was the wonderful thing about Michael, and Jeri, too. They were willing to take risks on new talent. We all got our starts because of them. But that didn't mean we were well behaved. We were all very opinionated, a very willful bunch. And," he adds with a chuckle, "boys will be boys."

Indeed. "We were quaking in our boots when *Deep Space Nine* started," recalls Echevarria. "We'd walk across the lot to their sets and sneak in to look around, and say, 'Wow—look at that. Those are *soooo* cool.' We were very competitive with Ira and his team."

Deep Space Nine debuted to astronomical ratings—but *TNG*'s ratings held up, which clearly meant the public had an appetite for more *Star Trek*. Paramount was quick to notice. The studio quickly made plans for yet another spin-off: *Star Trek: Voyager*.

Once again, the writing staff was kept in the dark. "They wouldn't let us see anything," Shankar says. "Nobody would talk to us about *that* new show." But by now, the young guns knew just what to do. "One day, when Jeri went to lunch, René went in and stole the treatment from her desk. We read it over lunch," he continues, laughing like a schoolboy who just stole the answers to the big quiz. *"And then we put it back."*

Picard, Riker, Crusher, Troi, and La Forge travel to Earth's nineteenth century in hopes of finding Data before the android loses his head. They catch up with the Devidians first, and learn the aliens have assumed human form to sap the energy from dying cholera victims. That energy then is taken to the twenty-fourth century, and gobbled up by others of their species. Once the away team finds Data, the entire group heads for the cavern where his head will be discovered five centuries in the future. But even as they realize that the cavern is the focal point for the Devidians' time travel efforts, the aliens catch up with them and open their portal through time, in the process triggering an explosion that blows off Data's head, separates Picard from the rest of his crewmates, and seriously injures Guinan.

While Picard was busy exploring the Final Frontier of the twenty-fourth century, the frontier adjacent to Soundstages 8 and 9, where *TNG* was shot, was changing.

For many years, Paramount, like the other major studios, had a large "New York Street" area for outdoor filming, but a major fire destroyed that part of the lot in 1983. For nearly a decade, Paramount productions that required an exterior backdrop of old-fashioned brownstones, storefronts, and quaint cafés either had to take their actors to other studios or find a suitable setting on location. For example, the exteriors for the first part of "Time's Arrow" were shot at Los Angeles's historic Pico House and along Olvera Street, a restored area near the city's first mission.

For Part II, *TNG*'s producers had planned to use a section of Universal Studios' back lot for the exteriors. But during the show's hiatus, work was completed on Paramount's brand-new New York Street, erected in the same location as its old one. Stanley Jaffe, president of Paramount Communications from 1991 to 1993, had mandated the construction project, which was part of the studio's first expansion in more than twenty years. Jaffe astutely determined that the investment would save Paramount's productions a lot of money in location fees—and also earn the studio significant revenue by renting out New York Street to other studios' productions and countless television commercials.

The Next Generation was one of the first Paramount productions to shoot on the newly completed back lot. *TNG* would return to the location for "Emergence," as would *DS9*, *Voyager*, *Angel*, *NCIS*, *Monk*, and dozens of other productions in the years to come.

Below: A Klingon wouldn't have fit in on the streets of nineteenth-century Earth, but Michael Dorn did get to pay his coworkers a visit on the cavern set.

"Reg, transporting really is the safest way to travel." —Geordi

Perennially nervous engineer Reginald Barclay earns the respect of his peers by coming up with a plan to reach the crew of a starship that's trapped in a plasma stream. But his boost in personal esteem is nearly wiped out when he's invited to join the rescue team. Barclay's lifelong phobia of transporters won't allow him to accept. After a session with Counselor Troi, however, he bucks up his courage and joins the team, only to discover that his fears may have been well placed.

Nostalgia is the mother of many creative efforts. Add a little phobia into the mix, and you've got a Brannon Braga script for *The Next Generation*.

"My favorite TV show of all time—as I'm sure *many* science fiction writers would say—is *The Twilight Zone*," Braga says. "'Realm of Fear' is my homage to 'Nightmare at 20000 Feet.'"

That episode of the classic anthology series featured William Shatner as an airplane passenger recently recovered from a nervous breakdown. When he spots a gremlin on the wing of the plane, he tries to warn the plane's crew; not surprisingly, no one believes him. For the *TNG* episode, Braga playfully substituted "a thing in the transporter" for "a thing on the wing."

"I thought it would be fun to explore the notion that just as not everybody likes to fly, not everybody likes to *transport*," Braga explains. "'*Whaddya mean my molecules are gonna be taken apart? How do I know I'm gonna come back together in exactly the right way?*'" he says, laughing. "Barclay seemed like the right guy to have that kind of neurosis."

Braga should know. He's one of those guys who doesn't like flying, although he's better now than he was when he wrote the episode. "I'm still not fond of it," he admits. "It's not really the act of flying—it's being trapped in a small compartment and not being able to get out. More claustrophobia than anything else. I'm just not comfortable with it."

"I'll run a scan on the Heisenberg compensators." —O'Brien

In 1927, German theoretical physicist (and Nobel Prize winner) Werner Heisenberg wrote, "The more precisely the position is determined, the less precisely the momentum is known in this instant, and vice versa."

In layman's terms, this tidbit of insight—known today as the Heisenberg uncertainty principle—means that it's impossible to measure the present position of a particle and accurately determine its future momentum. Or, for the troglodyte layman, "You probably can't get there from here." Unfortunately, if true, it means that Transporter Chief O'Brien would be out of a job—because he couldn't accurately calculate just where an away team would beam to. And that would render transporter technology impractical, if not downright deadly.

Of course, this didn't deter scenic artist Michael Okuda when he designed the transporter system schematic that went behind O'Brien's console.

"Note that I included a block for the 'Heisenberg

compensator,'" Okuda says. "I thought of it as a gag, years before I worked on *Star Trek*, because I'd read that Heisenberg's uncertainty principle would make the transporter impossible.

"I was hoping that someday Gene [Roddenberry] might point to the compensator, if anyone tried to invoke Heisenberg in order to criticize the transporter. If nothing else, Gene could have used it to indicate that the show's staff at least knew about the problem. As far as I know, he never did. However, a writer for *Time* magazine once asked me how the Heisenberg compensator would work. I haven't a clue, of course, so I answered, 'Very well, thank you!' A few weeks later, I was delighted to see the quote printed in *Time*!"

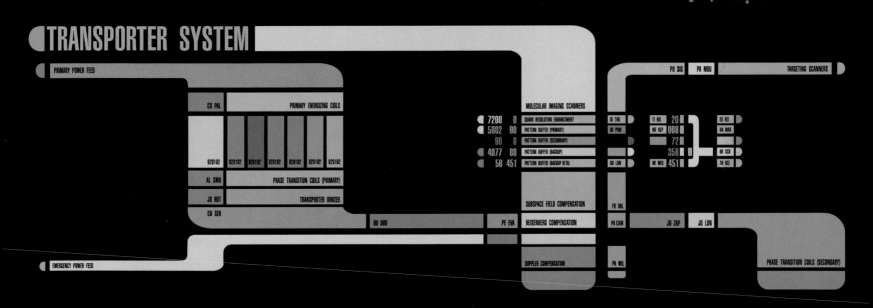

TRANSPORTER SYSTEM

PRIMARY POWER FEED

PR SIG | PA MOU | TARGETING SCANNERS

CD PAL | PRIMARY ENERGIZING COILS

MOLECULAR IMAGING SCANNERS

7200	0	QUARK RESOLUTION ENHANCEMENT
5802	90	PATTERN BUFFER (PRIMARY)
90	0	PATTERN BUFFER (SECONDARY)
4077	80	PATTERN BUFFER (BACKUP)
56	451	PATTERN BUFFER (BACKUP BETA)

DI THO | TI HEI 20 | ED REI
DE POW | WE KEP 008 | DA MAR
| 72 |
| 358 | BR SCH
GA LUN | MI WES 451 | CH REE

929192 | 929192 | 929192 | 929192 | 929192 | 929192 | 929192

AL SMU | PHASE TRANSITION COILS (PRIMARY)

JO ROT | TRANSPORTER IONIZER

CH SER

SUBSPACE FIELD COMPENSATION

FR VAL

HU DUV | PE EVA | HEISENBERG COMPENSATION | PA CAM | JO ZAP | JO LON

EMERGENCY POWER FEED

DOPPLER COMPENSATION | PA MIL | PHASE TRANSITION COILS (SECONDARY)

The *Enterprise* transports Alkar, a Lumerian ambassador, and his aged mother, Sev, to Rekag-Seronia, where Alkar hopes to mediate a cease-fire between two warring local factions. When Sev unexpectedly passes away during the journey, Alkar asks the empathic Troi to help him perform a funeral meditation. Not long after, Troi begins to age rapidly as she experiences a tsunami of irrational emotions that lead her to outlandish behavior. Realizing that Troi is behaving very much like Sev did before she died, Picard orders Crusher to conduct an autopsy on Alkar's mother—without the ambassador's permission—in order to determine what's ailing the counselor.

As the stand-up comedian said to an unreceptive audience in Las Vegas: "It's a tough room."

But he could have been talking about another tough room, located in Paramount's Hart Building during the years *The Next Generation* was in production.

"The writers' room on *TNG* was very much like being on a high school athletic team," Joe Menosky explains. "It was a very intense, mutually supportive, mutually competitive, memory-imprinting time. Not like the football team, but more the wrestling team or the gymnastics squad, because no matter how collaborative the process could be, at some point you were out there alone and you had to perform—or you got cut from the team."

Frank Abatemarco was just one of many who faced both the room and the rarified atmosphere in which a *Star Trek* producer must not only survive, but flourish. Brought in as supervising producer to fill Jeri Taylor's staff role when she was moved up to the position of co-executive producer, Abatemarco was a seasoned pro, a writer/producer with a roster of hard-hitting shows on his résumé, including *Cagney & Lacey*, *Equal Justice*, and the second coming of *Mission: Impossible*. His credits, like those of Michael Wagner (whose departure begat the arrival of Michael Piller), Lee Sheldon (whom Taylor replaced), and others, were impeccable. But like those men and women who left the series without completing a full season, he soon found that the *Star Trek* method of turning out a TV show wasn't for him.

A shortened production window for "Man of the People," his first episode, may have set the tone for his tenure. As the writers had been conditioned to do in a crunch, the script—a kind of update on *The Picture of Dorian Gray*—was "gangbanged" by various members of the team, each taking an act of the episode, reportedly to no one's ultimate satisfaction. Abatemarco contributed to the far more successful hard-hitting two-parter "Chain of Command" two months later, but said farewell to his coworkers in mid-season. He went on to executive produce two made-for-TV movies and the television series *Poltergeist: The Legacy* and *Dellaventura* before transitioning to the real estate trade in Southern California. Today, he is the chairman of the Santa Barbara County Foodbank's Board of Trustees.

Opposite: A deadly threat . . . doesn't always look quite so deadly during the rehearsal.

Where would showbiz be without doubles? The stunt double, who performs on-camera feats of physical prowess; the photo double, who fills in as the back of an actor's head for a shot where the actor's face isn't going to be seen; and the stand-in, who's present only for blocking and lighting purposes while the actor is off doing something else.

But what of that other unsung hero: the hand double? Hand doubles most often appear in productions that emphasize an on-screen character's technical prowess; think about the hands of the guy (or girl) who opens a safe, deactivates a bomb, or repairs a ruptured aorta. On *TNG*, think about O'Brien sliding his fingers along the transporter controls or Wesley plotting a course on the navigation console. The hand double is the star that shines in the dozens of insert shots required for each episode. But this particular double's job doesn't start until after the regular actors are done with principal photography.

"Let's say they already have a shot of Data pointing at a monitor on the bridge, or in engineering," says Guy Vardaman, who has frequently filled in for Data's digits. "Now they want a tight insert, show-ing the image that's on the monitor, but with Data's hand in the frame. They can't get Brent Spiner to come back—he's filming the next episode. So they bring in the hand double to shoot those two seconds of footage."

A hand double's prep generally takes longer than the actual filming. "For Data, they would shave my hands," says Vardaman, "and then paint them gold, to match Brent's. I wear a gold uniform, because you can see the sleeves in the shot. We'll watch the footage with Brent in it, so I can see the position of his hands right before the insert. And then I replicate that position [see right] as they shoot my hands pushing buttons, or pointing at the monitor, whatever he did."

Opposite: A second unit crew sets up an insert shot of a crewman's hands in Ten-Forward. "A shot like this goes very quickly once it's lit," explains visual effects associate Eric Alba. "It's the lighting and getting the actions right that's the hard part. It's shot very tight, so the actor has to hit his mark very accurately. We use dailies from the show to match the lighting."

"NCC One-Seven-Oh-One. No bloody A, B, C, or D!" —Scotty

The *Enterprise* chances upon three historic finds in the same day: an immense artificial habitat known as a Dyson sphere; the wreckage of the *Jenolen*, a Starfleet vessel that crashed on the sphere's surface seventy-five years ago; and the *Jenolen*'s captain, Montgomery Scott, still alive after spending three-quarters of a century suspended in the *Jenolen*'s transporter system. "Scotty" was the chief engineer of Captain James Kirk's *Enterprise* and is considered a Starfleet legend, but it doesn't take long for him to get on La Forge's nerves as the younger engineer tries to do his job without input from the elder statesman. However, when the *Enterprise* falls prey to the same mistake the *Jenolen* made years earlier, Scotty demonstrates that he's still a "miracle worker."

Emmy Award–winning director Alex Singer, whose credits include such classic shows as *Mis-sion: Impossible*, *Hill Street Blues,* and *Cagney & Lacey*, approached "Relics" as an opportunity he'd missed out on during the run of *The Original Series*. "I was across the lot for a few years doing *Mission: Impossible* [like *Star Trek*, a Desilu production], and I wanted to work with *Star Trek*," recalls Singer. "I met with Gene Roddenberry and, for one reason or another, it hadn't worked out. So the aspect of the Scotty character and his resurrection had a kind of multiple resonance. Having Jimmy Doohan there, I felt I was in the middle of some kind of mythic experience myself."

With thirty-one years of series television under his belt, Singer possessed the unique perspective of having experienced the early days of television, while also anticipating future trends in the entertainment industry. At the time he was directing "Relics," he was a member of a National Academy of Sciences committee that was examining the convergence of computers and entertainment. Coincidentally, serving with him on the same committee was computer expert Esther Dyson, the daughter of physicist Freeman Dyson, whose theories motivated *TNG*'s writers to create the Dyson sphere in "Relics."

Inspired by science fiction writers from the 1930s, Freeman Dyson had envisioned an artificial structure that could capture a star's entire energy output. Dyson introduced his thoughts in the treatise "Search for Artificial Stellar Sources of Infrared Radiation," published in a 1960 edition of the journal *Science.* It postulated that acquiring the materials to build a sphere large enough to encompass a star at its center would require dismantling an entire planet the size of Jupiter. Impractical? Probably. Possible? Yes, at least in a fictional context like *The Next Generation*.

"As soon as I saw the script, I knew I had something that would be terribly meaningful both to the mythology of *Star Trek* and also peculiarly to me," Singer said. "Each of Scotty's shocking encounters, 'synthetic commanders' and 'synthetic drinks,' had meaning. I had a deep sense of where Scotty was, and where his sense of technological obsolescence was, as he related to young Geordi. That story was very moving to me."

Writer Ron Moore wanted to include a holodeck scene with Scotty walking onto the original *Enterprise*'s bridge, but budget estimates for building an entire set were deemed too expensive. However, production designer Richard James felt that if footage existed of the original bridge *with no one on it*, it could serve as a blue screen element, meaning he'd need to build only a portion of the set for the live action. Dan Curry located the perfect scene in the *TOS* episode "This Side of Paradise." Even so, building the pie-shaped wedge with all the appropriate details seemed cost-prohibitive until Michael Okuda contacted longtime *Star Trek* fan Steve Horch, who'd already built a perfect replica of the captain's chair, along with Chekov and Sulu's console, for use at conventions. "If not for Steve Horch," Okuda says, "we would not have that scene."

The much-lauded "authentic" bridge set wasn't the only way the production team reached into the past. For the sequence aboard the *Jenolen*, where Scotty is rematerialized, "We used the original *Star Trek* transporter sparkle," says Curry. "I used to work at [effects house] Cinema Re-search, and I remembered that in the bowels of their stock footage storage room was an old box labeled '*Star Trek* Transporter Sparkle,'" he says with a laugh. "We blew the cobwebs off, dug through, pulled out the strip of film, and discovered it was in perfect condition."

On the audio front, coproducer Wendy Neuss and sound editor Bill Wistrom disinterred the sound effects for the original transporter from Paramount vaults to enhance the visual. In the meantime, composer Jay Chattaway added his own flourish. "We decided it would be nice to open the holodeck and have Scotty react to the sound effects from the old *Enterprise* bridge, and then to have a quote from Alexander Courage's old *Star Trek* fanfare theme," he says. "I then paraphrased the theme into an emotional cue, with Scotty alone, many years out of his time element, experiencing the feeling that his comrades were no longer here."

Scotty wasn't the only one touched by the emotion. "I sat in the captain's chair and I was moved to tears," Ron Moore recalls. "It was like I was touching a piece of my childhood. Bob Justman came down, and Majel Barrett came down. People who had some relationship with *The Original Series* kept materializing to see the bridge we had re-created. It was a very special episode."

Opposite: Michael Okuda made certain that some die-hard Trekkers who worked on the lot had a chance to visit the re-created bridge—including one of the authors of this book.

When *TNG*'s Rick Sternbach and Michael Okuda penned the series' writers' technical manual, "we suggested all these bizarre things," recalls Okuda. "One of them was the Dyson sphere. We never thought anyone would be audacious enough to create one on film."

Until Ronald D. Moore's very audacious "Relics."

"As soon as we got the script, we started to analyze the different shots," says visual effects supervisor David Stipes. "We had to decide, 'What does this Dyson sphere look like? How big should it be?'"

"It was important for the audience to get a sense of the geography, and of being inside a sphere," Dan Curry adds. "We cheated the scale down a bit, because if it were real with the dimensions described in the script, there would be no visible curvature. It was a bit of artistic license."

"At first we talked about generating it with computers," Stipes recalls. "But we ran into some challenges, so we called in Greg Jein."

Master model maker Jein built an eighteen-foot by eighteen-foot panel that contained a six-foot by six-foot portal. "The master pattern is made out of sections of a Japanese model kit," Jein said in a 1992 interview conducted in his workshop, where Dyson sphere parts hung on the walls and sphere debris lay scattered on the floor. "We cast them into a larger pattern and then made a rubber mold," he explained. "Then we peeled it off and started pouring giant urethane bricks. We put the bricks on wooden frames and put the frames together once we got to the stage."

"Greg's model was huge," Stipes says. "But we needed it to be a hundred feet long to give us the required scale. So the crew shot a section of the panel and then digitally reproduced that section over and over, in cookie-cutter fashion, making the thing look like it stretched on for miles."

"The exterior was pretty straightforward, because all the panels were the same except for the door," Jein says. "We had more fun with the interior, because we made it look like an industrial city block. We put our high school names on some of the buildings, like 'Dorsey High School,' but the audience never saw that. We used a lot of pieces out of 'central casting'—that's what we call our stock molds that have lots of details in them—to break up the surface so that each panel wasn't exactly the same. I carved the main core around the door out of foam because we didn't have time to make molds," he says. "It's sort of free-form."

Opposite: Curry and Stipes (kneeling) examine the sphere's exterior, while Jein shows off its interior.

Geordi's experiment with channeling warp energy through the main deflection grid seems to be working perfectly until an explosion occurs in the cargo bay. While the damage appears to be minimal, it's just the first of a series of inexplicable events that take place over the next few days. Although they have no memory of it, crew members, including Riker, La Forge, Worf, and Data, disappear from the ship at different times. After they're returned to the *Enterprise*, the hijacked officers are changed in minute ways, some the victims of exhaustion, others suffering from mysterious pains—and worse. Stranger still, there's an unusual level of tetryon particles in the cargo bay, which seem to be causing a rupture between their universe . . . and something else's universe.

"My sensibilities have always been offbeat, weird, and macabre," Brannon Braga acknowledges. "And in my episodes of *Next Gen*, I was, thankfully, allowed to explore some of these things. And some of them were kind of wacky. But they were always interesting. The writers each had their own skills and interests. Ron Moore excelled at the political-type shows with Klingons. René Echevarria usually did the really emotional episodes. Mine were more conceptually driven— interesting conceptually, but not necessarily heavy on anything profound.

"'Schisms' was just a garden-variety UFO abduction episode," he notes. "There weren't a lot of them around at the time. *The X-Files* hadn't come out yet, so it seemed fresh. It wasn't a particularly original idea, but it was creepy, and well executed."

Opposite: The masks used for the creepy unnamed alien species. Viewers never found out where they came from, but judging by their appearance, the Creature from the Black Lagoon may have been in their lineage. . . .

"Throughout the ages, from Keats to Jorke-mo, poets have composed odes to individuals who have had a profound effect on their lives. In keeping with that tradition, I have written my next poem in honor of my cat. I call it 'Ode to Spot.'" —**Data**

In keeping with that same tradition, we are pleased to share Data's memorable poem with our readers:

ODE TO SPOT
by Data

Felis catus *is your taxonomic nomenclature,*
An endothermic quadruped, carnivorous by
* nature.*
Your visual, olfactory, and auditory senses
Contribute to your hunting skill and natural
* defenses.*

I find myself intrigued by your subvocal
* oscillations,*
A singular development of cat communication

That obviates your basic hedonistic predilection
For a rhythmic stroking of your fur to demonstrate
* affection.*

A tail is quite essential for your acrobatic talents;
You would not be so agile if you lacked its
* counterbalance.*
And when not being utilized to aid in locomotion,
It often serves to illustrate the state of your
* emotions.*

Oh Spot, the complex levels of behavior you
* display*
Connotes a fairly well-developed cognitive array.
And though you are not sentient, Spot, and do not
* comprehend,*
I nonetheless consider you a true and valued
* friend.*

Opposite, far right: Spot, as painted by Data (actually *TNG* scenic artist Wendy Drapanas) in the style of Picasso. The portrait appeared in the seventh-season episode "Inheritance," and in the film *Star Trek Generations*.

New intern Amanda Rogers is smart, pretty, and tremendously enthusiastic about her job. But although she appears normal, Amanda has some unusual abilities that she's kept to herself. After she's forced to reveal her secret in order to prevent a warp core breech, Amanda receives a visit from Q, who rocks her world with the news that she's a member of the Q Continuum. And the Continuum thinks it's time for her to "come home" . . . or else.

"Q was not my thing," admits writer René Echevarria. "I didn't live and breathe it like I did other elements of the show. But I liked this particular episode because it had a different spin to it. The character Q had a mischievous and maleficent presence, but it was more about the girl and her journey. It had elements of *Bewitched* and an adolescent coming into her own and becoming empowered and all of that good stuff. And a really lovely performance by Olivia d'Abo."

"'True Q' was my first episode *on staff*," René Echevarria says. "The pitch came from a seventeen-year-old high school student named Matt Corey. I remember picking up the phone and calling him, saying, 'Hi, I'm a writer on *Star Trek*. . . .' I'd gotten a call like that just a few years earlier, so I was thinking how excited and happy this guy must be."

Today, Echevarria is a highly respected writer/producer who's worked on shows like *Deep Space Nine, Dark Angel, The 4400, Medium, Castle*, and *Terra Nova*. But back in 1992, he had a lot to learn, and one of his first lessons was how different the job of a staff writer was from that of a freelancer. "It was my first time seeing a script all the way through," he recalls. "Sitting in Rick Berman's office and getting his notes. Going to a production meeting for the first time—and realizing what things cost and the resulting choices you'd have to make. Just beginning to comprehend what it takes to make an hour of television. It was an eye-opening moment. And now," he adds with a chuckle, "it's a lecture that I give to young writers all the time.

"At the time, *The Next Generation* cost close to two million dollars per episode. When you hear a number like that, you think, 'That's a lot of money. Why are we sitting here counting how many phaser shots the episode has?'"

Here Echevarria slips into the hypothetical "conversation" that he—as the experienced producer—might have with his younger self.

"'How many phaser shots are in the script?'"

"'It looks like about twelve.'"

"'Well, each one costs three thousand dollars. You can have *six*.'"

Back then, he notes, young René would have said, "'Three thousand dollars? We've got two *million*!' I didn't understand that just to shoot for seven days on the sets, and pay the rent, and pay everybody involved—just to have the things we have every week, the film in the camera, the craft service table, the secretaries—everybody that needs to be paid to *make* an episode, and *nothing extra*—that alone represents maybe *1.8 million dollars*. Which means your *real* budget is only about *two hundred thousand dollars*. And with that you have to build any new sets, which might

cost you fifty thousand. And you want to hire a guest star, which might cost you ten thousand dollars. And do all the effects.

"You begin to realize that there's a reason why an extra doesn't get to say 'Here you are, sir,' when he hands something to one of the regulars on a TV show. The extra just nods, because if he spoke you'd wind up paying him *two thousand dollars* instead of *two hundred dollars*.

"That's what the budget was, back when *The Next Generation* was on," Echevarria says. "It's more now. Shows today are north of *three* million."

Still, even today, we're guessing he wishes he could have more phaser shots.

Opposite: A few of those pricey effects shots that make the story more fun for viewers.

A transporter accident transforms Picard, Ro, Keiko O'Brien, and Guinan into twelve-year-old children who retain the minds of their adult selves. After La Forge researches the situation, he determines the transporter can be used to safely bring the group back to normal. But before they can attempt it, the *Enterprise* is attacked by a group of renegade Ferengi, who disable the vessel and announce that they're claiming it for salvage!

If the premise "*The Next Generation* meets *The Little Rascals*" seems a little odd, imagine being assigned "Rascals" as your very first directing job.

That dubious honor went to Adam Nimoy, who was happy to receive the *TNG* assignment, despite the prospect of working with four children. As a child, Nimoy—the son of actor Leonard Nimoy—had watched his father struggle with his chosen profession. "My father never had job security when I was growing up," he stated in a 1994 interview. "People who are workaholics and then end up *not* working are not happy."

Rather than face similar career instability, the younger Nimoy attended law school, but, ironically, the seven years he practiced law were anything but secure. Opting to specialize as a music attorney, he repeatedly fell victim to the volatility of that particular industry, rife with management changes and insolvency. Between jobs, he tried relaxing by sitting in on some acting classes—and caught the "bug." But not the acting bug. What he really wanted to do . . . was direct.

He went back to school, taking classes in directing, acting, writing, and film editing, and shadowed director Nicholas Meyer during the making of *The Undiscovered Country*. When that film wrapped, Nimoy's father suggested he talk to Rick Berman, who allowed the ex-lawyer to go through "Paramount University," *TNG*'s unofficial directors' training program. Nimoy spent a year watching, learning, and listening. And ultimately, with "Rascals," he was given the opportunity he'd been waiting for.

On the whole, the effort was very successful. Viewers liked "Rascals," and Berman gave Nimoy a second directing assignment later that season ("Timescape"). He went on to direct more than forty-five hours of television, including episodes of *The Practice*, *NYPD Blue*, *Ally McBeal*, and *Gilmore Girls*. He currently teaches writing, directing, and acting at the New York Film Academy in Los Angeles.

"I'm beginning to see the appeal of this program." —Worf

With some spare time to kill, Alexander convinces Troi and Worf to participate in his "Wild West" holodeck program, and La Forge conducts an experiment to see if Data's neural network could be used as an emergency backup to the ship's computer. It's soon apparent, however, that La Forge's experiment isn't going to pan out. System glitches are appearing all over the ship, most dramatically in Alexander's holodeck program, where the safety protocols have shut down and all of the bad guys resemble Data—right down to his superhuman android abilities.

Right: Brent Spiner's lovely barmaid costume from "A Fistful of Datas," which sold at the 2006 Christie's auction, although probably not to Brent Spiner, who stated of his appearance in it, "I was so utterly homely as a woman."

"Y'all must be mistaken." —Data

On April 3, 1968, just prior to starting *Star Trek: The Original Series'* ill-fated third season, Gene Roddenberry wrote a letter to NBC's current programming manager, describing future plans for the show. "To help counteract any 'sameness' about the ship," Roddenberry wrote, "we are presently planning the addition of new and interesting ship areas, including a 'simulated outdoor recreation area' complete with foliage, turf, running water, and etc."

Roddenberry's 'recreation area' didn't come to fruition on that show, although an animated version of it did in 1974, in *The Animated Series* episode "The Practical Joker." Viewers wouldn't step into the full-blown concept until *TNG*'s 1987 pilot—where it had gained a name: the holodeck.

How *Star Trek*'s creator developed his futuristic recreation area hasn't been recorded. Perhaps it came to him as he read the short story "The Veldt," by his friend Ray Bradbury, in which a children's nursery could transform into any landscape the children desired. Or perhaps he'd read recent works by computer scientist Ivan Sutherland, who'd predicted a room that could "control the existence of matter." However he developed the idea, Roddenberry's plan to enhance his sets was revolutionary.

"*The Next Generation* was something of an anthology show, in that we could tell any kind of story, especially with the absolutely brilliant addition of the holodeck," states Brannon Braga. "Virtual reality was a rather new idea at the time, and with a holodeck on the ship, we could even do a *western*."

Which is just what recent UCLA graduate Robert Hewitt Wolfe had hoped. "I got my masters in screenwriting, and I'd pitched to *TNG* a few times," Wolfe says. "I didn't sell anything, but Michael Piller liked my pitches enough that he invited me back. Finally, I came in and pitched two stories, one of which I was sure they'd buy—but didn't—and another one which they actually *did* buy. I called that one 'The Good, the Bad, and the Klingon.'"

After Wolfe turned in a draft of the script, now titled "A Fistful of Datas" in tribute to the Sergio Leone spaghetti westerns, Braga did a finishing pass. "I loved Robert's idea that Data was *everybody* at the end," Braga says. "Even the zaftig barmaid, Annie."

As for the second story Wolfe pitched that day (a time travel story about Captain Picard and Geordi landing in twentieth-century Los Angeles just before the Watts Riots), it eventually found a home on *Deep Space Nine* as the two-parter "Past Tense," with Captain Sisko, Julian Bashir, and Jadzia Dax time-traveling to twenty-first-century San Francisco just before the fictional Bell Riots.

You can't be two places at once. Unless you're Data. In a holodeck program. With a cadre of photo doubles.

"There were three of us doubling as different aspects of Data that day, all wearing gold makeup," notes Guy Vardaman. "I was listed as 'Data Eli' on the call sheet, but they also had me do 'Data Frank,' with the mustache and the black vest and coat. That was the first time I'd ever had Data's makeup on my face and everywhere else that showed. Usually it's just hands, or the neck and back of the head. All the close-ups were Brent, of course."

The day that Vardaman mentions was the single day that *TNG*'s producers had booked to shoot on Warner Bros. Studios' "western street" in Burbank. Patrick Stewart—a fan of American westerns since childhood—had the good fortune to draw "A Fistful of Datas" as his third directing job. Because he had a large number of scenes to shoot at Warner's, he scheduled the crew to start early—as in *pre-sunrise* early—to prep. That would leave the maximum of daylight hours free for actual filming.

Unfortunately, the cool of early morning didn't last long. "The temperature must have been a hundred and thirteen in the shade," recalls production designer Richard James. "It was awful. The guys in makeup, particularly Michael Dorn, were just miserable."

"Everybody felt for Michael," Vardaman agrees, "because of the Klingon headpiece and the wig and all that. It all came down to the heat, with all of us periodically running back to stand in front of whatever air-conditioning unit was functional—anything to avoid sweating makeup onto the wardrobe. Data should *never* be observed sweating," he adds with a grin.

Despite initial fears that there wasn't enough time to get everything done, the day was a success. "The western street was in pretty good shape," James recalls. "We had to make the saloon look like it was being used, so we added signage and replaced a few broken windows. I added my own saloon doors and then took them back to Stage 16 at Paramount and put them on our saloon set there."

"The highlight of the day for me," Stewart says enthusiastically, "was the beginning of this classic western shoot-out in the street. It was a crane shot. The operator said to me, 'Do you want to ride on the crane? You might as well be up here with me.' I was buckled into the spare seat alongside the camera, and someone actually found a *megaphone* for me. I was able to call *'Action!'* [from up there] through a *megaphone*, on the *Warner Bros.* lot!" he states, still clearly thrilled at the experience.

"Doctor, what is the definition of life?" —Data

Dr. Farallon, the director of an orbital mining station, has created a computer tool she calls the "exocomp." The small mobile device can solve problems and replicate parts on its own as it deals with dangerous situations that might harm humanoids. But Data realizes that these machines are actually sentient—as "alive" as he himself is. Because no sentient being's life is worth more than another's, Data prevents Farallon from forcing the exocomps to participate in a hazardous rescue mission, even though the lives of Picard and La Forge are at stake.

During *TNG*'s fifth and sixth seasons, science consultant Naren Shankar was responsible for helping to fill in the "tech" blanks in the writers' scripts (Andre Bormanis took over those chores in the seventh season, when Shankar became a full-time story editor on the series). "I always thought it was hilarious," notes Shankar, "because every-

one was way more concerned about being consistent with how the *fake* science worked than actually being faithful with how *real* science worked. The technobabble is one of the things that hasn't aged particularly well about *The Next Generation*."

Shankar's first solo script for *TNG* contained quite a lot of technobabble, as, for example, in this conversation Data has with Dr. Farallon:

Farallon: "Is it true that your computational speed is limited only by the physical separation of your positronic links?"
Data: "Actually, that is no longer the case. I have recently converted my interlink sequencer to asynchronous operation, which removed the performance constraint."
Farallon: "I see. But how did you resolve the signal fragmentation?"
Data: "The interlink sequencer is now bi-directional. It compensates for the asynchronous mode distortion arising from the resonant field."

But beyond technobabble, the script has a lot of heart—primarily exhibited by the episode's non-

human characters: Data, and to a lesser degree, the exocomps. The initial concept, pitched by L. D. Scott, triggered in-house conversations, Shankar says, "about artificial intelligence, and what really defined something as a living being, even if it was a cybernetic organism. At what point would machine intelligence be described as 'alive'? What we eventually arrived at is, it's when something develops a survival instinct, showing that it's afraid to die. And that's the point where Data decides that these widgets are a form of life that is worth saving."

The subject, of course, had been broached in "The Measure of a Man," one of *TNG*'s most acclaimed episodes. "We were very conscious of that," acknowledges Shankar. "And Data does bring that up, how Picard fought to preserve *his* status as a sentient being, so how could he *not* act on behalf of the exocomps? It was a *logical* conclusion," he points out. "Those are nice moments with Data, when you can couch something emotional within the framework of a logical deduction—it becomes that much more moving for an android to make that kind of decision."

"There . . . are . . . four . . . lights!" —Picard

Starfleet orders Picard, Crusher, and Worf to leave the *Enterprise* and participate in a top-secret mission: investigate a facility where the Cardassians are thought to be creating biological weapons for use against the Federation. Picard's replacement on the *Enterprise* is Captain Edward Jellico, a tough martinet who immediately butts heads with members of the command crew, particularly Riker. On Celtris III, Picard, Crusher, and Worf infiltrate the hidden facility, only to discover that they've walked into a trap. Worf and Crusher manage to escape the ambush, but Picard falls into the clutches of a sadistic Cardassian interrogator named Gul Madred.

Madred reveals to Picard that the rumor about biological weapons was spread in order to lure someone like the *Enterprise*'s captain to the site. The Cardassian wants to know what strategy the Federation will use if his world actually *does* attack the Federation—and he plans to torture Picard until he hears what he wants to hear. On the *Enterprise*, Captain Jellico relieves Riker of command when the first officer voices strenuous objections to the captain's plan to mount a first strike against the Cardassians, a move that could endanger Picard's life.

With "Birthright, Part II," visual effects producer, matte painter, martial arts consultant, and weapons expert Dan Curry added one more title to his *TNG* résumé: director. "I'd been directing second unit, inserts, and stunt sequences," Curry says. "I finally got an episode of my own."

The story focuses primarily on a group of young Klingons who know little of their heritage. That's exactly the kind of blank canvas Curry likes. "I got to invent things, like the hunting game," Curry says. "It was very loosely described in the script, so the specifics were my invention. It started out like bocce ball or bowling, where they were just trying to hit things with the hoops. Worf teaches them to throw their spears *through* the hoop when it's rolling, as if they were aiming at running animals. Whenever the camera showed a close-up of a spear doing something, like going through the hoop, that was me throwing it from off-camera. I could do it because of my protracted misspent youth learning how to throw knives, axes, and spears," he notes with a chuckle.

Curry's background also included martial arts,

ing the Klingon discipline of *Mok'bara*. He'd taught it to Michael Dorn earlier in the season (for "Man of the People"), and now Dorn, as Worf, would teach it to the young Klingons. "There's a scene where Toq comes up to Worf from behind and puts his hand on his shoulder," Curry recalls. "We were rehearsing and there was some discussion about having Worf toss him with a very elaborate throw. I said, 'No, the whole point is that Worf is such a skilled warrior that with someone at Toq's level, it would be [a simple move] just like batting a fly.'" An undisclosed crew member, Curry recalls, "said that would be ineffective. So I said, 'Put your hand on my shoulder,' and I just flipped him over. Then he said, 'Okay, that works.'"

Curry's directorial approach wasn't all weapons and fighting, however. He does have a softer side. "I wanted to use lighting to underscore the emotional shifts in the episode, and I must thank [cinematographer] Jonathan West for being such a great ally in the project," he says. "Particularly in the scene where Worf is with Ba'el, and they're getting interested in each other. There's romantic

her hair . . . and suddenly discovers that she has a pointed ear—she's part Romulan!—and he steps back into the shadow. As his mood darkens, he essentially becomes a silhouette."

For the soundtrack, Curry says, "I gave [composer] Jay Chattaway several musical instruments that I'd gotten in Laos in the 1960s, some bamboo-reed mouth organs called *khenes*. Jay sampled the instruments—which sound like a cat being disemboweled—and some of those sounds are built into his score."

Opposite: Curry's prep included the usual storyboards, sketches defining the look of the Klingon spears, and discussions with Jay Chattaway regarding the composer's Klingon music.

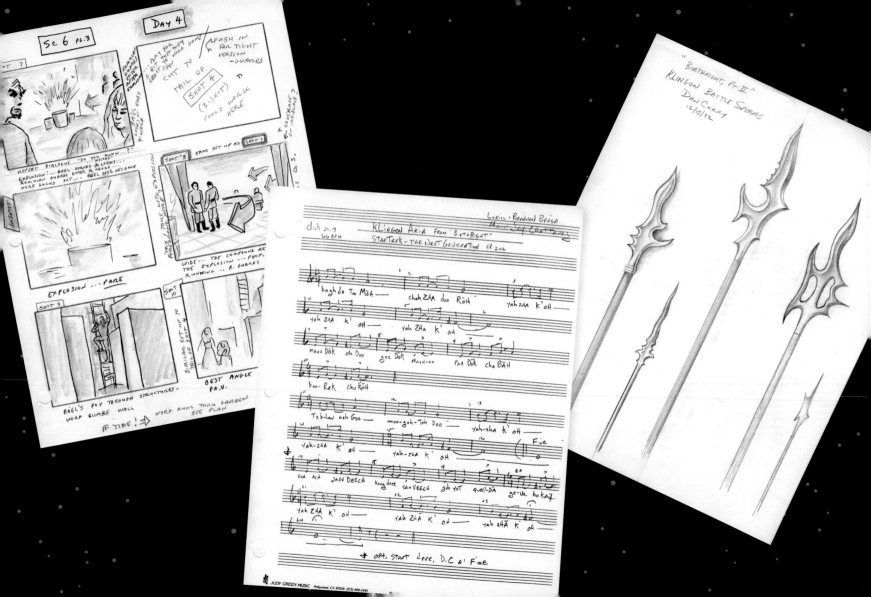

The *Enterprise* docks at the Remmler Array for a routine baryon sweep, a procedure that is part of the normal maintenance on a starship. Because the irradiation procedure is deadly, the crew is required to temporarily evacuate the ship, but Picard returns to retrieve something from his quarters before the sweep begins. To his surprise, he discovers a group of terrorists on board who are intent on stealing the ship's trilithium resin, which they plan to use to create a deadly weapon. With none of his crew around to help him, Picard sets out to foil the plans of the cold-blooded thieves—on his own.

Actor Tim Russ auditioned (unsuccessfully) for the role of Geordi La Forge when the cast of *TNG* was being assembled in 1987. It took six years for him to make it to the *Enterprise,* but after that, his route to the stars began to seem more like destiny than random casting. Following his appearance as Devor, one of the bad guys in "Starship Mine," Russ quickly won the role of a Klingon mercenary in the *Deep Space Nine* episode "Invasive

Procedures." The following year brought him back to the *Enterprise*, albeit the *Enterprise*-B in *Star Trek Generations*. Not long after, Russ won his signature *Star Trek* role as the Vulcan Tuvok on *Star Trek: Voyager*, a role he happily performed for the show's full seven-year run.

Was there a master plan in place? Russ humbly suggests that it was pure serendipity. "Rick Berman liked me," he says. "That's all there is to it. This business is so precarious—ten guys come in and read the hell out of a part, and the producers may like only one of them, and who knows what their reason is? The scenes I originally read for the *TNG* pilot were subtle, quiet scenes, nothing that gave me a chance to really get up and do some fireworks. But apparently there was something about it that Rick liked."

Ironically, a prop got more screen time than Russ did—at least, it got talked about so often that it *seems* as if it did. Picard's precious English riding saddle receives nineteen mentions in the script, and is the subject of four separate conversations (Picard, Hutchinson, Troi, and Geordi; Geordi and Riker; Picard and Kelsey; and finally Picard, Worf,

Riker, Crusher, and Troi). To add insult to injury, at one point Picard whacks Devor with it. But that probably wasn't nearly as humiliating as the fact that Picard eventually knocks out the future Vulcan with what looks suspiciously like a Vulcan nerve pinch (although it's described in the script as a carotid artery block).

Apparently, Picard's meld with Sarek left some interesting residual skills.

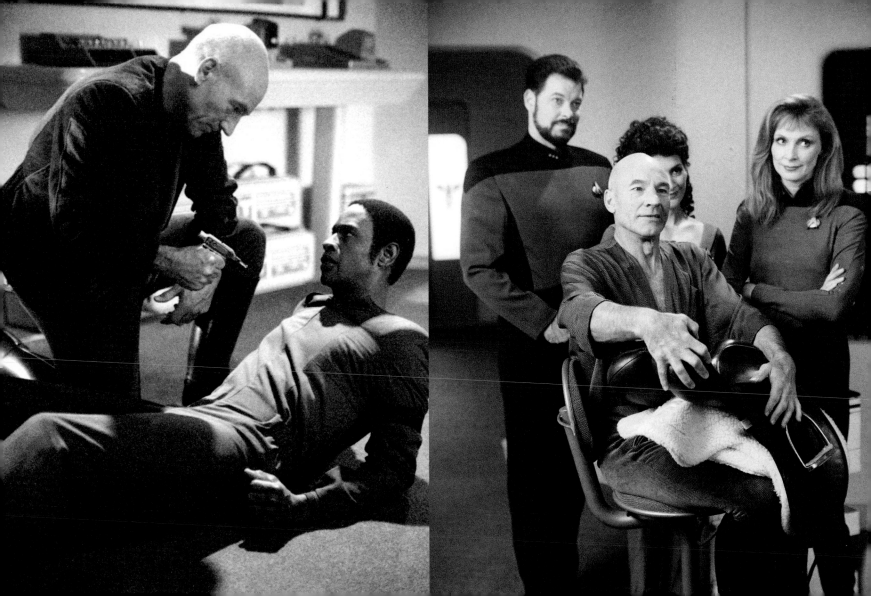

"Relationships with coworkers can be fraught with consequences." —Picard

Although uncertain about the wisdom of becoming involved with a subordinate officer, Captain Picard enters into a romantic relationship with the ship's new chief of stellar sciences, Lieutenant Commander Nella Daren. Picard vows he will be able to separate his responsibility to the ship from the dictates of his heart, but when the time comes to send Daren on a deadly mission, he realizes that duty and love do not mix.

Captain Kirk was always ready to engage in close encounters with the female guest alien of the week, but he avoided fraternizing with female members of his own crew. His behavior was in line with U.S. Naval regulations forbidding "unduly familiar" relationships between personnel of different rank and grade.

But as *Star Trek* moved into the twenty-fourth century, shipboard protocol—only loosely based on existing military models in the first place—grew even more tolerant. If Riker and Troi had been able to set aside their messy emotional baggage, they *could* have hooked up—even though Riker was a commander and Troi (until season seven) only a lieutenant commander. Ditto Geordi and Christi Henshaw, and even Data and Jenna D'Sora.

Picard had *only* subordinates to choose from in the *Enterprise* dating pool. Even so, he, too, was allowed to date—so long as he didn't let it interfere with his responsibilities.

But there, alas, was the rub.

It's hard enough to order a member of the crew to risk his or her life for the sake of a mission. But, as Picard discovers, it's unbearably painful when it's someone you love. As captain, his responsibilities must come first . . . so bye-bye, Nella.

Perhaps the old rules were better after all.

Right: Nella's portable piano, portrayed by two different props, both made by MEL. One was a flat strip of stretchy elastomeric plastic (used when Nella rolled out her instrument), and the other a solid prop that the actress could pretend to play. The detailing on them was identical, but although they looked great on-camera, something was amiss.

"No one here plays piano," MEL's Don Coleman says, chuckling, "so we didn't know what the layout of the keys should be. We just worked off of the sketch we got from the *Star Trek* art department, and whoever did it probably didn't play piano, either. No one noticed until they brought in the musician who was going to help the actress rehearse her hand movements. He had a fit because the keys were all wrong. We got a bit of flack on that one!"

"The Kurlan civilization believed that an individual was a community of individuals. Inside us are many voices, each with its own desires, its own style, its own view of the world." —Picard

Captain Picard is pleased to receive a surprise visit from Professor Galen, his old archaeology professor, but he's puzzled by the old man's request. Declaring that he's on the verge of a discovery so profound that it will rock scientific beliefs across the galaxy, Galen asks Picard to abandon the *Enterprise* and accompany him on a lengthy archaeological hunt. Picard regretfully declines, but a short time later learns that Galen has been mortally injured in a raid on his ship. Galen's secret work dies with him, leaving Picard determined to find out what his friend was searching for. Soon the captain and his crew find themselves vying against Cardassians, Klingons, and Romulans in a race to solve a four-billion-year-old genetic puzzle.

Professor Galen's gift to Picard of a complete set of rare Kurlan *naiskos* certainly impressed the captain—although not enough to convince him to join the professor on an archaeological goose chase. Galen charitably allowed him to keep the priceless *naiskos* figurines anyway, and Picard cherished them for a good two years—before abandoning them in the *[Spoiler Alert!]* wreckage of the *Enterprise*-D, on the surface of Veridian III (*Star Trek Generations*).

The beautiful *naiskos* props were made of high-strength gypsum cement fabricated with fiberglass cloth to give them an authentic look, according to Don Coleman, the senior prop maker and fabricator for MEL. Chris Bergschneider and Mark Sisson did the original sculpts, molds, and castings.

"Joe Menosky was intrigued with this notion of why there's a common humanoid ancestry for all the bipedal races we've encountered in *Star Trek*," says writer Ron Moore. "Why *was* the show filled only with people with bumps on their foreheads? We looked to give that an answer. And I was fascinated with the notion of something being written into the very fabric of their genes, that there was a code in there waiting to be established.

"We wanted to do a big chase," he continues. "We kept talking about doing an episode like *It's a Mad, Mad, Mad, Mad World*—a madcap romp across the universe with all these characters trying to find something. Rick [Berman] and Michael [Piller] kept telling us to take the comedy out, and bit by bit it just kept going away. By the time all was said and done, it was much less of a romp. And it wasn't much of a chase."

Menosky recalls working on the episode just prior to departing for his sabbatical to Italy. "Ron and I split the work," he says. "I took the scenes between Picard and his old professor. I based them on my memories of the complicated emotions I'd observed between students and mentors in college. I think those scenes had a kind of 'emotional truth' to them."

They also held an emotional resonance for director Jonanthan Frakes. "I *loved* working with Norman Lloyd!" he states emphatically. "His career goes back all the way to the Mercury Theatre with Orson Welles. He was a wonderful storyteller and a *brilliant* actor. We were so lucky to have this guy on our show. He's what I remember best about the episode."

Right: Although the "madcap" aspects of the episode were eliminated, the traditional silly stuff between scenes remained.

Opposite: In addition to Frakes's favorite, Norman Lloyd, "The Chase" featured appearances by a wide mix of nonhuman humanoids, including Klingons, Romulans, whatever species the hairless hologram played by Salome Jens was (perhaps, shades of "The Paradise Syndrome," a Preserver?), and Cardassians. Viewers had already met female Klingons and Romulans, but Gul Ocett (Linda Thorson, best recalled as the woman who replaced Diana Rigg in *The Avengers*) was the first adult female Cardassian depicted in *Star Trek*. Not to mention, the first Cardassian seen sporting pumps and a fluffy bathrobe. . . .

"Don't be afraid of your darker side. Have fun with it." —Troi

On the eve of an undercover mission to rescue Federation hostages held on the planet Tilonus IV, Riker experiences bizarre reality shifts, bouncing between life on the *Enterprise* and life in an alien mental asylum. As if that weren't confusing enough, his time on the *Enterprise* is spent practicing for an amateur theatrical production in which he plays a mental patient trapped in an asylum. Soon the thin walls between reality and fantasy seem to disappear, and Riker begins to believe the alien therapist who tells him that he is indeed a patient—and that he's been locked up because he's a murderer!

If there's a quintessential Brannon Braga *TNG* episode, it just may be "Frame of Mind." "That one was right up my alley," he confesses. "It was a really good concept: waking up in an insane asylum and being told that everything you think is real is just a delusion."

Waking up in an insane asylum . . . Where does an idea like that come from?

Braga, who used to have a sign on his office door that read THE PRINCE OF DARKNESS, chuckles. "I don't know. If I did, I would be selling infomercials on it. It popped into my head, just that nugget. And I took it into the writers' room."

To be fair, there were a number of so-called "dark" episodes produced during *TNG*'s sixth season, not all of them conceived by Braga; of "Man of the People," "Chain of Command," the upcoming "Descent," and "Schisms," only the last one is his. However, as his time with the *Star Trek* franchise continued, that "Prince of Darkness" reputation would grow.

But hey, every writer's got his "thing."

Although the premise was admittedly thin— that "nugget" was all he had—the producers took a chance that Braga would be able to weave a convincing episode around it to fill a last-minute dropout in the schedule. Braga credits the rest of the writing team for helping him out. "No one really just went off and did it," he says. "The initial in-

spiration here may have been my own, but we all contribute to the success of each other's episodes. Ultimately, it was a very complicated story, which took Riker down several different avenues that might have been real or might not. Ron [Moore] and I sat in a room and hammered it out together."

Besides providing the audience with "a real mind trip," as Braga so aptly puts it, the episode gave Jonathan Frakes an opportunity to show off his acting chops in a bravura demonstration of Riker with half of his marbles missing. "I thought it was his best episode," offers Braga. "A real tour de force."

"I was beginning to find out that investigating a murder was a little more perilous than I'd thought. And for everything I'd been through, I didn't have any more insight than I did before I started." —Crusher

Doctor Crusher invites a group of scientists to the *Enterprise* to hear the theories of Dr. Reyga, a brilliant Ferengi who claims to have invented a shield that will protect a ship from the deadly effects of a star's corona. After a scientist named Jo'Bril is killed testing Reyga's theory, the Ferengi vows to prove that his shields didn't fail; something else must have killed Jo'Bril. But not long after, Reyga is found dead, ostensibly the victim of suicide. Crusher doesn't believe his death was self-inflicted, but when Reyga's family forbids her to perform an autopsy, she opts to risk both her career and her life in order to clear his maligned name.

"They" (the literary deities who define such things) decree that when a production resorts to using the deadly duo of flashback *plus* voice-over narration to move a story along, it's an obvious attempt to plug holes in a less-than-brilliant script. That's not always the case, of course; a number of successful Hollywood films combine the techniques, including *Sunset Boulevard*, *Stand by Me*, *Goodfellas*, and others.

But in the case of "Suspicions," the deities were correct. For some reason, the combination just didn't work particularly well. The core idea of doing a "murder mystery" came from Joe Menosky shortly before he left the staff, and Naren Shankar was assigned to work on the tale. Discussions with the producers sent the script through many iterations. Initially, Worf was to be the central character—until he was replaced by Beverly. And when the producers learned that Whoopi Goldberg had become available, Guinan was worked into the mix.

"It was a misery," Shankar says. "It was a troubled script. There'd been two other attempts to do similar murder mysteries and they hadn't worked out—then we tried to do this and the whole thing was a clusterfuck."

Shankar laughs at a particular bit of irony. "I remember telling Jeri Taylor when we were breaking the story, 'If I had to do a murder mystery every week on the show, I'd kill myself.'"

This from a man who would go on to become an executive producer on *CSI: Crime Scene Investigation*—doing murder mysteries every week for nearly a decade.

"I am Kahless . . . and I have returned."
—*Kahless*

A disillusioned Worf takes leave from the *Enterprise* and travels to a Klingon monastery, where he hopes to "find Kahless" via meditation. But although the Klingon Empire's legendary spiritual leader has been dead for many years, Worf discovers what appears to be a real flesh and blood Kahless at the monastery, one who wishes to rally his followers to unite under his leadership. While Worf finds merit in the plan, Gowron, the Empire's current leader, sees it as a potential threat to his own rule, and sets out to prove that the reborn Kahless is a fake.

Much like their creator, Gene Roddenberry, most of the characters who live and work on the *Starship Enterprise* are secular humanists. They may hold personal religious beliefs, but they typically don't voice them. It's ironic, then, that the one character aboard who seems the most uncivilized is the one who holds and expresses the deepest orthodox beliefs.

Per Jeri Taylor, "Rightful Heir" wouldn't have worked with anyone *but* Worf. An examination of spiritualism and faith on *Star Trek* almost seems antithetical, and certainly unprecedented. But teleplay writer Ron Moore relished the assignment.

"It was intriguing to me *because* of the religious stuff," Moore says, "and because of what it would mean to meet someone from the past who's been re-created through cloning. What would happen if you could bring Jesus back? What would it do to the faith of his followers? What's true and what's not, what's authentic and what's not? It was an opportunity to get deeper into the Klingon mythology and the Klingon political sphere. And say, let's establish that they have a constitutional monarchy—and yet these people worship this guy Kahless. They worship him in a literal sense. So what would bringing him back do to his people?"

All good questions, all answered in that uniquely oblique way that *Star Trek* so often utilized to bypass controversy.

Right: Nope, not the craft service table. More of Alan Sims's Klingon grub, featuring lots of tantalizing tentacles. "The trick to making Klingon food look edible, yet at the same time totally revolting, is you mix and blend it," Sims says. "I use things like octopus, huge squid tentacles, and very bizarre-looking dried Asian vegetables. Into this, I mix edible items, things that you could stomach and find palatable."

Opposite: Director Rick Kolbe prepares Worf and Kahless for their battle.

Like many of his other contributions to *TNG*, the matte painting representing the Klingon monastery's exteriors was inspired by Dan Curry's extensive travels throughout Asia—in this instance, Nepal and the bordering Himalayas. "Several years ago I did some conceptual designs for a feature that was never made," Curry relates. "I thought of that art when I read the script for 'Rightful Heir,' where Worf goes to a Klingon monastery." That early design featured Himalayan-type architecture, with its distinctive pagoda-style tiered towers and multiple eaves, which Curry set into a craggy mountain range. The resulting image suggested a graceful yet formidable presence in very rough terrain. Using the original work as an inspirational springboard, Curry did a similarly themed Photoshop freehand painting of Himalayan structures on top of a photograph he took in the Canadian Rockies.

Right: Richard James's quasi-Byzantine interiors for the living quarters of the monastery rendered Planet Hell's familiar caverns completely unrecognizable . . . one might even say sumptuous.

Commander Riker returns to Nervala IV, intending to recover data from an away mission he was forced to abandon years earlier. The planet's peculiar atmospheric conditions allow transportation on and off the world only during a brief period every eight years. When Riker arrives, he's shocked to discover an exact duplicate of himself who, because of the planet's unique distortion field, was created the instant that he beamed off the planet. This Riker has spent the last eight years alone on the desolate planet and is understandably eager to pick up his life where he left off, particularly his passionate relationship with Deanna Troi. All of which troubles Commander Riker, who's not sure he wants to share his life—or his former love.

"One of my fondest memories of 'Second Chances' is how I was trying to find subtle differences between the two characters," recalls Jonathan Frakes. "And to this day, Marina [Sirtis] always reminds me of that. She says, 'I liked Thomas Riker better.'"

If Sirtis and the writing staff had their way, the episode might have had a completely different ending—one that would have allowed the Thomas/Deanna romance to continue indefinitely. "Most of us were advocates of killing Will Riker and having Tom take his place," Ron Moore reveals. "We thought it would be bold and shocking, and something for the fans to chew over. But Rick Berman, and to an extent, Michael Piller, didn't want to make such a big change." It was Piller, however, who made the unusual decision to allow Tom to survive at the end of the episode. Tom would make one further appearance in the *Star Trek* universe: in a *DS9* episode titled "*Defiant*."

Right and opposite: Visual effects couldn't handle all of the scenes with multiple Rikers. For that, the producers used Frakes's regular body double, Geoffrey Mutch, and two stunt doubles: Tom Morga and Mark Riccardi.

"We bought the idea of a transporter accident," teleplay writer René Echevarria says, "and that became the basis of a love story for Riker and Troi. We'd always talked about the fact that they used to be involved, and now they weren't. And 'Second Chances' was *our* chance to tell a story about them, and what a big love this really was for this man and woman. Tom *is* Riker. He's spent the last eight years thinking about being reunited with her. It was a very romantic story, and obviously a lot of fun for Jonathan and Marina."

"Second Chances" was a fan favorite, drawing accolades for the episode's writer, whose track record, which included "The Offspring" and "I, Borg," gave him a reputation for being an expert at the "touchy-feely stuff," as he refers to it. "I started getting letters saying that *Star Trek* 'needed more women writers' like me," Echevarria says with a chuckle. "Jeri Taylor was delighted by that. 'Just us girls,' she would say. I took it as a great compliment. We all had our specialties: Ron with his great muscular style of storytelling, Brannon with those weird mind games with an erotic tinge. And I, apparently, was doing the girlie stuff."

The episode represented a personal triumph for neophyte director LeVar Burton. "I'd had my eye on directing for a long time," Burton says. "Jonathan [Frakes] was the first of us to cross that line. When I finally mustered the courage to approach Rick Berman about doing it, he told me, 'I've been waiting for you to come walking in that door—now get your ass to Paramount University.'"

His first episode turned out to be more technically challenging than many, "a real baptism of fire," as Burton puts it. "I had one actor playing two different characters, and those characters continually interacted throughout the course of the story. It was incumbent upon me to figure out how to accomplish that. I felt that if I could pull this off without sinking the ship, I really had a possible future as a director."

One example: In an early scene, he recalls, "We had one Riker do a 360-degree walk around the other Riker. Of course, the visual effects people were there to assist, but I was pretty proud when I nailed the methodology for doing it. I recognized that there was a rhythm—beats that made the effect possible—so we recorded a click track and played it back for everybody. One-two-three-four-five-six. That was the blueprint. And then the rest of it was establishing 'Well, what can I do that uses a photo double, and what's going to be a visual effect.' It was a lot of pressure, but I felt I rose to the occasion and delivered. Directing the episode was the most fun, the most exhilarating, and the scariest time that I'd ever felt on the set."

Opposite: Burton and Dan Curry co-orchestrate one of the episode's many effects sequences.

In a 2005 CNN interview, astronaut Mae Jemison reported that she'd found inspiration for her life's work in the original *Star Trek* series. "What was really great about *Star Trek* when I was growing up as a little girl is not only did they have Lieutenant Uhura, played by Nichelle Nichols, as a technical officer—but she was *African*. So that helped to fuel my whole idea that *I* could be involved in space exploration as well as in the sciences." Twenty-some years after watching Nichols, Jemison became the first African American woman to reach outer space. As science mission specialist on the *Endeavor* Space Shuttle STS-42 Skylab J flight, she spent eight days, from September 12 through September 20, 1992, conducting bone cell, weightlessness, and motion sickness experiments—while orbiting the Earth 127 times.

Less than a year later, in April of 1993, she became the first *real* space traveler to step before the cameras on *Star Trek*, when LeVar Burton cast her to play Ensign Palmer in *TNG*'s "Second Chances."

"I knew how important seeing Nichelle in *The Original Series* had been for Mae," Burton says.

"Just as it was for me, as a child of the fifties and sixties, in formulating my own self-image. This was an opportunity that I didn't want to pass up— to complete that loop and close the circle. And I knew that Nichelle would be thrilled because of her previous commitments to NASA. I thought, 'Let me call Nichelle and say, "Mae Jemison, the first African American woman in space, is going to be on the *Star Trek* set. Would you like to meet her?" And then I'll just stand back and watch that happen.'

"So Nichelle came to the set and met Mae—and it was magic," Burton says, smiling. "I remember thinking, 'Oh my God, this is *so* cool.'"

"It's going to take a little time to explain, Number One." —Picard

Picard, Troi, Data, and La Forge return from a Federation conference to find the *Enterprise* and its crew frozen in time with a warp core breach in progress in engineering, and a Romulan warbird apparently firing on the starship. This strange scenario seems to be caused by the presence of a peculiar alien species whose young have taken up residence in the warbird's engine core. But ridding the Romulan ship of the alien presence won't solve everyone's problems: the minute that time "unsticks" and begins to move forward again, the *Enterprise* will be destroyed!

"'Timescape' was my second stab at time travel," says Brannon Braga. "Or in this case, 'time frozen.' I suspect that by this point, when the audience saw my name on the screen, they knew they were in for some sort of bizarre ride."

And bizarre is what they got: Picard sprouting

Fu Manchu–length fingernails; embryonic lifeforms trapped within an artificial black hole; Beverly Crusher bisected by a disruptor blast; and the *Enterprise* destroyed by a warp core breach (from which it—and Beverly—miraculously recover). Oh, and did we mention Picard drawing a smiley face on a thick cloud of gas escaping from the *Enterprise*'s warp core?

Reportedly, Braga's complicated script generated the longest list of required opticals the visual effects crew had ever received, but somehow they—and returning director Adam Nimoy—managed to put together an episode that was visually stunning, if not altogether logical.

"It was one of those episodes that read better on paper," Braga admits with a laugh. "And there's nothing worse than a bunch of extras standing around pretending to be frozen. You can see in some of those big shots, people wavering, trying not to move, but moving. People standing as if they're in mid-stride but it's obvious that they're about to topple over. We were able to do some shots where we froze the frame and then combined it with a blue screen image of someone walk-

ing through the action, but we couldn't afford to do that with all the shots."

For viewers who could never get enough of this beautiful ship, "Timescape" provided spectacular onscreen images of the *D'deridex*-class Romulan warbird, frozen in time and poised for salacious scrutiny. The ship made its debut in the season one episode "The Neutral Zone." The thirty-six-inch by twenty-five-inch by ten-inch shooting model—seen here all lit up and ready for postproduction close-ups—was built by Greg Jein from cast resin and acrylic plastic. Note the beautiful detailing on the ship's back and interior wing surface. Not quite visible is a fixed bottom-mounted rod used to attach the warbird to motion control equipment for visual effects filming. The model sold for $30,000 at Christie's 2006 auction.

An *Enterprise* away team finds the inhabitants of a science outpost, brutally dispatched by a group of Borg still present on the station. Unlike their unemotional brethren, these drones are individualistic and vicious. As the team fends off their attack, Data experiences a surge of rage and kills one of them. The rest of the Borg escape in a vessel that leaps through a strange subspace distortion. Startled by his own behavior, Data takes himself off-duty, while the crew tracks the Borg. They manage to capture a drone and lock him in the brig, but a short time later, the Borg escapes in an *Enterprise* shuttlecraft—accompanied by Data. Following the shuttle to an unexplored planet, Picard leads the search party for Data. He quickly finds himself surrounded by a horde of Borg commanded by Data's unstable android "sibling," Lore—and Data!

Let's play "Guess the Writer."

"I liked the idea of 'Descent' a lot. It was an opportunity to go very dark with a character. There were overtones to it that I was drawn to. Finding that Lore and the Borg had joined forces was a creepy proposition, and there was something delicious about that scene in the brig with Data talking to the Borg about killing. I liked taking Data to a very dark place."

You might think that's "Prince of Darkness" Brannon Braga talking, or perhaps the psychoanalytical Joe Menosky.

But no—it's Ronald D. Moore, proving that there are many options in a writer's toolbox. But while Moore enjoyed conducting Data's descent into the heart of darkness, he wasn't pleased with the way the "Descent" action sequences turned out. "The phaser fights were *so* static," he moans. "There was just no 'wow' to any of the phaser battles we produced on our show. It was frustrating. I remember sitting in production meetings, arguing, trying to get more energy into those scenes. But the characters would ultimately stand next to bookshelves and lean around them, fire once, then duck their head back. Then you'd cut to the other side, and the other character was doing pretty much the same thing.

"We tried to make the scripts as exciting as possible, but then I'd see it all get stripped away, for time, or for budget, or somebody thought it was too complex. There were a thousand reasons why the action sequences got cut back. The problem was, we were shooting on seven-day schedules. Later, when I did *Battlestar Galactica*, we shot an eight-day schedule; that's actually pretty standard in the industry. But with seven days, you had to shoot ten pages a day, a huge amount of work. And action sequences take much more time to set up and plan—for safety reasons, for choreography, and camera moves, getting the stunt player ready. We just didn't have the time to devote to realizing an interesting action sequence.

"But we were always trying," he swears. "If you read the scripts, you'd go, 'Ooh—that *sounds* exciting!'"

Over the years, eminent stars of stage, screen, and even the scientific community managed to parlay their interest in *Star Trek* into cameo appearances on the series. None was more noteworthy than theoretical physicist Dr. Stephen Hawking, who appeared as a holographic version of himself in the teaser for "Descent, Part I."

Visiting the Paramount lot in 1993 to help promote Paramount Home Video's upcoming release of the documentary *A Brief History of Time*, Hawking expressed a desire to see the sets for *Star Trek: The Next Generation*. Studio security contacted *TNG*'s production office, and executive producers Rick Berman and Michael Piller hustled over to meet the professor on the *TNG* soundstage.

Although he cannot speak nor walk due to the debilitating effects of Lou Gehrig's disease, Hawking, a longtime *Star Trek* fan, took full advantage of his visit. "I asked if I could sit in the captain's chair," he said (via his speech-synthesis computer) in an interview that took place after the tour. "It is rather more comfortable and a lot more powerful than my wheelchair." The interview took place in front of the *Enterprise*'s warp core, a component

that Hawking was quite taken with. "I'm working on that," he noted wryly. Before he left, Hawking conveyed to the producers that he would like to be in an episode. After checking to see that Hawking's schedule jibed with the show's production, the producers instructed writer Ronald D. Moore to add a scene to the teleplay he was working on for "Descent." Moore quickly constructed a holodeck poker match between the greatest minds of Earth history—plus Data, no slouch himself in the IQ department.

Appearing in the brief scene with Hawking was, says Brent Spiner, "perhaps my favorite moment in the entire experience of doing *Star Trek*."

Right: Hawking's electronic cardholder, seen at Einstein's elbow, was created by MEL's Paul Elliott. "What we do at MEL is build great stuff that doesn't exist," says Don Coleman.

In preparation for production of *TNG*'s pilot and opening title sequence, model maker Greg Jein and an Industrial Light & Magic crew supervised by Ease Owyeung built the "six-foot" (actual dimensions: seventy-eight by fifty-nine by fourteen inches) model of the new *Enterprise*-D from Andrew Probert's design. The model, molded of clear fiberglass, was engineered with ribs rigid enough that it could be hung or mounted at any angle for photography. The spacing between the ribs was filled with expandable foam, adding to the strength but not the weight. Prior to painting the ship, the crew carefully masked numerous areas, such as the "windows," leaving them transparent so an extensive array of interior lights could shine through.

They also built a two-foot-long model, although they did not equip it with lights; 3M reflective strips served as windows.

The six-foot model ultimately proved to be inconveniently large. Technicians at Image G, the motion control photography facility, quickly realized that they couldn't get their cameras far enough away from the ship to accommodate a requisite variety of interesting angles and moves. So Jein duplicated the model on a smaller scale, this one four feet in length. It, too, was fully outfitted with interior lights, although unlike the previous models, it could not be used for a saucer separation sequence. The four-footer was introduced in the show's third season.

Also pictured is a "gooseneck" model used for detailed close-ups of the *Enterprise*'s battle section when the show portrayed a separation sequence. Although producers had hoped to make such sequences a regular feature of the series, shooting them proved to be time-consuming and prohibitively expensive, so separation was seldom seen.

Opposite: The three *Enterprise*s and the gooseneck, docked in their usual berths at Image G, awaiting their close-ups.

By season seven, *The Next Generation* was on everyone's radar, even that of the Academy of Television Arts & Sciences, which at long last recognized the series with a nomination for Outstanding Drama Series (it lost to *Picket Fences*). Audience interest in the show was at an all-time high, elevated by Paramount's announcement that this would be *TNG*'s final year on television—and that the first *TNG* movie would bow in November 1994.

The move made financial sense for the studio. Escalating costs over the years had rendered the series much less profitable. "It was definitely a decision by Paramount," said Rick Berman in a 2006 interview. "The afterlife of a first-run television show is to go into stripped syndication. And once you have 175-odd episodes, it's considered enough. I had been contacted a year earlier by Sherry Lansing, who ran the motion picture division, and told that they wanted us to do a *TNG* motion picture. So it was all very clearly designed to end after seven years and to go right into production on the movie."

The accelerated pace was hard on everyone involved in the show's production. To accommodate the schedule for the motion picture, shooting for the series was pushed up by a month, meaning everyone got that much less vacation time between seasons. Many behind-the-scenes personnel were working on both *TNG* and *DS9*, and some, like writers Ron Moore and Brannon Braga,

were also involved with the new film. At the same time, Paramount tapped Berman, Michael Piller, and recently promoted executive producer Jeri Taylor to create another *Star Trek* series that could pick up the slack when *TNG* went off the air. "The studio asked us—or maybe 'told us' would be a better choice of words—to create what eventually became *Voyager*," Berman remarked.

But even with all the stress, it was a period that many of the participants relished. "It was a bittersweet time," says LeVar Burton today, "because we were having such a great time on the television series. None of us really wanted to stop production. The opportunity to do feature films was sexy, but at the same time we were really at the height of our popularity when we stopped production. The decisions that were made were way above my pay grade."

Given the chance, would he have been willing to do another year of *TNG* the series?

Burton doesn't need a moment to think. "We would *all* have done another year, absolutely!"

Opposite: At the beginning of every season, Paramount Television diligently scheduled a new "gallery"—or publicity—shoot for *TNG*. By the seventh season, the actors, reportedly a little bored with the process and the amount of time the sessions carved out of their increasingly busy days, didn't seem to take it terribly seriously.

"Goodbye, Lore." —Data

Following their capture by Lore and Data, Picard, Troi, and La Forge learn that it was their release of the Borg drone Hugh a year earlier that triggered the evolution of the very twisted Borg group led by Lore. When Hugh returned to the Borg cube, his newly awakened individuality destroyed the hive's sense of shared identity, leading to chaos. Lore's subsequent encounter with the group gave them a much-needed sense of united purpose. With the drones doing his bidding, the android set out to bring Data into the fold by covertly instilling him with negative feelings generated by Dr. Soong's emotion chip. Now Picard and the others must find a way to reboot Data's ethics program before Lore launches his plan to end "the reign of biological life-forms."

Things didn't go as planned in this follow-up to season six's cliff-hanger.

"There were too many balls in the air after Part One," says René Echevarria. "And I was stuck trying to catch them."

And, inevitably, some of the balls were dropped. "Part Two was built off the return of Hugh," Echevarria explains. But Hugh's through-line would take a backseat to Data's trip to the Dark Side, courtesy of his irredeemable "brother," Lore. A subplot about Beverly's moment in the sun (literally as well as figuratively) also would steal precious time from Hugh's story. Thus, the little Borg that viewers had fallen in love with in "I, Borg" gets to play only a supporting role here. He doesn't even have a chance to visit with his friend Geordi.

And that's because Geordi is once again the victim of an evildoer (Lore) who seeks to "hack" his neural implants in order to further some nefarious plan (Lore feels Geordi's implants make him "an ideal test subject" for the android's efforts to turn a human into an artificial life-form).

Back in season four, the Romulans used Geordi's implants to turn him into a remote-controlled would-be assassin ("The Mind's Eye"). And about a year *after* the events of "Descent, Part II," mad scientist Tolian Soran would utilize Geordi's VISOR to turn the engineer into an unknowing live video transmitter (*Star Trek Generations*).

It's no wonder Geordi eventually replaced his im-

plants and VISOR with ocular prostheses (*Star Trek: First Contact*).

Below: Jonathan Frakes and director of photography Jonathan West take a break during location filming near sunny Simi Valley, located northwest of Los Angeles.

Worf: "They look like dresses."

Riker: "That is an incredibly outmoded and sexist attitude. I'm surprised at you. Besides, you look good in a dress."

An encounter with several Iyaaran ambassadors creates confusion for members of the *Enterprise*'s senior staff, who are assigned to facilitate a cultural exchange. Troi finds that her ambassador is interested only in the gluttonous intake of food and drink, while Worf is goaded to violence by his charge. Meanwhile, Picard, who was en route to the Iyaaran homeworld, finds himself trapped on a desolate planet with a love-starved woman who would apparently do anything to keep him there.

"Liaisons" began as a pitch with potential: a *TNG* take on *Misery*, the bestselling Stephen King novel in which a disturbed fan holds a novelist captive. But freelance pitches seldom retain their original shape, and during the episode's difficult break session, this tale expanded into an unwieldy episode about the Iyaarans, a peculiar species that admits they don't know much about history (of the Federation)—or biology (they procreate through "post-cellular compounding"), pleasure (via an overabundance of tasty desserts), antagonism (apparently the Iyaarans don't have tempers to lose), and especially not love (which is where the original *Misery* theme ultimately led).

Brannon Braga did the polish on the script by *TNG* interns Jeanne Carrigan Fauci and Lisa Rich, and he attempted to lighten it up with the subplots about Byleth, the obnoxious Klingon-baiting ambassador, and Loquel, the ambassador who can eat a *lot* more chocolate than Troi. A few years after this episode, Braga would weave similar themes into the B story of the *Voyager* episode "Someone to Watch Over Me."

But while the revelation of what the Iyaaran ambassadors were up to was interesting, most viewers found the episode somewhat lacking, particularly in comparison to the ambitious territory the writers had explored during season six. And post-episode, there were any number of unanswered questions. Like: if your assignment was to explore pleasure and you were paired with Troi, would sampling peach cobbler *really* be the most interesting way to spend your visit on the *Enterprise*?

Below: Cosmo Genovese discusses a point of continuity with Michael Dorn. As the show's script supervisor, Genovese was charged with keeping track of all the minute details of the shooting day, including, perhaps, how Worf's sash was draped in the previous take.

As Geordi prepares to test a new technology that will allow him to use his VISOR as an interface between his mind and a mechanical probe, he receives word that his mother's starship, the *Hera*, has been lost with all hands aboard. Geordi refuses to postpone the experiment because it could save the lives of seven men and women aboard the *Raman*, a science vessel caught in the atmosphere of gas giant Marijne VII. The probe establishes that the *Raman*'s crew is dead, but it also indicates that La Forge's mother is aboard the *Raman*—and she wants Geordi to use the probe to send the vessel deeper into Marijne VII's atmosphere, where she claims the *Hera* is trapped.

James Cameron did it better, but Joe Menosky did it first.

"The core idea of 'Interface'—an *Avatar*-type interface used to function in an extremely inhospitable alien environment—was something I had wanted to do for a very long time," Menosky says. "After I left *TNG* to live in Europe, my colleagues very generously allowed me to continue to contribute—an inconvenience for them because this was *pre*-Internet, so we had to deal with faxes and FedEx. The staff gave me the 'Geordi's mom' idea as a character subplot, but I never really found a way to make that combination work," he adds with a sigh.

"There was some creative burnout during the last season," admits Ron Moore. "There was all this attention being paid to *Generations* and *DS9*, so we'd start doing things like, 'Well, we haven't talked about Geordi's mother—bring in Geordi's mother!' 'What about Worf's brother?' The relatives were coming out of the closet because we were looking for things to do with people."

Nevertheless, the 'Geordi's mom' idea did make one interested party happy, although he felt it didn't go far enough. "We just touched the tip of the iceberg where Geordi's background is concerned," LeVar Burton notes. "I wish we'd gotten deeper into his relationship with those parents. Geordi's mom, played by Madge Sinclair, and his father, played by Ben Vereen, were high-powered overachievers in Starfleet—as was their son. He was born blind, and due to the stature of his parents, he was able to be one of the first recipients of this *phenomenal* technology that allowed him to see. In spite of his physical challenge, Geordi was able to go through Starfleet Academy, and to *excel*, becoming a high-ranking officer on the Federation flagship. It's a great story. I wish we'd had an opportunity to *really* explore it."

The actor did get the opportunity to experience a kind of family reunion on the set. Like Burton, Sinclair and Vereen had played significant roles in the seminal 1977 television epic *Roots*—with Sinclair playing the wife of Burton's character as an adult (John Amos played the older Kunta Kinte), and Vereen his character's grandson—although they didn't share any scenes in the miniseries. Sinclair did, however, play Burton's mother in three different television movies.

The crew receives word that Captain Picard has been killed by mercenaries while on an archaeological trip, but Riker refuses to accept the report without investigating. Traveling to Barradas III, Riker finds evidence of Picard's attackers—right before he's taken captive himself. On board the mercenaries' ship, Riker discovers that Picard is part of the crew, posing as a smuggler. Following Picard's lead, Riker also takes on a false identity—a corrupt Starfleet officer—in order to gain the trust of the cutthroat group. Together, the two imposters hope to discover the real reason behind a string of archaeological lootings conducted by the mercenaries.

Although their ruse fools most of the raiders, Tallera, a Romulan crew member, soon demands to know Picard's true identity. She reveals that she is actually a Vulcan security agent; she's been tagging along with the mercenaries in order to track down fragments of the Stone of Gol, an ancient psionic superweapon that is powered by thought. She claims that her mission is to keep the weapon out of the hands of a destructive Vulcan isolationist group. But as the mercenaries near their goal, both Picard and Riker begin to have doubts about Tallera's identity and her motives.

Right: Makeup artist Michael Key touches up actress Robin Curtis as Tallera. Tallera (a.k.a. T'Paal) is actually a Vulcan masquerading as a Romulan, presumably because a Romulan identity is more plausible if one is trying to pass as a ruthless mercenary. Curtis made a convincing Romulan-Vulcan in the two-parter—but then, she'd already worn pointed ears as Saavik in two *Star Trek* movies: *Star Trek III: The Search for Spock* and *Star Trek IV: The Voyage Home*.

During his time at Paramount, Rick Berman had, on his desk, a bust of *Star Trek* creator Gene Rodden- ███ "I think the man who made the bust made two of them," Berman told StarTrek.com in early 2011. "He gave one to me and one to Gene. One day, I was in a meeting with the writers and somebody took a little piece of cloth, like a ribbon that was wrapped around something, and put it over Gene's eyes. Like, 'God forbid he see or hear what's going on in this room.' It was a joke, but it has been knotted around his eyes ever since."

According to Jeri Taylor's comments in the *Star Trek: The Next Generation Companion*, "Gambit" was one of the episodes that necessitated the blindfold. The staff had gone back and forth on a year-old pitch from Chris Hatton regarding "space pirates," a topic that had always been a big no-no in Roddenberry's eyes. Finally, Taylor was summoned to Berman's of- fice to discuss the story germ. Upon entering, Taylor saw a bright red bandanna across the Great Bird's eyes ██ Gene *always* said he'd never do space pi- rates," Taylor quotes Berman as saying, "and this is a space pirate story, and I don't want Gene to see this or hear it!"

INT. SHUTTLEBAY

The KLINGON SHUTTLE has now been brought into the bay. Worf and BEVERLY approach the shuttle door and wait. The door to the shuttle OPENS and Koral begins to step out . . .

24A ON BEVERLY

as she looks up . . . and up . . . and up . . .

24B RESUME SCENE

Revealing Koral as he stands before Beverly — he may be the tallest Klingon we've ever seen. He stands there towering above Beverly like some kind of displeased skyscraper. She is a little taken aback...

There's no "may be" about it. At six feet, nine inches, Koral is, indeed, the tallest Klingon ever seen on *TNG*, largely because he was played by Los Angeles Lakers star forward James Worthy. This choice bit of stunt casting was made possible when actor Robert O'Reilly (Gowron, leader of the Klingon High Council) found himself aboard the same plane as Worthy. As O'Reilly has related at many a *Star Trek* convention appearance, he introduced himself to the basketball player, who admitted to being a *Star Trek* fan, and the two men reportedly exchanged autographed pictures of themselves during the flight (per O'Reilly, he had to trade two Gowrons for one Worthy). Upon hearing that Worthy would love to be on *The Next Generation*, O'Reilly urged him to call Rick Berman. Subsequently, Ron Moore, who wrote the teleplay for Part II, was asked to find a part for Worthy; the result was the surly Klingon mercenary Koral, who made a big impression on everyone he met.

"Sometimes a cake is just a cake." —Troi

Data's dream program begins to generate disturbing nightmares that all seem to involve the crew's frighteningly bizarre eating habits. But even after Data deactivates his dream program, the strange images won't go away, and one of them drives him to stab Troi! Only after Troi is taken to sickbay and closely examined does Doctor Crusher realize that there may be a reason for Data's visions. The ship is infested with invisible leechlike creatures that are extracting vital amino acids from the bodies of the crew. But how can they rid the entire ship of parasites that no one can see or feel?

"Everyone remembers Troi as the cake," Brannon Braga relates proudly.

Indeed, how could *TNG* viewers ever forget the cake scene?

                    TROI

lying on her back on the tabletop. She is staring up at Data with a frightened expression on her face. Her legs are gone and HER TORSO IS A GIANT CAKE — made to look exactly like her real torso, blue uniform and all. A piece has already been cut out of her chest where the communication pin usually is.

Yes, the sequence owes a lot to the iconic 1985 music video for Tom Petty's song "Don't Come Around Here No More." But that was on MTV, a destination where surrealistic visuals inspired by mind-altering substances was far more commonplace.

Brannon Braga pushed for the sequence, which caused a bit of consternation in those crew members charged with bringing it to life. "I remember sitting in the production meeting with this team of fifty people," Braga says, "and with all this stuff we'd done—with aliens and alien worlds, and flying starships, all this weird stuff—they couldn't figure out how to make Troi into a cake. There was this long discussion about 'How are we going to do this?' And I'm like, 'Guys! It's an old magic trick. She's under the table. Her head's *on* the table.'"

Braga begins to chuckle. "I've got to tell you," he says. "Does a career get any better than that? To be able to write stuff like that? Doing episodes like this was so much fun!"

Below: And for dessert, a nice order of Riker's brains!

Opposite: Director Patrick Stewart supervises last-minute refinements to Troi's confectionary appearance by hair designer Joy Zapata and makeup artist June Abston Haymore.

In the 1939 film classic *The Wizard of Oz*, the Tin Man finds the Scarecrow with portions of his straw body strewn throughout the woods by flying monkeys. In a mixture of exasperation and distress, the Tin Man exclaims, "Well, that's you all over!"

Which could easily have been the comment of viewers as they watched "Phantasms." Data previously had lost his head on *TNG*—several times, in fact—and he'd temporarily lost an arm (in "Measure of a Man"), but "Phantasms" marked the first time the audience saw so many of the android's disembodied components in one episode.

Perhaps the most striking visual was Data's chest phone, an ingenious prop built by MEL. "They brought in the old phone they wanted me to use," recalls Don Coleman, "and one of Data's uniform shirts, and a sketch of what they had in mind. They said they just needed a chest that would open up and have a phone inside of it. I said, 'Okay, sure,' and did a vacuform pull over the top of an existing body mold, cut the chest open, and fabricated a box behind it to hold the phone. Then I applied the tunic over the top of that."

It was a weird request, he admits, "but you just kind of take it in stride."

Below: Michael Westmore helps Brent Spiner get into character as a one-armed android.

Opposite: Hair designer Josée Normand transferred from *TNG* to *Deep Space Nine* in 1993, but she came back for a visit during the filming of "Phantasms."

After Data begins experiencing disturbing night-mares, he visits a Sigmund Freud holodeck program for advice. "Freud," who is less than helpful, makes some rather outrageous claims about the Troi cake dream's symbolism, and refers to Data as "a poly-morphously perverse individual."

Data eventually works out for himself what his subconscious is trying to tell him, but not before he actually stabs Troi and scares the bejeezus out of his fellow crewmates, not to mention the show's fans. Over the course of *The Next Generation*, viewers had gradually experienced a shift in how they perceived the character of Data. His calm, stable persona ini-tially had led them to trust him implicitly. But with episodes like "A Fistful of Datas," where a computer interface with his neural net almost leads to Worf's death on the holodeck; "Descent," where a jolt of broadcasted emotion from the Soong emotion chip makes him fly into a murderous rage; "Descent, Part II," where a shutdown of his ethical subroutines al-lows him to casually implant nano-cortical fibers into his best friend's brain; and this one, where he as-saults a fellow crew person, Data had become a bit like a once-trusted family dog who's developed an unpredictable propensity for biting.

Was it really a good idea to have Data stab Troi?

"There was some concern about the scene," ad-mits Brannon Braga. "It *was* violent and disturb-ing." But there was a reason for it, he adds, and story-wise, it did lead to the revelation of the invis-ible creatures plaguing the crew. Which apparently was enough rationalization for the producers to let it through. While the U.S. version included the scene as is, the more cautious BBC opted to edit the actual moment of stabbing for the episode's British broadcast.

Troi's mother, Lwaxana, returns to the *Enterprise* when the ship plays host to a delegation of Cairn. The telepathic species is new to the spoken word, and Lwaxana serves as both escort and tutor to the group. Although Troi notices that her boisterous mother seems atypically despondent, she's shocked when Lwaxana falls into a coma. Close contact with a young Cairn girl has triggered repressed memories from the past—and the only way to help Lwaxana get past the psychic trauma is for Deanna to enter her mother's psyche and find the awful truth she's been hiding.

While a number of women held prominent positions in the *TNG* production office, the writers' room was primarily male turf. Over the years, women like Dorothy "D.C." Fontana, Hannah Louise Shearer, Melinda Snodgrass, and Jeri Taylor had a seat at the table. However, with the exception of Taylor, they all moved on to other projects after a year or two.

Hilary J. Bader, who wrote "Dark Page" and two earlier *TNG* episodes, came to the show as a writing intern during the third season, and although she didn't stay long, the series was an important stepping-stone in her career. Post-*TNG*, she went on to a successful career that included episodes of *Deep Space Nine* and *Voyager*, and a long stint on *Xena: Warrior Princess*. But Bader really made her mark writing for animated series like *The New Batman Adventures*, *Superman*, and *Batman Beyond*. In between TV assignments, she wrote scripts for the interactive video games Star Trek: Borg and Star Trek: Klingon, and thirty-eight superhero comic books for DC Comics.

"I didn't always plan to write for TV," Bader told *Batman: The Animated Newsletter* on ToonZone.net. "I came to L.A. with a couple of spec scripts, including a *Star Trek: The Next Generation*. *Star Trek* was the only TV show that would read specs submitted without an agent. Fortunately, mine was read by the executive producer, who called me in to pitch. On my second pitch, they were interested in one of the stories and asked me if I wanted to be the Writers Guild intern. Like anyone would say no to that! So my first job in TV was writing a script for *TNG* while spending twenty weeks as the intern."

Over the course of a busy dozen years as a professional writer, Bader received seven nominations for a Daytime Emmy Award, with two wins. She passed away in 2002.

Opposite, left: "Dark Page" was the last *TNG* guest appearance for Majel Barrett, seen here with Amick Byram (Ian Andrew Troi). She also played Lwaxana in three *DS9* episodes, and, of course, continued to serve as the voice of Federation computers in all *Star Trek* productions until her death in late 2008.

Opposite, right: Guest Kirsten Dunst sits with episode "costar" Simon (from Critters of the Cinema). "Kirsten was only twelve at the time, but we all knew she was going to be a major star," says Dan Curry. "She conducted herself with great professionalism."

Casting a dog isn't all that different from casting a person. Contact Rob Bloch, of Critters of the Cinema, and he'll bring over a candidate like Simon, the Pomeranian mix who played Kestra's dog in "Dark Page."

A wolf, however, is another matter. "None of the animal training groups have everything," explains Bloch, "so we call one another when we need another species. I sub-rented the wolves from Bobi and Chris Edrington of Steve Martin's Working Wildlife. They trained Teddy and Buck."

Teddy and Buck, both gray timber wolves, were already stars. Teddy had appeared in the Oscar-winning movie *Dances with Wolves* as Kevin Costner's four-footed "dance partner," with Buck as his backup. "Teddy was exceptional," says Bobi Edrington. "He was born in captivity and performed everything that a wolf *can* perform."

But as exceptional a performer as Teddy was, he was a *wild animal*, requiring very particular shooting conditions. "We did most of the shots with split screen," explains Dan Curry. "First we walked Kirsten Dunst down the corridor, then the wolf, doing a traveling matte line to make sure the animal was always close to where she'd been." When the episode

aired, it looked as if the two were walking together.

"To get a close-up of the wolf growling," Curry continues, "we used a wide-angle lens, which gave us flexibility with depth of field and depth of focus. But it meant the lens had to be physically close to the wolf.

"Teddy was very well-behaved, so we wondered how we were going to make him growl," Curry says. "Chris Edrington put a chain around the wolf's waist, and attached it to a big stage bolt in the floor so he couldn't move much. Then he set a box in front of the wolf. When Chris lifted the box, there was a big, meaty beef bone under it. Teddy started sniffing, and then chomping and licking it. Chris said, 'Ready for the wolf to growl?' and we said, 'Sure.' And Chris took a hook, pulled the bone away, and put the box back over it. The wolf went ballistic!

"Tom Denove, our camera operator, was the closest to the wolf," Curry says with a chuckle. "Teddy was growling and snarling, extremely excited. Finally, Tom looked back at me and said, 'Don't you have enough? I'd really like to back away from this thing!'"

Right: Teddy (left) and Buck in more natural surroundings.

Two societies reside on the planet Kesprytt: the Kes, who wish to join the Federation, and the Prytt, who are extremely suspicious of their neighbors. Picard and Crusher respond to a diplomatic request to meet with the Kes, only to find themselves in a Prytt prison after their transporter signal is intercepted. The xenophobic Prytt implant electronic devices in Picard and Crusher to learn the truth behind the Kes-Federation alliance. But after the pair escape, Picard and Crusher learn a different truth. The devices allow them to hear each other's thoughts—and Crusher finds that Picard was once deeply in love with her.

Ever since "The Naked Now," viewers were conscious of the romantic attachment that Beverly and Jean-Luc carried deep within their psyches, if not their hearts. But the writers waited until "Attached" to finally nudge that potential toward passion. Alas, a nudge was all disappointed viewers got. A fuller relationship would remain unrequited—at least for now (see "All Good Things . . .").

There was, on the other hand, nothing unrequited

about *Star Trek*'s attachment to Bronson Canyon. Starting with the *TOS* episode "This Side of Paradise," *Star Trek* producers regularly expressed their passion for this location. After all, they grew up in the same neighborhood.

Located only four miles from the Paramount lot, Bronson Canyon had been a Hollywood darling since pioneer filmmakers traveled from the East Coast to take advantage of the climate and to escape from Thomas Edison's control of most motion picture patents. For decades, filmmakers had been drawn to the scenic canyon and to the man-made caves blasted into its walls.

But romance with any exterior location was always limited. "We only went out once or twice a year," "Attached" director Jonathan Frakes says, fretting that even with those caves at hand, he was required to shoot interior cave scenes in "Planet Hell."

"We also were limited in the number of days we could use a crane," Frakes adds. "The rental of the crane, and the hot head [to remotely control pan/ tilt], and the power generator, et cetera, is a part of the show's budgetary strength." Nevertheless, crane shots certainly enhanced an episode's look.

"Rick Berman didn't like us to cut out of a moving shot," he notes. "So when we did a crane shot, you got to see the *whole* crane shot. Nowadays, with all the quick cuts on TV, you only see the beginning and end of crane shots, so there's almost no point to it."

The *Enterprise* is forcibly boarded by a pair of scientists who demand the Federation halt the use of warp drive near their world. Warp fields, they say, are destroying the fabric of space and rendering their planet uninhabitable. Data suggests the matter be referred to the Federation Science Council, but one of the frustrated scientists opts for quicker action, triggering a dangerous rift in space that threatens the lives of the *Enterprise* crew.

"Fifty-five. It's a law we can live with."
Ring a bell?
In 1973, the United States faced an oil embargo enacted by members of the Organization of Arab Petroleum Exporting Countries. Foreseeing a long-term possibility of high oil prices and disrupted supply, the Nixon administration put forward several proposals designed to reduce America's gas consumption, including a national speed limit, based on the belief that motor vehicles achieve maximum efficiency at 55 mph. The following year, the National Maximum Speed Limit (NMSL) was enacted as part of the Emergency Highway Energy Conservation Act.

"Force of Nature" was written in 1993, when the NMSL and depletion of the ozone layer were hot topics of conversation. It's not surprising that *TNG* would address a similar issue under the guise of twenty-fourth-century metaphor. Although many viewers found it a bit heavy-handed, some had a good time with it, as evidenced by the proliferation of fan-produced bumper stickers at *Star Trek* conventions stating WARP 5—IT'S A SPEED WE CAN LIVE WITH.

The episode originated with *TNG* story editor Naren Shankar, who readily proclaims, "It was a bad idea."

The denouement—which established a prohibition against starships traveling above warp 5—quickly hamstrung the drivers of the *Star Trek* franchise, "at least until everybody began to ignore it," says Shankar. He isn't disappointed that the precedents set in his episode were eventually swept under the rug. "It's a cautionary tale on why you should not let an issue drive a story. We were trying to talk about the environment. When you start from an inherently nondramatic premise and try to craft a nondramatic premise onto a message, it hardly ever ends up well.

"Initially we thought it would be a good thing, because it's good to have limitations. It was going to give us some dramatic complications that would be useful. But it worked in the opposite direction. It became more annoying than anything else. So we just mitigated the damage and moved on."

Likewise, those federal speed limit controls were officially lifted in 1995.

Below: LeVar Burton goes over the next scene with director Robert Lederman (standing) and cinematographer Jonathan West.
Opposite: The next scene.

"If she knew she were an android, we would have something to share. I would no longer be alone in the universe." —Data

Data discovers that one of the scientists working to reignite the core of the planet Atrea IV is Juliana Tainer, former wife of Data's inventor, Noonien Soong. Data doesn't recall her, she explains, because Soong wiped the android's memory just before the attack of the Crystalline Entity. Although Juliana says she thinks of herself as Data's "mother," she admits that she was against his creation; she was afraid he'd turn out badly, like Lore. For that same reason, she and Soong left him behind when they abandoned Omicron Theta. But while Data believes Juliana, he feels that something about her isn't right—and ultimately, that something leads him to a long hidden message from Soong.

"Inheritance" was "yet another touchy-feely episode," admits *TNG*'s resident touchy-feely guy, René Echevarria. "But I enjoyed it very much," he adds. Echevarria shaped journalist Dan Koeppel's premise into an emotional teleplay about Data's reunion with a mother he never knew he had. When he learns that she is also an android, he sees the potential for a kinship unlike any he's ever known, save the one he briefly experienced with Lal. But Soong—in an interactive prerecorded message—asks him to leave Juliana in the dark about her true nature, and Troi counsels the same.

"Data has to decide whether he should take away from her the one thing he's always wanted for himself—the desire to be human—by telling her the truth," says Echevarria. "It was a nice moment to get to."

Ultimately, Data decides not to tell her. Is it fair? Not really, but we all know that life's not always about what's "fair." Troi's rationalization—that he'd be robbing Juliana of the one thing *he's* always wanted—doesn't quite hold up. Data is self-aware. He knows what he is, even though he wants to be something else. He can handle the unique reality of his situation. The supposition, by Soong and the others, is that Juliana can't. She is blissfully unaware of her own reality, and doesn't comprehend that she's a copy of another being. As a scientist, wouldn't she want to know the truth? In a way, she's got the best of both worlds: the virtually unlimited abilities of an android packaged in a body that includes the emotions of a human. Perhaps Soong underestimated her ability to cope.

In the end, viewers can't know what the "right" decision was. We can only judge Data's actions and his decision to spare Juliana from the forbidden knowledge—which, as always, speaks more to his own humanity and compassion than to his lack of it.

"Captain, we're receiving 285,000 hails."
—Wesley

Worf inexplicably finds himself hopping from one alternate universe to the next after he returns to the *Enterprise* from a *bat'leth* competition. After Worf experiences realities where Deanna Troi is his loving wife, La Forge is dead, and Picard was never rescued from the Borg, Data concludes that on Worf's return from the contest, his shuttle inadvertently passed through a quantum fissure in the space-time continuum. Worf must take the shuttle back through it and return to his own *Enterprise*. But as the fissure begins to destabilize and hundreds of *Enterprise*s appear, that may be easier said than done.

"I remember thinking when I wrote 'Parallels' that it would probably never be made," says Brannon Braga. "It would be too expensive, especially the ending with all the realities collapsing into one, and thousands and thousands of *Enterprise*s appearing in the same space. In fact, I remember writing a stage direction in an early draft of the script: '[line

producer] Merri Howard's jaw drops to the floor.' Because that was a really super-expensive gag. But it was one the fans remembered. They seemed to like that, and also seeing crazy Riker aboard the *Enterprise* from the alternate reality where the Borg had destroyed Earth."

A certain contingent of fans, however, didn't like "The Worf/Troi thing," as Braga refers to the relationship. "The *Imzadi* fans—the ones who were really into the *Riker*/Troi relationship—they were up in arms," he explains. "But *we* really liked it because of the unlikely nature of their relationship. It was initially meant to be in only that one episode—'What if in one reality Worf is married to Troi?' But the chemistry was strong enough that we thought, 'You know what? Maybe we should do this for real.' The actors really enjoyed it. Anything new for them to do besides pushing buttons at their stations was always warmly welcomed!"

"For any event, there is an infinite number of possible outcomes. Our choices determine which outcomes will follow. But there is a theory in quantum physics that all possibilities that can happen, do happen in alternate quantum realities." —Data

Michael Piller was a tough taskmaster. "There was a rotating door on the writers' room," states Joe Menosky, "a kind of 'Great White Hope' situation where Michael would hire somebody he thought was going to work out great, and then fire them as soon as they turned in a script that he, inevitably, hated. None of us was really secure in our jobs until we proved ourselves to Michael in some dramatic fashion."

For the writers that remained with *TNG*, however, Piller's occasional glowing approval on a script was a moment to savor.

"When he read the script for 'Parallels,' he said to me, 'This is your crowning achievement,'" Brannon Braga recalls. "Michael loved it, particularly the idea behind it, which was based on parallel alternate realities. Quantum physics was a pretty radical thing to present to television viewers at the time. The whole idea of branching realities had to be explained with a graphic presented by Data."

It was one of several *TNG* episodes that triggered intense internal discussions: *"Will the audience get it?"*

Braga chuckles at the memory. "We'd be like, 'Okay, how are we going to explain this in a way that's graph-able and doesn't just sound like a load of crap?' But in 'Parallels,' it was more than just technobabble. It was based on a real theory. I think we may have introduced that theory to the mainstream for the first time."

The episode's mini lesson in quantum physics had a big impact on at least one young *TNG* fan: Roberto Orci, cowriter (with Alex Kurtzman) of the 2009 *Star Trek* movie. Plot elements in the movie collide with traditional *Star Trek* historical landmarks, thus establishing a new timeline of events for Kirk, Spock, millions of Vulcans, et cetera. Orci, aware that fans of *TOS* might be unsettled by this dismissal of the familiar timeline, stated in a 2008 interview with TrekMovie.com's Anthony Pascale that the changes established in his movie didn't actually impinge on the original timeline. Referencing Data's speech (and graphic) from the *TNG* episode "Parallels," Orci said, "Data summed up quantum mechanics as the theory that 'all possibilities that can happen, do happen' in a parallel universe. According to theory, there are going to be a much larger number of universes in which events are very closely related, because those are the most probable configurations of things."

Asked Pascale: "So everyone in the 'prime' timeline, like Picard and Riker, are still off doing their thing?"

Responded Orci: "Yes, and you will notice that when the movie comes out, that whatever DVDs you have purchased will continue to exist."

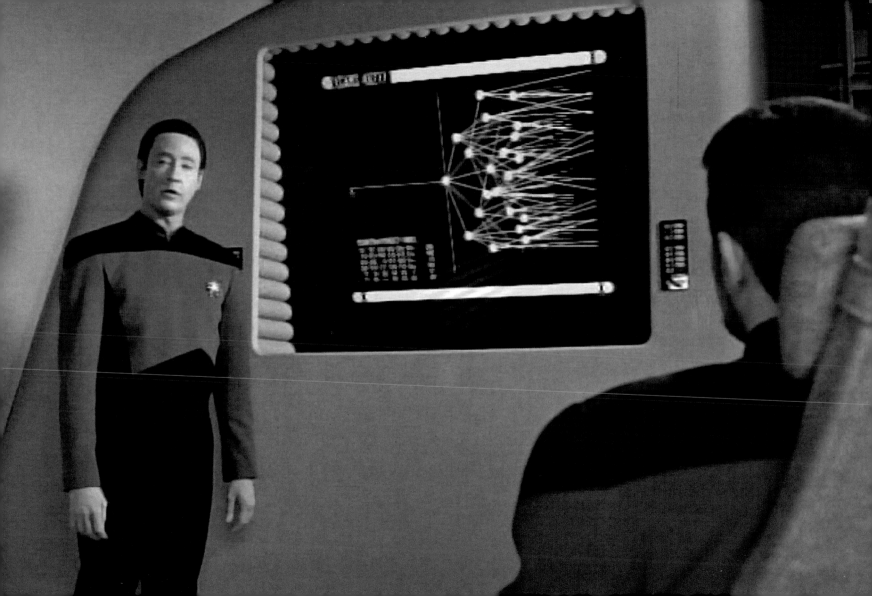

"I know Klingons like to be alone on their birthdays ▮ *I'm sure you have to meditate, or hit yourself with a painstik or something."* —Troi

For your next Klingon karaoke party—from the "Parallels" shooting script:

```
    PRONUNCIATION GUIDE FOR KLINGON
              BIRTHDAY SONG:
    Sung to the tune of "For He's A Jolly
Good Fellow"


    "Cha Worf Toh'gah-nah lo Pre-tOk"
    chaw worf toe-GAW-nah low pree-TALK
    (REPEAT)
    "Tu Mak Dagh Cha doh Borak"*
    too mock daw chaw dough bore-AWK


    *"Dagh" is articulated with a very
coarse, strong rasp — just like the ch
sound in ▮the name of the German composer
Bach or ▮ the Yiddish toast l'chaim.
```

Erik Pressman, Riker's first captain—now an admiral—leads the *Enterprise* on a mission to retrieve his and Riker's old starship, the *Pegasus*, lost a dozen years ago with most of its crew. Time is of the essence; the ship has been spotted by the Romulans, who also hope to salvage it. But only Riker and Pressman know there's a secret on board that could destroy the Federation's tenuous truce with the Romulans: a Starfleet-developed prototype cloaking device that violates a long-standing treaty.

Ron Moore had two wishes when he wrote "The *Pegasus*." One was granted—and one wasn't.

"I wanted to get to the heart of why the Federation didn't have a cloaking device," Moore states. "I mean, were they stupid? Everybody *else* in the galaxy had these devices. Gene Roddenberry's philosophy was that they don't have cloaking devices because it's sneaky and the Federation isn't sneaky. But that's an illogical argument, and I never bought it. I liked the idea that there was a reason, an arms control treaty saying that as a way of preserving a certain balance of power, the Federation would not

go in that direction.

"Of course, in 'The *Pegasus*,' some faction in the Federation was trying to figure out a way of developing one anyway, and Riker knew about it," Moore continues. "I loved that. It put Riker in a bad light—which I thought was good for his character. A lot of times we would play the drama of one of our officers doing something to get the job done by defying regulations and breaking the rules. I always thought that when they did that there should be consequences. They should get taken down a peg. There should be a reprimand. It's something I fought for a lot. I wanted to put Riker in jail for quite a while after the end of '*Pegasus*,' where he's been found guilty of a large conspiracy. And I wanted Picard to leave him in the brig for about the next three months.

"But there was no way I could convince anybody to do it."

Opposite: Terry O'Quinn, Jonathan Frakes, and first assistant director Adele Simmons find another use for the transporter pad. Notes director LeVar Burton: "If you have the opportunity to work with Terry O'Quinn, that's not something you pass up. The guy's got the goods."

Two decades ago, Michael Mack was an aspiring actor living in Washington, D.C. "I didn't like a lot of the roles that were available to black actors there, and I wanted to go to Hollywood," Mack says. "I didn't know how to act my way there, so I decided to *write* my way there."

The head of the screenwriting program at Maryland University took a liking to Mack's work and gave him a valuable suggestion: "Write the best script you can, enter it in the Nicholl Fellowships [a competition sponsored by the Academy of Motion Picture Arts and Sciences], do well, and then write to *Star Trek* and say you want to write for the show, because they're the friendliest to outside writers."

Mack wrote a historical drama for the competition, and made the final cut. "I sent the Nicholl confirmation letter to Rick Berman, and heard back: 'Congratulations on doing so well! Send your script to Jeri Taylor.' A year later, I was in Hollywood as a writing intern."

During his first conversation with Taylor, Mack mentioned that he'd like the opportunity to act on the show. "I showed her my demo reel, and she said, 'Let me know if there's a role you're interested in auditioning for,'" he recalls.

Mack spotted a few interesting roles, but he wasn't right for them. Then came Commander Sirol, in "The *Pegasus*." "It was originally written for a woman," Mack notes. "I said, 'I'd like to audition for this.' Jeri said, 'Well, there's no reason why the character *has* to be female, but we've never had a black Romulan.'" Nevertheless, she set him up for an audition.

"We really liked Michael," says René Echevarria, "and we wanted him to get an acting break. But when we heard about it, Ron Moore and I looked at each other and said, 'Yeah, but we've never seen a black Romulan.' We told Jeri, 'Shouldn't you give Michael an audition he could actually *get*?' And Jeri said, 'There are black and white humans—why *wouldn't* there be black and white Vulcans and Romulans?'

"We said, 'Oh. Yeah. Good point,'" Echevarria confesses sheepishly. "Of *course* we could have multi-races in *any* species. It had never occurred to us."

It had occurred to Mack, however. "In *Star Trek V: The Final Frontier*, when Spock relives his birth, the Vulcan midwife is black," he states. "The Vulcans and Romulans are cousins, so *of course* you could have a black Romulan."

With his deep, mellifluous voice, Mack turned out to be a perfect choice for the smoothly threatening Sirol. "I didn't know he was an intern on the show," director LeVar Burton says with a laugh. "I'm glad I *didn't* know, because I was just looking for the best Romulan to be on that screen. *Star Trek* has always pushed the boundaries of what *we as a people* look like. Gene Roddenberry's vision of the future has always been really comforting for me."

Worf is dismayed to learn that his adoptive brother, Nikolai Rozhenko, has violated the Prime Directive while stationed as a cultural observer on Boraal II. Although the planet is doomed, Rozhenko has fallen in love with the inhabitants of a small village, including a local woman who's carrying his child. He has kept them alive long enough to summon the *Enterprise* to Boraal, and now he wants Picard to relocate the villagers to a different world. The Prime Directive forbids such intervention with a pre-warp society, but Nikolai won't take no for an answer.

"*The Original Series* violated the Prime Directive all the time," writer Naren Shankar says. "And *The Next Generation* hid behind the Prime Directive all the time. Things that Kirk wouldn't even blink at doing, Picard would agonize about, and then do nothing.

"It was just a function of the eras in which the shows were created," Shankar points out. "Each series reflected where the United States was culturally at that particular time. Towards the end of *TNG*'s run, we tried to push at the boundaries. We felt there was a certain level of gutlessness and cruelty behind the

Prime Directive that was unnecessary, and sort of intolerable. So we dramatically encapsulated that in terms of Worf and his adoptive human brother. Nikolai was somebody trying to straddle those things. That was the core of 'Homeward.'"

Right: Michael Dorn makes his only appearance in *TNG* sans Klingon "turtlehead."

While attending her grandmother's funeral on Caldos IV, Beverly Crusher is seduced by a ghostlike alien life-form that has romanced the women of her family for centuries. When she abruptly resigns her post on the *Enterprise* and announces her intention to remain on Caldos, Picard steps in to find out the truth about Crusher's phantom lover.

Not really a fan favorite, but the people who worked on "Sub Rosa" had a good time. From the department of disinterred memories:

"Maybe a bodice-ripping, gothic haunted house romance featuring Beverly Crusher *was* a little 'out there' for our show," writer Brannon Braga admits. "I was obsessed with the movie *The Innocents*, which was based on *The Turn of the Screw*, one of my favorite novels. I thought we could pull it off. We ended up with an interesting experiment. Most of my *Star Trek* friends still make fun of me for it. René Echevarria still likes to recite a line of technobabble I put in Ronin's mouth: 'I can travel on the power transfer beam.' Technobabble combined with gothic romance—just sublimely absurd. I loved doing it,

but really, a spectacular failure."

"I loved it," states production designer Richard James. "We created a little church on a hill on Stage 16. I had to build the entire set on a platform, because we needed to be able to lower the coffin into the ground. The platform was quite high, probably twenty feet at the point of the hill, and the church was above that. We built enough wall and front entrance that when the actors were walking up toward the grave you would see the church and the buttresses and the stained glass windows. I wanted an enormous oak tree by the iron gate. Well, you can't 'travel' a big tree, so you bring in a trunk and then hang branches from the grid. And, of course, you have to shoot it before the greenery goes bad."

"Gates was fabulous, and she looked spectacular," notes director Jonathan Frakes. "And Duncan Regehr brought some real sex to the table. The episode was big on candles, which made [cinematographer] Jonathan West and me happy, because we were outside our safety zone for lighting. Any set we hadn't been in before became the thing that we most looked forward to. It was a wonderful out-of-the-box non–*Star Trek* episode."

The *Enterprise* senior staff considers four junior officers for possible promotion. However, Ensign Sito Jaxa is an unlikely candidate. She was involved in the same Starfleet Academy cover-up that blackened Wesley Crusher's record, and Picard seems to despise her for the weakness of character she showed at the time. Her mentor, Worf, encourages her to stand up for herself, but Sito ultimately finds that proving herself to Picard could come at the price of her life.

What's it like to be one of those nameless lower-level crew members who live and work aboard Starfleet's flagship, but stand forever in the shadow of the well-known senior staff?

"That was a great pitch from Ronald Wilkerson and Jean Louise Matthias, the same couple who did 'Lessons,'" enthuses René Echevarria, who wrote the teleplay. "Essentially, 'The *Enterprise* through the eyes of these lesser officers.' It was their version of an *Upstairs Downstairs* episode."

While the premise seemed like a winner, no one could predict how *TNG*'s viewers would react to an episode told from the point of view of non-regulars. But the audience really seemed to embrace the characters, particularly Taurik (well played by Jeri Taylor's son, actor Alexander Enberg) and Sito Jaxa (Shannon Fill), the Bajoran ensign previously seen in "The First Duty." In fact, had the series continued into an eighth season, Taurik likely would have popped up in additional episodes. (Enberg later appeared on *Voyager* as Vorik, a different Vulcan; Taylor suggested at the time that Taurik and Vorik were "twin brothers.")

Casting a Vulcan was tricky, notes Echevarria. "There were big shoes to fill," he says. "We didn't use many Vulcans on *TNG* because Leonard Nimoy's Vulcan was just so specific and indelible. It's hard to play a Vulcan without looking like you're doing an imitation. But Alex really pulled it off."

Sito made an even bigger impression, on both the viewers (who expressed dismay over her offscreen death) and the staff. "There was a lot of talk about bringing her back," Echevarria says, "but we never got around to it. This was always meant to be a story of loss, a coming-of-age story for those young people, and the death landed it for them."

But if there was no time to rescue Sito on *TNG*, there *could* have been on sister show *DS9*. While developing the script for the *DS9* episode "Hard Time," Robert Hewitt Wolfe began pulling in threads from a pitch that dealt with Sito's outcome. The original take was that Sito had been imprisoned by the Cardies. Although now free, she was suffering from post-traumatic stress disorder. The pitch hadn't established a motivating incident for Sito's condition, so Wolfe postulated that she'd killed her cellmate, a person to whom she'd become very close. Although the Sito tale was never produced, her plight was given to Miles O'Brien. "I took the end of the Sito story and threw away the rest," Wolfe says. "And I incorporated that ending into 'Hard Time.'"

A few years after *The Next Generation* ceased production, Naren Shankar went to work at CBS's powerhouse series *CSI: Crime Scene Investigation*. "It was pretty early on in the run of the show, but it was blowing up big," he says. "The producers had decided to do the *CSI: Miami* spin-off and they realized they would need an upper-level writer on the original show. By that point, I'd been working in the business for ten years, and I'm sure my science background also counted."

Shankar remained with *CSI* for nine years. While he admits that creating tales of "murder and dismemberment and dark stuff" can wear on a person after a while, he positively lights up when asked about the episodes that featured the nerdy "lab rats"—the lowly grunts who provide support to the flashier lead investigators. "That was just about my favorite thing on *CSI!*" he enthuses. "And you know what? The inspiration actually came out of *The Next Generation*, from René Echevarria's great episode 'Lower Decks.'"

Shankar began pushing for an episode "about the geeks"—the *CSI* equivalent of "Lower Decks" midshipmen—a few years into his tenure. "I liked their characters," he explains. "We finally had the right mix of people to do a story about—actors Wally Langham, Liz Vassey, Archie Kao, Jon Wellner, and the others. Finally, the opportunity presented itself and the premise really turned into this cool little series of weird black comedies, romantic comedies. We did one a year for about four years."

If there's one *CSI* lab rats episode that stands out over the others, it would have to be "A Space Oddity," the ninth season's take on murder at a science fiction convention. The story ostensibly pays loving tribute to an old *Star Trek*–like cult favorite called *Astro Quest*, but it also included sly references to a proposed reboot of that show, which, in an edgy new guise, would bear a striking resemblance to the reimagined *Battlestar Galactica* of recent years. Shankar's episode featured cameo appearances by some of the actors from *Galactica*—and a cameo by one of the key forces behind its relaunch, Ronald D. Moore. Shankar wrote "Oddity" along with two additional *Star Trek* franchise alums, David Weddle and Bradley Thompson, who wrote for *Deep Space Nine* and also (surprise!) *Battlestar Galactica*.

"It was a really sweet episode," says Shankar. "And I got the nicest letter from D.C. Fontana about it. I got a big kick out of casting Ron, too. It was all very incestuous and fun."

As Troi struggles to earn a promotion to command status, Data travels to the preindustrial world of Barkon IV to retrieve radioactive debris from a downed Federation probe. A power surge from the probe causes Data to lose his memory, leading the android to inadvertently endanger the inhabitants of a nearby village by bringing the radioactive substance into their midst. With the townspeople getting sick, Data searches for a way to help them, despite the fact that the increasingly suspicious locals now see him as a threat.

The best story ideas can be expressed with a minimum of words, and freelancer Christopher Hatton's pitch, "Data as Frankenstein," certainly fit the bill. Instantly calling up images of a "monster" pursued by villagers with torches, it's almost Tamarian (see "Darmok") in its metaphoric simplicity. Expanding on the pitch, however, wasn't easy.

"It seemed like a simple concept, but in execution it turned out to be excruciating," teleplay writer Ron Moore recalls. "With the setup scene cliché, it felt as though it wasn't about anything. I kept struggling as I was rewriting. At one point, Michael Piller called me into his office, sat me down, and said, 'You know, I just feel that you've hit a wall.' I was looking at him like, *'What?'* He said, 'You know, writers sometimes hit a wall. And they either push past that wall and they keep going, or they can't push back and their career is over. And at that point—you're out.'

"That really set me back on my heels," Moore says, the discomfort still evident in his voice. "I knew it wasn't a great script, but I didn't think it was the moment my *career* was about to explode.

"The fact is," he continues, "the seasons were very long on *Next Gen*. Now when I look back and remember that we did twenty-six shows a season, it just seems so exhausting. I can't even connect with the energy level that we all had to summon. We were always aware that the fatigue in the marathon would hit you and you would be running on fumes. At that late point in the season we were all feeling it. The writers' room was tired. The production staff was tired. We were low on money. Everyone was irritable.

"So by the time we did 'Thine Own Self,' I was burned out. It wasn't a happy experience. But," Moore says, sighing, "they didn't fire me."

Opposite: The last thing Moore wanted was to see his own name added to "The *Star Trek* Memorial Wall," listing the *TNG* writers who'd been kicked to the curb over the years (see Ron Moore's introduction). Larry Nemecek, author of the *Star Trek: The Next Generation Companion*, shot this photo in March 1994, as production on *TNG* was winding down. The poster was located in the restroom of Moore's office suite in Paramount's Hart Building.

Star Trek: The Next Generation Memorial Wall

Johnny Dawkins	Hannah Louise Shearer	Maurice Hurley
David Gerrold	Leonard Mlodinow	Michael Wagner
D.C. Fontana	Scott Rubenstein	Richard Danus
Greg Strangis	Burton Armus	Shari Goodhartz
Sandy Fries	Michael Gray	Melinda M. Snodgrass
Robert H. Justman	John Mason	Hans Beimler
Herbert Wright	Tracy Tormé	Richard Manning
Robert Lewin	Robert L. McCullough	

Troi: "I've been thinking about taking the bridge officer's test and becoming a full commander."
Riker: "What brought this up?"

"It was one of those ideas that had been kicking around the writers' room for quite a while," Ron Moore states, as if in answer to Riker's question. "I'd wanted to do something with both her and Beverly, to raise their ranks as officers and expand their duties on the ship beyond being just doctor and therapist. They were the women, the female characters, but they were both slotted into these quote-unquote 'softer roles' without the formal lines of authority that all the other line officers had. That rubbed me the wrong way, so I was always looking for opportunities to make them more like the guys.

"The actresses wanted to expand out from their medical and therapeutic roles, too," he says. "So I liked the idea that Beverly enjoyed being the officer of the deck periodically, just to keep her hand in it and to keep her proficiency going so that she always would be rated to stand watch on the bridge.

"I also wanted to establish that Troi had authority over many things," Moore adds. "She wasn't just the captain's therapist; she had people to talk to and things to do. I was determined to get Troi her commander rank, and make her a deck officer, especially after 'Disaster,' where she was in charge of the bridge. That episode played her as if she was in over her head because she didn't have the training and the experience to operate in that environment. Well, that was unfair to the character."

The story line about Troi's promotion was conceived months earlier, for the episode "Liaisons," but ultimately bumped from that episode. When "Thine Own Self" needed a B story, Troi got her much-deserved promotion.

Opposite: Troi's new pip.

While scanning a comet, the *Enterprise* crew inadvertently activates and downloads an alien society's archive of information about its mythological characters. Immediately, the program begins to transform portions of the ship into a facsimile of the civilization's temple, and Data becomes the repository for the personalities of the assorted gods and goddesses.

Joe Menosky admits to being the man behind "Masks"—but he's not happy about it.

"Over the years, 'Masks' has appeared on any number of 'Worst of *TNG*' lists," Menosky says. "If I can't bring myself to even watch it, how can I disagree? I hated the final shooting script. I'd tried to duplicate the very rich and ambiguous dynamic from Shakespeare's *The Tempest*. But since I was not there at the studio to fight for it, the script lost a crucial character arc: the 'Ihat' character that came through Data originally was written as *The Tempest*'s Ariel to Picard's Prospero. That gave depth and emotion to their personal arcs, and poignancy to the entire story—but it was stripped out during the on-set revisions. As a result, nothing was left but an intellectual exercise: a kind of puzzle with no real drama. It's not an exaggeration to say I was crushed with what happened to it.

"I still believe in the core premise. An alien culture's founding myth attempts to technologically re-create itself on the *Enterprise*, and our characters must find a way to enter into the myth—to participate in it—in order to deconstruct and shut it down.

"Some essence of that idea must have been present in the final result," Menosky adds. "After 'Darmok,' 'Masks' is probably the most 'written about' episode I did for *Star Trek*. I've seen chapters about it in academic-level books. If some university professor can write an entire chapter about a *failed* episode like 'Masks,' that speaks to the range and intellectual depth of the entire *Star Trek* franchise overall. Good luck saying that about pretty much any other TV series you can think of."

Although Menosky's characters were shaped around classical archetypes, their names were not. "I named 'Ihat' and 'Korgano' after James Iha and Billy Corgan of Smashing Pumpkins," Menosky confesses. "That was one of my favorite bands at the time."

Opposite: Masaka's beautiful sun mask, crafted by MEL, was a piece of vacuformed styrene, painted with leather dyes. "The direction we got from the studio was for a Venetian look," Don Coleman recalls.

The suicide of seemingly well-adjusted Lieutenant Dan Kwan surprises the crew, and when Troi investigates the scene of his death, she experiences an overwhelming sensation of panic and fear. Crusher notes that Kwan was a partial empath—like Troi—and wonders if the counselor was picking up an "empathic echo" of his feelings before he died. As Troi continues the investigation with Worf assisting her, she experiences visions that suggest Kwan's suicide may be related to a crime of passion that took place on the *Enterprise* during the starship's construction.

"During the seventh season, while Brannon and Ron were working on writing *Generations*, I wrote or polished something like thirteen episodes," says René Echevarria. "Brannon got 'Eye of the Beholder' started, and I wrote the teleplay.

"In the episode, there's a guy who commits suicide on the ship and his girlfriend tells Troi, 'It's not like Dan to take his own life.' It sounded very reasonable on the page. And it played just fine. It was only later on that the actress who played the girlfriend—who was actually my sister-in-law at

the time—started teasing me about what a weird line that actually was. It was like a commercial: '*It's not like Dan to have a second cup of coffee.*'"

Echevarria breaks into laughter. Clearly he feels he deserved the ribbing. "Sometimes, when you're trying to write something very clean and concise, it just comes off incredibly goofy," he admits.

Right: Dan Curry inspects part of the freshly painted control room set to see how it will work when juxtaposed against the blue screen, which will be set up behind the warp coil chamber door (shown closed).

Opposite: The dialogue may not have been perfect, but the people behind the scenes did their best to make it *look* perfect. With the finale just a few weeks away, production designer Richard James contributed a brand-new two-level set: the nacelle control room and plasma injectors where the suicide takes place. Scenic artist Anthony Fredrickson designed the warp coils, a two-foot by one-and-a-half-foot miniature based on Rick Sternbach's drawing in the *Star Trek: The Next Generation Technical Manual*. Visual effects supervisor David Stipes executed the composited shots.

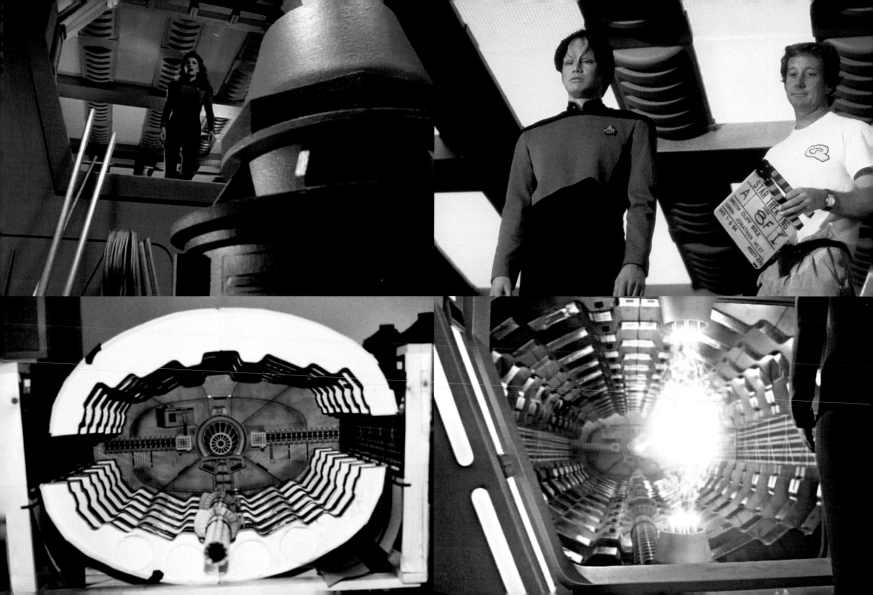

During a brief lull in the *Enterprise*'s busy schedule, Picard and Data depart in a shuttle to recover a wayward torpedo, and Doctor Crusher gives Lieutenant Barclay a synthetic immunizing agent to help him fight a flu bug he's contracted. When Picard and Data return to the ship, they find the *Enterprise* drifting unpowered in space, and every member of the crew devolved into a bizarre lower life-form. Data deduces that something has triggered the crew's long-dormant genes to cause the transformation. And now that Picard's been exposed to that something, he's beginning to change as well.

"'Genesis' falls into the category of wacky ideas gone bad," Brannon Braga says with a chuckle. "It's a 'B-movie-monster-flick-Saturday-matinee' episode. But I stand by it—and it was very well directed by Gates McFadden."

"I loved the episode," McFadden said in 2002. "It was really different. It was spooky. And what a supportive environment to have your first film directing experience!"

Directing was the next logical step for McFadden, a show business professional whose career had taken her from studying physical theater, movement, and mime at the International Theatre School in Paris, to serving as director of choreography and puppet movement for the Jim Henson Company, before returning to acting for the role of Beverly Crusher. After working with nonhuman characters in *The Dark Crystal*, *Dreamchild*, *Labyrinth*, and *The Muppets Take Manhattan*, she felt right at home with Braga's devolving human menagerie.

"[Gates] went to the zoo and did a lot of things to research what each one would turn into," Michael Westmore points out. "You could pick up from their body language what was going to happen to them."

"The (*TNG*) actors are very good," McFadden says. "With a couple of people I made suggestions, but I honestly didn't spend much time doing it. I would just give certain ideas. They know how to run with an idea, so you don't want to stand in their way. My greatest experience was being able to direct that episode."

Opposite: McFadden checks out an upcoming scene from an appropriate vantage point. One of the drawbacks of being an actor/director is that you might have to helm a scene before you've completed your own hair and makeup.

The term "introns" refers to sequences of DNA found in human genes that currently have no known purpose. Undoubtedly, scientists one day will discover the reason these sequences exist, possibly contradicting Data's explanation that introns are "evolutionary holdovers." But lack of concrete evidence didn't deter Brannon Braga from writing about them.

"The concept that we have dormant genetic material from other species inside us that *could* manifest itself because of some virus is kind of 'out there,'" Braga admits, "but it made for a good, fun piece of science fiction. I really loved the moment when Data informs Picard that he's going to become a pygmy marmoset. And with the Barclay spider, Jurassic Worf, and Troi with gills, I mean, c'mon—that's awesome!"

"The hair and makeup people did an extraordinary job," director Gates McFadden says. "I think it's the best work I've seen on the series." Indeed, the episode received an Emmy nomination for Outstanding Individual Achievement in Makeup for a Series, but lost to *Babylon 5*. "There's an awful lot of work for just a few frames of seeing something," McFadden notes. "But it was much more frightening if you didn't [give the audience] enough time to really stare at it."

"I wish we could have seen more of Worf's character," Michael Westmore says, "because there was tremendous detail. It's like an exoskeleton of a prehistoric thing from some Klingon planet."

With the exception of Michael Dorn, whose character was involved in some stunt-heavy sequences, all of the actors who usually appear on-camera played their transformed characters. One of the creatures that the camera *did* linger on was Commander Riker's australopithecine. Jonathan Frakes didn't find portraying the apelike creature all that taxing. "It wasn't much of a stretch," he says with a characteristic grin.

Perhaps the oddest transformation involved Troi's metamorphosis into an amphibian. "Marina had such a tough part," McFadden says. "She had to go in the water, in the bathtub, in her uniform, with her contacts and all the prosthetics. Wonderful stuff!"

Even odder: the sudden appearance of a bathtub on the ship. "We'd never shown a bathtub because they supposedly took sonic showers," Braga admits. "But Troi seemed like someone who'd like a good old-fashioned bath. And nobody asked about it. Believe me, we were questioned on *plenty* of things. I wish I'd kept a list of the insane stuff that came up that never saw the light of day. But nobody questioned the bathtub."

Data never seemed to notice that his cat suffered from identity uncertainty. Over the seasons, viewers saw Spot not only evolve into a different breed, but also change gender. This was not, as one might suspect in a sci-fi show, because Spot was a shapeshifter. No, in the time-honored tradition of ever-regenerating Doctor Whos and new incarnations of James Bond, it was all because of casting.

"The show originally used a Somali," says Karen Thomas of Critters of the Cinema, the animal training company that began supplying two- and four-footed creatures to *TNG* in season four. "But we didn't know that when we were brought in. We were just told it was an orange cat. We had tabbies," she says with a chuckle, "so the cat morphed."

In fact, Critters of the Cinema provided three orange tabbies—three *male* tabbies—notes Critters' founder Rob Bloch. "We used Monster for the action shots with running and jumping. And we used Brandy for the 'in the arms' and lying-around scenes. The cats were pretty interchangeable as long as the editor didn't do a quick cut from one to the other."

"A third, younger cat named Tyler was the stand-in," Thomas says. "The show did a lot of rehearsals, which can burn out a cat because we reward them with food while they're working. So we used Tyler while they were lighting the scenes. But he never ended up on-camera."

The two feline actors had different personalities. "Monster was a complete food freak," Thomas explains. "He would do *anything* for food. When he had to jump up on Data's desk in 'A Fistful of Datas,' I was under the desk trying to hold him still. He knew they were going to be calling him—and he was a handful. When he wanted to go, he would give me a little nip, like, 'Let me go, I want to run for my food!'"

Brandy was much more easygoing—although the show's makeup extremes sometimes threw him. "He took a while to get used to Data's eyes," Bloch recalls.

"Animals communicate by body language and facial expression," Thomas explains, "and Brandy knew something wasn't quite right about Data. But Brent Spiner was so awesome to work with that over time the cat was fine."

But "ol' yellow eyes" was nothing compared to a certain costar's turtlehead.

Thomas laughs at the memory. "When Worf picked Brandy up [in 'Phantasms'] and told Data, 'I will feed it,'" she says, "the cat gave him this long, low growl, like, 'What the heck are *you*?'"

Brandy managed to complete the scene—although Thomas is certain that Monster would have lived up to his name. "I wouldn't even have *attempted* to do that scene with him," she says.

As for Spot getting pregnant in "Genesis" . . . "They always referred to the cat as a 'he' in the earlier episodes," Thomas says with a sigh, "but I just thought, 'Oh well, it's *space*, right?'"

"Mozart . . . as a small child wrote astonishing symphonies. A genius beyond the understanding, the abilities of others. Wesley is such a person. Not with music, but with the equally lovely intricacies of time, energy, propulsion, and the instruments of this vessel. He should be encouraged."
—The Traveler, "Where No One Has Gone Before"

Picard's orders to remove a colony of Native Americans from a planet annexed to Cardassia—the result of a new Federation-Cardassian peace treaty—are challenged by the uncooperative colonists and a surprisingly sullen Wesley Crusher, who is visiting the starship while on leave from Starfleet Academy. As Picard battles with an intractable Starfleet admiral, a stubborn Cardassian commander, and his own troubled conscience, Wesley has a vision of his dead father that leads him to make a radical decision.

Sometimes art imitates life. Ask Ronald D. Moore. "Back in the first season, the show established that Wesley possessed some unnamed special ability, a super-secret thing that the Traveler was hinting at," Moore notes. "I said, 'Let's pay that off. Let's find out that he's not doing well at Starfleet Academy, that he's not happy there, and send him in a different direction.'

"Some of that came out of my own experience, going to college and realizing it wasn't the path I wanted to be on, and being miserable with it, but being afraid to make a jump out of it. Whenever we touched on the Wesley story line, even after Wil Wheaton left the show, I argued that just because his father was a Starfleet officer, it didn't mean *he* had to be one. Starfleet Academy isn't for everybody, and being a Starfleet officer isn't a perfect fit for everyone. I wanted him to realize where he was, and make a shift and say, 'I can do something else.' I identified with the character.

"There were various political minefields that we navigated as we told the story in 'Journey's End.' But I was glad we did it, because it took Wesley in a different direction and paid off the promise that had been set up by the Traveler. Of course," Moore adds with a chuckle, "we left it pretty vague. He and the Traveler went off and had some 'very special adventures' together. There were lots of strange jokes told with raised eyebrows about 'What was Wesley *really* doing with the Traveler?'"

With *TNG* nearing its denouement, and sister show *Deep Space Nine* parked comfortably at the edge of space, the producers set about laying the groundwork for their upcoming series, *Star Trek: Voyager*.

"We knew that we wanted to include a renegade element in *Voyager*, and that the show would involve a ship housing both Starfleet people and these idealistic freedom fighters that the Federation felt were outlaws," says Jeri Taylor. "So in order to avoid weighing down *Voyager*'s pilot with some burdensome backstory, we decided to plant relevant story threads in the shows that were already on the air."

Viewers were introduced to the Maquis—the aforementioned freedom fighters—on both *TNG* and *DS9*. "Journey's End," the first of these episodes to air, established a group of Native Americans who had moved from Earth to preserve their cultural identity, only to find their new home threatened by the Federation's treaty with the Cardassians. When *Voyager* debuted ten months later, it would feature a Native American character named Chakotay, a former Starfleet officer who turned Maquis in order to defend his home colony—one settled by Native Americans, much like the Dorvan V colony depicted in "Journey's End"—against the Cardassians.

In the meantime, the *TNG* staff fell in love with the notion of finding a planet that had been settled by Native Americans, Ron Moore recalls. "This group had left our world because the Earth of the twenty-fourth century was not a place they felt connected with. Their entire culture was predicated on a different understanding of man's relationship to nature. But that," says Moore, "was somewhat controversial because it flew in the face of Gene Roddenberry's notion that by the twenty-fourth century *all* of humanity was very happy, and everything had worked out perfectly for everybody. I was always the guy on staff saying, 'Well, it wouldn't work out perfectly for *everybody*.' Some human beings were bound to say 'This doesn't work for us.'

"The idea here was that the Native Americans were particularly put off when they started to control the weather on Earth, that the technological embrace had reached the point of controlling the actual elements of nature themselves. That's when they said, 'This is not our belief system. It's not the way we want to live. We're out of here.'

"Michael Piller became intrigued with the parallel that Native Americans had founded this colony and then here comes Picard—whose job is to kick them out," Moore says. "There were these really disturbing, problematic historical parallels."

The producers chose to base their colonists on the Hopi culture of Arizona. "Jeri Taylor put me in touch with a consultant who talked to me at length about their culture, and gave me books and literature. So the sweat lodge and the underground chamber had elements based on Hopi traditions. But we were careful not to say 'Hopi,' because they are a particularly private and sensitive tribe."

Worf: "How have you done this, come to this time?"

K'mtar/Alexander: "I met a man in the Cambra system. He gave me a chance to change the past. He had the ability to send me here, to this time."

Hoping to increase his son's interest in warrior training, Worf takes Alexander to a Klingon festival where the boy can engage in ritualistic battle play. All goes well until a trio of assailants attempts to kill Alexander. The attack is thwarted by the sudden appearance of a stranger named K'mtar, who claims to be a close friend of Worf's family. A knife left at the scene of the attack suggests that the Duras sisters are involved. But Worf's trust in his new ally is shaken when the origins of the knife are called into question, and Worf catches K'mtar poised to kill Alexander in his sleep.

Time travel is dicey. There are so many things that can go wrong and screw up the temporal flow for everyone. And yet, there isn't a Starfleet crew (not one with its own TV series, at least) that hasn't at-

tempted it at some point. James T. Kirk holds the record for the most temporal violations (seventeen), but each and every infraction, whether by accident or design, has the potential of causing repercussions within the space-time continuum. Which is why the jaunt taken by a future version of Alexander in "Firstborn" is so odd.

For one thing, it's never established *how* he jumps four decades into the past. His explanation is frustratingly vague: he met this guy who could, you know, *send him there*. Cool. Was that via time travel pod? A silver DeLorean? Magic? All we know is that apparently the trip came with a return ticket.

Ignoring the "how," there's the "why." Any student of (science fiction) history knows that you can't expect to radically change things without chronometric blowback, whether you're trying to save Worf, Edith Keeler, or Abraham Lincoln. Alexander thinks that getting his younger self to become more of a warrior will eventually save his father's life. But grown-up Alexander has forgotten what a stubborn little boy he used to be. When he fails to convince the boy to get more serious about killing, he moves on to plan B: killing young Alexander, thus removing them both from the space-time continuum. For-

tunately, Worf manages to prevent this from happening, and after a brief father-son chat, he sends mature Alexander back to the future with the suggestion that he'll be more understanding of young Alexander from now on.

Which apparently translates to sending the boy back to live with his grandparents on Earth (it's easy to be understanding from a distance). The next time we see Alexander, on *Deep Space Nine*, he's resentful—so resentful that, ironically, he enlists in the Klingon Defense Force, so that he can become more of a warrior.

Sometimes things work out the way you want even *without* the benefit of time travel.

Opposite: Stunt coordinator Dennis "Danger" Madalone demonstrates a defensive move for Brian Bonsall. Obviously, blue denim is timeless, even among Klingons.

Newly released from prison, vengeful DaiMon Bok sends a disturbing message to Picard: He plans to avenge the death of his son by killing Picard's own offspring, a young man named Jason Vigo. Although Picard is unaware of the existence of any offspring, he tracks down Jason. When Crusher establishes that the young man is indeed his child, Picard attempts to protect Jason by keeping him on board until Bok is captured. But he doesn't figure on Bok's possession of a subspace transporter capable of moving a person across billions of kilometers of space.

TNG's Ferengi hadn't worked out. A species whose culture was dedicated to lining their pockets just didn't fit on a series where the heroes didn't even *have* pockets. Although meant to represent a serious threat, no one took them seriously. And although given humorous mannerisms, they weren't particularly funny. They were the Rodney Dangerfields of space—they didn't get no respect from *Star Trek*'s audience.

But that was beginning to change.

As "Bloodlines" went into production, there were quite a few Ferengi earning a living across the street from *TNG*'s soundstages. On Stage 18, where *Deep Space Nine*'s beautiful Promenade set was situated, a different genus of Ferengi had emerged, its progenitor a bartender named Quark. His conception had taken place two years earlier, when Michael Piller began thinking about the characters who would reside on the space station.

"It was clear to me that having a Ferengi aboard *Deep Space Nine* would provide the show with instant humor and built-in conflict," Piller told the authors of this book in 1994. "I saw Quark as the bartender who is a constant thorn in the side of law and order, but who has a sense of humor about it."

The key word there was "humor." Brought on as *DS9*'s showrunner, Ira Steven Behr took that ball and ran with it, developing the psyche, motivation, and culture of his alien charges. Behr and his staff took the theme "Greed is good" to a hysterical extreme, codifying it into a sort of Ferengi Constitution: "The Rules of Acquisition." All 285 of them. And what a set of rules it was: "Once you have their money, you never give it back," states Rule #1. Words every Ferengi lives by. Suddenly, Ferengi avarice not only made

sense—it explained everything about their social development. In *TNG*'s "Bloodlines," Birta tells Picard that Bok was able to buy himself out of prison. No doubt that was covered by Rule #177: "Know your enemies . . . but do business with them always."

"Bloodlines" *could* have been the last Ferengi episode. But *DS9* gave this species a chance to evolve, and miraculously, viewers actually began to *like* them. In fact, they became so popular that a branch of Quark's bar opened on Earth (as part of the Star Trek: The Experience themed attraction) in 1998. Did good business, too.

But then, it was Las Vegas, a place where every schmo on the Strip understands Rule #284: "Deep down, everyone's a Ferengi."

"The holodeck was full of metaphoric imagery, like it was having some kind of daydream. It may not make literal sense, but symbolically it probably does have some kind of logic to it." —**Troi**

A string of bizarre and unexplained malfunctions leads Data to postulate that the *Enterprise* may somehow be on the verge of achieving sentience. The holodeck provides all the clues. There, the passengers aboard an antique train car seem to represent different aspects of the ship. As Troi attempts to find out what the passengers are looking for, the *Enterprise* takes itself into warp and heads for a white dwarf star for reasons unclear to the Starfleet crew. Is it possible that the ship is protecting and nurturing a new life-form that's growing in one of the cargo bays?

⌘

"Brannon's original story was insane; my teleplay was worse."

That's how writer Joe Menosky describes "Emergence."

The episode was another long-distance teleplay assigned to *TNG*'s unofficial "Italian bureau" when Bran-

non Braga, hard at work on the series finale with Ron Moore, had no time to bring "Emergence" to culmination. "It was kind of a stab at artificial intelligence," Braga says now, "but it wasn't wholly successful. Just kind of a 'Let's go all out and do this wacky thing and put all sorts of incongruent elements together,' but to be quite honest, it didn't cohere."

Right: The mean streets of New York: you never know who you might run into.

After graduating from Starfleet's advanced tactical training program, Ro Laren is sent to infiltrate the Maquis, a group of self-professed freedom fighters. Inflamed by treaty-sanctioned changes enacted at former Federation colonies, the Maquis are attacking Cardassian vessels near the Demilitarized Zone established by the Federation. Ro's mission is to gain the trust of the members of a Maquis cell and lure them into a Starfleet snare. But can Ro, whose people were oppressed for decades by the Cardassians, resist becoming a part of the Maquis cause?

The closer they got to the end, the higher the stress levels got in the writers' room. "At this point, we were really up against it," says René Echevarria. "We were all covering for Ron [Moore] and Brannon [Braga]. The movie was a bigger job for them than any of us realized. They were pulled in all these directions. It was all for the show, and the franchise. So Naren [Shankar] and Jeri Taylor and I stepped up and did what we could. We did so much writing, I don't even remember some of the last few episodes."

He *does* remember the Maquis plotline of his script

for "Preemptive Strike." "It was going to help platform *Voyager*, give it some background," he says.

"We were trying to tee up the other shows," adds Shankar, who wrote the episode's story. "That was the mandate. I really liked Michelle Forbes as an actress. With Ro, we'd wanted to create a character to spin off into *Deep Space Nine*, and give her some history with what they were going to be doing. A lot of the Maquis elements in 'Preemptive Strike' were like that, too. They were going to be laid into *Voyager*'s world."

But Michelle Forbes hadn't wanted to commit to *any* series, be it *DS9*, *Voyager*, or a generic cop drama. She was having too much fun playing the field, so to speak. "I think I made the right decision," she commented at Creation Entertainment's 2008 Las Vegas *Star Trek* convention. "As I said at the time, 'I was too young to get married.'"

In fact, Jeri Taylor had to personally get the actress on the phone and pitch her on "Preemptive Strike" in order to get Forbes to commit to *TNG*'s penultimate episode. But the effort was justified, as was the decision to focus the episode on Ro, rather than the *TNG* regulars. Without Forbes's sympathetic presence and the devastating emotional

impact of her betrayal of Picard—the man who'd reinstated Ro's Starfleet career—this final link in the quartet of Maquis-themed episodes wouldn't have been nearly as strong.

Below: "Preemptive Strike" was Patrick Stewart's last directing assignment for *TNG*.

He was the man who inherited the captain's chair. Following Gene Roddenberry's death, Rick Berman was responsible for keeping the *Star Trek* franchise afloat. His mandate from the studio was to expand that franchise by creating new *Star Trek* movies and television shows.

It's a big universe, and Berman could have taken the franchise in any of countless directions. Paramount execs—who never really understood what made *Star Trek* so popular—wouldn't have stood in his way.

But Berman felt a responsibility to the man who'd made it possible for him to take up the mantle. And that often clashed with the creative instincts of his staff. Particularly when he was developing *Voyager* with Michael Piller and Jeri Taylor.

In *TNG*'s final year, both "Journey's End" and "Preemptive Strike" suggested aspects of discord within the Federation—policies that didn't sit well with every twenty-fourth-century citizen, and rankled some within Starfleet's ranks. Those seeds of discord were to provide a major subplot of *Star Trek: Voyager*, where a group of Maquis dissidents—many of them ex-Starfleet officers—would be forced to work alongside a group of dedicated

Starfleet men and women on the show's titled starship. Over time, on that long, long voyage back to the Alpha Quadrant, they would grow to trust each other, and to see the value of each other's beliefs.

But once the series debuted, that process of mutual discovery was truncated. The Maquis characters quickly fell into line with Federation policy and the Starfleet captain's point of view. Before long, the Maquis and Starfleet crew members were practically indistinguishable.

What happened?

"Gene had very, very strong ideals about what he wanted *Star Trek* to be," Rick Berman stated in 2006, "and he wasn't going to let anybody mess with that. And I never messed with it. Or let me rephrase that: I *rarely* messed with it."

"Rick was very dedicated to the idea of preserving what he saw as Gene Roddenberry's vision," explains Ron Moore. "I thought that sometimes he was mistaken, and sometimes I thought that Roddenberry's vision was wrong. But Rick took it seriously, and he fought vociferously for things that he felt were important to Gene. And he really thought that Gene wouldn't have liked the whole Maquis story line. I know that Michael and Rick had a lot of

arguments about that—the whole thing with the rebellion against what the Federation was doing with the Bajorans and the colonists and the Cardassians. Michael really liked it. He was always arguing for something more complex, more nuanced, more character-based, more sociologically interesting. The initial idea for *Voyager* was that the Maquis who joined the crew would not put on the Starfleet uniforms. Michael lost that fight, and they put on the uniforms at the beginning of *Voyager*—which, depending on your point of view, was or wasn't a huge mistake."

Captain Picard has become unstuck in time—slipping back and forth between three distinct periods: his mission to Farpoint Station seven years in the past; the present on the *Enterprise*; and his retirement years in France, twenty-five years in the future. After a few dizzying trips backward and forward, he discovers that Q is causing his involuntary time-shifting, and that humanity is *still* being judged by the Q Continuum. But according to Q, Picard himself is responsible for the impending doom of humanity, not the Q.

Q takes Picard to the dawn of time—the exact moment when life sprang into being on Earth—except this time, the events that triggered the creation of life never happen. Q allows that the presence of a peculiar spatial anomaly spotted by Picard in his present day is somehow involved in the end of all things. But because the anomaly is even larger in the past—and not present at *all* in the future—Picard can't understand the relevance. All he knows is that if he doesn't solve the conundrum, he personally will bring the evolution of mankind to a screeching halt.

"We knew we wanted the finale to be a valentine to the fans and to the show," says Ron Moore. "It was going to be about the journey we'd taken together, and bookend the series. That's why we wanted to bring Q back, and resolve the trial that he set in 'Encounter at Farpoint.'"

"It was a strong concept," recalls Brannon Braga, Moore's writing partner for both "All Good Things . . ." and *Generations*. "Structurally, I guess the closest thing to it would be Vonnegut's *Slaughterhouse-Five*. It was not an homage, per se, but the idea of jumping between past, present, and future was a perfect framing device to end a science fiction show. You could be nostalgic, you could show what was going to happen to these people, and you could tell a story in the present."

"Michael Piller got interested in this notion of the three stages of a man's life—Picard's life—and that defined the show," continues Moore. "There was a fourth story line in the initial draft, about Picard's time with the Borg when he was Locutus. But Michael thought it was one too many."

"I believe that I contributed the time travel aspects of the story, and Ron contributed the Q and the final trial for humanity—but I really don't know *how* we did it, because we were still working on *Generations*!" Braga says, laughing. "I mean, why in the world would *we* be tapped to write the final episode?"

"Neither Brannon nor I thought that we were going to do the finale," Moore confirms. "There was an assumption on everyone's part that Michael would want to write it himself. Why wouldn't he? And then a month before the episode was due to film, Michael dropped the bomb and said he *wasn't* going to—he was too busy with *DS9* and *Voyager*. And he asked Brannon and me to do it."

"Having to satisfy the ending of a franchise and the beginning of another—it was a real challenge," Braga admits.

"We were shocked," notes Moore. "And honored. It's a big feather in your cap to write a final episode. We only had a couple weeks to work on the story, break it, and start writing. But it flowed very quickly. The one thing that I regret we lost was where the old gang gets back together and steals the *Enterprise*-D from a Starfleet museum. It was sort of a tribute to *Star Trek III: The Search for Spock*, where Kirk's crew steals their *Enterprise*. But I liked that idea so much that I worked it into the pilot I wrote for *Battlestar Galactica*!"

Quelle différence!

Duplicating the sets from seven years earlier? No problem!

Bringing back some of the actors who had since moved on? No problem!

Making the cast members look exactly the way they'd appeared in the pilot episode? No pro— Well, okay—not quite as easy.

People change in seven years—be it from 1987 to 1994, or 2364 to 2370. A jawline may have become a little softer, a set of abs more (or less) taut. Hair and makeup techniques may have changed. And so the actors who played their younger characters in "All Good Things . . ." naturally looked a *bit* different than they had in the pilot. The differences were as subtle as the less angular cut of Tasha Yar's no-nonsense do, or the more graceful styling of Deanna Troi's curly mane. Or as dramatic as the technical advances in prosthetics. While Michael Dorn once again was coiffed with Worf's first-season wig, Michael Westmore chose to use the Klingon's seventh-season "turtlehead" (as his fellow actors referred to

Frakes of the pilot. What could be done about the visually compelling facial hair the commander sported post season one? Buy Frakes a razor? No, there was a simpler fix. The writers set the action of the 2364 segment of the episode *before* the *Enterprise* picked up Riker, Geordi, and Doctor Crusher at Farpoint Station. That decision eliminated the need to send the commander to the barber—or Alan Sims to the props locker to find Geordi's original VISOR, or a hairdresser to Gates McFadden's trailer to restyle her signature auburn locks. A film clip of young Riker was all that was needed for the scene where Picard lets Riker know that the *Enterprise* has been delayed. They found it in "The Arsenal of Freedom."

Fortunately, the ship herself had retained her girlish figure—so no problem with the early scenes. But by 2395, even the *Enterprise* would require a few nips and tucks. Check out that sassy new nacelle!

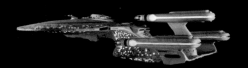

In the *TOS* episode "Return to Tomorrow," Captain James T. Kirk defended his mandate as a Starfleet officer and the inherent risks in that position. It was undoubtedly his most powerful speech: a brief motivational oration that inspired his crew to take on a challenge that they'd been arguing against.

"Risk," Kirk concluded, "risk is our business. That's what this starship is all about. That's why we're aboard her."

In "All Good Things . . . ," Captain Jean-Luc Picard—an equally powerful orator—hopes to inspire the same feeling in his understandably reluctant compatriots aboard the *Enterprise*-D. Unlike Kirk, he's at a distinct disadvantage. Kirk's crew had served with their captain for years; they knew his capabilities and trusted his judgment. Picard, on the other hand, is a man who's been thrown out of his regular time frame. He must motivate a crew to whom he is still very much a stranger. He knows *their* capabilities—but they don't know his. It's a different speech than Kirk's, but the subject matter is the same: *risk*.

"I understand your concerns, and I know if I were in your position I would be doing the same thing. Looking for answers. But you're not going to find any because I don't have any to give you. I know it is difficult for you to understand, but we have to take the ship into the very center of the phenomenon and create a static warp shell. Now, this will put the ship at risk. Quite frankly, we may not survive. But I want you to believe that I am doing this for a greater purpose, and that what is at stake here is more than any of you can possibly imagine. I know you have your doubts about me, about each other, about the ship. All I can say is that although we have only been together for a short time, I know that you are the finest crew in the fleet and I would trust each of you with my life. So, I am asking you for a leap of faith, and to trust me."

Do they take that leap of faith?
Need you ask?

"Ron and I were at that card table scene when it was being filmed," recalls Brannon Braga. "It was the final scene and everybody wanted to be there.

"There was a lot of emotion on that set, a strong bittersweet feeling. Which was strange, given that most of the people were going to be doing the movie soon. But with the TV show ending, everybody just knew that it was different. The family was breaking apart. The analogy I used at the time was, 'Instead of being a family living together day to day, we're going to be a family that sees each other every two years at Christmas.' We knew we were going to continue, but *The Next Generation* was never going to be the same."

Right: Jeri Taylor pays a last visit to the set; Brent Spiner, still wearing his poker visor, adds his own unique touch to the portrait.

If you ask anyone who worked on the final season of *TNG* to define "hell," the response most likely would be "March 1994."

Thanks to the overlapping shooting schedules of the series finale "All Good Things . . ." and the motion picture *Star Trek Generations*, that month was a frenzied period for dozens of talented people who suddenly found themselves doing two jobs at once. And then there were the folks who *also* were putting in hours on *Deep Space Nine* and *Voyager*. As costume designer Robert Blackman so succinctly stated at the time, "I don't have a life!"

"We were writing both projects simultaneously and we kept getting lost," says Ron Moore, laughing. "I remember racking up long hours at Brannon's house and at my house. There literally were moments when we were working together on a scene and we'd forget which project it was for, because we were dealing with the same group of characters on the same set. We'd go, 'Picard is talking about some tech thing down in engineering with Geordi . . . ,' and we'd have to stop because we couldn't remember if it was a scene for the movie or for the finale."

They weren't the only ones. The *TNG* actors found themselves being fitted for movie costumes even as they memorized their lines for the series finale, a task made more arduous by the complicated story line that required the actors to keep track of where their characters were in time on any given day of shooting.

"It was a chaotic, exhausting juncture," recalls Moore's writing partner Brannon Braga. "At the same time they were shooting our sets for the TV show, they were revamping them for the big screen, because they knew they wouldn't hold up for that."

"The difference between a thirty-foot-high, eighty-foot-wide movie screen and a twenty-inch diagonal video screen meant that the level of detail had to be increased," explains production designer Herman Zimmerman, who returned to the sets he'd created while Richard James took on the task of designing the interiors for the good ship *Voyager*. "Film has a much higher resolution; the TV medium is much more forgiving."

"It was always a thrill to be on the *Starship Enterprise*," Brannon Braga says today, "but I didn't get to the set too often. I didn't take pictures. I have no actual evidence that I ever worked on the show. Just pay stubs and some screen credits. I didn't even leave with a souvenir." Braga knows that a lot of the physical history of *TNG* is gone forever, sold at auction like the hero model of the NCC-1701-D (opposite). "And now there are no models," he says. "They're all done on the computer."

Whatever else it was, 1994 marked the end of a phenomenal era.

Right: Newly found evidence that Braga worked on the show.

Riker: "I always thought I'd get a shot at this chair one day."

Picard: "You may still, Will. Somehow I doubt this will be the last ship to carry the name Enterprise. Picard to Farragut. Two to beam up."

As filming came to a close on *Star Trek Generations*, the inevitable happened: the crew had to say goodbye to the sets they'd worked on for the past seven years. The last scene in the movie was, ironically, the last one that was shot on the (now trashed) *Enterprise* bridge. Stills photographer Elliott Marks caught Patrick Stewart and Jonathan Frakes in what appears to be a bittersweet moment of reflection on the end of an era.

To Paula, with love.

to Rachel

Jonathan Frakes

Rumor has it that an actor's career ends after disembarking from the *Starship Enterprise*. It's called "the *Star Trek* curse." But while it may have affected the careers of some of their predecessors, it doesn't seem to have touched the next generation.

"I don't think any of us were even aware of this curse," LeVar Burton says with a laugh. "I've spent my whole thirty-five-year career in popular-culture pieces like *Star Trek*, and I don't feel like I've been cursed. I've tried to make sure my efforts in that arena have brought something positive to the conversation. All TV is educational. The question is, 'What are we teaching?'"

Indeed, Burton's involvement in *Reading Rainbow*, the award-winning children's series he hosted and executive-produced, is a prime example. "It's the epitome of what one can accomplish with the communication medium," Burton says. *Rainbow* ran its course in 2006, but Burton is currently working on relaunching the show as a children's app, soon to appear on a small screen near you. Although he's dedicating all his time to that effort, he's continued to thrive as a television director.

As for his compatriots:

Following *TNG*, Patrick Stewart starred in three blockbuster *X-Men* movies, and television productions of *The Canterville Ghost*, *A Christmas Carol*, *The Lion in Winter*, *Moby Dick*, *King of Texas*, and *Macbeth*. In 2004, he relocated back to Great Britain, where Queen Elizabeth knighted Stewart for his "services to drama."

Jonathan Frakes directed episodes of *Star Trek: Deep Space Nine* and *Star Trek: Voyager*, plus two *TNG* films: *Star Trek: First Contact* and *Star Trek: Insurrection*. He has become a much-in-demand television director, helming episodes of such series as *Roswell*, *Leverage*, *Burn Notice*, *Dollhouse*, *Castle*, *NCIS: Los Angeles*, and *V*.

Brent Spiner cowrote the final *TNG* film, *Star Trek Nemesis*. He has appeared in the Broadway revival of *1776*, in films as diverse as *Independence Day*, *The Aviator*, and *Dude, Where's My Car?*, and in the television series *Law and Order: Criminal Intent*, *Leverage*, and *Threshold*, as well as the new web series *Fresh Hell*.

Michael Dorn appeared as the president of the United States on *Heroes*, and plays a recurring role on *Castle*. His distinctive baritone voice has been heard in dozens of computer games, in television commercials, and in animated shows such as *Cow and Chicken*, *Superman*, *Justice League*, and the revival of *Duck Dodgers in the 24½th Century*.

Marina Sirtis played a recurring role in the syndicated comedy *Girlfriends*, and has guest-starred on shows such as *Without a Trace*, *Three Rivers*, and *Grey's Anatomy*. Most recently she starred as the Wicked Queen in a theater production of *A Snow White Christmas*, with Neil Patrick Harris.

Gates McFadden was named artistic director of Ensemble Studio Theatre–LA and spearheaded the building of the Atwater Village Theatre Collective. As a teacher, she's held faculty positions at the American Academy of Dramatic Arts, Brandeis University, Harvard, the Stella Academy in Hamburg, and the University of Pittsburgh. McFadden was awarded the George Burns Teaching Fellowship at the University of Southern California, where she continues to teach today.

They're well known in the entertainment industry today, but twenty-something years ago, Ronald D. Moore, Brannon Braga, René Echevarria, and Naren Shankar were just four young guys with no professional writing credits. Without the open-door script submission policy established by Michael Piller, the road to success might not have existed.

"It was a unique situation," Shankar says, "certainly unique when compared to my subsequent years in the business. I've never seen another staff like that, where almost *everyone* started that way, fresh off the boat, as it were."

Shankar was the first to go out "into the real world," as he puts it. "After *TNG*, I left the gang and started to do other things," he says. "At the time, *Star Trek* was considered some weird little ghetto. You had to write something else or nobody would look at you." Shankar got hired on staff for *SeaQuest*, then *Farscape* and *The Chronicle*. He later became an executive producer on *CSI: Crime Scene Investigation* and *Grimm*.

Following the end of *TNG*, "I thought it would be neat to go to *Voyager*," says René Echevarria. "But Michael Piller said, 'You're going to *Deep Space Nine* and I think you're going to flourish there.' I was really

mad, because I wanted to be a part of the new uncharted territory. But Michael said, 'You're going to learn a lot more by working with Ira Behr. One day, you're going to come back and thank me.' And he was absolutely right." Following *DS9*'s wrap, Echevarria became a writer/producer on *Now and Again*, and an executive producer on *Dark Angel*, *MDs*, *The 4400* (a series he cocreated), *Medium*, *Castle*, and *Terra Nova*.

Fresh off his collaboration with Brannon Braga on "All Good Things . . ." and *Generations*, Ron Moore shipped over to *DS9*, while Braga went to *Voyager*. The pair reteamed in 1996 to write the second *TNG* movie, *Star Trek: First Contact*, and in 2000, to cowrite the screenplay for *Mission: Impossible II*. Moore later joined the production teams on *Good vs Evil*, *Roswell*, and *Carnivàle*, codeveloped and produced the reboot of *Battlestar Galactica*, and created the *Galactica* spin-off *Caprica*.

Braga stayed with *Voyager* for its entire run, eventually sharing executive producer responsibilities with Rick Berman. With Berman, he cocreated *Star Trek: Enterprise*, the fifth live-action series based on Gene Roddenberry's creation. Then he moved on to executive produce *Threshold*, *24*, *FlashForward*, and

Terra Nova. "To this day," Braga admits, "I think *TNG* had the best writing staff I've ever worked with."

For all the ups and downs of working with Michael Piller, no one downplays the influence he had on their careers. "After Michael died in 2005, a bunch of us got together at his memorial service and talked about the things he used to say to us that *we* now say to our own staffs in our own rooms," reminisces Shankar. "In sports, they use the term 'coaching tree.' It's like *your* coaches give rise to other coaches. Michael was the ancestor for the *Star Trek* coaching tree."

Opposite: "The young guns," circa 1993. Left to right: Moore, Braga, Echevarria, Shankar.

Star Trek licensing flourished after the debut of *The Next Generation* in 1987. As it had with *The Original Series*, publishing led the way, with *TNG*-related comics and paperback fiction titles quickly finding their way into the hands of eager fans.

Pocket Books, a division of Simon & Schuster (like Paramount, once a part of the Gulf and Western conglomerate and later the studio's Viacom sibling), obtained the license to publish *Star Trek* books in 1978. The first *TNG* novel out of the gate, in October 1987, was an adaptation of "Encounter at Farpoint," written by celebrated *Star Trek* screenwriter David Gerrold. "There was a mad scramble to get the book finished on time," recalls the novelization's editor, Dave Stern. "Script changes were taking place even as we were preparing to go to press. I recall standing by the fax machine, waiting for dialogue changes that had to then get rushed down to our production department. And the approved cast photo didn't make it to us in time to use as a cover. We had to go with a simple picture of the show's logo for the first paperback run of the tie-in."

The novels proved to be extremely popular, repeatedly landing on the *New York Times* bestseller list. At their height, Pocket Books announced that it was printing a quarter-million copies of each *Star Trek* title it released.

TNG aficionados also eagerly snapped up comic books. DC Comics published the first issue of a six-part *TNG* miniseries in late 1987, and in 1989 launched a regular monthly *TNG* comic, which ran until 1996.

For several years, publishing was the most lucrative part of Paramount's *TNG* consumer products business, but with the advent of interactive gaming, publishing soon shared the limelight with game publishers like Interplay, Activision, MicroProse, and Simon & Schuster's interactive division.

Star Trek was equally successful in other venues. In 1998, Star Trek: The Experience opened at the Las Vegas Hilton. The themed attraction, which included a *TNG* virtual reality ride, a futuristic restaurant, and retail outlets, won a tourism development award from the State of Nevada shortly after its debut. During its ten-year run at the Hilton, the Experience was the site of numerous Trekker weddings and a large, annual *Star Trek* convention.

To date, cumulative retail sales for *Star Trek* merchandise top $4 billion worldwide. Beyond publishing and gaming, you'll find the usual toys, collectibles, apparel (including costumes), trading cards, role-playing games, magazines—and a few oddball items like Borg air freshener and a *Galaxy*-class "pool lounge."

Below: Some *Star Trek* products, like comics, required likeness approval from the actors, who, understandably, could be particular about their appearance. After viewing a series of disappointing facsimiles, Patrick Stewart finally signed off on a cranium that he appreciated.

"The challenge working on *Star Trek* was trying to stay ahead of the technological advances happening in the real world—especially in computer technology and communications," says Andre Bormanis, *TNG*'s science consultant during the final season (he served the same role on *DS9* and *Voyager*). "When *TNG* premiered, nobody had ever heard of the Internet," he points out. "That's the kind of thing that is almost impossible to anticipate. But I think we did a good job anticipating some of the ways technology would become such a regular part of our daily lives."

One obvious example was the personal access display device, or padd. This updated version of the "electronic clipboard" created by Matt Jefferies for *TOS* had no mechanical buttons; the screens had only to be touched to "work." Rick Sternbach's simple, compact design, highlighted by Michael Okuda's cool and colorful screen graphics, defined portable access to stored digital information, and it didn't take long for such a device to take shape in the real world. Just as flip phones—starting with Motorola's StarTAC in 1996—bore a distinct resemblance to *TOS*'s communicator, the ever-growing number of "tablet devices" on the market, such as the iPad, Xoom, and PlayBook, certainly *look* as if *TNG*'s padd

figured in their genetic makeup.

"It's like the 'chicken and egg' paradox," Bormanis says. "Neither came first. They evolved together, and each side needed the other. Mike and Rick were technically savvy guys. They read the science journals, tried to extrapolate what the world would look like in the future, and designed their devices. Then scientists, engineers, and students who were into the show said, 'Wow, I wonder if *I* could build something like that.' A few years later, here it is."

Not all of *Star Trek*'s technological wonders have been achieved—but they're on people's minds. "If you ask computer science and artificial intelligence researchers what they hope to someday achieve," Bormanis says, "most of them will answer, 'We're trying to make Commander Data.' Because he's the ultimate user-friendly computer. The most relevant example is Robonaut Two [developed by NASA in conjunction with General Motors], the newest crew member aboard the International Space Station."

Robonaut 2 launched up to the station on the space shuttle *Discovery* as part of the STS-133 mission in early 2011. It is the first dexterous humanoid robot in space, and the first U.S.-built robot at the space station. But, as NASA states on its website,

"that was just one small step for a robot and one giant leap for robot-kind."

"Astonishing things are happening," Bormanis concludes. "I'm sure we're going to have androids that will be more sophisticated than Commander Data *way* before the twenty-fourth century. We can only hope *TNG* doesn't end up looking too dated. *The Original Series* may look dated today, but the ideas are still very current, and still recognized as being way ahead of their time."

Opposite: Robonaut 2, NASA's own gold-faced robot, in the International Space Station's Destiny laboratory, November 2011. Data's grandpa?

Gene Roddenberry was no longer physically present when *Star Trek: The Next Generation* completed its original mission on the small screen. Yet it's only fitting that Roddenberry be remembered at the close of this book as well as the beginning. On August 19, 1987, a month before the fledgling show's premiere, the cast gathered to celebrate the shared birthday of Roddenberry (age 66) and his new "first officer," Jonathan Frakes (age 35). To commemorate the event, the crew presented "the Great Bird" with a framed dedication plaque—a duplicate of the plaque that would be displayed on the *Enterprise* bridge for the first few seasons.

"Space . . . the final frontier. These are the voyages of the Starship Enterprise. Its continuing mission: To explore strange new worlds . . . to seek out new life and new civilizations . . . to boldly go where no one has gone before." —the Star Trek: The Next Generation "preamble," as spoken by Captain Jean-Luc Picard

Acknowledgments

This book would not have been possible without encouragement, cooperation, and direction from a community of gracious people who readily lent their time, talent, and personal tales. To them, we extend our heartfelt gratitude and thanks.

First of all, for keeping the night-light aglow in a lonely photo archive, and for that spark of liveliness in her voice no matter how often we whined, "Just one more thing . . . ," we must thank Marian Cordry at CBS Consumer Products. We couldn't have done it without you, Marian—again!

For memories, some dredged up during the hours of conversation you allowed us, others dug out of long-forgotten personal photo books or garaged boxes, we humbly say thank you to: Eric Alba; Allan A. Apone; Ira Steven Behr; Rick Berman; Rob Bloch; Andre Bormanis; Brannon Braga; Kate Brambilla at Christie's; LeVar Burton; Don Coleman; Dan Curry at dancurrygallery.com; Kevin Dilmore; Doug Drexler; René Echevarria; Bobi Edrington; Paul Elliot; Jonathan Frakes; Kim Gottlieb-Walker; Gary Hutzel; Beth Jacques at mptv images; Richard James; Greg Jein; Alan Kobayashi; Joyce Kogut; Mark Lenard; Michael Mack; Dan Madsen; Elliott Marks; Dave McDonnell; Joe Menosky; Ronald D. Moore; Larry Nemecek; Neil Newman; Marc Okrand; Michael and Denise Okuda; Alec Peters at Propworx; Andrew Probert at probertdesigns.com; Tobias Richter at thelightworks.com; Robbie Robinson; Dave Rossi; Naren Shankar; Jo Ann Smith; Dave Stern; Rick Sternbach at ricksternbach.com; Eric Stillwell; Jeri Taylor; Karen Thomas; Guy Vardaman; Dayton Ward; John Wentworth; Michael Westmore; Wil Wheaton; Robert Hewitt Wolfe; Durinda Wood; and Herman Zimmerman.

We owe unbounded attribution to the authors of previous *Star Trek* tomes whose great works provided enlightenment when we needed it most: Robert H. Justman; Joe Nazzaro; Larry Nemecek; Denise and Michael Okuda; Herbert F. Solow; Judith and Garfield Reeves-Stevens; and Michael Westmore.

At CBS Consumer Products, we wish to thank John Van Citters and Risa Kessler. And at CBS Digital: Nicki Kreitzman and Wendy Ruiz.

To those fan-driven *Star Trek* sites across the web universe, keeping the flame alive for generations past and generations to come, thank you.

At Abrams, we wish to thank our dauntless, resolute, and persevering editor, Eric Klopfer, as well as managing editor Scott Auerbach and copy editor Rob Sternitzky and, of course, Charles Kochman.

And a special thank you for your friendship and assistance: Hua Curry; Cassandra DeCuir; Dani Dornfeld; Jeff Erdmann; Hallie Lambert; Ben McGinnis; Paul Ruditis; Paul Simpson; and Drago Sumonja.

Editor: Eric Klopfer
Project Manager: Charles Kochman
Photo Archivist: Marian Cordry
Designer: Seth Labenz and Roy Rub of Topos Graphics
Production Manager: Ankur Ghosh

Library of Congress Cataloging-in-Publication Data

Block, Paula M.
  Star trek, the next generation 365 / by Paula M. Block and Terry J. Erdmann.
    p. cm.
  Includes bibliographical references and index.
  ISBN 978-1-4197-0429-1 (alk. paper)
1. Star trek, the next generation (Television program) 2. Star trek (Television program) I. Erdmann, Terry J. II. Title.
  PN1992.77.S73B56 2012
  791.45'72—dc23
    2012008244

TM ® and © 2012 CBS Studios Inc.
© 2012 Paramount Pictures Corporation. STAR TREK and related marks are trademarks of CBS Studios Inc. All Rights Reserved.

All images provided by CBS Studios Inc., with the exception of the following:

Eric Alba: Spreads 247, 250, 272 [right-hand page], 295 [right-hand page, at left], 311, 314, 342 [left-hand page; right-hand page, bottom left], 343 [right-hand page, at left], 365 [right-hand page]

Paula M. Block: Spreads 100 [left-hand page], 274, 359, 362 [left-hand page]

CBS Digital: Spread 020 [left-hand page]

Christie's, Inc.: Spreads 027 [right-hand page, at right], 028, 035 [right-hand page], 103 [right-hand page, at right], 116 [right-hand page], 132 [right-hand page], 136 [right-hand page], 148 [right-hand page, at left], 200 [right-hand page], 262, 281 [left-hand page], 295 [right-hand page, at right], 297 [right-hand page], 358 [right-hand page]

Dan Curry: Spreads 042 [right-hand page], 048 [left-hand page], 103 [right-hand page, at left], 121, 134 [right-hand page], 192, 193, 239 [right-hand page], 244 [right-hand page, at left], 245, 254, 298

Doug Drexler: Spread 242 [right-hand page]

Bobi Edrington/Steve Martin's Working Wildlife: Spread 326 [left-hand page]

Getty Images: Spreads 001, Richard Howard; 003, George Rose; 037, George Rose [right-hand page]; 039 George Rose [right-hand page, at left]; 069 George Rose [right-hand page, at left]; 287, Henry S. Dziekan III [right-hand page]

Graphic Imaging Technology, Inc: Spread 362 [right-hand page, upper right]

Hallmark Cards, Inc: Spread 201, Courtesy of Hallmark Cards, Inc. [left-hand page]

Richard James: Spreads 106 [right-hand page], 143 [right-hand page]

The Light Works/Tobias Richter: Spread 013 [right-hand page, at right], Back Cover Image

Makeup & Effects Laboratories: Spreads 064, 265 [right-hand page], 289 [right-hand page], 300 [left-hand page], 301, 323 [right-hand page, at right], 341 [right-hand page]

Joe Menosky: Spread 266 [left-hand page]

mptv: Spreads 008 © 1993 Gene Trindl/mptvimages.com [right-hand page, at right], 034 © 1987 Gene Trindl/mptvimages.com [right-hand page], 069 © 1987 Gene Trindl/mptvimages.com [right-hand page, at right]

NASA: Spread 363

Larry Nemecek: Spread 339 [right-hand page]

Michael and Denise Okuda: Spreads 029, 270

Andrew Probert: Spreads 014, 016, 021, 036, 063, 065 [right-hand page, at left], 066, 233 [right-hand page]

Propworx: Spreads 030 [left-hand page], 046 [left-hand page], 181, 226 [right-hand page], 276, 277 [right-hand page, at right], 349 [left-hand page]

Naren Shankar: Spread 361

Rick Sternbach: Spreads 041, 054 [right-hand page, at left], 059 [right-hand page], 101 [right-hand page, at left], 105 [left-hand page], 110 [left-hand page], 119 [right-hand page], 130 [left-hand page], 138 [left-hand page], 195 [right-hand page], 196, 233 [right-hand page], 265 [left-hand page]

Eric Stillwell: Spread 136

Karen Thomas/Critters of the Cinema: Spread 277 [left-hand page]

Time & Life Images: Spreads 004, Alan Levenson; 055, Robert Sherbow [right-hand page]; 082, Alan Levenson [right-hand page]

Dayton Ward: Spread 262 [right-hand page, upper left]

John Wentworth: Spread 329 [left-hand page]

Durinda Wood: Spreads 072 [left-hand page; right-hand page, at left], 104 [right-hand page, at left], 112 [right-hand page, at left]

THE ART OF BOOKS SINCE 1949

115 West 18th Street
New York, NY 10011
www.abramsbooks.com